The Knights of the Golden Circle in Texas

How a Secret Society Shaped a State

GREAT SEAL OF THE K'S OF THE C. C.
UNION · POWER · BICKLEY · AMER'N · LEGION · 1858.

Randolph W. Farmer

The Knights of the Golden Circle in Texas

How a Secret Society Shaped a State

VITA HISTRIA

Vita Histria

Las Vegas ◊ Oxford ◊ Palm Beach

Published in the United States of America by
Histria Books, a division of Histria LLC
7181 N. Hualapai Way, Suite 130-86
Las Vegas, NV 89166 USA
HistriaBooks.com

Vita Histria is an imprint of Histria Books. Titles published under the imprints of Histria Books are distributed worldwide.

Library of Congress Control Number 2020949925

ISBN 978-1-59211-087-2 (hardcover)

Contents

Chapter One

Beginning a Great Tragedy

The greatest tragedy in the history of the United States burst into its full and deadly force on April 12, 1861 with the first cannonade fired upon Fort Sumter, a Federal military outpost located in Charles-ton harbor in the State of South Carolina. A war that would surpass all other wars in terms of the savagery inflicted upon citizens of the United States, and in numbers of total casualties, the American Civil War was precipitated by the concerted action of a secret organization known as the Knights of the Golden Circle, or "KGC". By the beginning of the secession crisis, the KGC had established the base of its power and its de facto international headquarters at San Antonio, Texas. Its Texas leadership was well represented in the aggressively violent action at Fort Sumter, most notably by Louis Trezevant Wigfall, a United States Congressman from the East Texas town of Marshall. Wigfall had done much behind the scenes to instigate the violence and afterward toured the south taking credit for forcing the surrender of the Federal troops at Fort Sumter, an action that precipitated a war that consumed more than 600,000 American lives.[1]

Wigfall, however, was not the only Texan KGC member working behind the scenes to achieve the dissolution of the United States and an all-encompassing disaster for its people. Fellow Texan Ben McCulloch had partnered with Wigfall in secretly securing armaments for KGC operatives who took Texas out of the United States. McCulloch had planned and directed the seizure of the federal arsenal in Texas and the complete expulsion of Union troops from the Lone Star State weeks before the attack on Fort Sumter. By the time of the actual attack at Charleston Harbor, rumors had circulated that McCulloch and a company of

Texas Rangers were in the area of Washington, D.C., preparing to attack and capture the Capitol and install their own President. This would not happen, but it later became known that KGC members had apparently planned to kidnap or kill President Abraham Lincoln at the beginning of the war. KGC members and sympathizers regarded Lincoln as a tyrant and would-be monarch. For them the usurpation of such a tyrant was a righteous defense of the Constitution. Failing to execute their plans in 1861 members of the KGC were implicated in Lincoln's murder before the end of the war. Unlike many in the Deep South, there were those in Texas that applauded and celebrated Lincoln's assassination. Unlike the Deep South, Texas was never successfully invaded during the war, nor was it successfully occupied afterward.[2]

Rumors and mythology have always surrounded the KGC. This should be expected as one of the goals of a secret organization is to remain secret, leading to speculation by outsiders as to the true intentions of the organization and the identities of its members. By the close of the Civil War it had become standard practice to blame the KGC for virtually any disaster that befell the Union or its loyal supporters; it was also an effective way to demonize one's enemies or political rivals by accusing them of association with or membership in this secret organization. This overreaction eventually led to a revisionist movement among conventional historians that downplayed the power and importance of the KGC. As the pendulum of opinion swung to the opposite extreme, the role of the KGC and those interested in it became the occasional subject of mockery by establishment historians who thought the KGC of minor historical interest. In part, this diminution was the result of a preoccupation with the personal life and antics of George W. L. Bickley, who many mistakenly believed was the founding father of the KGC. There is now more than sufficient evidence to show that Bickley was employed by the KGC's true founders to spread their treasonous organization across the United States. Bickley was an effective public speaker; a good front man and mouthpiece for men who desired to retain their legitimate positions of power by remaining in the shadows. His personal foibles and failings should be no surprise to anyone who has ever known or experienced interaction with an aggressive salesman. Military matters would be left to military men like Ben McCulloch, a veteran of the Mexican War and frontier battles against Comanche Indians while with the Texas Rangers.[3]

As with any effective criminal organization the KGC utilized a hierarchical structure that would isolate and protect its true leadership from prosecution. The entity that George Bickley was selling to the American public found a full-fledged and battle-hardened military organization in Texas that was more than receptive to his message; they had heard it from others before Bickley ever appeared on the national stage. It was only a matter of time before the organization Bickley promoted and the pre-existing organization of Texans would merge; the KGC was to achieve its greatest power in Texas under the direction of pro-secession extremists. Many of these extremists were foreign-born or originally from the northeastern United States.[4]

It is precisely because Texas and much of its history have been obscured or mythologized by most Americans that the KGC and the extent of its influence in the State have remained hidden. While the KGC had little or no influence in the rest of the United States, the case may be made that this organization ran Texas before, during, and after the Civil War. Why should anyone care? Texas has grown in size and influence to the point that it is now the second most populous State in the Union, and is continuing to grow faster than the rest of the country. There are those in the older sections of the United States that do not understand the prevalent attitude that drives its people. Why is Texas so different? The answer lies in the echoes and nuances of the culture that the KGC built in Texas. It is a fact that the KGC had as its goal the construction of a new world order that by necessity required Texas as its touchstone. Texas was to be the base of operations and jumping off point for a series of invasions that would convert Latin America into a slave empire run by and for the benefit of a privileged class. Once the war for slave owner's rights was lost, the KGC adapted and informally continued to influence and occasionally control matters in Texas until well into the 20th century. The KGC had sought to establish its members as leaders in the political, economic, and military structure of a new society. This secret organization thought of itself as offering the best solution to the problem of slavery in the United States. The KGC is gone now, but its legacy remains. There are lessons to be learned from the story of its rise to power in Texas.

Chapter Two

Legacies and Antecedents

The conditions that led to the formation of the KGC were in place at the very beginning of the colonization of North America. The KGC was to encourage the preservation and expansion of slavery in the Western hemisphere. Slavery was brought by the Dutch into New Netherland, which later became New York, in the 1620s. It arrived in the British colony of Massachusetts in 1624, when Samuel Maverick became the first slave owner in New England; his descendant, also named Samuel Maverick, became one of the leaders of the KGC in Texas. Samuel Maverick of Texas would play a key role in the expulsion of United States troops from Texas in February 1861, months before the Civil War started with the attack on Fort Sumter.[1]

France would also participate in the extension of slavery from the Old World into the New. By the late 1600s slavery was steadily increasing in the French West Indies, with colonies established at Saint-Domingue (Haiti), Guadeloupe, and Martinique. In 1685, the French king instituted the Code Noir, an early attempt to prevent the mistreatment of slaves, but it was never strictly observed. Mortality rates for French colonial slaves were much higher than those in colonial America. In the 1700s, the French investment in colonial slavery increased greatly, with 864,000 Africans imported into Saint-Domingue alone. Only 6% of the slaves taken from Africa arrived in the United States; 40% wound up in the 3 French offshore slave colonies. The first slaves in mainland French Louisiana arrived in 1719 but did not make it any farther north than Natchez until the following year. In the French possession of the Illinois Country, the Roman Catholic Church encouraged religious education of slaves so that they were integrated into the moral and social life of the community. In the French Caribbean colonies, however, slaves were typically under absentee ownership, subject to physical and mental abuse, and lived in chaos. Many of the Caribbean-based owners were Protestant Huguenots, not interested in the dictates of the Catholic Church. The situation on the islands in French possession would eventually result in bloody slave uprisings that drove refugees both white and black from the Caribbean into the port cities of New Orleans, Savannah, Charleston, Norfolk and Baltimore. The refugees carried their legacies and fearful stories of brutality with them. The ongoing fear of slave revolts led in part to the formation of the KGC, accelerated by John Brown's raid on Harper's Ferry.[2]

In 1664, the British took New Netherland from the Dutch and renamed it New York. From that point, the slave trade was greatly increased in New York City to the point that slaves made up 21% of the city's population in 1746. By that time, slaves had been traded on Wall Street, sold at auction, for 35 years making New York one of the most active slave trading centers on the Atlantic Coast. Under British rule, conditions greatly deteriorated for New York's slaves. In 1741, thirteen Africans were burned at the stake, accused of conspiring to burn New York City and murder its inhabitants in an uprising; seventeen more slaves were hung and 70 more were sold into the brutal environment of Caribbean slavery. Consequently, in the near future slaves in the city would be rounded up and whipped as punishment for gathering in groups. The New York slave conspiracy trials had much in common with the Salem witchcraft hysteria of 1692. Suspicious fires in Texas towns in 1860 and the slave revolt hysteria that resulted directly led to an increase in KGC membership and power – not just in Texas but across the South.[3]

George Washington, one of the Founding Fathers, was a slave trader; he owned and bred slaves for sale in his native Virginia. Just as many of the leaders of the KGC would do later, Washington went into war against the government he had once served as a professional soldier. Washington had fought the French on behalf of the British government, whom he subsequently opposed in the Revolutionary War, just as many West Point trained American veterans of the Mexican War joined the Confederate forces in opposition to their former government. During the colonial era conflict, some slaves had rebelled against their owners by running away and joining the British army to fight against their former masters. At the end of the war, Washington was in New York looking to recapture some of his escaped slaves. Once Texas gained its independence from Mexico it counter-manded the Mexican government's opposition to slave ownership. Texas became a slave republic. One of the KGC's goals was the creation of a police state to prevent the escape of slaves. It is no wonder that many KGC in Texas and other southerners looked upon George Washington as the first "rebel."[4]

Washington was also involved in the formation of an early organization that had some interesting parallels to the Knights of the Golden Circle. This was the Society of the Cincinnati, formed May 13, 1783, with George Washington as President of this somewhat secret society. Just weeks before the date of the Cincinnati's founding, an idea for a similar society had circulated in newspapers: a so-called Order of Freedom with Washington as proposed grand master and the state governors as "knight companions." The motto of the organization was to be *sic semper tyranis* (thus be it ever to tyrants), the same phrase shouted by KGC member and presidential assassin John Wilkes Booth after the killing of Abraham Lincoln in Ford's Theater. The Order of Freedom was never directly connected with the Society of the Cincinnati, but the timing of its proposed formation was significant. This demonstrates that there was an undercurrent in American culture, even in early 1783, for the formation of a European-styled knightly order. Oddly enough, the first "Castle" (or lodge) of the Knights of the Golden Circle allegedly was founded at Cincinnati, Ohio in 1854.[5]

The Society of the Cincinnati membership was open only to Revolutionary War officers and their descendants; the only apparent benefit of membership was access to a planned charitable fund for use by the membership. The aspects of the Society that troubled patriots like Benjamin Franklin were the exclusivity of an essentially military organization and its hereditary nature, so reminiscent of the British aristocratic society they had fought against in the war for independence. The organizational structure of the Cincinnati appeared to be that of a shadow government and so alarm was publicly registered by men like Benjamin Franklin and John Adams. Soon George Washington was compelled to repudiate the Cincinnati even though he had accepted its presidency and approved of its bylaws and insignia. Behind the scenes, Washington continued to serve as President of the secret society until his death. Rumors circulated that the Cincinnati would usurp the republic in favor of a police state. Slavery was not universally a burning issue at the time as it was an accepted aspect of colonial life and so the slavery question had no bearing on public consideration of the Cincinnati. However, it should be noted that the Society was named in honor of Lucius Quintus Cincinnatus, a Roman general and sometime dictator who distinguished himself by defeating a revolt of ordinary citizens against the aristocracy of the Roman Empire. Rome was built upon slavery. The governing body of the Society, called the general society, was established at Newburg, New York, just up the Hudson River from New York City. The society had been formed in part as a result of the Newburgh Conspiracy and was suspected by some of initiating Shay's Rebellion in 1787, both revolutionary movements that involved former military officers. After George Washington was inaugurated as the first President of the United States in 1789, attacks against the Society faded. Reforms promised to the alarmed public were never adopted by the state societies of the order. Critics of the Society of the Cincinnati, in particular Benjamin Franklin and the Viscount de Mirabeau, brother of one of the society's sharpest critics, were made honorary members of the Cincinnati which no doubt had a quieting effect on their earlier apprehensions.[6]

Once the Society was exposed to public suspicion and repudiation, a new organization that can be directly tied to the KGC arose from the ashes of the Cincinnati. Its name was the Society of Tammany, or Columbian Order of New York. The Tammany Society was organized "under a Constitution and Laws in 1789." There are no surviving lists of members from its initial meetings, other than the name of William Tapp, the Secretary pro tem in 1789; very little is known of him, except that he was a member of the Society of the Cincinnati. Other prominent members of the Cincinnati joined the Columbian Order of New York. There were informal meetings in which the organization of the Tammany society was proposed as early as 1786 under the guidance of William Mooney who many believed served as a tool for Aaron Burr. Burr it was said "used the Society to secure his own political preferment." Burr, a former Revolutionary War officer who served as Vice President of the United States under Thomas Jefferson, took what was basically a social club and converted it into a political machine later known as Tammany Hall. Several noted members of the Columbian Order of New York were KGC, and the highest echelon of the KGC in Texas and elsewhere across the United States were designated Knights of the Columbian Star. Some members of the Tammany Society were also members of the Order of the Lone Star, which later merged into the KGC. The Order of the Lone Star was dedicated to the expansion of the United States via the con-quest of Spanish territory in North America and the Caribbean. This too, was one of the goals of the KGC. [7]

The Tammany Society or Columbian Order of New York enjoyed a close and friendly relationship with the Cincinnati in 1789. It was the Columbian Order of New York that first proposed an annual celebration of George Washington's birthday, beginning upon the end of the first year of his Presidency. The Society, supposedly named after an Indian chief known as Tammany, had its leader designated as 'Grand Sachem". The toast given by the Society on Washington's Birthday called for "the auspicious birth of our Great Grand Sachem, George Washington, be ever commemorated by all the loyal Sons of Saint Tammany." Washington at the time was President of the Society of the Cincinnati. As the Tammany Society spread across the young republic, the local chapters in other states slightly adapted or changed its name: in Virginia it was called Sons of St. Tammany in the Columbian Order and in Kentucky it was titled Sons of Tammany or Brethren in the Columbian Order. Those two states in particular would set a precedent that increased the likelihood of a civil war at a later time in the nation's history. In 1798, then Vice President Thomas Jefferson anonymously and secretly wrote the Kentucky Resolution of 1798; James Madison secretly authored the Virginia Resolution of 1798. Both documents seriously challenged the authority of the Federal government by arguing for state's rights and strict constructionism. Strict constructionists argued that the states had the right to declare any act of Congress not authorized by the original Constitution to be null and void – thereby unenforceable. In effect this meant that any Federal antislavery laws would be unenforceable. As slavery was never specifically mentioned in the original Constitution, this nullification doctrine led to the eventual secession of Texas and the rest of the South. The authors of both of the 1798 nullification resolutions were slave owners, as well as signers of the Constitution; both favored the spread of slave ownership into the western territories. The KGC be-came a leading force of the secession movement in the United States by 1860 and its leadership often cited the Kentucky and Virginia resolutions of 1798 as proof of legitimacy of slave-owners rights. In their eyes, secession and westward expansion became necessary to extend and protect the institution of slavery.[8]

Another warning signal flashed in 1798 with the release of *Proofs of a Conspiracy Against All the Religions and Governments of Europe, Carried on In the Secret Meetings of Free Masons, Illuminati, and Reading Societies* written by John Robinson, a professor of philosophy and secretary to the Royal Society of Edinburgh. It was first printed in New York. This provided an American audience with an introduction to the Illuminati and led to the necessity of George Washington denying any involvement with the Illuminati. Washington, like Ben Franklin, was a Freemason. Washington wrote in a letter to an acquaintance, "I have heard much of the nefarious, and dangerous, plan, and doctrines of the Illuminati, but never saw the book until you were pleased to send it to me…. I believe notwithstanding, that none of the Lodges in this country are contaminated with the principles ascribed to the Society of the Illuminati."[9] A contemporary Masonic historian has written of the Illuminati:

> The original order of the Illuminati was suppressed in Bavaria in 1784. It has been called a 'quasi-Masonic' association because it infiltrated Freemasonry yet was never officially recognized by any Masonic body. The founder, Adam Weishaupt, was a professor at the University of Ingolstadt with an ambitious plan for modernization of German society who proposed to bring his goals to pass by utilizing the secrecy and social discipline of the Masonic lodges.

Weishaupt was especially attracted to the existence within German Freemasonry of defined grades of illumination and the doctrine of obedience to unknown superior authorities. He recruited a number of men who held important positions in the German government and society. He sought to employ Masonic secrecy to achieve leftist political objectives.[10]

Professor Weishaupt founded the Illuminati in 1776 coincidentally the same year that the American Revolution began. John Robinson, in his expose published in 1789, wrote that in addition to numerous Illuminati-infiltrated Masonic lodges in Germany there were 8 such lodges in England, 2 in Scotland, "many" in Holland, Switzerland, and France; several in Italy and "several" in America – before 1786. According to Professor Robinson, the secretly stated objective of the Illuminati was to create a global organization that would rule the world. Robinson also identified numerous European members by name; one such person – Count Mirabeau, was a known correspondent and ally of Benjamin Franklin. Franklin enlisted Mirabeau in his crusade against the Society of the Cincinnati by supporting Mirabeau's republication of Franklin's arguments in a French edition titled, *Considerations sur l'Ordre de Cincinnatus…* par le Comte de Mirabeau. The French edition premiered in Paris in late 1784, London in 1785 and Philadelphia in 1786. Although the Society of the Cincinnati had already lost in the court of public opinion by 1786, with its hereditary principles in disfavor, Mirabeau and Franklin, who was the Minister of the United States in France at the time, knew that the hereditary principle still reigned in France. When the French Revolution began in 1786, the Society of the Cincinnati (indirectly), and the Freemasons (directly), played a role in inciting it. According to one historian,

> Freemasonry thus became the bond between the Revolution of 1688 and the Revolution of 1776, then between the Revolution of 1776 and the French Revolution of 1789….Freemasonry itself did not make the revolutions, but prepared and achieved them. It impelled its members to play their part in the revolution, but when the revolution actually started it disappeared, to appear again later more brilliant and alive than ever.

Although the typical Masonic lodge was devoted to charitable work and community based Masonic initiatives that were exclusive of politics, the political initiatives of the Freemasons "…have been applied either through puppet societies – such as the Committees of Correspondence and the Sons of Liberty during the American Revolution…or through some of its great heroes…. there was the instance of Benjamin Franklin in France."[11]

The KGC was one such puppet organization of a certain faction of Masonry that followed the example of the Illuminati in executing its agenda. As early as 1789 this faction was bespoken of in John Robinson's expose: "ILLUMINATUS DIRIGENS, or SCOTCH KNIGHT." [sic] Robinson explained that the "Scotch Knights" were not one of the lower degrees of Illuminated Freemasonry, and outlined its objectives:

> In No. I it is said that the 'chief study of the Scotch Knight is to work on all men in such a way as is most insinuating. II. He must endeavor to acquire the possession of considerable property. III. In all Mason Lodges we must try secretly to get the upper hand. The Masons do not know what Free Masonry is, their high objects, nor their highest Superiors, and should be directed by those who will lead them along the right road.

> In preparing a candidate for the degree of Scotch Knighthood, we must bring him into dilemmas by catching questions.—We must endeavor to get the disposal of the money of the Lodges of Free Masons, or at least take care that it be applied to purposes favorable to our Order—but this must be done in a way that shall not be remarked.

In addition, the candidate for such knighthood must "'consider and treat the Illuminati as the Superiors of Free Masonry, and endeavor in all Mason Lodges which he frequents, to have the Masonry of the Illuminated, and particularly the Scotch Noviate, introduced into the Lodge."[12]

This blueprint for covert revolutionary societies derives its inspiration from an even older story, locked away in the Vatican archives since 1312. These were the records of the suppression of the Knights Templar, a medieval crusading (read: military) order that was destroyed by the King of France with the cooperation of Catholic clergy. Certain French mystics, some with Masonic connections, believed that the Knights Templar modeled themselves after "the military Masons of Zerubbabel, who worked with a sword in one hand, and a trowel in the other." These warrior Masons, the Templars, were led by Jacques de Molay, who was thrown into prison for blasphemous activity and sentenced to death. However true or not, the legend grew that

> …the Templars real crime was betrayal of the great secret to the profane through Masonic lodges. Legends arose that de Molay, who was burned at the stake on 18 March 1314, had organized four such secret societies in prison awaiting execution. These lodges… were located 'at Naples for the East, Edinburgh for the West, Stockholm for the North, and Paris for the South.' De Molay's charge to these 'Templar Masons' was to carry out the revenge of the Templars, regardless of how long this might take, and 'to exterminate all kings and the Bourbon line, to destroy the power of the pope, to preach liberty to all peoples, and found a universal republic. According to these legends, these Masons eventually infiltrated other lodges whose members did not know their secret design, and, over the centuries, infiltrated many organizations….

This story implies that there were "Scotch Knights" placed in Edinburgh, Scotland from the early 14th century, sent there by the Templar leadership to fulfill their destiny as warrior Masons. It was also claimed that the latter-day Templars, in contemporary Masonic incarnation, had launched the French Revolution by storming the Bastille because "it stood on the site of the place where de Molay was confined."[13] The French Revolution had been aided and abetted by Ben Franklin, in conjunction with a known member of the Illuminati, Count Mirabeau. The goal of the Illuminati had been accomplished in France with their help.

The "Scotch Knights" spoken of by the Illuminati were refugees from 17th century warfare in England and Scotland who had immigrated to France, where they continued their Masonic practice. The first "Scottish Lodge" was established at Bordeaux in 1732. From there the order spread first to the French slave colonies in the West Indies in 1763, and then to Albany, New York by 1767. The Albany lodge was originally known as a "Lodge of Perfection" and was considered a fore-runner of the Scottish Rite Masons in America. In 1783 another Lodge of Perfection was founded at Charleston, South Carolina; that city soon became the location of the first Scottish Rite Supreme Council in the world, officially in 1801. The Supreme Council consisted of eleven founding members, four of whom were Jewish, five Protestants, and two Roman Catholics. Eventually in 1813 a Northern District was established with a separate Supreme Council. The original Supreme Council became responsible for all Scottish Rite lodges in the South and continued to be based in Charleston, the slave trading capital of the United States.[14]

Membership in the Scottish Rite was open to all Masons who had completed the requirements for the three degrees of Blue Lodge Masonry, the lower degrees; the highest degree in the Scottish Rite was the 33rd degree, attainment of which entitled the Mason to learn the secrets of the Order that were deliberately withheld from the lower degrees. As it was stated by the Illuminati,

> The great strength of our Order lies in its concealment; let it never appear in any place in its own name, but always covered by another name, and another occupation. None is fitter than the lower degrees of Free Masonry; the public is accustomed to it, expects little from it, and therefore takes little notice of it. Next to this, the form of a learned or literary society is best suited to our purpose, and had Free Masonry not existed, this cover would have been employed; and it may be much more than a cover, it may be a powerful engine in our hands. By establishing reading societies, and sub-scription libraries, and taking these under our direction, and supplying them through our labors, we may turn the public mind which way we will.[15]

The membership of the lowest three degrees below the Scottish Rite, the Blue Lodges, were useful tools for subversive political projects because their members were in the dark as to the ultimate goals of the hierarchy above them; they could be manipulated. This blue-print for revolution laid out by the Illuminati also depended heavily on control of the printed word; in 1776, printing was still in its infancy, but by the time of the founding of the KGC in 1854-55, newspapers would be a most accessible media for propaganda purposes. Through the Blue Lodges and sympathetic newspaper publishers, the KGC would further its expansionist objectives in favor of a slaveholding aristocracy. Until that time, the tide of expansion of the American empire would build to a crescendo aided by the phenomena of the filibuster, only to break with the country divided and at war. Before that would happen the KGC itself would experience a schism within itself, with members forced to choose sides between the Republic founded by George Washington or one to be founded by secessionists. The issue that divided the KGC was whether slavery would be allowed to continue within individual states under state sovereignty, or whether slavery could only continue in a new country severed from the old.

Chapter Three

A Culture of Filibusters

In 1784 Spain closed the Mississippi River to free navigation for American citizens. This was intended to curb further expansion of the newly created Republic by strangling the fledgling western states' economies. This greatly angered southerners and almost led to the secession of several states. The controversy continued amid threats of violent intervention by armed westerners until 1795 when a treaty with Spain was negotiated and reopened the Mississippi. However, the conflict with Spain over its North American territories would not end there. Events subsequent to the Spanish Conspiracy would create the culture of "filibusters" that infested Texas before the Civil War and filled the ranks of the KGC. An East Texas newspaper defined the word filibuster in the context of its time, below:

> "Filibuster – We are often inquired of as to the etymology and precise signification of the word filibuster. The Boston Advertiser says the term… was derived from a Spanish name for a light boat, a vessel formerly in common use in the West Indies. It was similarly used in the French and other languages as descriptive of a class of freebooters of all European nations who infested the West India Islands and the coast of Central Ameri-ca for purposes of piracy, during the last half of the 17th century. In English they were commonly called Buccaneers."[1]

The above clarification was published in 1851, an indication that the term "filibuster" was used for years in describing some of the more adventurous persons immigrating to the West in search of plunder. Others had come for different reasons – so much so, that new arrivals were often asked, "…what have you done that you have come to Texas?"[2] Some came to Texas to escape the consequences of a duel or criminal act. Others, those known as "filibusters" saw in the vast resources of the unmanaged territory of Spain and later, Mexico, the opportunity of personal gain through plunder. As one early writer put it:

> No tales of border romance contain more thrilling adventure than the sim-
> ple record of these land buccaneers, who set out like the sea rovers of old
> to carve their fortunes from the gathered treasures and domains of the
> Spanish race….many of them – instance Travis, Crockett, and Cameron –
> were true patriots as well as filibusters….The line between the filibuster and
> the patriot is not easily drawn. Houston and Bolivar are national heroes
> because they succeeded; Walker and De Boulbon are remembered as fili-
> busters because they failed.[3]

Using this archaic definition of a filibuster, the earliest such character in Texas was a Kentuckian from the tobacco country: Philip Nolan. Between 1791 and 1801, Nolan led four expeditions into Texas from Louisiana that are now regarded as being "horse-catching operations motivated by personal profit rather than as revolutionary efforts to free Texas from the rule of Spain."[4] Regardless of whether or not political motivations are deemed necessary for one to meet the accepted definition of a filibuster, Philip Nolan inspired others that were to follow his exploits. No doubt he was considered a heroic figure by many of his fellow Kentuckians; the fact that historian Wentworth Manning began *Some History of Van Zandt County* with Nolan's story is an indication of the influence Nolan's exploits had on former Kentuckians like Manning. *Some History* not only concerns one county in Texas; it provides the insight of an early frontiersman of Texas on the major events of his day; Manning came of age during the Civil War. The particulars of Nolan's story are worth addressing to understand the filibuster element in Texas.[5]

Philip Nolan's life as a filibuster began with his introduction to James Wil-kinson, a man born to a wealthy planter's family in Maryland in 1757 who served as a captain in the Revolutionary War under Benedict Arnold. Wilkinson was in-volved in the Conway Cabal against George Washington and was forced to resign his commission in the army in disgrace. Moving to Lexington, Kentucky in 1783,[6] he secured a virtual monopoly over tobacco shipments from Kentucky to New Orleans, then under Spanish control, by swearing allegiance to the King of Spain in 1787. In 1788, he sent a large shipment of Kentucky tobacco down the Missis-sippi in care of his agent and business partner, Major Isaac Dunn.[7] During the year

1788, Wilkinson was the instigator of a scheme to separate Kentucky from the United States to ultimately become a territory of Spain; this became known as the Spanish Conspiracy. The majority of delegates to the Kentucky Convention rejected this proposal, opting instead for cooperation with Virginia. The following summer Wilkinson met with the Spanish governor of Louisiana, Esteban Miro, to complain about financial aspects of their trade agreement and to ask that he and twenty-one other Kentuckians be made pensioners of Spain. Miro advanced $7000 in silver to Wilkinson, which was entrusted to Joseph and John Ballinger to convey back to Kentucky for Wilkinson, while he and Philip Nolan returned home via the Natchez Trace. During the year Major Dunn committed suicide, presumably over the state of his financial situation, and Philip Nolan became Wilkinson's agent in the tobacco trade.[8]

Wilkinson abandoned the tobacco business in 1791 and re-entered the United States army. This left Philip Nolan at loose ends, and sometime after August 7th it is recorded that he sold a slave to Joseph Ballinger to raise money for travel.[9] Nolan then departed for Texas, then part of the Spanish province of Mexico, by means of a passport issued by Governor Miro. In late 1793, Nolan returned to Louisiana with fifty wild mustang horses that he had captured in Texas.[10] The cattle business was booming in Louisiana, but there was a chronic shortage of horses necessary to conduct that trade. Wild horses were abundant in Texas.[11] Nolan had found an intriguing way to make money. In June 1794, Nolan was given a contract to supply horses to the Louisiana militia regiment and armed with a passport issued by Miro's successor Governor Carondelet, re-entered Texas, returning in1796 with 250 horses which were sold at Natchez and Frankfort, Kentucky. A third expedition, begun in 1797, netted over 1,200 horses, but garnered political opposition from the Spanish governor-general of Louisiana.[12] Nolan had, however, attracted the favorable attention of Thomas Jefferson, then Vice-President of the United States, who began corresponding with him in 1798.[13] Nolan then began his fourth, and fatal, expedition to Texas in 1800, fully intending to visit Thomas Jefferson at his home in Monticello before he left, but the meeting apparently did not occur.[14] The expedition was doomed from the start, for at least two reasons that can be identified.

The Texas horse trade was technically illegal, although it was encouraged by Spanish officials who profited from it. The reason was that hard currency was in shortage in Louisiana, so the horse trade in Texas was conducted by barter, with Nolan bringing useable goods into Texas to trade for the horses he would sell in

Natchez and Kentucky. Barter did not result in a taxable transaction, so the Spanish government saw this as tax evasion. These horses were contraband, and Nolan was trading in them.[15] Secondly, the suspicious Spanish authorities would not grant Nolan an official passport for this last expedition, but Nolan undertook the journey anyway with an armed party of men. One Spanish official in particular, Jose Vidal of Natchez, undertook a letter-writing campaign with the intent to portray Nolan's expedition as a hostile one. In a letter dated October 6, 1800, Vidal wrote that "little by little the Americans will proceed to eat away those precious possessions of His Majesty."[16] Vidal, who has been described as "...a small, vindictive man, very proud of his key role in exposing the plot...." did base his argument on information from a defector from Nolan's expedition, who stated that its real intent was not to gather horses, but to conquer the province with the backing of either the English or James Wilkinson, who was now general-in-chief of the Federal army of the United States.[17]

With conspiracy theories gaining currency, the Spanish sent an expedition of 120 men armed with artillery to confront and arrest Nolan in Texas. Eventually they found his stronghold in what is today Hill County, near the present-day town of Blum in north central Texas. Nolan and his party of approximately twenty-seven men put up a fight until Nolan was killed by cannon shot. His men surrendered, with a few unnamed individuals possibly escaping. The Spanish commander had Nolan's corpse mutilated by cutting off his ears, which were sent to the governor.[18] Historian Wentworth Manning confirmed the mutilation story, listed the names of all the participants in the doomed expedition and wrote that Nolan was likely killed on Nolan's River in Johnson County, Texas.[19] Although rumors arose that Thomas Jefferson had authorized Nolan to undertake a filibustering expedition, the evidence points to horse smuggling as the reason for the undertaking. Historians have argued over the historical significance of the events, with one writing in 1901, "I believe that this murder of Nolan in 1801 was the beginning of that hatred of the Spanish and Spain which characterises [sic] the whole of the Southwest up to the present moment."[20] Others have stated that the Nolan expedition was the precursor of many other filibusters – the Burr Conspiracy, the Gutierrez-Magee expedition, the Long expedition and many others that involved Texas.[21]

Not long after Philip Nolan appeared, another soldier of for-tune with designs on Spanish land made his presence known at Fort Miro, now known as the city of Monroe in northern Louisiana. He called himself the Baron de Bastrop, a.k.a. Felipe Enrique Neri.[22] In truth, he was an international fugitive from justice without any royal titles. His real name was Philip Hendrik Nering Bogel, born 1759 in Dutch Guiana. After moving to Holland with his parents in 1764, he served in the Dutch cavalry before taking an appointment as a tax collector. Accused of embezzlement in 1793, "the Baron" came to Spanish Louisiana in 1795 after a reward of $1,000 gold ducats was offered in Europe for his arrest. With the self-imposed title of Baron de Bastrop, he passed himself off as a Dutch nobleman to the Spanish authorities.[23] It is one of history's ironies that the State of Texas owes so much to the accomplishments of a confidence man like Bastrop, for he was a major facilitator of the Anglo-American colonization of Texas. It is also of interest to note that "the Baron" was a major person of interest in the Burr Conspiracy.

The Burr Conspiracy was hatched by the treacherous General James Wilkinson, who in secret had become a Spanish citizen before taking command of the United States army. On the payroll of both the United States and Spain, he began to play the two countries against one another for his own profit. Wilkinson had already played a role in the downfall of Philip Nolan but was not yet finished with his international intrigues. Aaron Burr had taken control of the leadership of the Tammany Society or Columbian Order of New York in 1797, was the Vice President of the United States from 1801 to 1804 under Thomas Jefferson, had been convinced by Wilkinson that he could take the territories of Texas, New Mexico, and possibly Mexico away from Spain and establish an independent country.[24] Burr was also an original member of the Society of the Cincinnati. He had previously advocated that the United States seize Spanish possessions in the Southwest, and after leaving office, declared in Kentucky and New Orleans that he would spend the rest of his life in the cause of ending Spanish power in America.[25] Burr was warmly received in Kentucky, but even more so in New Orleans, where some three hundred citizens were members of the Mexican Association, dedicated to providing information and support to anyone who might invade Mexico.[26] The Baron de Bastrop figured in the scheme as an intermediary; in the transition period before Spain transferred possession of Louisiana to the United States, Bastrop had somehow convinced the last Spanish governor to grant him some 1.2 million acres of land in Louisiana and present-day Arkansas. Bastrop sold most of it – some two thirds to a Kentucky banker named Charles Lynch[27] and retained 100,000 acres for himself, with most of it being in present-day Arkansas. The Bastrop land was formally surveyed and conveyed in writing to the Baron on October 9, 1805. Bastrop was then permitted to enter Texas and establish a colony between the

Trinity River and Bexar, granted on October 18, 1805. Bastrop's land was to be used as a base of operations for Aaron Burr's invasion force, which was being financed and assembled by various individuals.

Future President Andrew Jackson had been hired by Burr to build five large boats for the expedition, paid for with a loan from the Kentucky Insurance Company. Other financing sources included George M. Ogden of New York.[28] After encouraging Burr in this filibuster, Wilkinson kept in contact with Burr and had several secret meetings with him. The result of one of these meetings was that Wilkinson sent Zebulon Pike on a mission to map a trail to Santa Fe. Zebulon M. Pike thus became the first Mason known to have entered Texas, in 1806 and 1807.[29] Before the proposed invasion took place, Wilkinson sent a letter to President Thomas Jefferson disclosing Burr's plans and Burr was arrested along with Peter V. Ogden, described as "a young Burr lieutenant." 30 Burr was indicted for treason against the United States and for a misdemeanor offense related to filibustering on June 24, 1807. He was found not guilty on the treason charge based on technicalities on October 20, 1807.[31] Before Burr's trial concluded, Wilkinson had negotiated a treaty with General Herrera, commander of Spanish forces in East Texas, supposedly to prevent an international incident over Burr's planned invasion of what was then Spanish territory. Wilkinson had no legal authority to do this and was secretly being paid by the Spanish government. The agreement created a buffer zone between the United States and Texas and essentially gave territory to Spain by moving the U.S. boundary back seven miles to the east. This buffer zone in Texas became known as The Neutral Ground, which extended between the Sabine River and the Arroyo Hondo, a small tributary of the Red River. Neither Spain nor the United States had legal authority in the Neutral Ground, so it became a natural haven for outlaws who flocked to the area in droves. By the time the 1810 revolution against the Spanish Crown broke out in Mexico, the Neutral Ground was so infested with murderers and thieves that the U.S. army was sent in to clean up the area. Commanded by Lieutenant Augustus Magee, the gangs were broken up by the army and order was restored.[32] Wilkinson would later face court martial by President Madison in December 1811 for actions taken by him as governor of Louisiana. His traitorous employment as a Spanish agent would not be discovered until long after his death. His niece, Jane Long, would become known as "the mother of Texas" and Wilkinson would support one more filibustering expedition to invade Texas – the Long expedition of 1820. Apparently, Wilkinson had some business dealings with Stephen F. Austin, for whom the Texas State Capitol is named, the natures of which are not known. Wilkinson died in 1825 and was appropriately buried in Mexico City.[33]

Augustus Magee, the pacifier of The Neutral Ground, became a named principal in the next filibuster that was supposedly inspired by the death of Wilkinson's protégée Philip Nolan. The Gutierrez-Magee Expedition began in December 1811 when Jose Bernardo Gutierrez de Lara traveled to Washington, D.C. in search of support for the antiroyalist revolution then under way in Mexico. Gutierrez was led to believe that the United States would support him in some vague, undefined way. Armed with a letter of introduction he sailed to New Orleans where he met with Governor William C.C. Claiborne, who introduced him to William Shaler, an agent acting as "observer" for President James Monroe. Shaler was also the principal adviser to the expedition and assigned Lieutenant Magee to help Gutierrez. On August 8, 1812, an armed party of 130 men crossed the Sabine River and invaded Texas. Magee's contingent grew in size and strength as it traveled toward San Antonio. With a force of roughly 300 men, Magee easily captured La Bahia, present-day Goliad, Texas. Magee died of apparent natural causes on February 6, 1813, and Samuel Kemper took over command. Kemper, with a force now grown to 800 men, captured San Antonio after defeating a royalist army of 1200 men. Unfortunately, Gutierrez lost control of his men and they executed the Spanish Governor Salcedo, General Herrera, and thirteen other royalist officers. Kemper and his men abandoned the expedition in disgust and returned to Louisiana. On June 20, 1813 royalist forces were again defeated outside San Antonio by the remaining filibusters. As Spanish forces re-grouped for another campaign, President Mon-roe's agent Shaler intrigued to remove Gutierrez from power and install in his place a Spaniard named Jose Alvarez de Toledo.[34] By this time most of the American idealists who wished the annexation of Texas to the United States had abandoned the expedition. Those Americans who remained were common looters and thieves; this American contingent was led by Henry Perry, a slave-trader. On August 18, 1813, Toledo and Perry's forces were massacred in the battle of the Medina outside San Antonio by a combined Spanish force of 2000 men. Of the 850 American volunteers who had stayed, only 93 survived by escaping into the woods. Colonel Perry and Jose Toledo both escaped.[35] In the months that followed, the Spanish generals conducted a bloody purge, with 327 persons executed in San Antonio and a similar number in Nacogdoches.[36] The Spanish General Arredondo pledged to kill every Anglo-Saxon he found on Spanish soil. The territory of Texas outside of Bexar was virtually depopulated, as many had fled to Louisiana.[37] Peace was temporarily restored when Augustin de Iturbide led Mexico to independence from Spain in 1821 and had himself declared Emperor of Mexico in 1822.[38]

The last of the early filibustering campaigns into Texas by Americans would be the Long expedition which began in 1819 in the midst of growing opposition and concern over privateering and the slave trade. Privateering was the concern of the Grand Jury of Baltimore when in February 1819 it reached the following decision:

> The Grand Jury having, in the performance of their official duty, been called to investigate criminal charges against per-sons committed immediately after landing on our shores from privateers, assume the right, if even it should not be considered a duty, of proclaiming their detestation and abhorrence of the odious and demoralizing business of privateering and African trading. The diabolical system of privateering, and robbing on the high seas, (or rather, Piracy, for it results in nothing else) has brought down the character of American seamen, from the proud pinnacle of glory and honour, upon which they once stood, to the degraded and disgraced situation of culprits and criminals, in which they are often now found....[39]

The jury was referring to the principle business of Jean Lafitte, who would play a role in the Long expedition and the establishment of Galveston, Texas as a major slave-trading port. Lafitte's Louisiana operation had been confiscated in 1814 and he had traveled to Washington, D.C. hoping for aid from President James Madison in the winter of 1815. Failing in that, he gradually assumed control of Galveston Island and had consolidated his power by September 1817.[40] On August 1, 1817, the collector of customs at New Orleans had notified the Secretary of State of the U.S. of "...shameful violations of the slave act, as well as our revenue laws...by a motley mixture of freebooters and smugglers, at Galveston, under the Mexican flag." Lafitte procured his illegal African slaves by raiding slave ships off the West Indies and smuggling the stolen human cargo to Galveston. Agents of the slave trade in New Orleans would transmit orders to Galveston for a specific quantity of slaves, which were then shipped to depots at the mouth of the Sabine River, Calcasieu, Bayou Lafourche, or one of numerous locales in Barrataria Bay. Sometimes the prospective buyers or their agents would journey to Galveston in person to inspect the slaves before buying. There also existed an overland trade, in which slaves were taken inland for sale, herded like cattle.

Lafitte's principal agents engaged in transporting slaves into the Texas mainland were the Bowie brothers – Resin P. Bowie, John J. Bowie, and the future hero of the Alamo, James Bowie. Negroes sold from Galveston went for a dollar a pound, with the average price being one hundred forty dollars per man. Lafitte did business in bulk. Any slaves confiscated by U.S. Customs officials would be sold at auction in New Orleans, thanks to a proposal made by a Georgia politician that had been passed into law. Louisiana slave companies would surrender the slaves received from Galveston to the customs officials, who then re-sold them to the highest bidder, giving them legal title and permission to ship them up the Mississippi River. Intermediaries were used as buyers at these auctions by the slave companies, who then bought the same slaves back from the intermediaries.[41] There were many ways to circumvent the law and make money in the slave trade.

Lafitte's involvement in the Long expedition was a result of his friendship with Andrew Jackson, for whom he had fought in the Battle of New Orleans in 1815. Dr. James Long had fought at New Orleans also and was a favorite of the former U.S. President as well. Long had married a niece of James Wilkinson and was designated the leader of the expedition which was backed by Wilkinson and John Sibley. The names of Wilkinson and Sibley have been connected by some historians to almost every major filibustering expedition against Texas.[42] Gutierrez was also a member of the Long expedition, which was the largest and best equipped filibuster since Gutierrez-Magee.[43] The Long expedition was a reaction to the United States abandoning its long-held claim to Texas in 1819 as part of an agreement to purchase Florida from Spain.[44] This angered many in the Southwest who no doubt were speculating in land and other commodities in Texas. The Long Expedition began in stages with an advance force of one hundred twenty men crossing into Texas on June 8, 1819. General Long left Natchez on June 17th with a group of seventy men and arrived in Nacogdoches on June 21st. On June 23, 1819, Texas was declared an independent republic by the filibusters and their supporters with General Long as its Commander-in-Chief. Following this declaration of independence, a complaint against the treaty of February 22, 1819 be-tween the U.S. and Spain was published in newspapers in Kentucky, Philadelphia, and Natchez. Provisions of that treaty negotiated by Secretary of State John Quincy Adams had attached East Florida to the United States in exchange for the U.S. giving up all claims to Texas which remained with Spain.[45] Long soon left for Galveston to ask for help from "the real power in the region, Jean Lafitte." Lafitte had already aided an illegal expedition of Frenchmen that had tried to settle on the

Trinity River in 1818 and had been expelled. Lafitte absolutely refused to get involved in Long's expedition.[46] Expectations had been raised not only in New Orleans, but in northern slave states like Maryland, where the news was reported as in this story:

Natchitoches, Jan. 15, 1820.

Being near the Head Quarters of the late Republican Army of Texas, you will naturally expect me to make some mention of this formidable expedition. From the flattering accounts and pompous proclamation of Gen. Long, many people in the northern states, believed that a considerable degree of respect-ability was attached to this expedition – But it was, at best, a visionary project, conducted by a set of men, who though they were possessed of a tolerable share of talents and education, who were led away by airy castles and romantic ideas…. A part of this army were taken by the Spaniards and sent to Mexico for trial; a part of them ran away; and Gen. Long, with some of his officers, are now at Galveztown with the celebrated pi-rate Lafitte. I have seen some of the officers who made their escape from the Spaniards, and have arrived at this place; they have lost their fortunes, …ragged and almost starved.

Thus has ended this formidable army, which has at no time amounted to more than 70 men, officers included….[47]

Long began to reorganize his forces on Galveston Island in 1820 and on September 19, 1821, sailed with fifty-two men and captured La Bahia on the mainland of Texas. Four days later, Long was forced to surrender to General Perez. He was taken as a prisoner to Mexico City where he was shot and killed by a guard, supposedly by accident.[48] Jane Wilkinson Long had been left on Galveston to fend for herself and her two children with only one slave girl to help her. Against the odds, she survived, and finally receiving the news of her husband's death, she went back to the mainland. Settling near Richmond, Texas, sometime later, she ultimately was known as "the Mother of Texas". In 1821 the U.S. Navy ran Jean Lafitte off of Galveston Island, and he disappeared.[49] Events had been set in motion and Long's death was only the end of the first era of filibusters involving Texas and Texans.

The argument can be made that a culture born of these intrigues took root in Texas, a culture that was hostile to the ideas of freedom and justice for all men.

After each successive filibustering expedition, a residue of adventurers, mercenaries and criminals were left to settle in Texas. Pondering their uncertain future on what was then the Southwestern frontier these men no doubt retained a hatred of Hispanic people and their culture as well as a general disregard for international law. Some historians have writ-ten that the Burr Conspiracy was one of a chain of events that led to the formation of the Knights of the Golden Circle or KGC and ultimately, the secret organization popularly known in Texas as the Klan. In Texas the KGC attained a measure of power it never reached in other parts of the United States; it was essentially a Texas-based phenomenon initially dedicated to filibustering in the name of the expansion of slavery.[50]

Texas was not the first Lone Star Republic created by filibusters from former Spanish Territory; that honor belongs to the short-lived Republic of West Florida. Of the West Florida Controversy of 1810 one historian has written,

> By mere omission, historians and cartographers generally ignore the heated debate between the U.S. and Spain regarding ownership of the territory following the Louisiana Purchase. They ignore that the debate began with an unsubstantiated interpretation of the Louisiana Purchase, proceeded along with bribery, coercion, and threat, and was concluded with aggressive force. They surely ignore the subsequent U.S. covert operations to illegally seize West and East Florida from Spain. These filibustering operations were some of the first on the U.S. expansionist record....

West Florida comprised an area that included parts of present-day Louisiana, Alabama, Mississippi and western Florida. Between 1804 and 1810, Samuel Kemper and his two brothers attempted to seize this territory so it could be annexed by the United States. The fact that one of the Kemper brothers had also been involved in the Gutierrez-Magee Expedition in Texas indicates that the Kemper brothers were somewhat unofficial agents of U.S. territorial expansion. Finally, in September 1810, a group of some 70 Anglo settlers seized the Spanish fort at Baton Rouge. West Florida was declared an independent empire, under its own flag – the Bonnie Blue flag that later was incorporated into the Texas flag in 1836 and was revived by the KGC in Texas in 1861. Its design was a single lone star in the center of a solid blue background. On October 27, 1810, Secretary of State James Madison announced that the United States would acquire the Republic of West Florida. The successful but false pretext used by the U.S. to take this territory from Spain was later used in arguing for the acquisition of both Texas and California: "It learned that exploiting the weaknesses of its rivals proved more effective in making gains than diplomacy, negotiations, and treaties."[51] The KGC would attempt to use the established tactics of the Federal Government to create its own separate empire for slavery.

In December 1832, a U.S. Army veteran of Andrew Jackson's Indian campaigns in Alabama and Florida crossed over into Texas from the Indian Territory. His name was Sam Houston. In his native Tennessee, he had invested in the Texas Company, a consortium created to speculate in Texas land headed by Robert Leftwich. The Mexican state of Coahuila y Texas had authorized Leftwich to bring settlers into Texas but the Leftwich claim became more difficult to legally enforce due to changes in Mexican law. A speculator in the Texas Company named James Prentiss secretly hired Houston to organize a filibustering expedition into Texas; if Houston succeeded, both men would be rich. Houston first proceeded to Tennessee to visit his old mentor, Andrew Jackson. What was said in their meeting was never made public, but it is clear that Jackson supported Houston's illegal venture; he provided Houston with a cover story and $500, a considerable sum of money in those days. Once in Texas, Houston met and travelled with James Bowie, the slave-trader and provocateur and exchanged information. While traveling the state in order to make contacts and gather in-formation Houston became involved in Texas politics. By October 1835 he believed that war with Mexico for Texas independence was necessary; he therefore became commander in chief of troops for the East Texas Department of Nacogdoches. The following month, he was made major general of the Texas army. In the War for Texas Independence that followed he found the volunteer soldiers difficult to control, insubordinate, and sometimes mutinous; characteristics that would later plague the Texan Confederate Army. Eventually Houston achieved total success with his defeat of General Santa Anna at the Battle of San Jacinto on April 21, 1836. In gratitude to one of the revolution's primary financiers after the battle Houston sent the captured saddle and bridle of a Mexican general to William Christy of New Orleans. Two days after Houston's victory at San Jacinto a company of volunteers from Mississippi, the Natchez Fencibles, linked up with the Texas troops looking for a role in a battle that was already over. The leader of the Mississippi troops was John Anthony Quitman, who would later co-found the KGC in 1854. His partner and co-founder of the Natchez Fencibles, Thomas Jefferson Green, was a former Florida legislator who became a Texas Congressman before serving in the California leg-islature. Born in New York and descended from Prussian nobility, Quitman moved to Mississippi from Ohio after joining the Masonic brotherhood in Ohio in late 1821. In Mississippi, he ingratiated himself with plantation nobility, espe-cially the Runnels family; Hardin Richard Runnels facilitated the expansion of the KGC in Texas while serving as Governor of the Lone Star State from 1857-1859. When Hardin Runnels father Hiram left his post as Governor of Mississippi one month earlier than necessary in 1835, John Anthony Quitman took over as acting governor for the one month that remained, served as Grand Master of the Masons in Mississippi from 1826 to 1838 and again from 1840 to 1845. Quitman had en-couraged Sam Houston in his revolution and so the men became close friends. At the close of the Texas revolution, Houston offered to make Quitman his second in command; when turned down Houston then offered to make him judge advo-cate in the trial of General Santa Anna, the defeated commander of Mexican forces. Refusing this also, Quitman returned home to his plantations in Mississippi and became brigadier general of that state's militia, but Texas would always be a major concern for him. During this time, he became a major slave owner, with 311 slaves on his largest plantation.[52]

The independent Republic of Texas became a reality in part due to the sup-port of businessmen and a smaller group of Mexican political exiles in New Orle-ans. Some of these benefactors were Masons; the Scottish Rite had been estab-lished in Mexico itself in 1806 by a group of French Masons. By 1828, the Mexican government had outlawed all secret societies which included the Scottish Rite Ma-sons. In New Orleans the Masons continued their revolutionary activities; the no-torious James Wilkinson was a member of Concorde Lodge number 3 on Dau-phine Street as was Lorenzo de Zavala, a signer of the Texas Declaration of Inde-pendence, and Warren D. C. Hall, described as a "filibuster and close friend of James Bowie"; Hall later became an officer in the Texas army. William Christy, while a personal friend of Sam Houston was reportedly not a Mason but was chair-man and treasurer of a New Orleans committee to aid Texas in its rebellion. On October 13, 1835, Christy chaired a meeting in New Orleans that raised money for the Texas revolution as well as an armed company of men known as the New Orleans Greys. In January 1836, Christy helped the Texans secure two loans to-taling $250,000 for the cause. He was a close friend of the intriguing Mason, James Wilkinson and had served as a soldier of fortune in James Long's unfortunate Texas filibuster in 1819. After the war was over, Houston granted Christy's sons

William and George a league and labor of land in the name of their cousin, Vincent Drouillard, for his service to Texas in the New Orleans Greys. Christy himself was appointed an agent for the Texas Railroad, Navigation, and Banking Company; eventually, he too became a plantation owner.[53]

Sam Houston was elected the first President of the Republic of Texas serving his first term from October 22, 1836 to December 10, 1838. During that time, he played a key role in organizing the Masons in Texas. On December 20, 1837, President Houston chaired a convention of all three Masonic lodges in existence in Texas. This body elected Anson Jones the first Grand Master of Masons in Texas. Jones was elected President of the Republic of Texas after Houston's term expired and in 1844 had a rather strange encounter with an agent of the Federal government. Duff Green, a former member of Andrew Jackson's administration was appointed United States consul at Galveston, Texas and attempted to involve the Texas President in international filibustering intrigues. Green's plan was to form two joint stock companies to secure investors in an invasion and takeover of the northern provinces of Mexico, which would then become part of the independent Republic of Texas. When Jones refused a bribe, Green threatened to start a revolution and overthrow the legitimate government of the republic. Green was thereafter barred from Texas but would continue his filibustering tactics from his office in New York; he was a likely candidate for being one of the five co-founders, with John Quitman, of the KGC. The correspondence of two different operatives of the British government confirm Anson Jones' version of events in regard to Green's proposed invasion of Mexico in 1844. In a secret letter from Charles Elliot to the Earl of Aberdeen, the British operative in Texas wrote of Green's intent being, "…to transfer almost all the powers of the Constituted Authorities of this Country, with the use of its flag, for purposes of disturbance and spoliation in Mexico, to a Confederacy of political Speculators and Capitalists in the United States….," and further,

> Keeping in view General Green's implication in the Nullification Agitation, and intimate connexion with the leader of that party, the reflection will present itself that there may be in this strange Scheme some speculation of preparing for the disruption of the South from the North in the United States, and ultimately for the Establishment of a great Confederacy extending from the Atlantic to the Pacific, with possession of the Californias. [sic]

Charles Elliot stated in his letter the idea that would become the central goal of the KGC; it was obvious even to an outsider that Texas would serve as a tool for the creation of an empire for slavery. Duff Green had become an ally of John Calhoun of South Carolina, whose son had married Green's daughter; Calhoun was the champion of disunion, as was John Quitman who sided with both men during the 1833 Nullification Crisis. There were those who later believed that John C. Calhoun was the "spiritual father" of the KGC. In 1846, Anson Jones, as the last President of the Republic of Texas, presided as the Lone Star state was ushered into the Union. John Anthony Quitman had been a fervent champion of the annexation of Texas to be admitted into the Union as a slave state, as was Duff Green. Both men made public speeches on its behalf. Sam Houston served a second term as President of the Texas Republic from 1841 to 1844; served in the United States Senate from 1846 to 1859, and as Governor of Texas in 1860, when he was publicly rumored to be leading a proposed invasion of Mexico aided by the KGC. In January 1851, Houston had been made a member of the Columbian Order of New York, also known as the Tammany Society.[54]

Jefferson Davis eventually became the nominal leader of that "great Confederacy" mentioned in British correspondence in 1844, taking office in 1861, but in 1844 he was campaigning for the presidential campaign of James Polk. On August 13, 1844, Davis spoke at a democratic mass meeting among Monroe and Lowndes counties in Aberdeen, Mississippi; taking a lead role in the conduct of this meeting was a future leader of the Texas KGC, John Alexander Wilcox, then of Aberdeen. This may not have been their first meeting; Wilcox did not move to Texas until 1853. Wilcox, who was described as "a handsome, jovial fellow, popular with men, women, and children" was a well-spoken lawyer and political operative in Mississippi, as shown by his introductory speech for this meeting:

> Gentlemen:…We have met for the purpose of interchanging friendly salutations, and joining heart and hand to sustain the men and measures so happily adapted to the genius of our government – the preservation of our liberties. We have nothing to fear. Our cause is the patriot's cause… for it is the cause of Polk, of Dallas, and of Texas. In conclusion, permit me, as the representative of the democratic association of Monroe, to return you their sincere thanks for the zeal and interest which you have manifested upon the present occasion, and bid you a welcome, a thrice hearty welcome to their town, their homes and their firesides.

Polk was soon-to-be President of the United States; "Dallas" was George Mifflin Dallas, his Vice President. Both men favored the annexation of Texas; the city of Dallas, Texas, was named in honor of the Vice-President. After the dinner that followed, Jefferson Davis was introduced as speaker. One listener later wrote, "...when he took up the Texas question, the effect upon the audience was elec[t]rical, and he proved to the satisfaction of every sensible man that it was to the interest of every section of the country to annex Texas. Mr. Davis was cheered throughout the entire discourse."[55]

Prior to Polk's election, President John Tyler and Secretary of State Abel Upshur had successfully negotiated a secret agreement to annex Texas, on February 27, 1844. The agreement obligated the United States to send troops to Texas, an act of war in Mexico's eyes. Tyler knew that it would have been difficult to bring Texas into the Union before the nominating conventions in May; he also had no power to declare war on Mexico. To complicate matters, his Secretary of State Upshur was killed in an accident. Tyler did not sign the joint resolution for the annexation of Texas until March 1, 1845, just three days before the end of his term as President. In December, Texas formally became part of the union under President James Polk. War with Mexico soon commenced; its outcome would solidify the career of John Anthony Quitman, Jefferson Davis, and many of the leaders of the KGC in Texas and elsewhere. Jefferson Davis served in this war under General John Quitman; Elkanah Greer, military head of the KGC in Texas, served under his friend Jefferson Davis. Other Mississippi residents during the Mexican War that later became leaders of the KGC in Texas were John A. Wilcox and John J. Good.[56]

The second President of the Republic of Texas, Mirabeau Lamar, signed up to fight in the Mexican War upon its outbreak in 1846, but upon leaving office in 1842 and falling into depression upon his daughter's death in 1843,[57] he began a curious crusade to attract more slave owners to Texas. The germ for this idea may have been planted in 1839 by his cousin John T. Lamar, who wrote from Georgia to his "Dear Cousin":

> ...I cannot see the policy of compelling the people of Texas to pay 1200 to
> 1500 each for Slaves raised in the United States, when they may be obtained
> from Cuba & other places at 200 to 300$ each.... All I believe admit that
> slave labor is indispensable to Texas, and without it she cannot in a century
> rise in wealth and importance much beyond what she is now.... the republic
> is already repudiated & denounced by the abolitionist in the United States

& elsewhere as a Slave holding people. Why not give to your Citizens the means to supply themselves with laborers to enrich the Country and themselves – There is a strong and growing feeling in the South in favor of Texas and particularly in this State....[sic][58]

Mirabeau B. Lamar had been a slave trader in Texas at least since 1838.[59] Thomas M. Bradford of Alabama wrote to him in 1838 proposing an invasion of Mexico "...organized and carried on under the Texas flag, and by the approbation of the Texas government." Bradford even offered a cover story, saying that Lamar could justify the invasion as a response to "continued efforts on the part of that government (Mexico) to make war on you through hordes of indians [sic] on your borders...."

I can assure you, from information and observation in which I cannot be mistaken, that at the first tap of the Drum for volunteers, 50,000 men – (100,000 if necessary) will rally under your standard and bear it triumphantly and plant it immovably on the walls of the city of Mexico! ...a large portion of the inhabitants of that country would be pleased at a change of government....It can – it must be done. Do write me and let me know your views on the subject.

If you cannot go, what do you think of Gen'l. Hamilton of S.C. and Gen'l. Gaines of the U.S. army. I think either or both would go with us. ...I have consulted, confidently with some of the heaviest capitalists in the United States. The money can be had – Now is the time.[60]

The failure of Lamar's Santa Fe Expedition in 1839 proved that an invasion of Mexican territory, "organized...under the Texas flag..." was not practical, as the fledgling republic's government could not even enforce the laws within its own boundaries as demonstrated by the events leading up to the Regulator-Moderator War, a civil disturbance in East Texas over land titles and slave-stealing that claimed dozens of lives. Nevertheless, President Lamar began a working relationship with the man referred to in Bradford's letter as "General Hamilton".

His true name was James Hamilton, the former governor of South Carolina who had begun speculating in land in East Texas in 1836. The Texas Congress drafted a joint resolution that year directing Sam Houston to offer Hamilton the command of the Texas army as a major-general. Hamilton demurred and instead encouraged his godson to relocate to Texas. His god-son Bernard Bee became his contact man in Texas; several Georgia speculators became partners with Hamilton in the South Carolina Land Company, which made its first purchase of Texas land on Caney Creek in 1836 and added thousands of acres to its holdings in subsequent years.[61] As mayor of Charleston, the capital of the slave trade in the United States, Hamilton had presided over the arrest, prosecution and execution of slaves involved in the Denmark Vesey revolt. It is been written that "Within six weeks of Vesey's execution, Hamilton had, politically and literally, ridden the back of black re-volt toward his ambition of higher public office." His version of the trials and executions, Negro Plot: An Account of the Late Intended Insurrection Among a Portion of the Blacks of the City of Charleston, South Carolina, was published more than a month before the court's re-port that autumn, first appearing on August 16, 1822. He was subsequently officially proclaimed the "hero of Charleston" by the state legislature.[62] In 1822, he was elected to the United States Congress and served until 1829 when he became the nullificationist governor of South Carolina from 1830 to 1833, a state that had been hostile to the federal government since 1822. Hamilton was John Calhoun's protégée.[63] As Vice-President of the Republic of Texas, Lamar had appointed Hamilton to assistant commissioner of loans in December 1837.[64] Hamilton indicated to M.B. Lamar in a transmittal dated November 3, 1838, that he intended to ship "a gang of Negroes to settle a Plantation in Texas." His plantation became one of the largest in terms of total slave population in the republic. Hamilton also offered to sell an armed blockade running ship to the republic in the event Great Britain and France attempted to prevent shipments of slaves to Texas; his partner in this venture was Gazaway Bugg Lamar, the Texas president's Georgia cousin. Another recommendation from Hamilton to then Texas President Lamar was for the state Congress to meet "in secret session" to pass a resolution for financing of the ship and other matters related to expanding the slave trade in Texas.[65] Hamilton dropped out of South Carolina politics after 1839 to devote all his time to affairs in Texas. In 1842, he bought a half interest in Retrieve Plantation in Brazoria County and shipped another load of slaves there from South Carolina. He confided in March 1842 to Albert Sidney Johnston, another future member of the KGC, that he intended to lead a filibuster to conquer Mexico and overthrow the government of Sam Houston in Texas, an idea that suspiciously parallels Duff Green's plans in 1844.[66]

Other KGC founders played the Texas question to political advantage. In November 1843, George Nicholas Sanders called the first meeting in the United States in favor of the annexation of Texas; political aspirant James Polk responded to the call at Ghent, Kentucky as strongly in favor of Texas' admission to the

Union, a move that served him well in the Presidential election. After successfully campaigning for Polk's election, George N. Sanders then moved to New York City and established an office on Wall Street to continue his involvement in Democratic Party politics. Sanders was later closely linked to KGC member John Wilkes Booth and other KGC operatives. A close associate of James Buchanan, George Nicholas Sanders was very likely one of the 5 founders of the KGC. He was also the grandson of George Nicholas, a Revolutionary War veteran who convinced Thomas Jefferson to write the Kentucky Resolution of 1798; disunion was in his pedigree. Others espoused the Slave Power's rationale for the necessity of the Lone Star state's admission to the Union. Former Texas President M.B. Lamar made a speech at Macon, Georgia on August 1, 1844, in which he stated, "slavery is not established in Texas on an immovable basis…there is in reality no serious obstacle to its extirpation…the present condition of Texas is such as strongly to persuade her to a gradual surrender of her slaves for the obtainment of peace." Lamar, a fervent supporter of the slave trade, had observed in this speech "…the Negroes in Texas as yet are few in number, bearing but a small proportion to the white population….Mexico is hard by, and would furnish them a suitable and an acceptable home" should abolition come. "If Texas is left to stand alone" continued Lamar, "there is every probability that slavery will be abandoned in that country….And when slavery gives way in Texas, the ruin of the Southern States is inevitable." The central idea that Lamar was selling his audience of southerners was this:

> The abolition of slavery in Texas, will be effected in a quiet and peaceable manner, without the loss of life or property; whilst its extirpation in the South will be but another performance of the tragedy of St. Domingo. A half century will not roll away before the slaves will so accumulate in the South, and the lands so decline in fertility, that this species of property will not only cease to be profitable, but will become a burden to its owners. In this situation, what will be done with the surplus of blacks? If Texas were attached to the Union, as a slave-holding country, she would not only afford a safe outlet, but would be a profitable market for them.[67]

Mirabeau B. Lamar was proposing that Texas become the expansion market for slavery and a custodial haven for slave owners from all over the United States. The speech was being made in support of the annexation of Texas to the United States. Three months after this speech, James K. Polk was elected President of the United States. Texas was annexed "soon after Hamilton returned (to Washington,

D. C.) from a trip to Texas…" during which Hamilton, "…informed Polk of his indispensable services in selling the idea to the Congress at Austin and to the merchants at Galveston."[68] Galveston was the most active slave market in Texas; Sam Houston was President of the Republic of Texas during the time of annexation. Some have intimated that Houston had acted in the Texas war of independence as an agent for Andrew Jackson, who as President of the United States had claimed the Neches River rather than the Sabine River as the southwestern border between the U.S. and Mexico.[69] The Neches River rises in eastern Van Zandt County, Wentworth Manning's home, and lies further west of the Sabine River; claiming the Neches as the boundary represented an aggressive assumption upon Mexican territory and further extension of the slave trade. Sam Houston was favorably disposed toward the slave trade, as shown by his appointment of James Hamilton's son as consul for the Port of Charleston, establishing a Texan consulate at the capitol of the slave trade in 1838.[70]

Some historians view the 1846 war inaugurated by President James Polk between the United States and Mexico as "…a conspiracy, a disreputable plot, favored by Tyler and executed by Polk, with the aid of self-seeking and unscrupulous 'slave-drivers.'…Mexico has been generally understood to have been the harmless and almost pathetically helpless victim of a brutal and grasping assailant."[71] A subsequent migratory wave into Texas was occasioned by the Mexican War and its swift conclusion. One historian wrote,

> It is difficult to explain with certainty the great interest that the war aroused among Alabamans. They were stirred by the love of adventure, by the hope of fame, and by a ready and not too critical sympathy with their fellow countrymen who were beset by foreigners some doubtless foresaw with tolerable clearness an increase in slave territory and planned therefore.

> Whatever may have been their motive in waging the war, there is no question that it brought them face to face with the great problem of slavery in the territories, which involved the question of states' rights and was to find its solution only in civil war.[72]

New Yorker John Sayles had gone to Texas during the Mexican War and had written his brother Thomas a letter in August 15, 1847, extolling the virtues and pitfalls of living in the Lone Star State. "The population of the state" he wrote, "is something like a 100,000; by terms of the annexation treaty, she sends two representatives to Congress." Continuing, Sayles wrote, "The immigration is very great from nearly all of the Southern States. Some 6 or 8 thousand have come from Germany within the last year…" Describing the settlements, he wrote, "New Braunfels…settled entirely by Dutch, and Fredericksburg, 50 miles from the former place, contain each about 2000 souls, that is Dutch souls." These German settlers would later be persecuted by the KGC. Continuing, Sayles described the other settlers:

> The people here are as they are everywhere else, if they can make a good trade off then they are pretty sure to do it. They are very fond of talking of their honesty, hospitality, etc., but any scurvy trick by which a few dollars can be made will be cheerfully played by that class. Taking the whole population as a mass there is undoubtedly more general intelligence & high toned feeling than in any other new state, more than in most parts of Georgia.[73]

Born in Ithaca, New York, Sayles had taught school in Georgia before earning his B.A. degree from Hamilton College in New York. He soon moved to Texas and was admitted to the State Bar in 1846 and acquired a plantation near Brenham. A large slave owner, he became a Confederate general during the Civil War and was involved in the organization of the Baylor University School of Law afterwards.[74] He was a high-ranking KGC member, serving on Aztec Club founder John Bankhead Magruder's personal staff while Magruder was supreme commander of the Confederate forces in Texas during the Civil War. John Sayles wrote numerous published books, one of which was used by Wentworth Manning as source material for *Some History*.[75]

With Mexico conquered in 1848, and New Mexico, California, and Arizona acquired by the Treaty of Guadalupe Hidalgo, covetous eyes turned to the province of Sonora in Northern Mexico. It had been noticed by members of the wartime Doniphan expedition in 1848 that northern Mexico was especially well-suited for stock-raising.[76] The Doniphan expedition had been part of the three-pronged attack launched by the United States on Mexico in the Mexican War.[77] No doubt many other expedition members spread the word of the wonders of Sonora and its riches once they got home. The northern Mexico province of Sonora would become the future target of a generation of California filibusters, and men from Texas would join them.[78] By 1848, there were as many slave states in the United States as free states, at least temporarily. More free states would be created from the lands acquired in the Louisiana Purchase, especially to the north and west of

Missouri, upsetting the balance between slave and free states.[79] James K. Polk died in 1849, and that year the Gold Rush lured Texans to California. Some Texans established a settlement on the east bank of the San Gabriel River, twelve miles from Los Angeles. It became known as El Monte, and was known for "…an enviable success in agriculture, unanimous loyalty to the Democratic Party, and an enthusiastic readiness to hang suspected criminals."[80] El Monte would supply both filibusters and Southern sympathizers in the decade ahead; with Sonora as their target, the true prize that northern Mexico represented for the KGC was not cotton, as many have mistakenly believed; it was grazing land for cattle. The mineral interests were not to be ignored, either, as gold and silver were hard currency needed by what would be known in the future as The Confederate States of America. The men of the KGC were long-range planners. By 1850, Mirabeau B. Lamar was advocating the secession of Texas from the United States.[81] That was the year that saw the birth of the initial goals of The Knights of The Golden Circle, as secession sentiment was once again brought to bear by political elements in South Carolina; specifically, by Governor Whitemarsh Seabrook. The South Carolina governor secretly wrote to the governors of other southern states, advocating a disunion scheme in which Mississippi Governor John Anthony Quitman enthusiastically offered to assume a leading role. Having spent most of his time in East Texas in 1847 and 1848, by 1851 former South Carolinian James Hamilton was also advocating the secession of Texas. A veteran of the War of 1812, with a father who had been the President of the Society of the Cincinnati from 1828 to his death in 1832, Hamilton had earned a reputation as a "knowledgeable and experienced military man" and had commanded a regiment of South Carolina militia. He also shared the grand delusions of the founders of the KGC, as it was said of him that:

> …he became obsessed with a grandiose vision of a vast economic domain with its hub at Charleston and its spokes stretching along the Louisville, Cincinnati, and Charleston Railroad into the West and along steamship lines to Liverpool. Commerce and cotton would be the lubrication of this wheel of fortune and James Hamilton would be the animating force that would put it into motion with the establishment of an integrated network of commercial-financial-transportation units in Europe and the South which would ultimately secure control of all production, shipment, and distribution of southern cotton.[82]

James Hamilton's early fixation on these ideas and his successful actions in achieving international diplomatic recognition for Texas in Europe and Great Britain suggest that he, too, could have been one of the 5 original founders of the KGC in 1854. He certainly thought along the same lines as those who sought the creation of The Golden Circle. However, he never had the successful Mexican War military career one would expect from the founders of the paramilitary Order; nor did he envision Cuba as the center or hub of the Golden Circle. He did have something in common with many promoters of the KGC: he became one of the largest owners of slaves in the Lone Star state.

The Mexican War came to a close with the occupation of Mexico City. Once things had settled into a relative torpor for the occupying forces, on October 13, 1847, a meeting of U.S. military officers was called in what they called "the City of Mexico." The men in attendance formed an exclusive society known as the Aztec Club; it was the spiritual successor to the Society of the Cincinnati. In fact, many of its original members were sons or grandsons of the original members of the Cincinnati; and like that organization that had chosen George Washington as its leader, the Aztec Club incorporated the hereditary membership privilege that had so angered the American public, with its echo of European aristocracy and alleged role as a military-led shadow government. For its leader, the Aztec Club elected John Anthony Quitman, who served as its first president for one year. Other founding members of the club included Robert E. Lee, General John Bankhead Magruder, and Barnard Elliott Bee, James Hamilton's godson. The second president of the Aztec Club, General Persifor Frazer Smith, would serve from 1848 to 1852 before taking command of all U.S. forces in the Department of Texas, serving there from 1850 to 1856. In September 1847, Persifor Smith was advocating the annexation of all of Mexico; John Quitman was doing likewise in early 1848. Quitman and Smith had shed blood to conquer all of Mexico – why give it back? Persifor Smith is likely the 5th founding member of the KGC; his military experience in Mexico and the West would be useful for empire building. When Quitman left Mexico for the United States, Persifor Smith took his place as leader of the Aztec Club. The insignia for the Aztec Club would be similar to that of the KGC, with only slight alteration; both prominently featured the Maltese cross of the Knights Templar.

After his election to leadership of the Aztec Club, New York born John Anthony Quitman was summoned to South Carolina on December 22, 1847. As Major-General in the victorious army of the United States that had conquered Mexico, he was recognized as Past-Master of the Grand Masonic Lodge of Mississippi by a special committee of Masons in South Carolina the following day. On that day John Quitman was made an honorary member of the Grand Lodge of South Carolina; the following day he was awarded the 33rd degree, the highest designation of the Scottish Rite. Upon attainment of this degree he was privy to the inner secrets of the Masons. In conveying these honors upon the victorious general, the Most Worshipful Master of South Carolina made the following address to all assembled:

> The Masonic Institution, it is true, is devoted to the cultivation of those virtues which find their more common exercise amid the occurrences of ordinary life, and may seem hos-tile to the military profession. But nature has stamped on the human mind the principle of self-defense, and under the influence of that principle Masons may go forth to battle when the voice of their country summons them to conflict.

Quitman then spoke, saying, "...there were circumstances in which war, for the defense of one's country, liberty, and rights, was strictly in accordance with all the duties and obligations of the Mason." He then noted that at Vera Cruz, he had been "...invited to be present at a meeting of a Lodge whose warrant of constitution had been granted by the Grand Lodge of Mississippi." This was a statement of the reach of the Scottish Rite into Mexico, and his state's role in that expansion. In a special ceremony, John Anthony Quitman was subsequently made an active member of the Supreme Council of the Southern Scottish Rite at Charleston, South Carolina, the governing body of all Southern Scottish Rite Masons. He had joined their inner circle and was now privy to the Book of Gold, "the book in which the transactions, statutes, decrees, balusters, and protocols of the Supreme Council or a Grand Consistory are contained." His appointment solidified a link between the secessionist movements in South Carolina and Mississippi, the two most important in the United States at the time. Secessionists in his adopted state of Mississippi referred to him as "Cincinnatus of America." His new position also gave Quitman access to the entire framework of the Southern Scottish Rite, a capability to be envied by the most ardent Illuminati. From his new seat of power, he could proselytize for the formation of the Knights of the Golden Circle throughout the Masonic network across the South, following the blueprint provided by the Illuminati.

Not everyone was as sanguine in their assessment of the Mexican War as the members of the Masonic Supreme Council in South Carolina. On the same day that John Quitman had been summoned to South Carolina by the Masons, a young freshman congressman named Abraham Lincoln stood up to address the causes of the war as propagated by President Polk. In Congress, on December 22, 1847, Lincoln presented proof that the war had not been started by Mexico, but by U.S. troops, in an unprovoked attack on Mexican soil. President Polk, not Mexico, was therefore responsible for the deaths of American soldiers, Mexican soldiers, and civilians. According to Lincoln, Polk had lied in order to acquire territory for slave owners like him. Lincoln's arguments added fuel to a growing anti-war chorus voiced by journalists as well as soldiers; both had witnessed atrocities committed by Americans in Mexico, and Texas Rangers in particular. One especially merciless incident involved a company of Texas Rangers who reportedly hung more than 40 Mexicans. For the old Texians who would later join the KGC, the slaughter in 1846 and 1847 was the continuation of a blood feud that had started many years before. In less than 7 years from Lincoln's speech, the KGC would be born in the mind of John Anthony Quitman in Natchez, Mississippi, but brought to life in his one-time state of residence, Ohio. The State of Texas, whose concerns were Quitman's long-standing interest, would provide his organization's muscle and sinew.[83]

The KGC is Formed

There has been some dispute as to exactly when, how, and by whom the KGC was formed. One Texas historian wrote of the Knights in 1893:

> Many years previously, a secret order was formed for the purpose of estab-lishing a Southern empire, with slavery, and known as the Knights of the Golden Circle. Its empire was to have Havana, Cuba, as its center and ex-tend in every direction from that sixteen geographical degrees. It is said that the filibustering expeditions of 1850 and 1857 were undertaken un-der the auspices of this organization, and that now, in the anti-slavery agitation at the North, the disappointed Democrats began to turn to it for aid.[1]

Although most historians believe today that the KGC was organized in Cin-cinnati, Ohio or across the Ohio River in Lexington, Kentucky in 1854, it is un-derstandable how some would have thought that the date of origination was 1850. KGC founder John Anthony Quitman was involved in both the failed southern states' secession attempt in 1850 and the filibustering efforts against Cuba that took place between 1849-1855. The mention of the 1857 expedition is in reference to one of three attempts to colonize Nicaragua; Texans were heavily involved in both the Cuba and Nicaragua expeditions. On July 12, 1850, an armed force of 250 Texans put to sea to join an invasion of Cuba led by Venezuelan-born Nar-cisso Lopez. Sam Houston publicly canvassed for money to support the expedi-tion, while sitting Governor of Texas Peter Hansborough Bell advocated the in-vasion and annexation of the island. This filibuster campaign had been conceived in 1849 by a New York-based consortium called the Cuban Council. Lopez had been hired by the New York revolutionaries to conduct the invasion with John

Quitman as his broker and sponsor. In Quitman's papers is found a letter to Lopez from John J. Good dated May 30, 1850. Good is one of the first men to bring the KGC to Texas. In his letter to Lopez, Good wrote from Alabama, "I desire to join your standard and think at least one Battalion can be raised from this State. Will you need more troops? If yea upon what conditions can I join you with a battalion." [sic] After being elected a Brigadier General of the Alabama militia, John Jay Good left his home at an unknown date in 1851 to join with other American filibusters in Mexico fighting for Jose Carvajal; among these men were future KGC leaders John Salmon Ford and Chatham Roberdeau Wheat. John Good took his life savings and left Alabama for Texas, arriving in Austin in October; while in Austin "he obtained reliable information of the brigandish character of the movement," and decided instead to settle in Dallas, Texas, where he arrived on November 25, 1851. After calling for the organization of a "military company in this place" in the *Dallas Herald* in August 1856, he became the nucleus of the KGC in that town. Whether Good was a participant in any of the landings on Cuba is not known; however, he must have had an important position within the organization for Quitman to have kept Good's letter to Lopez in his personal papers. The May 1850 Cuban invasion was undertaken by about 600 additional men from Louisiana, Mississippi and Kentucky; the Kentucky regiment was by far the largest, consisting of from 300 to 400 men. The Louisiana Regiment was led by Colonel C.R. Wheat, described as "a member of the bar in New Orleans." Chatham Roberdeau Wheat was wounded slightly in the attack, became a close confidant of General Quitman in further filibustering schemes, and played a key role in organizing the KGC. Quitman was indicted by a Federal grand jury in June 1850 for financing the failed invasion, but was acquitted in 1855. Because of his embarrassing legal troubles with the U.S. government, Quitman resigned his position as Governor of Mississippi; in 1850, the Cuban exiles shifted their base of operations from New York to a friendlier locale in New Orleans.[2]

Narcisso Lopez was not finished yet, however. On July 4, 1851 he declared that Cuba was free and independent from Spain; he did so from the safe and comfortable confines of Washington, D.C. For his third and final attempt at the liberation of Cuba, Lopez departed New Orleans with 420 men on August 3, 1851, intent on conquering the entire island with just that small force. Upon landing in Cuba, he realized he was outnumbered and without support from the supposedly rebellious citizens of the island. After his capture, he was killed by garroting on September 1st; a Spanish firing squad also executed fifty American volunteer members of his army, including William S. Crittenden, the nephew of Kentucky born John Crittenden, the attorney general of the United States. The American press had initially swallowed the false reports of success of this expedition; once the truth was known that some 150 Americans were still being held prisoners, the press coverage became ugly; some of the farewell letters written by the executed Americans began to show up in print. A letter represented to have been the last words of William S. Crittenden to his uncle said, "In a few minutes some fifty of us will be shot. We came here with Lopez; you will do me the justice to believe that my motives were good. I was deceived by Lopez. He, as well as the public press, assured me that the Island was in a state of prosperous revolution...." Some of the living prisoners, when interviewed in Havana by U.S. Navy Commodore Platt, "...manifested much indignation towards General Lopez and Mr. Sigur, editor of the Delta, at New Orleans, for deceiving them with false representations that Cuba was in a state of revolt." Papers held by one of the prisoners also revealed that one of the officers of the expedition was Felix Huston, a former Texan who continued his involvement with Quitman in later filibustering operations, including the KGC. Citizens in Cincinnati, Ohio were fearful that "some seventy young men from that place" had joined the Lopez expedition; they had not been heard from since. Finally, the Cincinnati Commercial broke the story of how this tragic fraud had been foisted upon its citizens:

> Previous to the fitting out of the expedition, we were called on by prominent men, engaged in the enterprise, for the purpose of securing the influence of our columns. This led to an exposition, on their part, of the plan of the campaign, and the means by which it was hoped to carry it out. Among those we con-versed with on this subject was Gen. Hamer's son, now no more.... There are others living with whom we had better success, and would name if it were necessary....

> Money was to be raised, and the bonds of the CUBAN GOVERNMENT THAT WAS TO BE have been disposed of, it is said, to immense amounts, at ten cents on the dollar. This was to engage the interest of speculators and certain leading newspapers. Leading presses throughout the country were to be secured, and it was thought the others would be their echoes, until politicians took up the subject; when the moneyed interest, the press and politicians would force the Government into measures of the secret clique which were then urging it forward, and fancy letters were to be written to keep the "ball" in motion [sic].

The story illuminated the true motivations of the promoters of this filibustering scheme, and the others that would be undertaken by members of the Order
of the Lone Star, and its successor, the KGC. As for the compensation for the
"activist" soldiers them-selves, it was said that "the officers…were to receive sugar
and coffee plantations with slaves on them….the soldiers were to receive $5,000
and all supposed degraded enough…were promised the smiles and gratulations of
the Creole girls [sic]." The manner by which the plantations with slaves would be
provided to the officers required the seizure of such property from the Cuban
citizens that did not support the invasion. Rumors began to circulate that John
Quitman was now in charge of the continuing efforts to acquire Cuba, by force if
necessary. Quitman withdrew his name from the nomination for Governor of
Mississippi in September 1851; the exposure of the Lopez invasion had damaged
his political career. Quitman's rationale for risking his reputation was succinctly
stated by the General himself: "Our destiny is intertwined with that of Cuba. If
slave institutions perish there, they will perish here. Thus interested, we must act.
Our government, already distracted with the slavery question, cannot or will not
act. We must do it as individuals."[3] Quitman owned over 300 slaves, a substantial
personal investment and a large percentage of his personal net worth.

Because of the Lopez disaster in September 1851, (supposedly) a new filibustering entity was formed in New Orleans. It was called the Order of the Lone Star.
The *Daily Delta* newspaper in New Orleans printed a revision of the order's constitution and by-laws, noting they had been revised by a committee of the "Parent
Division, of the 'Order of the Lone Star,' City of Lafayette, La." The document is
dated "1851" with no specific month of origination indicated. It is possible that
the Order was formed at an earlier date. Led by Dr. John V. Wren in 1851, the
organization drew its name from the Bonnie Blue flag of the West Florida filibusters and the Lone Star flag of the Texas revolution of 1836. Newspaper reports
suggest that this organization, or its predecessor, existed before the revision of its
bylaws. A dispatch from Savannah, dated April 28, stated "…one expedition
against Cuba has been set on foot, and is marching South across the States." On
June 17, 1851, a Galveston, Texas newspaper reported the following strange account:

> An expedition allegedly bound on a gold hunting trip along the Gila River
> in Arizona went thru Jefferson, Texas 'last Tuesday' according to an item
> in the *Jefferson Herald*. The rumor was however that the party was headed

for a filibustering trip to Cuba. This outfit, consisting of 'officers' and 'privates' carried a banner upon which was inscribed "Secession Southern Rights." This flag was part of the division of an extinct 'southern rights' association, which 'was born, kicked (once) and died, in Montgomery, Alabama.' The members were well equipped with guns, one piece of cannon, wagons, provisions, etc…. [sic]

A follow-up article by the same newspaper on September 21, 1851 stated that, "A company who started from Alabama last spring, for the Gila, by way of the Red River, were met at the Pecos, nearly worn out with fatigue, famine and sickness. They are coming to San Antonio to recruit" [sic]. Was this the company that John Jay Good had offered to recruit in Alabama for Lopez in his letter of May 30, 1850? Jefferson, Texas was a port on the Red River and the destination for travelers to and from New Orleans to North Texas. Good had left Mississippi and moved to Alabama in 1850; if it was Good's company, it would explain how he got as far west as Dallas, Texas from Alabama, arriving November 25, 1851 after returning from Austin, a city much closer to San Antonio than Dallas. Supposedly Good had intended to join the Carvajal filibuster in Mexico that attracted fellow Texas KGC members John S. Ford and Hugh McLeod, but for some reason Good elected to change directions and head for Dallas. Dallas was just a tiny village on the Trinity River in 1851; a very unimpressive settlement on the edge of the wild frontier. If the remnants of the Alabama southern rights company got to San Antonio, it would also explain the early start both the Order of the Lone Star and KGC got in that city as the successor to the Order of the Lone Star. The Texas branch of the Order of the Lone Star became known as the Order of the Lone Star of the West and took on a distinct character of its own. Ultimately the Order spread to the Texas towns of Austin, Dallas, San Antonio, Houston, Henderson, Washington, Victoria, Indianola, Lavaca, Corpus Christi, Brownsville, Rio Grande City, Webberville, Laredo and El Paso. A strange poem was published in 1844, before Texas officially joined the Union, and republished in a Dallas newspaper in 1908, titled, "The Lone Star of the West". The last stanza of the poem seems to link the Lone Star of the West to the Knights of the Golden Circle:

Lone Star of the West: latest boon of that spirit
Who twined of such gems our own luminous wreath:
When linked with our circle thy rays shall inherit
Whole ages of glory, unstained by a breath.
Thou should'st not be left it: thy loneliness gleaming

While near thee are kindred so brilliant and blest:
Come, gild our cynosure – thy rays through it streaming,
Shall hallow the circle – Lone Star of the West.

The author of this poem, Edward John Porter, was born in Ireland around 1823 and did not enter the U.S. until 1845, landing at Charleston, South Carolina. From there he went to Kingstree, South Carolina, "with letters of recommendation from prominent men in Charleston," the slave trading capital of the United States. The 1850 census shows him as a resident of Kingstree, Williamsburg County, South Carolina, boarding in the Mouzon house with Neighbor D. Lesesne. It was said that he had many friends and acquaintances in Texas. He became a slave owner and a prominent attorney in his adopted home, "a frequent contributor to the leading newspapers and magazines of the country about the time this poem was written." He married Mary Jane Lesesne in May 1853; Joseph White Lesesne was one of John Quitman's Alabama agents in 1854, indicating a family connection through his wife to the Order of the Lone Star. During the Civil War, Porter served as a commissioner in the Confederate States court at Williamsburg and supplied at least one slave to help build the fortifications of Charleston. He died in 1873, so "The Lone Star of the West" was written during the formative years of the Order of the Lone Star; its Texas branch became known as the Lone Star of the West, and its successor, the Knights of the Golden Circle. The Lone Star of the West did have a chapter in Dallas, where this poem was republished, established sometime before 1856 by John J. Good. Not much else is known of the man who wrote the poem, but he seems to be yet another link between John Quitman's Charleston-Mississippi-Texas circle, facilitated by Masonic connections; the "prominent men in Charleston." As to the unidentified, Alabama-based filibuster attempted in 1851, some historians believe the KGC was incubated by the many southern rights organizations that sprang up, a movement first inspired by a convention of planters held at Montgomery, Alabama in February 1845. John Quitman made effective use of the planters' conventions, using them as a platform for his speeches on Southern rights. By 1850, Alabama was the leading cotton growing state in the country and began promoting the "Florida Plan" that proposed to create a cotton grower' cartel. Meetings were held in Montgomery in 1850 to discuss the planned Cotton Growers Association convention that did in fact take place in October 1851 at Macon, Georgia.[4]

On December 27, 1851, the *Daily Delta* announced that the Order of the Lone Star was holding a "Fancy and Dress Ball" at Lafayette, Louisiana. In May

1852, the Spanish consul in New York claimed that Dr. Wren, the leader of the Order was in the city enlisting new members in concert with some of Lopez' former collaborators; supposedly they were organizing a rendezvous of the Order for another Cuban expedition to sail from Mobile and New Orleans. In September of that year, the Spanish foreign minister complained to the U.S. State Department of a wide-spread recruitment effort in American cities for a Cuban invasion, supported by various newspapers; even advertising their schedules for military drills and target practice. In October 1852, New York-based Cuban exiles formed a new revolutionary organization. In January of the following year, the Democratic Review, a New York-based publication that served as a mouthpiece for the Young America movement, ran a 6-page article on the Order of the Lone Star, noting "We have no knowledge of the secret principles, as we have not been honored with the membership of this celebrated order.... We understand the purpose of the Lone Star to be, first and foremost, the liberation of Cuba from the despotism of Spain and her allies [sic]." Additionally,

> events are in preparation which will remove all necessity for violence in regard to Cuba. The order of the Lone Star…will not be called upon to exert itself openly. The spirit of the people is adverse to violence. If Cuba can be secured by purchase, it will be the glory of the next Democratic administration to accomplish its liberation.[5]

Efforts to purchase Cuba from Spain ultimately failed. In April 1853, the agents of the new Cuban junta recently formed in New York approached John Quitman in his hometown of Natchez, Mississippi to recruit him to lead another invasion. Quitman accepted and was appointed by the junta to be "civil and military chief" of a proposed invasion and uprising intended to overthrow Spanish rule from the island. He was also authorized to issue bonds backed by the replacement government of free Cuba, in order to raise money not only for the proposed new government, but also for his pay. Once it was made known that Quitman was in charge, members and supporters flocked to the Order of the Lone Star. Known members included Pierre Soule, a Louisiana Congressman; John Salmon Ford, Texas legislator, Texas Ranger captain, newspaper editor and future Texas KGC leader; Hugh McLeod, a future Texas-based fundraiser for the KGC; Charles Augustine Lafayette Lamar, a Georgia slave trader, son of New York banker Gazaway Bugg Lamar, and relative of former Republic of Texas President Mirabeau B. Lamar; and in New York the Order's leader was George Nicholas Sanders, a future co-founder of the KGC. The Order operated out of Tammany Hall in New York;

many members of the Columbian Order of New York were sympathizers if not members.[6]

The election of Franklin Pierce to the White House in 1853 seemed at first to be a filibuster's sweetest dream. Pierce packed his cabinet with expansion-friendly political operatives: Caleb Cushing, Attorney General; Jefferson Davis, future President of the Confederate States, as Secretary of War; James Buchanan, future President of the United States from 1856-1860, as U.S. Ambassador to England; George Nicholas Sanders, U.S. Consul in London; Pierre Soule, former Louisiana Senator, U.S. Ambassador to Spain; and William Leslie Cazneau, U.S. Consul to Santo Domingo. Boston-born William Cazneau was a soldier in the Texas war for independence from Mexico, served in the government of Mirabeau B. La-mar, served three terms in the Texas Congress, and fought in the Mexican War until 1847, when he partnered with filibuster Henry L. Kinney in Texas land acquisitions. Cazneau's wife, Jane, nee McManus, alias Cora Montgomery, had been Aaron Burr's agent in Texas and an agent for Stephen F. Austin's Colony in Texas. She acquired 1,000 acres of land there, which led her to speculate further in Texas' land and its future. Through her writings, published under a pseudonym, she actively promoted filibustering for Cuba and Nicaragua. Future Texas KGC leader John A. Wilcox shared her views, at least on Cuba and more than likely on Mexico. In 1852 she was living on the Mexican-Texas border, where she published unfounded accusations of Mexican atrocities in an attempt to encourage revolution in Northern Mexico. Caleb Cushing of Massachusetts was a pro-South leaning kingmaker in the Northern Democratic Party with ties to southern secessionists. Like John Quitman, Cushing was a General in the Mexican War. Their newly elected President, Franklin Pierce, took a strident tone in his inauguration speech, stressing the expansionist desires of his constituents. It was rumored that Pierce himself was a member of the Order of the Lone Star. [7]

Jane Cazneau's work as Young America's voice of expansionist propaganda had led her to Eagle Pass, Texas in 1852, a town she and her husband had helped found on the Mexican border. Revolution had already begun in Northern Mexico the previous year. A Texas newspaper had reported in September 1851 the existence on Mustang Island, off the Texas coast, of two companies of men from Narcisso Lopez's failed, and fatal, invasion of Cuba. Half of these beaten men decided to return to their homes, but the other half reorganized, elected officers, and intended to join the new revolution supported by Jane Cazneau and led by Jose Maria Jesus Carbajal. This attempt to revolutionize Northern Mexico became known as the Merchant's War, because it had commenced after Carbajal issued a pronouncement demanding that Mexican troops withdraw from the northern states of Mexico and allow a five-year grace period for American goods to flow duty-free across the border. After an arrest attempt by Mexican authorities, Carbajal took up residence in Brownsville, Texas. There he was able to recruit Texas merchants and filibusters such as the remnants of the Lopez Expedition; some 200 to 700 Americans joined his paramilitary force. On September 20, 1851, they attacked the Mexican town of Camargo, as excitedly reported by New Orleans newspapers:

> The whole force under Col. Carvajal was three companies, amounting to three to four hundred, if I am rightly informed. One company from Guerrero, under command of Don Jose Maria Canales, was placed in front; the second company, almost all Americans, was placed in the centre, under command of Capt. Tremble; and the third company, under the command of Don Tomas Cabazos. They were led to the plaza by Col. Carvajal, in spite of cannon and every other mode of defence which the Mexican troops could adopt [sic]. The houses on the plaza which could afford them any protection were soon taken, and every Mexican soldier who dared make his appearance above the house-tops was immediately shot by Texas rifles....

Carbajal's forces did succeed in taking Camargo that day, and the town became his temporary base where he waited for reinforcements from Texas. On October 1, 1851, John Salmon Ford, member of the Lone Star of the West and future KGC member, arrived in Camargo with twenty-nine other decommissioned Texas Rangers; Ford became a Colonel in the insurgent army; "Robert" [Roberdeau] Wheat also became a Colonel in this army. "Capt. Tremble," the leader of American forces at Camargo, was Edwin Trimble, another future KGC leader in Texas. Although Carbajal continued to receive recruits from Texas, it ultimately was not enough. John Quitman and Felix Huston jointly signed a letter in August 1852 to Texas Governor Bell offering the service of the Natchez Fencibles "for frontier service," offering to boost the state's military force with troops from Mississippi. Carbajal continued his raids from Texas into Mexico until March 26, 1853. He was arrested twice by U.S. authorities but was released both times; his attempt at revolutionizing Northern Mexico fell out of favor and he faded from prominence, living out his life on the border. One intended consequence of Carbajal's career may have been an increased likelihood of further revolutions; one such later revolution against Mexican dictator Santa Anna resulted in his acceptance of the terms of the Gadsden Treaty of 1854, which ceded a large part of what is now southern Arizona to the United States. It is said that Carbajal was a soldier in the 1854-1855 revolutionary movement against Santa Anna. The land Mexico ceded was needed for the right-of-way for the proposed Southern route of the Transcontinental Railroad. Jefferson Davis, as Secretary of War, wanted a southern route in order to encourage slavery in California. South Carolinian James Gadsden had been appointed to negotiate the treaty in May 1853; after his success in doing so, Gadsden returned to his plantation near Charleston to work, breed and occasionally sell some of his 300-plus slaves. After the Arizona land was purchased in 1854, President Pierce lost interest in the project, but Jefferson Davis made efforts to keep the southern railroad project alive for military reasons, an interesting decision for the future commander-in chief of rebel forces.[8]

Once Quitman was in charge of the Cuban invasion contemplated for 1854, he "absorbed" the Order of the Lone Star, as one historian put it. From the very beginning some of the seasoned filibusters in his command attempted to steer him towards the conquest of Mexico, which became the initial goal of the KGC. One of these was C. R. Wheat, a veteran of at least one of the Lopez expeditions who wrote Quitman in January 1854:

> Gen. Carrajal has authorized me to say that if the friends of Cuba will furnish him enough money say $200,000 to revolutionize the states of Tamaulipas, Nueva Leon & Coahuila, then he will then repay the $200,000 & give the ports of Tampico Matamoras & San Fernando to the friends of Cuba together with such artillery, small arms & other munitions of war as they may need. Now it seems to me that the longest way around may turn out to be the shortest way home. The Sierra Madre country can be revolutionized by November. Large bodies of men can be very easily thrown across the Rio Grande for the ostensible purpose of assisting the Mexicans to throw off the yoke of Santa Anna & nothing more; but that once done & Spain & the U.S. being thrown off their guard; how easy it would be to transport a well-organized force of six or seven thousand men from a port completely under our control to Cuba. There would be no necessity for you to appear in this minor movement in person; but the basis operation being se-cured by your Subalterns you could then take command [sic].

"Carrajal" was of course Jose Carbajal; Wheat further put his ideas in perspective by noting, "…in case you should not be able to raise the requisite amount

to make a movement directly upon the island then you might take into consideration this as a [last] resort."[9] Wheat's words would prove prophetic and were his
greatest contribution to the creation of the KGC by Quitman.

In the meantime Felix Huston was actively trying in the Baton Rouge area to
raise the requisite amount of money for the Cuban invasion, writing Quitman on
March 4, 1854, that "I have written a letter to our planters, in which I wish to refer
to the committee by name. But I do not know whether I ought to do so without
seeing Mr. S." Mr. "S" was Pierre Sauve, a St. Charles Parish sugar planter and
fundraiser for Quitman in the New Orleans area; others enlisted for this task in
New Orleans included Samuel R. Walker. Others worked to procure men and material for the invasion. Thomas Scott Anderson, another future KGC leader in
Texas, wrote Quitman from Austin, Texas in April, 1854 and by way of introduction noted that "…I am a brother of Col. J. Patton Anderson, formerly a representative in the legislature of your State, from DeSoto County – I was a resident
of Mississippi in 1851, and met you at Hernando during your canvass for Governor." T.S. Anderson made the following offer in his letter:

> I will confide this communication to Col. John S. Ford, who you will rec-
> ollect, commanded a company of Texas Rangers in the Mexican War, with
> honor to himself and to his State. He has received intimations from those
> friendly to the cause of freedom, that an expedition is being fitted out, the
> effect of which will be to render 'material' and effective aid to the oppressed
> and downtrodden Patriots on the island of Cuba – that this expedition will
> leave the shores of the U. States within a few weeks from this time, fur-
> nished with all the accoutrements of war, and commanded by yourself, and
> he has been solicited to join the expedition, with a corps of Mounted Rifles.
> With these assurances and solicitations he now proceeds immediately to
> Galveston and perhaps to N. Orleans to confer more fully with the leaders
> of this movement, and if possible with yourself [sic].

Anderson concluded by saying that "myself and others from your State would
be gratified with an opportunity to join the Expedition."[10] However, in the face of
all the enthusiasm and support rumored for Quitman, events soon conspired
against his venture. On May 20, 1854, the Kansas-Nebraska Act was signed into
law by President Pierce; a provision of the new law repealed the Missouri Compromise as it applied to Kansas and Nebraska territories, the net effect being that
whether those territories were to be "free soil" or slave states would be up to
voters within those states. This opened the prospect of the expansion of slave

territory within the United States; it also meant that President Pierce had used up his political capital with Northern, anti-slavery voters and could not support the invasion of Cuba. This undercut support for Quitman's expedition. One of those who began to personally back away from direct involvement was Texas newspaper editor John Marshall, who wrote Quitman on June 14th, "…I should not presume on the present occasion to say that I would desire strongly to be with you in effecting the independence of that oppressed country….I am now on business in Mississippi & have allowed myself at least a month's absence from my post in the *Texas State Gazette*." Marshall would continue to encourage Quitman in "striking a blow for Cuba under yourself as Commander…," just without him. Marshall would, however, strike a blow for the KGC in Texas.[11]

Quitman was not ready to give up just yet. On June 20th, a reporter found General Quitman and a brother of Jefferson Davis together on a steamboat from Vicksburg to Natchez. The reporter noted, "The conversation, of course, turned on Cuban affairs, from which I gathered that there is really a great cry, and likely to be little wool, from the filibuster movements. The general would like to see Cuba a slave republic; that is, a republic, in whose constitution the leading article shall be one guaranteeing the perpetual existence of slavery…." This article appeared in the *New York Herald*, and many articles similar to it appeared in many other newspapers across the country, making the illegal operation one of the worst kept secrets in the world. The lack of secrecy prompted the U.S. Supreme Court Justice in New Orleans, John A. Campbell, to convene a grand jury to investigate whether a violation of international neutrality law was occurring. Quitman was summoned from his home in Natchez to appear before the court to answer questioning. His attorney representing him in this case was Thomas Neville Waul, a Texas plantation owner who had lived in Mississippi from 1833 to 1850. Waul, who was by birth an Englishman, later became a KGC leader in Texas. On Wednesday the 28th of June, Quitman made his appearance and denied any knowledge of a revolutionary movement against Cuba and was dismissed by the Grand Jury foreman. However, on Saturday July 1st Judge Campbell decided to place Quitman and two other men, John S. Thrasher and Dr. A. L. Saunders, under $3,000 bond as assurance that they would break no laws in the future. The men flatly refused to sign the bonds, were taken into custody of the Marshal, and held in the City Hotel. On Monday, July 3rd, the men reappeared in court and signed their bonds, registering formal protest. No one had ever been indicted. By that afternoon they were free to go.[12] The question is now, was John A. Quitman able to make the July 4th meeting in Lexington, Kentucky, at which time and place the KGC was allegedly born?

George W. L. Bickley, whom many mistakenly have claimed as the founder of the KGC, is generally now considered to have been its front man, master salesman and recruiter. Born at Bickley Mills, Virginia in 1823, to a family of some local repute, he became the public face of the KGC by 1859; but in 1854 was a relative unknown. After his first wife died in 1850, he helped establish the first Masonic lodge in his home county of Russell, Virginia. A self-taught doctor, in 1852 he joined the faculty of the Eclectic Medical Institute in Cincinnati, Ohio; the following year he married Rachel Kinney Dodson, an affluent widow. In Cincinnati he set about to establish himself as a writer, editor, and public man, and was described as "a fluent and eloquent extempore speaker". He had a novel published in 1853, and using his wife's family's money, employed an editorial staff that enabled him to produce 2,700 pages of lectures and more than 200 pages for Physiological and Scientific Botany. He also served as editor of the Western American Review (in addition to his duties at the Eclectic Medical Institute) until his wife's family cut him off from any further money. He suffered a nervous col-lapse by mid-1853; in the spring of 1854, he left his job at the Medical Institute. Bickley, in his crusade to build the KGC into a national organization, consistently maintained that the organization "…originated at Lexington, Kentucky, on the fourth day of July 1854, by five gentlemen who came together on a call made by Gen. George Bickley, the President of the American Legion, K.G.C." Those who came in contact with Bickley over the years learned not to believe everything he said, and many soon said he was not the real man in charge. That man, the true founder of the KGC, was said to be John Anthony Quitman. Could Quitman have made the journey from the courtroom in New Orleans on the afternoon of July 3rd to Lexington, Kentucky by July 4th? The distance is approximately 750 miles; the only possible way to complete the journey would be by train. If a train could average 20 miles per hour, a non-stop trip (if that was possible) would consume about 38 hours, more than a day and half; it seems unlikely then, that Quitman could have made that trip on that day. Quitman did in fact go to Cincinnati the year before, exact arrival date unknown, from where he sent a letter to his wife on July 6, 1853; spending several days there "visiting foundries and talking to contractors"; by that time he had been engaged in his Cuban conspiracy for months. Bickley was in fact a contractor used by the KGC as a professional agitator and was living in Cincinnati when Quitman made his weeklong visit in 1853. It may not have been the last opportunity for Bickley to meet the general. Quitman was as far north as the Astor House in New York City by early October 1854, but his whereabouts until then are sketchy, as he travelled throughout the country at will. So why did George Bickley give July 4, 1854 as the day of origination? July 4th is Independence Day in the United States, a celebration of the successful revolution against Great Britain by which independence was obtained. The goal of the KGC was to establish an empire for slavery, independent from the United States, by revolutionary means if necessary. July 4th is also the day that Narcisso Lopez announced independence for free Cuba, and the Golden Circle was to have Havana, Cuba as its central point. It is also true that by July 4, 1854, John Anthony Quitman was a free man once again, having been held against his will by an officer of the United States Circuit Court.[13]

This is all very symbolic, and a Mason like George Bickley certainly understood the power of symbolism; the Masonic Order is built upon it. But when is it likely that the KGC was born, and was Lexington its birthplace? Judging from the June 20, 1854, reporter's comment in the *New York Herald* that the filibuster movement would likely produce "little wool," it was already becoming apparent that the proposed invasion of Cuba was set to fizzle out. The hoped-for support of President Pierce had been withdrawn by May due to political considerations from the passage of the Kansas-Nebraska Act. Because of the lack of any true secrecy surrounding the expedition, the Spanish government was well aware of Quitman's plans and had fortified the island. They had also threatened to free all the slaves in Cuba and arm them against an invasion by the pro-slavery forces under Quitman. On July 4, 1854, the *New York Herald* chronicled the futility of attempting an invasion of Cuba under these circumstances, noting:

> The whole population of the island is 1,130,000; of which the white population, chiefly creoles, is 500,000; free negroes 200,000; Bozales, the imported negroes, justly entitled to freedom, 180,000, and the slaves 250,000. The Bozales, most of whom are full grown males, are said to be among the most savage and bloodthirsty barbarians, and we may therefore add, in the case of war, 100,000 Bozales to their Spanish contingents, to say nothing of the other 200,000 free negroes. Furthermore, we have been admonished, that in the event of an armed invasion by the United States, the 200,000 slaves will be emancipated and turned loose on the common enemy…. the invading army will never get out of Cuba. …in this view, our readers may

rest assured that the war has been postponed till the first Monday in December next.

For all practical purposes, the Cuban campaign was over by July 4th, and the organization behind it had been exposed, with all its flaws made apparent. Quitman was a man of his word, however, and he continued for a time to pursue any possible means to revive the movement. July 4th would have been a great moment to have a meeting of the faithful, to reconsider strategy and plan new approaches. But would Quitman have come to such a meeting called by a relative lightweight like Bickley, who had no recognizable military experience? An old warrior like Quitman would have been able to size up Bickley very quickly. There is no record of any correspondence between the two men; but their meeting could have been facilitated by others in September 1854, at Lexington, Kentucky.[14]

By September 1854, it was known that the expedition had failed to raise the amount of money Quitman had stipulated for the invasion of Cuba. Texas KGC member John Marshall wrote Quitman a letter dated September 18th, in which he said, "I am deeply sorry that the want of funds prevents the consummation of our purposes. Cannot the Cubans make up the $200,000. I know they have contributed largely already, but then what is that additional sum, compared to the complete & permanent freedom of their island?" It was apparent to Quitman at this point that the creation of an empire for slavery in conjunction with the Order of the Lone Star was not happening; but he was still in contact with fundraisers, many of whom were Masons. The most likely time and circumstance for a meeting between Quitman and Bickley was at the Triennial Meeting of the Masons of the General Grand Chapter and General Grand Encampment of the United States, held at Lexington, Kentucky from September 13-20, 1854. This meeting drew Masons from all over the United States to Lexington at a time when Quitman dearly needed their support. This private meeting between Bickley and Quitman was likely facilitated by a high-ranking Mason well-known to John Anthony Quitman; Killian Henry Van Rensselaer.[15]

Van Rensselaer was the highest-ranking Mason in the Northern Scottish Rite, and he had moved to Ohio not long after Bickley, in 1851; Quitman was on the Supreme Council of the Southern Scottish Rite. Both men were 33rd degree Scottish Rite Masons, privy to the highest secrets of their order. Masonic sources identify Van Rensselaer as "the St. Paul of Scottish Rite Freemasonry, as he spread the Rite from the Connecticut to the Mississippi during his missionary labors of 1848-

1863." He founded the first Scottish Rite lodge west of the Alleghenies at Cambridge, Ohio in 1852, where he lived from 1851 to 1867. Killian Henry Van Rensselaer was descended from the family of Kiliaen Van Rensselaer, one of 8 men from Amsterdam that served in the governing body of the Dutch West India Company. In 1625, slaves owned by the Dutch West India Company cleared the land that became New York City. As Kiliaen Van Rensselaer was one of the major stockholders in the company, indirectly this made him a large slave owner. By the 1660s the company dominated the slave trade into Spanish America. His descendant Killian Van Rensselaer set up the first regional headquarters of the Scottish Rite, west of New York, at Cincinnati, Ohio in late December 1853. For much of the year 1854, Van Rensselaer was in Cincinnati, the place and time that George Bickley was said to have founded the KGC. Others have written that it was Van Rensselaer that founded the KGC. Several members of the Van Rensselaer family were members of the Society of the Cincinnati, the predecessor of the Aztec Club. Two of them, Jeremiah and Nicholas Van Rensselaer, were original members of the New York State Society of the Cincinnati, as was Aaron Burr and William Tapp. General Arthur St. Clair, another officer of the Pennsylvania Society of the Cincinnati as well as the Governor of the Northwest Territory, changed the name of the chief settlement of this territory from Losantiville to Cincinnati in honor of the secret society in 1790. The new name for the town survives to this day. Killian Henry Van Rensselaer died at Cincinnati in 1881. By some accounts the KGC was created by George W. L. Bickley in Cincinnati, the town named for a secret military society.[16]

It is more likely that Van Rensselaer introduced Quitman to Bickley at some undetermined time in connection with a Masonic gathering in Cincinnati or Lexington. All three men were Masons; Bickley and Van Rensselaer would have met in Cincinnati, and Quitman knew Van Rensselaer as they were both high level leaders in the Scottish Rite. Ohio was also where John Anthony Quitman had joined the Masons and began his law practice in 1821. Although Quitman and Bickley were two very different men, they needed one another. A newspaper article published on July 2, 1854 described Quitman as "In stature he is short, has a dim eye, and a very poor voice." Bickley was known to be an impressive speaker, not afraid to address large audiences; he had a good voice. Quitman needed a mouthpiece to be his front man, as he was still under indictment for his part in one of the Lopez expeditions and had been on the hot seat in New Orleans for his own intended invasion of Cuba, which cost him $3,000 in bond money. Bickley could work on commission and raise funds through membership fees from the members in the new organization, the KGC which was organized as a joint stock company, similar in that way to Kiliaen Van Rensselaer's West India Company and Duff Green's failed 1844 Texas-based filibuster into Mexico. The long-term objective was still Cuba, but Mexico would need to be taken first to supply a secure base of operations, as had been suggested by C. R. Wheat, an experienced filibuster and Quitman operative. The overland invasion of Mexico was less expensive and could easily be accomplished from a KGC base in Texas, which shared the longest border with Mexico making it virtually undetectable by the Federal government. The most likely time that Bickley, Quitman, and the other four founders could have come to an agreement on this in Lexington is December, 1854, or in the month following, for the simple reason that one of the five founders was out of the country until then – George Nicholas Sanders.[17]

Sanders had been born in Lexington and had spent most of his early life on the nearby Sanders estate. George's father had been a one-time business partner of conspirator Aaron Burr; his grandfather had worked with Thomas Jefferson on the 1798 Kentucky Resolution so treasured by secessionists. In 1846, George Sanders moved to New York City and kept an office on Wall Street, as did Duff Green, who had also been born in Kentucky. On August 26, 1853, a farewell party for George Sanders was held at the Astor House in New York, prior to George leaving for London to assume his position as Consul-General to that country. The Astor House was frequented by ex-pat revolutionaries from Europe and was where Quitman was staying in October 1854. George Sanders, like Jane Cazneau, was active in the Young America movement that had been inspired by Italian revolutionary Giuseppe Mazzini and his Young Europe movement. On February 21, 1854, Sanders and his wife hosted a dinner in London for their revolutionary friends Mazzini, Garibaldi, Felice Orsini, all of Italy, and several others from Russia, Hungary and other countries; James Buchanan, the American minister in London and future President, also attended. This and other radical activities angered Sanders' British hosts and his enemies in America, who influenced the United States Congress to reject Sanders' appointment, meaning Sanders lost his government position. This enraged him greatly, so rather than return home immediately, he stayed on in London and continued his revolutionary agitations against European monarchy. He even wrote a letter "to the people of France" encouraging the assassination of Louis Napoleon. In Belgium, from October 9-11, 1854, James Buchanan and Pierre Soule, both United States ministers, met in secret and drafted the Ostend Manifesto, which called for the acquisition of Cuba from Spain by force if Spain refused to sell it to the U.S. Buchanan signed the document, but according to one newspaper, George Sanders played a key role in organizing the Ostend Conference, more so "…than any of the Plenipos who signed the famous Manifesto." Once this was made public it prompted international outrage against the United States. Dejected and angry, Sanders returned to the United States in December 1854. Quitman was angry too; in late October, he had written, "A powerful party at the North now controls the House of Reps. It seeks to seize also the Executive arm of the Govt. It has declared war [against] the rights and the social systems of 15 states of this Union." The other members of the five founders – Quitman, Felix Huston, John Morgan, and Persifor F. Smith – could have traveled to Lexington in December, provided Smith obtained holiday leave from his military post as commander of the Department of Texas. There is a gap in Smith's official correspondence from November 1854 to January 1855, and Smith was originally from Philadelphia, Pennsylvania – near enough to New York. Smith graduated from what is now Princeton University in New Jersey where he studied law before embarking on his military career; he likely maintained contacts with friends and relatives in the region. With Sanders back in the eastern United States by December, it was possible for all five of these well-travelled men to have met George Bickley in Lexington in late 1854 or more likely, January of the following year. All of them were in favor of the preservation of slavery and the acquisition of the former territories of Spanish America. Texas was the key to the successful implementation of their strategy.[18]

Chapter Five

Meetings and Plans

After his release from incarceration in New Orleans on July 3, 1854, General Quitman left that city for his home in Mississippi. By early January the following year he was back in New Orleans pitching his new approach to creating an international empire for slavery. He confided this new mode of attack, an idea that had been given him by C. R. Wheat, in a letter to Charles A. L. Lamar, a wealthy and well-connected slave trader and heir to a banking fortune.

> Our great enterprise has been planned with the advice and approval of some of the most distinguished military men of the country. It contemplates aiding a revolutionary movement in Cuba with from three thousand well-armed and well provided men embarked in swift and safe steamers. To avoid a breach of our international neutrality laws the organization and arming will not take place in this country.[1]

The letter implied that Quitman and the four co-founders of the KGC had already met and reviewed this strategy. The General told Lamar in this letter that $500,000 had been raised but much of that would be lost if an additional $50,000 was not raised in time to meet the invasion window of 60 days. As the letter was dated January 5, 1855, it follows that the invasion was slated to take place in early March. Still, more money was needed to hire enough men and equip them; there was much to be arranged. In asking his help in lining up potential investors, Quitman asked that Lamar use "great secrecy" in future discussions of what he termed "this great Southern Movement." This letter to Lamar was written by Quitman in

New Orleans on January 5, 1855 – the same day George Nicholas Sanders was reported in that city by the New Orleans *Times-Picayune*.

Meanwhile, General Quitman and his right-hand man, Felix Huston were scheduled to make an appearance in New Orleans on January 9, 1855 at the opening day for the Southern Commercial Convention. It was more than just an appearance; Quitman was one of the Vice-Presidents of the Convention and C. A. L. Lamar's cousin from Texas, Mirabeau Buonaparte Lamar, was its President; a total of 212 delegates from across the South were present. Texans Hugh McLeod and Paul Bremond were Assistant Secretaries of the meeting and on the first day of this seven-day event Felix Huston was made Chairman of the Business Committee. Other members of the Business Committee were Texans Hugh McLeod and Jacob Raphael De Cordova. McLeod was C. A. L. Lamar's brother-in-law and a KGC member.[2]

It is generally considered that these Southern Conventions were the breeding ground for the early organization of the Knights of the Golden Circle; that is certainly true in the case of the New Orleans convention of 1855. Quitman and Felix Huston were founders of the KGC, and Hugh McLeod was a member. A slave owner, railroad promoter and developer like Paul Bremond would have at least been sympathetic, if not a member and his future involvement with the Confederate government and Democratic Party in Texas made Jacob De Cordova a likely member. Also serving at this meeting as a Convention Vice-President (like Quitman) was Jefferson Davis Howell of Baltimore, Maryland, the brother-in-law of future Confederate States President Jefferson Davis. J. D. Howell would later publicly proclaim his KGC membership in a widely-circulated "card" to various Southern newspapers in which he claimed to have worked with George W. Bickley, alleged founder of the KGC, in enlisting "between five and six hundred of our fellow citizens."[3]

Another member with a familiar family name was present at this event in New Orleans. His name was Charles Goethe (or Gano, by some accounts) Baylor, the brother of Texas KGC members John R. Baylor and George W. Baylor; he was also a cousin of Texas KGC leader George W. Chilton. Charles G. Baylor impressed the assembled convention members with his discussion of his treatise, "A Letter of Interest to Cotton Planters." In his speech, he advocated for direct trade between southern cotton merchants and producers and European countries, especially Germany; cutting out the middlemen in the northeastern United States.

Baylor assured his listeners that a German bank with multiple locations was interested in seeing this happen. A brilliant and prolific writer, Charles G. Baylor lived in Washington, D. C. where he also published the *State Rights Register*, a weekly, "conducted upon the principles of STATE RIGHTS as laid down by JEFFERSON." Endorsed by several Congressmen, including John C. Breckinridge, wrongly suspected by some as being one of the founders of the KGC (although he was said to be a member), the *State Rights Register* provided a strict constructionist interpretation of the Constitution; meaning it was pro-slavery on Constitutional grounds as was the KGC.[4]

On the first day of the convention Hugh McLeod offered a resolution to deepen Galveston harbor and to expedite the transmission of the United States mail to Texas; veteran Texan politician Memucan Hunt offered a resolution for the commercial convention, as a whole, to recommend "appropriations by Congress for suitable fortifications at the east end of Galveston Island for the protection of the inlet and harbor of Galveston, and on the Gulf of Mexico, opposite the city of Galveston, for its protection." Fortifications had suddenly become important on the heels of the passage of the Kansas-Nebraska Act. Mr. Estes, of Louisiana, then offered a resolution for the Convention to recommend Congressional appropriations for the improvement of navigation on the Red River, which formed the Texas-Louisiana border and offered access to the Mississippi River, and thereby New Orleans, for cotton producers, slave traders and citizens of Texas and Northern Louisiana. Then the meeting adjourned for the day.[5]

On the second day of the Convention, General Felix Huston stood up before the assembled body and offered his apology for his inability to serve as Chairman of the General Business Committee; something had come up that would prevent the further attendance of both General Huston and General Quitman, whose apology Huston tendered before his audience. The New Orleans *Times-Picayune* offered more detail:

Gen. Felix Huston, from the General Committee, stated that the committee had made considerable progress in the matters referred to them, and would report shortly. Gen. Hus-ton also stated that private business compelled him to resign his position of chairman of the committee. He also stated that his friend Gen. Quitman had requested him to present his apologies to the Convention for his non-attendance, and his regret that engagements of an imperious nature, previously contracted, compelled him to leave town.[6]

With Quitman and Huston gone by January 10, the stage was set for Albert Pike to dominate the rest of the proceedings – which he did. Pike was the convention's Chairman of the Committee on the Pacific Railroad, a topic near and dear to KGC leadership, who vied for the construction of a southern route for the nation's trans-continental railway. With General Quitman and Felix Huston missing in action, Hugh McLeod spoke at length on the role that "Texas and her resources...are to look for the construction of an important part of the Pacific Railroad." At the end of the day, a "Dr. McGimsey, of Louisiana" addressed the convention to call for a resolution that each convention member "strongly recommend our Senators and Representatives in Congress... to introduce a bill to repeal all laws suppressing the slave trade, and that they exert all their influences to have such a law passed." McGimsey recommended this "In view of the fact that African slavery is an institution clearly sanctioned by the Volume of Inspiration... and that it constitutes the best state of society...." He was advocating the re-opening of the African slave trade, that according to KGC doctrine, had been "ordained by God" (the Volume of Inspiration being the Bible) and had been illegal since 1808. Jacob De Cordova then followed McGimsey by introducing a resolution for the Federal government to craft a trade agreement with Spain and Mexico, "upon the same plan as that lately consummated, and known as the Reciprocal Treaty, with the Provinces of Canada, Nova Scotia, etc." The General Committee looked favorably upon De Cordova's proposal, but it would not be until December 14, 1859, that a reciprocal treaty with Mexico would be signed that was favorable to the KGC and its constituents. The McLane-Ocampo Treaty as it was called, was ultimately not approved by the Senate.[7] All of these ideas and resolutions introduced to this convention would have delighted General Quitman and his right-hand-man Felix Huston, as they were standard KGC concerns, so why had they left so soon? Where were they, and what were they doing? What was the "imperious" matter that so needed their immediate attention?

Newspapers continued to speculate that General Quitman was headed to Cuba with an invasion force but that was already a dead end by January 1855. Instead, Quitman was reported to be heading north from Mobile up the Alabama River. This river course could have taken him into the north Georgia town of Rome, where he could catch a train to Kingston, Georgia to link with the Western and Atlantic Railroad to points north and east. George N. Sanders had left New Orleans by January 21st, and was making his way North; by January 30, 1855 he was reported to be in Louisville, Kentucky, a short distance from Lexington, where

George W. Bickley met with the five founders of the KGC sometime around January 30. Sanders was born in Lexington, Kentucky and grew up in nearby Carroll County, so he knew the way to the meeting. Bickley at this time was somewhat at loose ends, having left his primary job in Cincinnati in May of 1854. From January 15 to January 19, 1855 he was speaking in New York City on "Doomed Cities of Antiquity." Sometime after that he returned at an unknown date to his wife's farm in Southeastern Ohio; on February 12, he checked into a hotel in Petersburg, Virginia. He was moving about the country and could have easily attended a meeting in Lexington in late January after his work in New York was finished. No doubt the host for the meeting in Lexington was a man of wealth and power with a military background. That man would likely have been John Hunt Morgan, the scion of an old Lexington family that was one of the most respected and wealthy in the state of Kentucky. Morgan, like Quitman, was a combat veteran of the Mexican War and was dissatisfied with his military experience; he wanted more. John Hunt Morgan had a friend of similar social and financial stature that saw trouble ahead for slave-owners. Morgan's childhood friend and business partner was Joseph Orville Shelby, who had moved from Lexington to live near the Missouri-Kansas border which was now threatened with warfare over the slavery question. Shelby needed help both in terms of men and materiale for a paramilitary campaign as well as organization. George W. Bickley also had a friend in the same situation: Henry Clay Pate, who like Bickley was a native Virginian. Both men had briefly dabbled with the Know-Nothing Party but found it lacking and had moved on. Pate had moved to Louisville, Kentucky in 1850 where he established business connections in the newspaper publishing business before moving to Cincinnati, Ohio in 1851 – the same year Bickley had moved to the same place. Both men authored books and tried their hands at newspaper publishing; Pate moved to the Missouri-Kansas border in 1855 as had Joseph Shelby previously, and later lived in Petersburg, Virginia as had George Bickley. Bickley, Pate, Shelby, and Morgan were moving in the same circles. What brought these men together on that day was the Kansas-Nebraska Act of 1854 and their perception of the need for a response to it.[8]

Introduced into the United States Senate in December 1854, the act virtually repealed the Missouri Compromise of 1820 which had maintained the balance of free states and slave states in terms of Congressional representation and thereby, legislative influence. The Kansas-Nebraska Act therefore left the question of whether slavery would be permitted in territories or new states to be decided by the voters within those territories. That set up a contest between the pro-slavery and anti-slavery forces to colonize the Kansas territory with people who would vote to ensure their respective interests. Initially the pro-slavery forces got the jump on the abolitionists. A slave owner named John Wilkins Whitfield had been appointed as Indian Agent to Pottawatomie Indians in late 1853 and moved to Independence, Missouri. He was a former Mexican War officer and was elected twice to the Tennessee State Legislature. It is said that General Whitfield brought the first slaves into the Kansas Territory. Whitfield had political ambitions in Kansas as a representative for the pro-slavery element and had the backing of many in Missouri and elsewhere. He would play a significant role in organizing Confederate military forces in Texas after the Civil War began in 1861. On June 15, 1854, an unidentified young man from Lexington, Kentucky, acting as a scout, sent a letter to the *Lexington Observer and Reporter* giving his account of the numbers of pro-slavery Missourians crossing the border into Kansas:

> At the Weston ferry alone, in one such day up to noon, up-wards of 500 people crossed. The immigration is immense to all parts of the territory. Associations are being formed for mutual protection. Many public meetings have been held and resolutions passed affording each other assistance in preventing the northern abolitionists from settling in the territory.

The report closed by extolling the virtues of Kansas land and its potential as a slave state; "No doubt it will be organized very soon – it will be a slave state, and persons would be safe in carrying slaves... as numbers are already there." The Lexington scout was no doubt aware of a meeting of transplanted Missourians that took place 5 days before his report at a trading post just 3 miles west of Fort Leavenworth. Among these 32 pro-slavery men from Weston, Missouri was one Sackfield Maclin, a man who later played an interesting role in the secession of Texas. At this meeting a Squatter's Claim Association was organized which proclaimed that slavery had always existed in Kansas Territory. They also appointed a Vigilance Committee of 13 unnamed men to help enforce that claim. Among the association's adopted resolutions was one that would offer no protection to abolitionists; protection was for slave owners only.[9]

Others claimed that secret pro-slavery societies had been conceived by Missourians for control of Kansas as early as autumn of 1853. These were known as "Blue Lodges" by the anti-slavery press, which coincidentally, is the term for the first 3 degrees of Masonic membership. The members of the Blue Lodges in Missouri who posed as settlers of Kansas became known as "Border Ruffians" because so many of them came from counties in Missouri near the Kansas border. When the first election was held in Kansas on November 29, 1854, J. W. Whitfield was chosen to represent Kansas as its delegate to Congress. Whitfield was elected in Kansas by Missouri residents. One such border ruffian, a man named Jordan Danison, later testified under oath that he had joined a Blue Lodge in Pleasant Hill, Missouri in February 1854, well before the founding of the KGC in January 1855. However, another former member of the so-called Blue Lodge, Mr. John Scott, testified under oath be-fore Congress that the early self-defense organization had subsequently been replaced by another:

> But since the 30th of March, 1855, I think that society has been superseded by another society, which has a fund for the purpose, of sending pro-slavery emigration to this Territory, and is regularly organized for that purpose. The fund is used in aiding emigrants, by loaning them money to get into the Territory, in providing claims, and entering the land. It is a self-defensive organization, intended to have a bearing upon the political institutions of the Territory, as far as slavery is concerned.[10]

This new pro-slavery, anti-abolition secret society created in early 1855 was the earliest version of the KGC. It marked an improvement over the Blue Lodges that were initially formed by Joseph O. Shelby and others like him. It was funded, and over time, would evolve to offer military training and drill instruction. An early resident of Greene County, Missouri described the new organization operating in their state and Kansas:

> This organization had many members in this county, and three or four lodges or "camps." These were in communication with other camps in other States, and performed an important part of the work for which the order was created. The order had its hailing signs, its grips, its passwords, and was near akin and auxiliary to the famous Knights of the Golden Circle. It did what it could to make Kansas a slave State. Some of its members, went from time to time to Kansas and voted every time a territorial Legislature was to be chosen or a constitution adopted, and as regularly returned to their Missouri homes after the election! [sic]

Years later, when the KGC had grown substantially in membership, George W. Bickley would tell his Knights that, "The Legislators, in destroying the Missouri-Compromise line, opened the political Pandora's box. The K.G.C. was originated to provide an antidote." The abolitionist Emigrant Aid Society sponsorees continued to pour into Kansas in large enough numbers to cause concern across the South. These Free-Soil societies also received shipments of weapons in Kansas to arm their anti-slavery voters. However, no one from either side was killed over any political matter in 1854, and in 1855 only 4 persons' deaths could be attributed to political disputes – 3 of whom were anti-slavery men. The following year would be much different. By December of 1855, it was rumored among Free-Soil (anti-slavery) Party members that General John Quitman had personally contributed $2,500, a hefty sum in those days, to Southern Aide societies, and would arrive in Kansas by spring of 1856 with several hundred men from Mississippi. That was the rumor; Quitman in fact spent much of the next year successfully campaigning for election to the U.S. House of Representatives for the State of Mississippi. Besides, General Whitfield, the Territory's Congressional Representative and some say, the defacto leader of the pro-slavery forces, had "called upon the President, and asked him not to send U.S. troops to Kansas...":

> ...or in any wise interfere with the local affairs of her territory; that the men of Kansas could maintain the laws, and would preserve order without the least assistance from with-out.[11]

This would prove to be a miscalculation on Whitfield's part. His thoughts may have been influenced by the Southern myth that "one good Southern man could whip 4 Yankees." He was echoed in his sentiment by General Quitman, who reportedly said he would "...never report a bill for sending troops to Kansas to butcher American citizens, whether of one side or the other of the question at issue." The abolitionist forces gained a very capable leader in 1855, in the person of one James Henry Lane, who would become an object of fear and terror for pro-slavery Texans as well as Kansans. He, too, was a Mexican War veteran and in 1855 was taking the measure of the situation in Kansas, biding his time. A pro-slavery man known only as Mr. Cook was killed by abolitionist forces at Easton, Kansas on January 17, 1856. One of his assailants was killed with an axe the same day in retaliation. This set up a series of tit-for-tat killings of 38 people, making 1856 the bloodiest year of the Kansas war. An equal number died on both sides that year, but the sensationalist press on either side greatly exaggerated the casualties in order to fire up their respective bases. The killings most sensationalized by the Southern media were those perpetrated by abolitionist John Brown at Pottawatomie, Kansas on May 25, 1856. In that one incident Brown and his men dragged non-combatant pro-slavery settlers from their homes and hacked 5 of them to death with swords, sometimes in front of their families. This was the same John Brown who would do much to increase KGC membership in 1859 when he killed more slave owners and raided the arsenal at Harper's Ferry, Virginia.[12]

By mid-1856 the violence in Kansas was escalating, and both sides found a ready outlet for biased accounts of the events through the media. One of these outlets was provided by George W. Bickley in Ohio, with the help of an enigmatic person named E. M. Horrel, from 1855 to 1856. Bickley had left his job at the Eclectic Medical Institute in Cincinnati in the spring of 1854 for medical reasons, and subsequently moved to his wife's farm in Scioto County, Ohio. The county was located at the conjunction of the Ohio and Scioto rivers, and among the various towns in the county was the crown jewel, the county seat, the town of Portsmouth. It was in Portsmouth that Bickley got his fingers into an established but struggling newspaper. Originally started in 1848 as the *Portsmouth Democratic Enquirer* it had been taken over by Captain Francis Cleveland until he sold his interest to Alexander Pearce in 1852. In mid-1854, about the time George W. Bickley left his job in Cincinnati, Pearce sold the paper to 'George W. Nelson.' In the July 13, 1855 edition, it was announced that the paper was having financial trouble (so was Bickley, coincidentally) and that the paper would restart and change its name to the *Ohio Pennant*.[13]

The *Pennant* attacked the Know-Nothing party and abolitionists; it was what was known as a "campaign paper," a newspaper that existed only for the length or duration of a political campaign – or, perhaps, a quasi-military campaign like the one being waged in Kansas at the time. By December 1855, the editor of its cross-town rival, the *Portsmouth, Ohio Spirit of the Times* began to publicly doubt the identity of 'George W. Nelson,' the alleged editor of the *Pennant*, as shown in this op-ed:

> There exists, somewhere in Scioto county, a clueless fellow who prints his name "Geo. W. Nelson." Who he is – what he is – what his antecedents – we know not. We know nothing about him, except that he publishes a very weak "egg-rum-and-toddy" paper...the "Ohio Pennant."...In turn, we expel him from the Democratic fold, and send him over to the disunionist fire-

eaters of South Carolina! That locality is just suited to his moral constitution. How admirably he would serve the purposes of some planter who
wanted a creature that could amuse him, and which he could despise!

George W. Nelson (or George W. Bickley, using an alias) had printed that
"The *Times* is one of the most bitter abolition papers published in Ohio." This
angered its editor, who countered that the *Times* was a "democratic paper, opposed
to the extension of slavery over territory now free." That last comment was a reference to the Kansas Troubles. Perhaps Bickley had been assigned by the real
founders of the KGC, to continue to present the pro-slavery side of events in
Kansas through his newspaper on the Ohio/Kentucky/Virginia border and help
raise money for the general fund that equipped and supplied the Border Ruffians.
By February 1856, the paper restyled as the *Daily Democratic Pennant* was published
"from the office of BICKLEY & NELSON, Portsmouth, O."; sometime in 1856
Bickley had developed and crafted the official seal of the KGC – its first ever
emblem.[14] It somewhat resembled the medallion given members of the Aztec
Club; both Generals Quitman and Persifor F. Smith owned such medallions, as
they were founding members. Perhaps they brought them to the January 1855
meeting in Lexington.

By the Fall term of 1856, Bickley was back on the faculty of the Eclectic
Medical Institute in Cincinnati. *The Daily Democratic Pennant* had shut down and was
replaced by his former partner's paper, *The Weekly Plaindealer*, published by "E. M.
Horrel, for the Committee" as reported in August 1856. Sometimes misidentified
as "Edwin Horrel" its publisher, Edward Horrell, continued publication until the
end of the 1856 Presidential campaign. Candidate James Buchanan was always
thought to be a warm friend of the KGC; some even thought he was a member.
He won the 1856 election and in 1857 became the 15th President of the United
States. But who was Edward Horrell?[15]

An early published history of Ohio states that "E. M. Horrel...subsequently
went into the rebel army." That seems strange for an Ohio resident, even if they
were a member of the Democratic Party. Prior to his involvement with Bickley,
E. M. Horrel was in Clarksburg, Virginia promoting the Washington Temple of
Honor, a secret temperance society in 1854. He and Bickley had a shared history
of involvement in secret societies in Virginia; perhaps that was how they met.
There are Civil War service records for an "Edwin M. Horrel" in the Confederate
army, joining at Montgomery, Alabama on May 7, 1861. In 1862, he transferred

from his unit, the 6th Regiment of Alabama Infantry, to the 20th Battalion of Alabama Light Artillery, where he eventually attained the rank of Sergeant. In 1863, he was captured but released at Vicksburg on July 9, 1863. By January 1, 1864, he had reenlisted in the 20th Battalion of Light Artillery, and the next month at Decatur, Georgia helped craft a reenlistment resolution for his unit that was sent to the Confederate House of Representatives and the daily newspapers at Columbus, Georgia. Then, his military record states "Killed by Provost Guard Sept. 2 1864." That would seem to be the end of it; but was it really? No information other than what has been stated previously, was ever found concerning Edward M. Horrell. If his business partner, George W. Bickley, used an alias during the time they published a Democratic campaign paper in a solid Republican state like Ohio, could "Edwin M. Horrel" (also known as Edward Horrell or E.M. Horrell) be an alias, too?[16]

The events in Kansas in 1856 were very distressing for those slaveowners who had family and property in Missouri. George W. Bickley's friend, Henry Clay Pate, had moved to Westport, Missouri after selling his Cincinnati newspaper, *The Weekly Patriot*, at a considerable profit. In 1855, he began publishing another newspaper, *The Star of Empire*, and opened a law office in Westport. Before long he was considered a wealthy man. On June 2, 1856, Pate was leading a company of about 25 men acting under orders of T.W. Hays, U.S. Marshal for the Southern District of Kansas. This was barely a week after John Brown perpetrated the Pottawatomie Massacre. Pate was endeavoring to capture the murderers. Brown rallied support from the anti-slavery element and attacked Pate's camp early in the morning of June 2nd with a superior force. Henry Clay Pate and his men fought for 3 to 5 hours before surrendering. Newspaper reports stated that Pate sent a call for help to Joseph Shelby and other local warlords before surrendering, and J.W. Whitfield took the field with armed volunteers searching for the enemy. Several of Pate's men were wounded but none were killed in the fighting. Eventually Pate was freed by Brown on June 5th under orders of the Governor, and Brown temporarily faded into the vastness of the Territory. Pate was advised to leave the area and go home to Missouri.[17]

U.S. military forces intervened in Kansas on June 17, 1856 by blockading the roads into the Territory to prevent the movements of the combatants. Joseph Shelby complained that Colonel Sumner of the U.S. Army, with 2,500 men, had "drove me clear out of the territory." Northern newspapers described it thusly:

A letter published in a St. Louis paper, dated Westport, June 17, says Col. Sumner has put the California and Santa Fe roads, and all the principal thoroughfares leading into Kansas under blockade, and has driven Mayor Buford, Gen. Jones' Col. Shelby's, and all other emigrant parties, not desirous of becoming peaceable settlers, out of the Territory. [sic]

"Mayor Buford" was actually Major Jefferson Buford, a lawyer and planter from Alabama and leader of one of the armed contingents of pro-slavery "Border Ruffians" recruited from other states. The victorious Colonel Sumner was rewarded for his service by being relieved of command by President Buchanan and Jefferson Davis – yes, that Jefferson Davis; at the time he was Buchanan's Secretary of War – in a few short years, he would be the Commander-in-Chief of Confederate forces. But in Kansas in 1856, they replaced Sumner with General Persifor Frazer Smith – one of the 5 founders of the KGC. Conventional histories of the Kansas Troubles note that Smith had "Southern sympathies." He was General Quitman's confidante, having served under Quitman in the Mexican War. Persifor F. Smith would pursue a policy of non-involvement of U.S. troops during his duty in Kansas – the policy requested previously by J.W. Whitfield and General John Quitman. General Smith formally took command on July 18th. Abolitionist Jim Lane, meanwhile, had gone to Chicago and other points north to recruit anti-slavery volunteers for the war in Kansas. On July 1, 1856 it was reported that he was in Council Bluffs, Iowa with 1,000 armed and angry men, designated as "buffalo hunters." These men were headed for trouble in Kansas, and pro-slavery forces anxiously awaited their arrival. Ironically, KGC leaders in Texas would soon use the "buffalo hunter" ruse for their own purposes. Before the vanguard of Lane's Army, as it was called, arrived in Kansas, Joseph Shelby and his men boarded a riverboat carrying their arms and supplies and stole them. More shipments were sent, nevertheless.

On August 16, 1856, pro-slavery forces rallied along the border. On that day, at Westport, Missouri, some of the leaders of the Border Ruffians issued a "call," or press release, that screamed the headline, "LANE'S MEN HAVE ARRIVED – CIVIL WAR HAS BEGUN! This was picked up and re-published by many pro-slavery newspapers across the South, such as the Dallas, *Texas Herald*, which ran the banner and a timeline of reported atrocities committed by the anti-slavery forces. *The Kansas Weekly Herald* reported on September 13th that Joseph Shelby was escorting a force of 40 men from Lexington, Kentucky into the Territory, and that all their expenses were being paid. The unnamed organization funding this movement also promised each man would "receive upon arrival 160 acres of land, and are guaranteed a livelihood for one year." This was a KGC company. The KGC later used such inducements as acres of land for its soldiers in Mexico to encourage the invasion of that country. On September 18, 1856, an extraordinary meeting was held at Lecompton, one of the few pro-slavery settlements in Kansas; this would not be reported for several weeks by the newspapers. "Colonel" Henry Clay Pate was one of the featured speakers at what was described as "a large and enthusiastic meeting of Southern men, for the purpose of encouraging and facilitating Southern emigration to Kansas...."

At this meeting resolutions were adopted, the first 3 of 5 pertaining to the colonization of Kansas by pro-slavery Southerners and the organization of armed self-defense groups; the 4th, and the 5th and final resolutions pertained to raising money from across the country to be distributed to the pro-slavery forces in the territory. Most importantly, the 5th resolution created a network of people to oversee the collection and disbursement of funds from the various southern states. Joseph Orville Shelby was one of two men appointed to oversee the funds raised in Kentucky; Henry Clay Pate and 4 others were assigned to Virginia; Albert Pike and 4 others assigned to Arkansas; John A. Quitman and two others assigned to Mississippi, and the following men assigned to Texas: "J. L. Hunter, F. W. Bowden, N. G. Shelly and G. Turner". Three of these men assigned to raise funds in Texas were former members of the Alabama State legislature: John Lingard Hunter, Franklin Welsh Bowdon (not "Bowden") and Nathan George Shelley (not "Shelly"). All three men were attorneys and prominent Democrats in Texas. Shelley and Bowdon were veterans of the Mexican War and Shelley moved to Austin, Texas in 1855. Bowdon had been a classmate of Texas Supreme Court Justice Oran Milo Roberts at the University of Alabama in 1836; he moved to Henderson in Rusk County in 1852. A brother-in-law of known KGC leader George W. Chilton, Bowden became a partner in Chilton's Tyler, Texas-based law firm. J. L. Hunter was General John L. Hunter, another veteran Democrat Party member in Texas who worked for the Lockhart Watchman, a newspaper in Caldwell County. Born in 1795 and raised in Charleston, South Carolina, he briefly served as a State Senator representing St. Bartholomew's Parish, the lowland plantation country of the Palmetto State. The population of the area was 84% slaves by 1820, so its Congressional representatives tended to be radical. By 1833 John Lingard Hunter was the largest slaveowner in Barbour County, Alabama. After serving briefly in the Alabama legislature and being promoted to Major General of the Alabama

Militia, he moved to Caldwell County, Texas in 1855. A graduate of South Carolina College school of law, he preferred to focus his effort on the promotion of agricultural practices, especially those related to cotton production. The Kansas meeting clearly shows the earliest workings of the KGC, the early involvement of Texans, and a clear connection between John Anthony Quitman, Albert Pike, Joseph Orville Shelby; and by association his close friend and business partner John Hunt Morgan; and Henry Clay Pate, the friend and associate of George W. Bickley. In addition to these men and the states they represented, the following states were also represented and had fund-raising operatives appointed by the committee: Alabama, Georgia, South Carolina, North Carolina, Missouri, Maryland, Delaware, Florida, Tennessee, Louisiana, and the Kansas towns of Leavenworth and Lecompton. The states most heavily represented in terms of fund-raising efforts were Alabama, with 7 appointees (not counting those three emigres to Texas), and South Carolina, with 6 appointees. Behind it all there was a working organization dedicated to the perpetuation of the struggle for the expansion of slavery and the protection of slave-owner's Constitutional rights.[18]

Was General Quitman actually present at the September 18th meeting in Lecompton? It is certainly possible; Congress had adjourned on August 30th. Quitman spent some time with his family before attending a banquet in New York City for the Montezuma Club on September 15th. The Montezuma Club was a spin-off from the earlier Aztec Club, of which Quitman was the founding force and first President. The Aztec Club had been founded by officers that had served in the Mexican War to be their very own Society of the Cincinnati, and like that earlier order, membership was hereditary and could be passed down to the closest living male heir. In Colonial America, this had been objectionable to many in the public, who were not members of this private, and somewhat secret, military organization; to the outsiders it smacked of monarchy, the very thing they had fought and died fighting against. The Montezuma Club had been formed in 1855, ostensibly to correct a stricture in the Aztec Club's constitution that prevented the recruiting of new members. Perhaps the Montezuma Club was formed to increase pro-slavery membership. One might assume the same public concerns that beset The Society of the Cincinnati would have been applied to the Montezuma Club. In any event, Quitman had two full days after the banquet in New York to travel to Kansas to attend the Lecompton meeting on September 18th. The House did not reconvene until December 1st. Quitman and family spent most of the remaining recess at Monmouth, his plantation near Natchez, Mississippi.[19]

Ultimately the contest for Kansas would tilt in favor of the Free-Soil movement. By spring of 1857, most of the players knew it was already decided. Operations began to wind down. By December, the *New York Times* opined on the situation in the town of Lawrence, one of the Free State strongholds:

> Several of the Pro-Slavery men in this town are beginning to despair of
> making Kansas a Slave State. They say that too many abolitionists have al-
> ready settled here, and slave property can never be safe while they remain,
> and there is no use to attempt to drive them out, for they are so determined
> on making Kansas a Free State they are sure to return. And so the cry is
> "Ho for Nicaragua." How many will go? [sic]

Several newspapers reported that General Quitman recommended to Henry
Titus, one of the leaders of the pro-slavery Border Ruffians, that he leave Kansas
to join William Walker's pro-slavery crusade in Nicaragua. Titus took him up on
that idea, with his men joined by 100 others at Leavenworth, to "...leave for 'Governor Walker's dominions,' to fight for slavery there, instead of persisting in their
attempts to establish the institution in Kansas, against the will of the people."[20]
But for many secessionists, the next big contest that year was the race for Governor of Texas, and the Kansas Troubles – the violence caused by the Kansas-Nebraska Act, would determine the winner.

Chapter 6

The KGC Goes Public in Texas

In March 1857, James Buchanan was inaugurated as President of the United States. In his history of Van Zandt County, Texas historian Wentworth Manning later wrote,

> James Buchanan was elected President of the United States, because he had advised the seizure of Cuba, a province of Spain, if Spain would not sell it to the United States, on terms dictated by the republic. During President Buchanan's administration, the Knights of the Golden Circle, a secret organization, was organized in this republic with a view to obtaining Cuba and perpetuating slavery.... I should think by the time the new administration came in on the fourth of March, there were fully fifty thousand men under muster in the south, by reason of the activities of the Knights of the Golden Circle.

Wentworth Manning wrote about what he saw in his early days in Texas as well as the state's verifiable history; but as he did not come to Texas until 1857, his knowledge of the KGC in that state was limited to the year 1857 onward. The Order of the Lone Star of the West had been in Texas for years before Manning's arrival and eventually merged (or morphed into) the KGC. Manning was aware of the KGC because several prominent members and by the end of February 1861 an entire division of the order were based at Tyler, Texas, just a few miles from Manning's home at Wentworth, Texas.[1]

In addition to the Lone Star of the West, there was another secret organization in Texas that preceded the KGC and upon its demise, contributed to and

increased KGC membership. This was the American Party, popularly known as
the Know-Nothing Party, as its members were pledged to secrecy, as were KGC
members. Like the KGC, members had secret signs, passwords, and grips (hand-
shakes).

Certain signs were used to enable fellow members to recognize each other,
such as scratching an eye with the right fore-finger and when gripping the hand
pressing with the middle finger upon the lowest joint of the other finger. This was
supposed to bring the reply of 'Where did you get that?' The answer being 'I don't
know,' to which the other returned, 'I don't know either.'

Thus, the term, "Know Nothings." Only higher echelon members knew the
true motives and plans of the order. There are other similarities between the two
organizations; they shared certain members, especially political leaders. Founded
in New York City in 1852, the "KNs" as they were called, spread rapidly across
the country into the South and into Texas by the latter part of 1854, filling a void
created by the demise of the Whig Party. Like the KGC, the American Party ("the
KN's") was modeled after the Blue Lodges, the lower three degrees of Masonry.
The first degree of the KNs, upon initiation, were said to be in "the august presence of Sam." First degree members were not eligible for office in the order, or
for any political office; second degree members were charged with helping (legally)
to "remove all foreigners, aliens or Roman Catholics from office or place". This
was an anti-immigration organization, especially anti-Irish. The third, or highest
degree, was the "Union degree" which was pledged to "support the ties which
bind together the states of the union and to oppose all men and measures adverse."
The beliefs of the third degree KNs were averse to those KGC members who
were secessionists. The presence of so many former KNs in the KGC would lead
to a split, or schism, within the KGC by 1858, as third-degree KN members believed in the preservation of the Union as well as preserving the institution of
slavery. By 1857, most KGC members in Texas felt that the breakup of the Union
was the only way to preserve slavery in their home states. This is demonstrated by
a letter written by former KN and aspiring Texas KGC leader John A. Wilcox to
Hardin R. Runnels, Governor of Texas:

> In my humble opinion the entire South should be placed in a State of mili-
> tary preparation to meet the crusade that awaits them. We will never have
> any more concessions from the North, other than those which our strong
> arms will exact....it is evident to my mind that we have had no Nationality
> since the administration of Gen. Jackson. Still for the sake of the Union

and the hope that the North would retrace its steps I have fought its battles. I shall fight them no more.[2]

Wilcox was ready for secession and war by 1857, as revealed in his letter, and had given up on the American Party and the United States. The failure of the KNs began almost as soon as they had reached the peak of their influence. By the Virginia political elections of early 1855, the American Party had begun to crumble be-cause of the dispute over slavery between the Northern and South-ern factions of the party. In the Virginia election it became obvious that the KNs would never control a Southern state. The party had experienced a meteoric rise; in 1855 the *New York Herald* estimated there were 1,375,000 voting members of the Know-Nothing Party in the United States. Other sources put the number at "not less than 1,250,000." The KNs had been more successful in Texas than in any other southern state, because foreigners were a concern for its early settlers. There was a large population of foreigners in Texas, and the State itself bordered a foreign country, with which it had been at war since 1835. There were two groups of foreigners attracted to Texas who generally held anti-slavery sentiments and were blamed for encouraging the escape of slaves into Mexico: those of German and Mexican origins. In some Texas counties in the 1850's the German inhabitants comprised as much as 85 per-cent of the population. Bexar County, site of the city of San Antonio, had in addition to its German population of 20 percent, a population that was 60 percent Mexican. Immigrants were seen as a threat to the "southern way of life." On a national level, slave owners had been attracted to the American Party because they realized that immigration into the port cities of the North would lead to greater representation in Congress for Northern states, which meant slave states would be outvoted in the legislature. Increased immigration endangered Southern wealth that was based on slave ownership. Restricting the voting rights of immigrants became important for this reason; the Texas American Party platform called for a 21-year naturalization period. The same party platform also called for "A strict construction of the Constitution of the United States, and the preservation of all the rights of the States," which meant protection for the property rights of slave owners, as the words "slave" and "slavery" were not mentioned in the original document written by the Founding Fathers, many of whom were slave owners themselves. KNs in Texas also specified in their platform that "Congress possess no power under the Constitution to legislate slavery in the States where it does or may exist, or to re-fuse the admission of a new State into

the Union" due to the slavery issue. The American Party lost almost all its Southern member-ship when it softened the proslavery language in its national platform to take a neutral posture on the issue. This prompted many to seek membership elsewhere, in either or both the Democratic Party and/or the KGC. Prominent Texas KNs who were known KGC included George H. Sweet of San Antonio, John A. Wilcox of San Antonio, Hugh McLeod of Galveston, Roger Q. Mills
of Navarro County, John S. Ford of Travis County, John Sayles of Washington
County, Trevanion Teel of San Antonio, Austin-based newspaper publisher John
Marshall and former President of the Republic, Sam Houston. Sam Houston actually ran for office as a KN, and John Anthony Quitman, his friend and the
founder of the KGC, was courted by the KNs to be a potential political candidate.
Duff Green, a close confidante to the founders of the KGC, wrote Quitman a
letter on August 11, 1856, encouraging him to use his influence to draw members
and voters away from the American Party "KN's" to support James Buchanan for
President. Soon thereafter Quitman publicly characterized the American Party as
a half measure for "timid and non-committal men." Buchanan campaigned in support of the KGC goal to capture Cuba, as Wentworth Manning noted, and later
tried to employ the KGC in a plan to control Mexico through the McLane-
Ocampo Treaty. At the National Democratic Convention held in Cincinnati in
1856, Buchanan was nominated as his party's Presidential candidate; Quitman was
nominated for Vice President by a member of the Illinois delegation. On the first
convention ballot, Quitman received the most votes at 59, to John Breckinridge
in second place with 51 votes. Illinois, South Carolina, Mississippi and Arkansas
had placed all their delegate votes for Quitman; Texas had given him 3 out of its
4 votes, Ohio 8 of their 23 votes and New York 7 of their 25 votes. On the second
ballot, Governor Matthews of Mississippi withdrew Quitman's name, and the
nomination went to Breckinridge. Buchanan's Vice President, John Cabell
Breckenridge, was described by a Texas KGC member as one of the order's "great
lights." The Democratic Party platform was strongly proslavery and supported
"the principles laid down in the Kentucky and Virginia resolutions of 1798," the
meaning of which was not lost on secessionists. Breckenridge would have been a
good candidate for being one of the 5 founding members of the KGC, had it not
been for the fact that he was a friend of Abraham Lincoln, through his cousin
Mary Todd, who became Lincoln's wife. Like John Quitman, a fellow member of
the Aztec Club, Breckenridge joined the Democratic Party in supporting Polk for
President in 1844. Quitman tended to be apolitical; Sam Houston eventually left

the KNs and joined the Democratic Party by 1859. The American Party was politically dead by late 1857.[3]

Houston had run for Governor of Texas in 1856 as a KN and had been
defeated by Democrat Hardin R. Runnels because of Houston's opposition to the
Kansas-Nebraska Act. Houston had correctly perceived that the Act would eventually result in Kansas becoming a free state, but hardline Democrats in Texas
didn't see it that way. In their eyes, Houston had failed an important loyalty test,
and Runnels thereby became the only man in history to defeat Sam Houston in an
election. Hardin Richard Runnels, part of a family that helped found the State of
Mississippi and had long-standing ties to John Quitman, was inaugurated as Governor of Texas on December 21, 1857; just days later former KN member John
A. Wilcox wrote Governor Runnels requesting armaments for the Alamo Rifles, a
known KGC company organized by Wilcox, who served as its Captain for several
years. Runnels, a substantial slave owner was himself later identified as a KGC
member, and Thomas Scott Anderson, his Secretary of State, was unquestionably
a member of the Lone Star of the West, which merged with the KGC. Anderson
had written John Quitman on behalf of John Salmon Ford, another known member of the Order of the Lone Star and the KGC who had offered to join Quitman's
forces for the invasion of Cuba. Anderson had indicated in this letter that he had
re-sided in Mississippi for a time, as had KGC leader Quitman, Texans John Wilcox, T. N. Waul, Hardin Richard Runnels, John Marshall, Felix Huston and others,
as well as the future President of the Confederacy, Jefferson Davis. His support
of the Order of the Lone Star and his other actions substantiate T. S. Anderson's
membership in the KGC. Anderson sometimes served as Acting Governor, as
when he corresponded in April 1858 with U.S. Secretary of War, John Buchanan
Floyd, who was later accused of being a KGC member, and did in fact later serve
as a General in the Confederate military. Runnels and Anderson were a formidable
team; together these two men did much to facilitate the expansion of the KGC in
Texas. One of their first actions in office was the passage of "An Act to incorpo-
rate all Military Uniformed Companies now organized, or to be organized in the
State;" a portion of which is below:

> Section1. Be it enacted by the Legislature of the State of Texas, that the
> Galveston Artillery Company, the Washington Light Guards, of the City of
> Houston, the Alamo Rifles, of the City of San Antonio, the Milam Rifles,
> of the city of Houston, the Lone Star Military Company, of Galveston, the
> Turner Rifles, of the City of Houston, the Refugio Riflemen, and all other

Uniformed Volunteer Military Companies now organized or that may be hereafter organized in this State, be, and they are hereby constituted bodies politic and corporate, under whatever style and name they may determine.... each to have a common seal with whatever motto and ensign they please, to elect in whatever manner they shall determine the Officers necessary to command them, to ordain and establish by-laws for the government and regulation of their affairs, and the same to alter and amend at will....

Section 1 of the law also required "that said company shall never number less than thirty-two, non-commissioned officers and privates, nor exceed one hundred, of the same." At least two of the companies named, the Lone Star Military Company and the Alamo Rifles formed by John A. Wilcox, were known KGC companies. It is possible that all of them were KGC; these were uniformed private militias. All but two were based in the Houston-Galveston area; both towns being ports on the Gulf of Mexico involved in the slave trade, adjacent to each other. This was the most likely port of entry for the KGC in Texas; in July 1854 (the month the KGC was supposedly started in Lexington, Kentucky), one KN group in Galveston had its charter revoked because its ritual included the skull and crossbones, which did not conform to the American Party national standard. This renegade Galveston KN lodge was displaying in its ritual a known KGC symbol used in its initiation ritual. At the beginning of the Civil War, most of the earliest companies formed in Texas had been organized under the law passed by the Runnels administration, which legalized private, unregulated, uniformed militias. This legislation encouraged the formation of even more of these private, uniformed military companies, as they had been legitimized, regardless of their ideology or intentions.[4]

By July 1856, Sam Houston smelled a rat within the Texas Democratic Party, as noted in this letter to John Hancock of Austin:

The democracy of today is a 'compound' of heterogeneous materials; it has dwindled down to mere sectionalism & is now but a faction. It has lost the principle of cohesion and boasts no longer a uniform policy.... Where is that democracy today? Swallowed up in...squatter sovereignty – in sectional bickering, and disputes – in disregarding compacts between different sections of the Union, the repeal of which has led to insurrection in Kansas – in getting up Indian wars wherever Indians could be found, as a pretext for increasing the regular army.... [sic]

Incoming Governor Runnels initial speech contained a blatant threat of secession from the Union by the State of Texas. His forbearance of this threat was predicated on the condition that slave owners' rights be assured in Kansas. This was certainly a taste of things to come during his administration. In February 1858, the legislature of Texas met and adopted a joint resolution favoring the rights of slave owners in Kansas. Presided over by the Runnels administration, Louis Wigfall was Chairman of the Senate side of this joint committee, and Hamilton Bee (son of Bernard Bee) was Chairman for the House. The defeat of slavery in Kansas was still a sore spot for Southerners, as was the arrest of William Walker by the United States government for his second invasion of Nicaragua. In Texas especially, Native Americans were the subject of much fear and scorn, and evidence will be presented that this fear was manipulated by the KGC to further their agenda of acquiring weaponry under the guise of defense against an exaggerated threat of Indian raids – as Sam Houston had mentioned in his July 1856 letter and in his later statements. The Great Comanche Raid into Texas that occurred in 1840 had been precipitated by the Council House Fight in San Antonio, which was basically a slaughter of un-suspecting Indians who had come to negotiate a peace treaty. This slaughter occurred during negotiations on March 19, 1840 that were under the direction of Hugh McLeod, a future KGC leader. After the Comanche peace emissaries, and accompanying women and children, were killed during this melee, other Comanche tribes undertook a war against Texas settlers. In the resulting Great Raid, the Comanches penetrated as far east into Texas as Victoria, which was sacked. Finally, on August 12, 1840, the Comanches suffered a major defeat at the Battle of Plum Creek, in which then future KGC leaders Ben and Henry McCulloch, John Henry Brown, Felix Huston and others played a part, but minor Comanche raids continued until 1844 when Sam Houston negotiated a truce. The oath taken by the political class of KGC leadership specifically designated Indians, along with Negroes, as being of the slave class. By 1858, there was little need for private, uniformed militias. Any Indian aggression was a problem for the Texas Rangers to deal with – not the militias. Like the Negro, there would be no freedom for Indians in Texas if the KGC had its way, but this was only known by the upper echelon members of that order.[5]

George W. Bickley, the public face of the KGC, still had not made any public appearances on the organization's behalf in 1858. Ill for most of 1857, he was virtually unknown in Texas until 1860, and by that time people suspected that he was only a figurehead and not the man in charge. Quitman and William Walker were at the forefront of the news in Texas, however. On February 1, 1858, John Quitman wrote a private letter to Texas newspaper publisher and KGC leader John Marshall that all of the Gulf States (including Texas) should meet in convention and declare their intent to secede, pending consultation with other slave states as to the timing, and "immediately assemble to form a Confederation or Constitution." William Walker had written Quitman a letter just two weeks prior which read more like a report from a subordinate to a superior than a request for aid. In the letter Walker defended his eligibility under Nicaraguan law to serve as President of the country, and concluded with "It is hoped that the State Department will not permit itself to become the dupe of diplomats who have a 'fatal facility' for deceit and falsehood." Walker need not have worried; President Buchanan publicly repudiated the actions of U.S. Navy Commodore Hiram Paulding for his arrest of Walker, calling it "a grave error." Walker was freed on December 29, 1857 and was at large in 1858. Southerners rallied around Walker, with a typical opinion piece published in Texas by the Columbus based Citizen in 1858:

> The British Government aided and assisted by our own, defeated Walker at first; but his second defeat must be attributed to our own. President Walker was invited to Nicaragua in the first instance; afterwards, if we mistake not, he was elected President of the Republic of Nicaragua, by the people. The Costa Ricans aided by British gold and British influence, waged war against him; when the United States authorities (while he was in a critical position) captured and took him back to the United States. Under these circumstances, is not Walker the rightful President of Nicaragua? Has he not been shamelessly ousted out of his rights?

Is this view William Walker was a symbol of the Federal government's encroachment upon Southern rights. In Congress, John Quitman of Mississippi and Lawrence Keitt of South Carolina decided to make Walker's case a rallying point for sectional agitation and did so during the first session of the House of Representatives in 1858. Quitman spoke to Congress in favor of repealing portions of the 1818 Neutrality Act that precluded filibustering activity. The discussion ultimately became heated and led to an altercation between Congressman Keitt and Republican whip Galusha Grow. Others took a different approach to Nicaragua; Randolph Runnels, the brother of Governor Hardin Runnels, wrote a letter to his brother the Texas Governor in January, 1858, asking for his help in securing an appointment as U.S. Consul to Nicaragua, perhaps anticipating the return of Walker to the helm of leadership of that Republic. He got the job. Sam Houston made a bold statement as to Texan intentions when on February 16, 1858, he introduced a resolution into the United States Senate proposing to establish a protectorate over Mexico, Nicaragua, Costa Rica, Guatemala, Honduras, and El Salvador. This idea was one that would have suited William Walker and Houston's friend, John A. Quitman. Adverse reaction to this suggestion resulted in Houston amending his proposal in April to include only Mexico, suggesting it could be achieved with five thousand troops. Houston ended his resolution with a veiled threat to "unfurl again the banner of the lone star." When brought to a vote, the resolution was defeated 30 to 17. Houston was then reported to have then threatened to take matters into his own hands, with the *Dallas Herald* reporting that Sam "was now ready to lead volunteers into Mexico, to restore peace and good government to that distracted country." Although nothing like that happened in 1858, Houston did not give up on the idea.[6]

In the meantime, William Walker stayed occupied while other filibustering operations proceeded in 1858. Down in the Mexican border town of Brownsville, Texas, the newspaper reported on January 27th an unusual influx of strangers "looking out for locations," and also noticed "signs of revolution in Northern Mexico". While the *Houston Weekly Telegraph* indulged in an inordinate amount of pro-slavery proselytizing in February; on March 17, 1858, it noted that a Waco newspaper "talks like a filibustero about Mexico. It says that country is ours by inheritance. No doubt of it, and we are consummate fools to let the lazy greasers cheat us out of our property." On the same day, the New York correspondent of the *Philadelphia Ledger* reported that "a military expedition of a formidable character is organizing in this city" to support the government of Ignacio Comonfort of Mexico. There was a full-scale civil war being waged in Mexico between Comonfort's Liberal Party and the Conservative Party backed by the Catholic Church. The leadership of the Liberal Party were all Freemasons: Benito Juarez, Melchor Ocampo, Lerdo de Tejada, Payno y Prieto, and Ignacio Comonfort, like many KGC were Masons. John Quitman, on the Supreme Council of the Southern Scottish Rite Masons, who were established in Mexico, had already approved of filibustering operations in Mexico as early as 1856. Quitman's rationale for seizing Mexico was that the chronic instability of that country made it an attractive target for acquisition by European powers, and to prevent that from happening, the United States should act first. However, in 1858, Quitman was advocating once again for Texas and the other Gulf States to secede, consistent with KGC dogma of using the Gulf States as a base for the creation of an agricultural empire built

on slavery, to include Mexico and Cuba. By January 1858, the Comonfort government was willing to sell, for $1 million in cash, enough of Northern Mexico to
create a railroad right-of-way clear across the continent, from the Gulf of Mexico
to the Pacific Ocean.[7]

Aware of these developments, and with KGC castles established in Texas by
1858, more private militias and ranging companies were formed in the State. John
A. Wilcox formed the Alamo Rifles in January 1857; in November 1857 the Colorado Cavalry Guards were formed, with William J. Herbert as Captain, John L.
Shropshire, 2nd Lieutenant, John Upton, 1st Lieutenant, and Howell A. Tatum as
3rd Lieutenant. John Shropshire's brother and business partner, Ben, was Captain
of the KGC castle in La Grange, Fayette County; John was probably a member of
one of the Colorado County castles, and both were in the Black Belt of slave ownership in Texas. Howell A. Tatum was a known KGC member and organizer and
had been one of the three men on the vigilance committee that condemned 5
slaves to death for their part in a suspected 1856 attempted slave revolt. It is highly
likely that the Colorado Cavalry Guards were an early KGC military company.
Thomas C. Frost, another likely KGC member, was appointed by Governor Runnels to the rank of Lieutenant in a ranging company for Coryell and Comanche
counties on December 31, 1857, to investigate alleged malfeasance by Indians on
the Brazos River Reservation. As Sam Houston had noted in 1856, Indian mischief
was invented in order to gain support for building up a military force in Texas. On
January 8, 1858, Lieutenant Frost wrote to Governor Runnels the following:

> In accordance with the conditions of my instructions…I herewith transmit
> my official report which was due a few days since…. it is almost proved
> that if the Indians on the reservation are not the aggressors they are un-
> questionably concerned in the numerous and recent atrocities…. The
> charge may be untrue in toto but it does seem that no evil could accrue
> from an investigation of the matter and I would therefore modestly suggest
> its consideration to your Excellency….

Frost was reaching; he had no proof that reservation Indians were involved
in any malfeasance, but he wanted to find something damning. In reality the "recent atrocities" he referred to were committed by four white men, who were hung
for their crimes in May. The harassment of the reservation Indians in Texas would
continue and intensify in the coming two years, culminating in tragedy and their
removal from the state. In the meantime, Governor Runnels had other things on

his mind; frequently during his 2-year administration he threatened to lead his state out of the Union. It was with that in mind that he appointed several men to attend the Southern Commercial Convention in Montgomery, Alabama, a Southern rights conclave that met on May 2, 1858. The men named included T.N. Waul, E.B. Nichols, and Nathaniel Terry, all KGC members.[8]

On January 16, 1858, known KGC leader Samuel A. Lockridge, a veteran of one of Walker's invasions of Nicaragua, posted a "card" in the Galveston News announcing an emigration to Northern Mexico was to take place by April 1st. "No arms nor organizations will be allowed," he said, "other than to insure mutual protection.... Large means and some of the most influential citizens of this country are engaged in this enterprise, which will insure its success, beyond doubt." By late March, Lockridge was still publicly calling for volunteers. At the same time, Texan Henderson McBride Pridgen was publicly calling for a war with Mexico in order to re-claim runaway slaves. Said to be "a splendid orator," Pridgen called for those like-minded citizens to meet him on April 22nd at Clinton, Texas in Dewitt County. Later in life, Mr. Pridgen would fondly recall his membership in the KGC. By early April 1858, the Mexican minister informed President Buchanan that a filibustering expedition against his country was being organized in the Southern United States. True enough, Samuel A. Lockridge, a veteran of one of William Walker's crusades against Nicaragua, was in New Orleans in March calling for an expedition to Mexico, and arrived in Brownsville, Texas by April. Amid these events, pro-KGC newspapers in Texas agitated for the reopening of the African slave trade, and more volunteer militia companies were formed. Newspapers told of the *Waco Southerner* advocating for the reopening of the African slave trade, as did the *Dallas Herald*, and made mention of two armed companies drilling in Waco. Another company, the Grey Eagle Guards, was reported to have "reorganized" in Richmond, Texas in May, with John T. Holt as Captain. On May 8, 1858, Malcijah Benjamin Highsmith, another known KGC leader, wrote Governor Runnels informing him that he had formed "...a company of Rangers for frontier service in the event there should be a call for them...I have about one hundred names enrolled from the counties of Bastrop Fayette & Burleson that hold themselves in readiness at a moment's warning...." Highsmith gave as his references two known KGC leaders, John Salmon Ford and Henry E. McCulloch; Highsmith had served under Ford in the Rangers previously.[9]

At about the same time a group of militia left North and South Carolina in April 1858 for Texas, led by John Taylor Coit of Cheraw, South Carolina. Coit sent a letter to 2nd Lieut. W. B. Smith of the Cheraw Company of the 28th Infantry requesting a list of all men and material belonging to the company, including books on military tactics and militia law. Smith was reporting to him as Coit was Lieutenant Colonel of said company; Coit then received the following letter from an A. Patterson dated April 17, 1858:

> If nothing prevents I expect to be over in your town by Wednesday next ready to start for Texas on Thursday morning. Maj. A. C. McIntyre expects to start at the same time and I hope it will suit your convenience to start then. I have been trying to persuade Col. Malloy to go but I am very doubtful about his going, he will not say positively whether he will or not....

John T. Coit and J. H. Malloy had played a major role in the September 1856 trial and deportation from South Carolina of two men named Caldwell and Malone, who were accused of uttering antislavery sentiments. Coit did not leave South Carolina for Texas until sometime in May, 1858, indicated by a letter he received at Cheraw from W. L. T. Prince, asking him to bring back "two negroe men of mine now in Austin, or if Dr. Patterson or Mr. McIntyre would find it more convenient get them to do so." Colonel W. L. T. Prince was the driving force behind the prosecution of the antislavery men in Cheraw in 1856; he was a large slave owner. The Coit family history states that John Coit arrived in New Orleans sometime in 1858, "and from there by boat up the Mississippi and Red Rivers to near Jefferson, Texas. He bought a horse and rode over the country to Bonham, McKinney, and southward." Coincidentally, the towns of Bonham and McKinney had KGC "Castles," or lodges; those towns being early adopters of that order in North-east Texas. Austin being in Central Texas, it is feasible that Coit and his party had gone further south of Austin to participate in Samuel A. Lockridge's proposed filibuster into Mexico. Charles Anderson, an early citizen of San Antonio, wrote that in the spring of 1858 the KGC was in South Texas looking for recruits and stirring up resentment against the government of the United States. Ultimately, they were unsuccessful in their Mexican emigration scheme, but they had succeeded in bringing more would-be warriors to Texas, some as permanent settlers. John T. Coit wrote his wife Catherine from Dallas on June 18, 1858, informing her that he had bought land in Dallas and adjacent Collin County. It has been previously thought by some historians that the Collin County town of McKinney, Texas was the point at which the KGC first gained a foothold in Texas. This is because McKinney is the first place that the KGC was reported by name in a Texas newspaper, in January 1860. Others believe that Greenville, Texas, in

Hunt County adjacent to McKinney and southeast of Bonham, was the earliest point of entry for the secret order, due to the mention in a private letter by a member who was recruited there in 1859. Known KGC member Isaiah T. Davis had begun organizing his "volunteer company" in the nearby East Texas county of Upshur as early as June 1859. Still others point to Marshall, Texas, the home of Louis Wigfall and his business partner and ultra-military knight Elkanah Greer, as having a KGC Castle by 1858. Harrison County, where Marshall is located, had the largest slave population of any county in the State. By early June 1858, the predecessor of a military company that be-came known as the Knights of Guada-lupe was being organized East of San Antonio in Seguin, by Nathaniel "Nat" Ben-ton and H. B. King. Nat Benton led a company of men from Seguin into Mexico in search of escaped slaves as part of the notorious Callahan Expedition in 1855. He must be considered an early KGC organizer in Texas. Evidence has been presented thus far by this writer that the KGC was firmly established in Texas by 1858, and most likely entered the State through the largest Texas slave trading market at Galveston, which was also the largest Texas port city, sometime very soon after the secret society's formation in 1855. It is also more likely that Dallas had a KGC chapter, or Castle, before its neighboring town McKinney because of the presence there of John Jay Good, a member of the Lone Star of the West who came to Dallas in 1851. John Coit may have been one of the first KGC to settle in Collin County, but he wasn't the first.[10]

That honor likely belongs to William Mack Weaver or Joseph Ponsol Bickley. William Weaver had resided in Tennessee where with his father he was a large raiser of cattle but dealt more in horses and mules. It was not unusual for livestock dealers to also deal in slaves. At William's age, 21, his father died while in Hunts-ville, Alabama, where he had driven a herd of livestock. William married that year. On February 7, 1855, he wrote a letter to John A. Quitman in New Orleans, asking if he could be Quitman's Aide de Camp for the Cuban invasion. He concluded by asking Quitman to write him in Selma, Alabama, where he might have driven live-stock. Sometime that same year Weaver moved to Plano, Texas where he became known as a Democrat and substantial cattleman. This put Weaver, a member of the Lone Star of the West, in Collin County sometime in 1855, three years before John T. Coit. In June 1858, Weaver became one of the original members of the first Masonic lodge in Plano. Weaver rose quickly in the officers' ranks during the Civil War after organizing a company for the war in Collin County and eventually was promoted to Colonel in command of 4 companies. As the KGC was most heavily represented in the officer class of the Confederate forces, given his other activities, Weaver was most likely a KGC member. Fellow Collin County resident Joseph Ponsol Bickley was a cousin of George W.L. Bickley, the master recruiter and public face of the KGC and its alleged leader by 1859. Joseph P. Bickley was descended from William Bickley, the founder of Bickley's Mills, Virginia, as was George W. L. Bickley. Born in 1827 in Scott County, Virginia, by October 1857 Joseph Bickley was living in Collin County but exactly when he arrived is not known; there is evidence he was there at least occasionally as early as 1854. He eventually settled at Farmersville, Texas where he became a farmer and stock raiser. Described as being "a great organizer" who "knew that he was able to direct others and his life proved it," he served as an enlisted man in the Confederacy in the same company of Partisan Rangers founded by William Mack Weaver. The few Bickley family letters that survive show that he kept in touch with his cousins and other relatives in Scott County, Virginia and at Bickley's Mills. A natural organizer, he could have helped spread his cousin George W.L. Bickley's message in Collin County at an early date, before the public face of the KGC was revealed there in January 1860. Not much else is known of Joseph P. Bickley.[11]

Although John Taylor Coit made his new home at Plano, Texas in Collin County he kept his 14 slaves on his land in adjacent Dallas County. The town of Dallas was a nest of KGC; Thomas Scott Anderson moved from Austin to Dallas and made his home there from 1858 to 1860, even while serving as Secretary of State in the Runnels administration miles away in the State Capitol at Austin. John Jay Good had written Governor Pease from Dallas on June 20, 1854 indicating that in the event of war with Spain, Good could raise a company of men for the war, and that it "would be a matter of pride and pleasure to myself...." Good may have anticipated recruiting the Dallas Citizens Militia, of which he was a member in 1854; he later organized the Lone Star of the West in Dallas in 1856. John Coit later helped organize another military company in Dallas County, at the nearby town of Breckenridge, now known as Richardson, Texas. The Breckenridge Guards, as they were known, was more than likely a KGC company. Dallas had at least two other KGC companies: the Dallas Light Artillery Company, commanded by John Jay Good, and the Lone Star Company (also known as the Mesquite Light Horse company) commanded by Ashley (or Asher) Carter, composed of men from the eastern part of the county, specifically the town of Scyene, today's town of Mesquite, Texas. Another possible KGC company in Dallas was the Dallas Minute Company, commanded by Colonel John M. Crockett, who served as State

Representative for Dallas County from 1851 to 1857 and Mayor of Dallas from 1859 to 1861; in September 1861, he was elected the first Lieutenant Governor of the Confederate State of Texas. Nicholas Henry Darnell, a career politician who represented Dallas County in the State Legislature from 1859-1861, also became known as one who had "taken a bold stand in defense of Southern Rights and has been a tower of strength to the cause." He, too, became a high-ranking officer commanding Confederate forces. Dallas County, with its meager 1859 population of 7,729 whites and 1,080 slaves, and the city of Dallas, with an 1859 population of 581 whites and 97 slaves, produced eight men who rose to the rank of Colonel in the Confederacy: Nicholas Henry Darnell, B. Warren Stone, T.C. Hawpe, Nathaniel M. Burford, John Jay Good, John T. Coit, George W. Guess, and W.E. Hughes. George W. Guess, a known KGC member from Dallas, served as one of the five city aldermen from 1859 to 1861. Guess was born in North Carolina and became a Mason in 1857. Within his private papers is found an undated oath of allegiance to the KGC, titled "Obligation of the Knights of the Golden Circle," which states,

> You of your own free will and accord do solemnly swear before almighty God and these witnesses that you will bear true allegiance to the C S C & that you will serve her faithfully… if in your power to do so. That you will observe and obey the orders of the officers appointed over you according to the rules and articles of war. You further swear that you will forever abjure all allegiance to the government of the United States or any other enemy we may have either foreign or at home and that you will not give aid or comfort to the government of the U.S.A. or any other enemy either directly or indirectly and you further swear that you will aid and assist the government of the C S C & by all means in your power both in and out of the army and you further swear that you will aid all southern men and southern families in the protection of both person and property at a reasonable risk of your own life. You further swear that you will aid and assist a Knight of the Golden Circle in any distress to the greatest extent that you can without injury to yourself. You further swear that you will not reveal any of the secret signs grips or words or any of the secret works of the Knights of the Golden Circle or any secret order…. binding yourself under the no less penalty of being taken by your brethren and being hanged by the neck until you are dead, dead, dead and your bones to bleach upon the plains as unworthy of being if you should be so vile as to reveal these obligations etc. so help you God [sic]

This handwritten, undated oath is not in the handwriting of Mr. Guess and appears to have been meant for new recruits in the months leading up to the Civil War, with its reference to the C.S.C. and "articles of war." The official KGC oath was first publicly published in 1860. There was some variability regionally in the oaths taken by KGC members, and certainly due to their relative position within the organization, which may have also depended upon events as they evolved; but the common denominator of the oath was its pledge of secrecy, and the fact that it was a lifetime oath to protect the members and their families. This in itself had long-term consequences and influence over life in Texas. As one member later wrote, "'Once a Knight, always a Knight,' is a standing axiom of the Order. When you go in, you know not what you are doing, but are led along step by step, to assume obligations… that every honest man would scout with scorn, could he see them as a whole…." Another former Texas Knight made similar statements in writing that was published only after his death, that "The ramifications of this secret society, which in its constitution was something like the Italian Mafia, of evil notoriety, were very wide, but though the leaders were perfectly well-known, the rank and file, who obeyed their behests without question or hesitation, were difficult to identify." The writers of both these statements were members of the KGC in Texas, and one referred specifically to the Order as "A Texan Mafia." Like the Mafia, one might have found it very difficult to get out alive once one joined.[12]

The disturbance caused by the KGC on the Texas-Mexico border may have taken a brief respite upon the death of its founder in 1858. John Anthony Quitman died at his plantation in Natchez on July 17, 1858, under suspicious circumstances; some suspected poisoning. His death certainly created a vacuum within the organization, as revered as he had been across the South. Shortly before his death a new military company had been organized in Austin, Texas. Calling themselves the Quitman Rifles, this probable KGC company led a procession through the state capitol in honor of their fallen leader on July 28, 1858. An enlisted member of the company, N. G. Shelby read the eulogy. Other members of the company included W. L. Hill, X. B. DeBray, J. Martin, F. Arlitt, B. Herzog, E. D. Walker, O. Flusser, T. J. Paterson, W. T. Masterson and C. H. Ruston. Xavier Blanchard DeBray later rose to the rank of Colonel in command of the Twenty-Sixth Texas Cavalry in the Civil War, after brief service in the Fourth Texas Infantry and Second Texas Infantry. Flusser, Masterson and Rushton also became members of the Fourth Texas Infantry, and Flusser died in battle. Most KGC companies became the core of the

early Texas military companies organized for the Civil War, such as the Second
and Fourth Infantry. The KGC continued to expand across the country without
Quitman, gaining sympathizers as well as members. Unlike the KNs, the KGC did
not discriminate against the Irish. Irish born writer John Mitchel had attended the
Southern Commercial Convention at Montgomery in May and was quoted by the
Houston Weekly Telegraph as espousing the KGC party line in 1858:

> I am a moderate man, and confine my views for the present to a Dissolution
> of the Union – Revival of the African Trade – Americanization of Cuba,
> Central America, Mexico and the West India Islands – and establishment
> of a potent Southern Confederacy, based on Slavery; that's all. As for the
> conquest of the Northern States, I would defer that.

Mitchel was a former admirer of Young Italy's Giuseppe Mazzini, as well as
Italian revolutionary Garibaldi, and a member of the Young Ireland movement,
the Old Sod's branch of Young Europe. Upon moving to New York in 1854 he
commenced publication of a pro-slavery newspaper. During the Civil War he edited the Richmond Enquirer, the mouthpiece of Confederate President Jefferson
Davis, and was particularly fond of the Jefferson Davis Guards, a mostly Irish unit
based in Galveston, Texas that held off an 1863 Union naval invasion of Texas at
the Battle of Sabine Pass.[13]

Texas newspapers, especially the *Weekly Telegraph*, continued to agitate for the
reopening of the African slave trade, and to hint at the goals of the KGC in Texas
by April of 1858:

> The time may yet come when Texas will resume her nationality. The world
> is full of changes. What will become of the United States, no one can tell.
> That they will stand as now many years is rather hoped for than expected.
> In the divisions that may occur Texas have nothing to lose…. we have
> within ourselves the resources of a great nation, and if ever we are again
> called to stand alone we can do so and bid defiance to the world.

Independent military companies continued to form across the state, like the
Frontier Guards formed at Weatherford, in the Northwest Texas county of Parker,
in June 1858. It was designated a volunteer rifle company, with elected officers
comprised of Captain C. L. Jordan, 1st Lieutenant W. L. Pendleton, and 2nd Lieutenants J. W. Curtis and I. B. Turke. John Jay Good, who was traveling the State
practicing law, may have had something to do with the formation of this rifle

company, as the notice of its formation was found in his private papers. Newspapers sympathetic to the arms buildup in Texas continued to encourage other counties to start private military organizations. On October 1st the Harrison Flag published one such article, titled, "To Be Prepared for War is one of the Most Effectual Means of Preserving Peace." The title was attributed as a quote from President George Washington and the article noted that the State Legislature had passed an Act "authorizing the Governor, upon the application of any company regularly organized and uniformed, to furnish the same with arms."[sic]

> San Antonio has her "Alamo Rifles".... Houston has her "Washington Life Guards" who for their discipline, good order &c are the pride and boast of the "Bayou City". Galveston has her "Continentals" which for discipline &c, is unequalled by any Company in the Union. Austin boasts the "Quitman Rifles" (newly organized) who are self-constituted guardians of the "Capitol City". Waco's "Rifle Rangers" are said to be on a firm footing and bid fair to rival any of the former in a short time – all commanded by such men – as Wilcox, Edwards, McLevi, Hill and Smith, all men who have "done the State some service." Why should Marshall be behind hand in this measure? [sic]

The town of Marshall was the county seat of Harrison County, and that county, the article stressed, "now occupies the position of being the largest slave owning county in Texas." The gist of the article was that these independent, uniformed military companies were needed to control the slave population, not as defense against hostile Native American tribes, as some have supposed. James A. Wilcox, William C. Edwards of Houston's Light Guards and J.M. Smith of the Waco Rifle Rangers were all known KGC members; perhaps McLevi and Hill were also.[14] Other members of the KGC had plans for the Indians, and they were already in motion.

Chapter 7

Genocide

Upon his election to the office of President of the Republic of Texas, Mirabeau Buonaparte Lamar's first address to the Texas Congress had called for a war of extermination and expulsion of the Native American tribes residing in the republic. In serving as the second President of the Republic, his administration reneged on previous treaties with the Indians to force them off their lands in East Texas. Lamar served one term, which ended in late 1841; by 1850, he was a prominent and vocal advocate of secession; he died on December 19, 1859. Violence perpetrated by KGC members against Lamar's non-white enemies would not be quelled upon his death. The "land sharks," as one historian termed them, would realize his dream of forcing the Indians out of the state in 1859. The closure of the Brazos Reservation where several tribes had been relocated was accomplished by men aligned with a well-known KGC commander: John R. Baylor, and his partner in crime, a little-known KGC functionary named Harris A. Hamner. These two men used the betrayal of the Brazos Reservation tribes as a springboard to organize and expand the KGC in Texas.[1]

Much is known of John R. Baylor. The sympathetic Texas media treated him as if he were Southern royalty:

Capt. Baylor is a gentleman by birth and education--is a descendant of the Baylor family of Va., whose ancestors came over from England during the time of the Colonial government, settled near Old Point Comfort, and received large grants of land from Charles II, for their services as Cavaliers during the troubles of Charles I. The family has always been influential, and of the highest respectability. The Captain has made a very favorable impression on the minds of our citizens. He is a gentleman and a scholar, and subscribed for the Herald. [sic]

So said the pro-slavery, pro-KGC *Dallas Weekly Herald*, in dressing up their man with the proper ties to royalty. This blue-blood conceit was a common factor for many of the KGC leadership. The Baylor family was an historic one, with John Baylor III serving in the Virginia House of Burgesses, maintaining a 20,000-acre tobacco plantation with more than 180 slaves while enjoying an English gentleman's education at Cambridge. General George W. Baylor had served with George Washington and was said to have died from battle wounds in 1784. Through this ancestor, KGC member John Robert Baylor was eligible for membership in the Society of the Cincinnati through its Virginia society. John Baylor IV lost the family fortune due to the interruption of the tobacco trade during the Revolutionary War and died in debtor's prison in 1808, an ignoble end for colonial gentry. This sense of lost nobility was also shared by other KGC leaders – George W. L. Bickley, Philip Ignatius Barziza, John Anthony Quitman, and untold others who claimed families with a glorious past. The descendants of Walker Baylor started over in Texas. Not all newspapers would be as sympathetic to Texans John R. Baylor and his brother George W. Baylor as the *Herald*, however. They were a far cry from their titled, genteel, Virginia ancestors.[2]

Much less has been written about Baylor's partner, Harris A. Hamner, although his life was one of intrigue. H. A. Hamner was born in South Carolina in 1827, and moved with his family from Mobile, Alabama to Texas around 1854.[3] At some point, he settled in Johnson County, just southwest of present-day Ft. Worth, where he was released from the County Militia prior to his next move further west to Jack County. This locale at the time was considered far West Texas; there he settled on the headwaters of Lost Creek, near several springs.[4] On legal documents, he listed his address as Keechi Salt Works. His neighbor and friend was James Cambern, a Mexican War veteran; together they served as officials in the first election held in Jack County on July 4, 1857. On April 18, 1858, it was believed that Indians were responsible for attacking their homes, killing Mr. and Mrs. Cambern and three of their children. Hamner subsequently became the Jack County Tax Assessor and Collector and posted his bond on August 17, 1858. He served two terms in that position, but problems with nomadic Indians continued, so Hamner became the Captain of what were known as the Jack County Volunteers, a local self-defense organization.

John W. Middleton, an early settler of East Texas, left there in 1856 and became a stock raiser along the Brazos River near Hamner in nearby Parker County. Also a participant in Hamner's anti-Indian crusade, Middleton blamed an old rival from Shelby County, where both men had been involved in the Regulator-Moderator War, for the murder of the Cambern family; his name was John Walker. According to Middleton, "Walker and four others, Joe Robertson, Bob Tucker, Covington and Dordy were the men who, pretending to be Indians, murdered Cameron [sic] and his wife in Lost Prairie." All those men were eventually either executed or killed while resisting arrest, except Walker, who escaped.[5]

At this point the slave-owning tribes - Southern Cherokees, the Choctaw, Chickasaw and Creek - were in present-day Oklahoma, having been pushed out of Kansas, where they had been previously allowed to own slaves. In Indian Territory they formed a secret organization to encourage the emigration of like-minded people on the slavery question, and to discourage those who thought otherwise.[6] If not initially organized as the KGC, it certainly was its forerunner. Land had been leased from the Choctaw and Chickasaw tribes, just north of the Red River, for an Indian agency for the Wichita tribe. On this land with the Wichita lived some Comanche Indians that were hostile to the settlers across the river in Texas. It was desired by some to eventually move all of the Indians still left on reservations in Texas into the Wichita Agency North of the Red River.[7] Those Indians still residing in Texas at this time were located on two different reservations: the Comanche Reservation on the Clear Fork of the Brazos River and the Caddo Reservation on the main fork of the Brazos River. Living with the Caddo on their reservation were Indians from the Anadarko, Keechie, Tonkawa, Waco, Tawakoni, Delaware, and Shawnee tribes (the Shawnee having been slave owners in Kansas). These Indians were friendly to the Texans and served as a buffer against the hostile Comanches and their Kiowa allies. Unfortunately, the Texas Comanche Reservation Indians sometimes interacted with their wild relatives from north of the Red River. These predatory tribesmen became known to Texans as the Northern Comanches. This hostile group of tribesmen from north of the Red River stole livestock from the Reservation tribes as well as the white population.[8]

On October 30, 1858, the schoolteacher on the Caddo Reservation on the Main Fork of the Brazos wrote the following in his diary:

> Several gentlemen from Jack county here today. Professing to have traced some of their stolen horses to the Caddoe Village which trails turned out

to be only Capt. Roys'es returning trail from Fort Arbuckle whether they were satisfied or not I am unable to say but if their appearances argue anything I cannot believe they were satisfied as such men are seldom satisfied without they can injure someone. [sic][9]

The reservations in Texas were under the supervision of Major Robert S. Neighbors, in charge of Indian affairs in the state. He in turn worked closely with the commander of Federal Troops in the area, Lieutenant Colonel Robert E. Lee, destined to be a hero to many in the Confederate states. Assisting Major Neighbors as Special Agents to the Reservation Indians were Shapely P. Ross (referred to as "Roys" in the teacher's diary) and Captain John R. Baylor, who reported for this duty in 1855. In his report for 1856, Major Neighbors commended both men and generously credited their work for the satisfactory state of Indian affairs that prevailed at that time.[10] The following year, John Baylor was dismissed from the service, allegedly for quarreling with Major Neighbors; his rivals later stated that Baylor was fired for stealing money from the Reservation, money meant for the Indians.[11] Purely out of spite, Baylor began a smear campaign against Major Neighbors and the peaceful Indians on the Texas reservation. Baylor and Hamner teamed up to lead a movement among the white settlers to pressure the government to close the reservations in Texas and move the Indians across the Red River into Indian Territory. It had been Baylor and Hamner's men who had visited the reservation in October 1858 looking for trouble; they had done so before. On December 23, 1858, Hamner and his men committed an atrocity; that night some of their party killed seven harmless Indians, including three women as they lay sleeping.[12] Six more Caddo and Anadarko tribesmen were wounded; their attackers let their intentions be known: to "kill all the Indians on the Reserve and all their American friends there."[13] John Salmon "Rip" Ford, one of the organizers of the KGC in Texas, had been authorized by Governor Runnels to raise a company of Rangers to protect the settlements in West Texas; Judge N. W. Battle of Waco, who heard the testimony of a survivor of the attack on the defenseless tribesmen, ordered Captain Ford to arrest the perpetrators. Ford refused to do so on the grounds that the Judge's order was a civilian order, and this was out of his jurisdiction as a State ranger.[14] No arrests were made; a month later Captain Ford came to the Brazos agency: Mr. Coombes, the agency schoolteacher, wrote in his diary on February 22, 1859, "I had as leave not be honored with his company as he is nothing more than a magnificent ass."[15] Coombes entry for March 4, 1859 is as follows:

...almost all of the officials of Jack County are interested and engaged in the raising and outfitting of men to come here and wipe out this reserve, both red and white.... Well I hope if they do come, that they will at least some of their Dare Devil Leaders may be sent to their long, their last and their final homes. For if these innocent and harmless Indians cannot be protected and left undisturbed by outlaws it is to be hoped that said outlaws may be sent to their final home, their last long farewell to all outlawry. [sic][16]

Not all the citizens of the frontier supported Baylor, Hamner and the Jack County Rangers: over the next few weeks, prominent frontiersmen like George B. Erath, Colonel Middleton T. Johnson and others toured the surrounding counties counseling restraint, using the public forum; unfortunately they were followed by Baylor and Hamner and their adherents who publicly advocated just the opposite.[17] On April 25, 1859, one-hundred twenty-eight men signed a petition calling for the resignation of Major Robert Neighbors; among the signers were John R. Baylor, J. A. McLaren, John Funderburgh, John Hittson, Oliver Loving, William B. Eubank, J. J. Cureton, and G. W. Slaughter. Most, if not all, the signatories were cattlemen - they coveted the grazing land along the Brazos River that was occupied by the tribes and their livestock. They certainly coveted Indian ponies. On May 5, 1859, Captain S. P. Ross informed Major Neighbors by communique that John Baylor and a party of armed men had raided the reservation with the intent to take Indian scalps but were driven off by United States cavalry there to protect the reservation. Commenting further, Ross wrote:

I had hoped when it was made known that the government intended to remove the Indians from Texas as soon as practible, that the agitators would become quiet; but they are now more clamorous than ever. It seems that ponies, and not protection, is the groundwork of this move. Some of these exasperated men have succeeded very well in the pony move.[18]

Captain S. P. Ross, a well-known and respected pioneer citizen was of the opinion that the whole affair was an excuse for Hamner, Baylor and the cattlemen to steal Indian ponies. There is support for his opinion. The Nacogdoches Campaign Chronicle printed a letter from the son of David G. Burnet, the former President of the Republic of Texas. His son was an officer among the U.S. troops assigned to protect the reservation. Lieutenant Burnet stated in his letter that Baylor had been "discharged from the Agency for stealing public money" and that "his followers are engaged in stealing cattle." Of the Indian's oppressors, Burnet wrote "They deserve hanging. They would as soon rob the mails as anything else." An-other source also reported that Oliver Loving and other cattlemen in nearby Palo Pinto County were prepared to fight to protect the murderers that had been led by Peter Garland, leading one to wonder if the cattlemen had been behind the attack on the Indians all along.[19] The Clarksville Northern Standard reported that "Baylor and his party have been killing cattle and taking horses belonging to the Indians."[20] Then, around May 8th, tragedy struck again:

> ...a noble young man named Holden was killed and scalped about halfway between the two Indian reservations. His slayers were trailed into the Co-manche reservation. It was either Peter Garland or Captain Hamner who was in charge of a group of men doing the trailing, when they came to a camp of Indi-ans. The pursuers were all mad and asked no questions but commenced firing, killing four warriors, two squaws and one child. These Indians were friendly Caddoes. This hastened the war with the reservation Indians.21

War was what Baylor and Hamner wanted, and they got it on May 23, 1859. Gathering forces at what became appropriately known as Filibuster Creek, they led a force of 250 to 300 men and boys from several counties to the Brazos reser-vation on that day and were confronted by United States Army troops led by Cap-tain C.C. Gilbert. John W. Middleton wrote in his account of the incident that "Hamner and his company came first, and finally all came forward except Sutton's company from Weatherford which refused to proceed further and returned home."[22]

After some incendiary dialog back and forth, Baylor decided not to attack the troops; however, as Hamner passed through the reservation, he killed a feeble old Indian man and farther on, an old Indian woman in her garden. This enraged the once friendly Indians who gave chase with seventy of their best warriors; fifty of the Indians chased the cowardly attackers for two miles and scattered all 250 of them, chasing them for another eight miles. The Indians killed seven whites at a loss of three warriors. Lieutenant Burnet then sent a second letter to the Nacog-doches newspaper that con-firmed this account of the battle.[23] This story would not have a happy ending, and it wouldn't be the last of the KGC's fake Indian crises.

In the meantime, Governor Runnels campaign for reelection was not going well precisely because of his handling of the Indians and his constant threats of secession from the United States. On a national as well as a state level, the KGC had been growing and was about to publicly manifest itself. On May 25, 1859, the *San Antonio Daily Herald* mocked the editor of its nearby publishing media rival, John Marshall of the *Austin State Gazette*, as being a fear monger. "Marshall of the *State Gazette*" it opined, "is terribly exercised at information received from San Antonio, of the existence of a 'secret organization, formed there,' whose object is to destroy the democratic party."[sic] The editor of the *Daily Herald* apparently didn't know at that point that the KGC was indeed entrenched in San Antonio, the largest city in the state of Texas at that time; or that John Marshall himself, was a member of the KGC. The by-laws of one of the KGC Castles in San Antonio list J.M. Carolan as Captain, George Cupples as Lieutenant, Albert Wood as Secretary, J.A.G. Navarro as Treasurer, J.H. Beck, Jr. as Inspector, J.M. Smith as Guide, and J. Marshall as Sargent [sic]. The Knights of the Golden Circle had not yet been mentioned by name by a Texas newspaper, but they were certainly a secret Order that intended to not only destroy the Democratic Party, but all political parties, as well as democracy itself. After running that op-ed piece ridiculing Mr. Marshall, less than a month later the editor of the *Herald* reprinted an op-ed from the Nacogdoches Campaign Union, as shown by this excerpt of June 16, 1859, titled, "Disunion":

> We believe that a great and dangerous party, hostile to the Union, now exists in the South and Texas, and that it is high time for the people to rise in their strength and crush it out. That party is thoroughly organized, and drilled in the ways of cunning and deceit.... It cannot be denied that a large majority of the leading organizers are in favor of the reopening of the African Slave Trade, and other disunion issues – that per se they are for disunion – and that they are lead on by such men as Gov. Runnels, Jno. Marshall & Co., and that they are in league with a horde of conspirators in other states, and for years have operated together to carry out their objects.

The Campaign Union concluded by further implicating Governor Runnels and newspapers that were certainly friendly to the KGC; those being *The State Gazette*, the *Galveston News*, and others. Continuing, the Union alleged the conspirators "hope to 'precipitate' the south into a dissolution" and:

> But, they whisper, 'don't make the issue yet, we are not ready: let us bind, hand and foot, the old party first, then we'll unfurl our banner, and 'let slip

the dogs of war.' It was just such men as many of this party that Gen. Jackson threatened to hang as high as Haman, in Nullification times. And yet they call themselves 'Jackson Democrats.' [sic]

That is exactly what would happen inside of 2 years, when former Governor Hardin Richard Runnels would play a very key role in binding, hand and foot, the old Democratic Party, as would be seen, and in precipitating the withdrawal of Texas from the union.

The article may have been dismissed at the time as partisan rhetoric in an election year, which was possible because the general public was unaware of the existence of this secret organization. Less than a month later, however, awareness was partially raised as the KGC was finally identified by name in a Texas newspaper, the July 13, 1859 issue of the *Dallas Times Herald*, in an article titled, "Another Filibustering Scheme":

> The *New York Tribune* announces the discovery of a filibustering project on a most extensive scale. The general name given to the new association is the 'K.G.C.,' or 'Knights of the Golden Circle.' It is to consist of two legions, one of which is to number ten thousand men, when it is completely formed. It is to have an abundance of officers, and commissary, surgical and conveyance departments – quite a standing army. The American legion is to be composed of one regiment of cavalry, one of mounted riflemen, one of artillery, five of infantry, and a reserve guard. The brigadier generals are to constitute a war board, and the headquarters are to be in the city of Baltimore.

Still, the Order had not been identified by name in Texas. Until then, the KGC in Texas would content themselves with a small but significant victory, just one step in their long-range plan for white supremacy, by bulldozing the Indians out of the state. On August 1, 1859, Major Neighbors of the Brazos Indian Reservation began to resettle the tribes in Indian Territory, outside of the State of Texas. Neighbors concluded the resettlement on September 4, 1859, and tendered his resignation. In his farewell address to the Indians, one of their chiefs, a Tonkawa named Placido, cried like a child. Friends of Major Neighbors pleaded with him not to go back to Texas, but their efforts were in vain. One attempt had already been made on his life before he even crossed the Red River going north; he and his military escort were attacked by hostile Indians and renegade whites, but the attack had been repulsed. After re-crossing the Red River and reaching Fort

Belknap in north Texas, friends there warned him not to go into town. He did anyway, and within minutes of leaving the Young County courthouse on September 14th, he was assassinated, shot in the back with a double-barrel shotgun after being distracted by an accomplice. The man who killed him, Edward Cornett, had never met him before that day. Cornett escaped in the confusion and went into hiding but was later killed by the Young County Sheriff.[24]

Sam Houston used the mishandling of the Indians on the frontier to his political advantage in the election campaign for governor. Houston told the Texas Republican that "The Indians have been charged with an aggressive and hostile spirit towards the whites; but we find upon inquiry that every instance of that sort which has been imputed to them, has been induced and provoked by the white man...." This he tied to the Runnels administration. The *San Antonio Daily Herald* during this time consistently opposed Runnels, who was the official candidate of the Democratic Party; Sam Houston ran as an independent. The *Herald* referred to John Marshall, chairman of the state Democratic Party, as "chairman of the Central Committee of African Slave trade revivalists and disunion agitators" and soundly mocked him and other KGC members. Referring to Hardin Richard Runnels as "Little Dickey," and fellow KGC member John Carolan as "a little man with a large cane," a July 19, 1859 article predicted a landslide for Houston and ignoble defeat for Runnels. The article concerned a political meeting at the Menger Hotel in San Antonio, a raucous affair where Trevanion T. Teel, a high-profile KGC member, was jeered and shouted down when he tried speaking to the assembled crowd. The pro-Houston crowd on that Saturday night, as well as the editor of the *Daily Herald* had no idea who they were dealing with when they mocked those men; they would find out soon enough when the KGC revealed itself in Texas. John M. Carolan may have been "a little man" in physical appearance, but in 1859 he was District Deputy Grand Master for two Masonic Districts; the one man responsible for examining the operations of Masonic lodges in eleven counties in central and southwest Texas. This necessitated periodic travel to those lodges and contact with their members, a perfect position from which to recruit new members for the KGC. An influential merchant and auctioneer in San Antonio, also involved in the slave trade through that position, Carolan was the District Clerk in Bexar County under Judge Thomas Jefferson Devine, a very powerful KGC leader in San Antonio and in the secession movement state-wide. Carolan was also Captain of one of at least four KGC Castles in San Antonio. Sam Houston did prevail in the Governor's election, beating Hardin Richard Runnels on August 1, 1859. He would not assume the office until December 21st.[25]

In the meantime, the KGC held its first national conference at White Sulphur Springs, in what is now West Virginia, on August 8th and 9th, 1859. Now freshly unseated, former Governor Hardin Richard Runnels was one of the attendees from Texas, along with the famous Texas Ranger Captain, Ben McCulloch. The conference had been set up by George W. L. Bickley, who had seen an opportunity to put himself at the center of things after the death of General John Anthony Quitman, the original founder of the KGC. Prior to that, Bickley had been little more than a paid agitator in the hire of the original five founders, composed of Quitman's trusted associates, two of whom had also died in 1858, leaving a vacuum Bickley filled. Now calling himself "General" Bickley, unlike the original founders, he had no actual military experience that can be documented, but was a talented public speaker, as alluded to in this article from an Alabama newspaper:

> We are told by the Charleston News that a meeting was held on the 8th instant, at the Virginia Greenbrier Sulphur Springs, to consider, in the language of the circular, Mr. George Bickley, "the steps necessary to render the political standing and material interests of the South more permanent." The American Legation is called a Southern Military Organization, of which General Bickley is the head, and numbers some thirteen thousand members, mostly armed and ready to march on short notice.... It appears, from the proceedings of the convention, that the purpose of the Legation is to get possession of Spanish America, *vi et armis*, it being a political and commercial necessity that the United States should have entire control of the Gulf. Bickley is described as a young man of thirty-five, full of enthusiasm and confidence in the success of his mission, and a radical disunionist. He is said to possess that magnetic influence that attracts others to his cause, and is regarded as a dangerous man, because he so successfully plays with the liveliest passions, and arouses the most ardent hopes among the Southern people. So we have at last the meaning of the mysterious initials, "K.G.C." and a full exposition of the purposes of the association.[26]

The convention at White Sulphur Springs is thought to have been the first meeting of the top tier of the KGC; those members designated as Knights of the Columbian Star, a designation borrowed from the Tammany Society of New York. Attendance at this meeting meant that both Hardin Richard Runnels and Texas

Rang-er Captain Ben McCulloch were members of that most secretive and powerful degree of the Order. This is significant because previous published research into the Texas organization stated that none of the members of the Knights of the Columbian Star have been identified. The Third Degree, as the Knights of the Columbian Star was also known, was essentially the political function of the KGC. There were said to be 80 to 100 men in attendance at White Sulphur Springs, all "military men and noted political leaders." Two other Third Degree members in Texas have been identified by this writer from private correspondence written in 1861; members of that degree were sworn not to reveal their status to anyone except a fellow member of the Third Degree. The formal designations and their corresponding functions within the KGC were more than likely delineated at the White Sulphur Springs conference, by the attendees, and then left to George W. L. Bickley to take to the printer, thereafter to be disseminated by him and others to existing members and new recruits. A sixty-page booklet soon appeared, titled, *Rules, Regulations and Principles of the American Legion of the K.G.C.* issued September 12, 1859, "By Order of the Congress of the K.C.S. [Knights of the Columbian Star] and the General President."[27]

Still unknown by name in Texas, the KGC had not yet exerted its influence over daily life in that state. In fact, its supporters and members were still the object of ridicule and mockery by the *San Antonio Daily Herald* in a post-mortem election article published August 10th, titled, "Obituary":

> Died, in the city of Austin, on Monday, the 1st day of Au-gust, for the want of votes, the grand COLLARITE, HOUSTON CONVENTION, RE-OPEN AFRICAN SLAVE TRADE, OPPOSITION DEMOCRACY. The chief mourners are "little dickey," F. R. Lubbock, T. N. Waul, and Major John Marshall. Sub-mourners in this city, Hons. Dr. Graves, J. G. Martin, M. G. Anderson, "T. T. T-eel," and Messrs. E. G. Huston, A. McLeod and N. A. Taylor of "Tar River" N. C. (A. B.) [sic]

KGC Knight of the Columbian Star "Dick" Runnels had been the Democratic nominee for reelection as Governor, as decided by the Democratic Convention, which was held in the town of Houston. "A copy of the African Slave Trade Resolution," the article continued derisively, " which was 'laid upon the table of the Houston Convention,' and a copy of the Gonzales Platform will be buried with the corpse." Other known KGC members mentioned in the article include Francis R. Lubbock, T.N. Waul, John Marshall and Trevanion T. Teel.[28] Although this might have seemed, at the time, a low point for the organization in Texas, the turning point was soon to come, gift-wrapped and handed to the KGC on a silver platter by northern abolitionists. Until then, the Order continued its military build-up in Texas based on the trumped-up Indian scare inaugurated by John R. Baylor. His reputation had taken a beating in the press, as reflected in a letter written to him by his uncle Robert Emmet Bledsoe Baylor, the man for whom Baylor University in Waco, Texas was named. A judge and an ordained minister, concerned for the family name and his nephew's salvation, Uncle R. E. B. wrote John R. Baylor on September 7th. "Feeling uneasy and suspistious about your welfare when I first heard of your troubles," the distinguished gentleman wrote, "and the part you was takeing in them I wrote to you by Capt. Erath, beging you to be prudent and do no act that you would regreat in after life." [sic] Baylor's uncle must have been ignorant of the fact that Captain George B. Erath, also a respected citizen, had informed Governor Runnels back in May through an intermediary (Edward J. Gurley) by letter, "confirming my worst suspicions in regard to the designs of the frontier people, or rather those that control them." The letter continued:

> There is in progress a conspiracy to Massacre, not only the Indians but the whites upon the Reservations. The determination is that the Indians shall not be removed, but be killed either at the Reservations or on their route to Red River. These are not idle threats of an excited populace, but the determination of their leaders, of which the mass of people are ignorant. Their plan is to use as many of the Minute Companies as they can – take advantage of the general excitement to enlist the whole frontier.... These leaders make it their business to watch closely the public sentiment from one extent of the frontier to the other, and immediately following any pacific demonstration, they take steps to counteract it, and to increase the excitement and animosity against the Reservations.[29]

John R. Baylor and his partner Harris A. Hamner were the leaders obliquely referred to by George Erath through his intermediary Edward Gurley. Uncle R.E.B. Baylor's admonitions had fallen on deaf ears. The Northern Standard reported, "Baylor and his party have been killing cattle and taking horses belonging to the Indians. Baylor has publicly threatened to hang Capt. S.P. Ross, Mr. Chas. Barnard and Major Neighbors, also threatens James Duff, U.S. Deputy Marshal, Harvey Matthews, Wm. Marlin, Mr. Bandy, the Sheriff of Young county and others, all of whom are among the best citizens in the country" [sic]. John R. Baylor was never prosecuted for his actions: Major Neighbors was killed exactly a week after Baylor's uncle's letter was written, and the Brazos reservations in Texas were closed.[30]

Governor Runnels, although defeated for reelection, was still in the seat of power until December, and receiving letters from KGC organizers around the state, like the one from John J. Good of Dallas on August 7, 1859, asking about a shipment of arms for The Dallas Light Artillery: "We were informed that we would be notified of their arrival at Hempstead" Mr. Good wrote, "We are as yet without any advice as the members of the Company are anxious to continue drill...." The letter from Good to Runnels was effective, perhaps indicative of John J. Good's stature as a member of the Order of the Lone Star, and now the KGC. A letter in Governor Runnels' possession documents the response of the chain of command in fulfilling Good's request, from "C. Waller jr."[sic] at Hempstead to "R. H. K. Whitely Esq, Capt. Ordinance, San Antonio" [sic], informing Whitely that he (Waller) had corresponded with the Governor and written to "General Goode of Dallas"[sic]. Waller concluded his letter with "I am now in receipt of a letter from him in regard to the manner of handling the arms etc., & will examine the boxes & report to you forthwith." As John J. Good was not actively serving in the U.S. Armed Forces, the title, "General Good" must refer to his standing within the KGC. Good's company got their arms while others did without. The Federal arsenal in San Antonio was located in a building owned by Asa Mitchell, who would become infamous during the coming Civil War for his actions as the KGCs chief secret policeman in that city.[31]

While the KGC persecuted the peaceful Indian tribes of Northwest Texas, members of the Order were actively involved in religious persecution in Northeast Texas; at issue was the anti-slavery beliefs of members of the Methodist Episcopal Church, North. The Methodist Church in the United States had previously split into two factions in 1844 over the slavery question, with the Methodist Episcopal Church, South in favor of the "peculiar institution." However, the Methodist Episcopal Church, North, had made significant inroads into Northeast Texas, and on March 11, 1859, its Arkansas Annual Conference was held at Timber Creek, in Fannin County, Texas, near the town of Bonham. Geographically this entire conference was within slave states; it comprised 20 ministers and approximately 1,257 members; most of the members were Germans who were anti-slavery. Bishop Edmund Storer Janes, a New England Yankee by birth, attended the conference and was conducting Sunday worship services when confronted by the KGC en masse. A committee had been formed in Bonham the previous day to confront the

Bishop while on his visit from New York to Texas. For their chairman, and lead spokesperson, the committee had elected Judge Samuel Alexander Roberts, a local man who had attended West Point Military Academy with Jefferson Davis and was also a personal friend of former Republic of Texas President Mirabeau Buonaparte Lamar. It was Roberts, serving as Secretary of State of the Texas Republic, who had drawn up the plan for the disastrous Santa Fe Expedition, a state-sponsored filibuster in which Texas tried to conquer New Mexico in 1841. In Bishop Janes own words, this is what happened when Judge Roberts showed up with the KGC as the Bishop addressed a packed house of his brethren:

> While reading the Scripture lesson, I accidentally lifted up my eyes in the direction of the window, and saw the mob approaching the church. They were mounted on horseback, and marching with considerable regularity, as I judged from the momentary side-glance I had of them, in platoons of from three to five. The Bonham paper states their number to have been about two hundred. I think most of them were armed. The revolvers and bowie knives of some of them were exposed. During prayer they gathered around the church.

> While singing the second hymn, as many as could crowded into the church. At the close of the singing I commenced giving out my text. At the same time their 'spokesman,' as he termed himself, standing about half-way up the aisle, said, 'Do I address the Bishop!' I made no reply, but continued giving out my text. He repeated, 'Do I address the Bishop!' I then replied, 'I am the Bishop of the Methodist Episcopal church.' He then said, 'I have an unpleasant duty to perform, and I presume it will be equally unpleasant to you.' He then described the meeting at Bonham the previous day, when, looking around upon his associates, and pointing me to them he said: 'This large and respectable committee was appointed to wait upon you and the conference, and to make known to you the determination of the meeting.' He then called upon one of his company to read to us the resolutions adopted by the meeting.

The resolutions presented had been drawn up with the assistance of Leonard C. DeLisle, who played a leading role in the pro-slavery committee meeting, and who would later be revealed to be the Captain of the KGC Castle in Bonham. Many who had participated in compiling the resolutions, which banned the Methodist Episcopal Church, North, from existence in Texas, were likely KGC members also. Many involved in this anti-religious debacle were members of the local

Masonic organization, Constantine Lodge No. 13 in Bonham. Those likely KGC members, in addition to known KGC member and Mason, J. L. Smith, who had infiltrated the local Masonic organization were H. A. Hoffer, Gideon Smith, Alfred E. Pace, B. F. Davidson, Joshua Cox, R. H. Lane, and B. F. Fuller; all had participated in compiling and presenting the resolutions to Bishop Janes, and all were or had been Masons. Gideon Smith in particular is suspect as he was the largest slave owner in the county and would be one of the first to raise a company of Confederate cavalry when the war began. Other members of the Smith and Cox families were known members of the Bonham KGC. Joshua Cox and R. H. Lane are known to have owned slaves as well and were concerned that someone in the Methodist Episcopal Church, North had been "tampering with their slaves" - trying to convince them to run away from the plantation. The disruptors of the Sunday service threatened violence if their wishes were not fulfilled, and Judge Roberts issued an ultimatum to the Methodist clergy, giving them 2 hours to give the KGC mob an answer: would they go or were they going to stay. Roberts then publicly assured the Bishop in front of the congregation that, "nine-tenths of all the respectable men in the county were engaged in it; that they were determined to carry it out; and he forewarned... if we did not cease to prosecute our church organization among them – blood would be spilt, and the responsibility would be on us." Another of the likely KGC members at the Bonham committee meeting, William M. Wood, admitted to have been a Border Ruffian active in Kansas, and had urged his fellow disrupters "to adopt similar measures towards those in this county, and drive them from our borders." Leonard C. DeLisle, also known to the Northern press as one of the Missouri Border Ruffians, chimed in after William M. Wood and added that the Northern Abolitionist Societies sent "their 'wolves in sheep's clothing' among us, professing to preach the gospel, but, in reality, to spread abolition documents among the people, and endeavor to abolitionize the country." According to Bishop Janes, DeLisle continued:

> All their operations were carried on in the 'underground railroad system;' that if we waited to catch them in the overt act, we would wait until it was too late, as did the people of South Carolina and Virginia before the fearful negro insurrections that took place in portions of those States, instigated by emissaries of Northern abolition societies. He believed those in our midst to be but spies and forerunners of the invading army of abolitionism, and mentioned the peace and safety that resulted to the people of Marion

county, Missouri, from routing just such a nest that had organized in their midst.

Ultimately, the KGC was successful in discouraging the Northern Methodists; two of the ministers did respond to the mob within the 2 hours allotted, and called it quits in North Texas. The rest of the conference, led by Bishop Janes, agreed to suspend services until the Quarterly Conference could be consulted. Interestingly, perhaps quite tellingly, Bishop Janes took great pains to disassociate himself from the Masonic Order by later writing, "I state that the report extensively circulated through the papers, that when the mob came upon us I made the Masonic sign of distress and thus subdues [sic] them, is wholly without foundation. I am not, and never was, a Mason. The report is pure fiction." His congregation had only temporarily escaped the violence promised by the Fannin County Masons and their comrades. Sadly, one of the few full-time local employees of the Methodist Episcopal Church, North in Texas, sat quietly in the church that day in March, listening patiently to the demands of the mob. His name was Anthony Bewley, and in the following year he would become the victim of a disgraceful atrocity at the hands of the mob. No doubt many of the men at the Timber Creek confrontation were involved. Fear of the anti-slavery unionists and abolitionists in Kansas pervaded North Texas.[32]

John Brown, the noted abolitionist of infamy from the Pottawatomie massacre of slave-owners in Kansas, committed more anti-slavery atrocities later in the year- this time in Western Virginia, at a place called Harpers Ferry, on October 16th, killing more slave owners and seizing a Federal arsenal. His actions were not spontaneous – his Northern financial backers hired a military strategist as his consultant. English revolutionist Hugh Forbes, as that consultant, counseled Brown to make a series of smaller strikes into the border slave states over a longer period of time; but Brown disagreed and instead pursued his own path hoping to gain recruits from among the slaves in Virginia. As a result, he and his men were either killed or captured by Federal troops under the command of Robert E. Lee. John Brown was hanged on December 2, 1859 after standing trial. Among the spectators at his execution were John Wilkes Booth and Edmund Ruffin, one of the 5 founding members of the pro-slavery philosophical society called the Sacred Circle. At least one Texas KGC member, J. Mayrant Smith, was there also. John Brown's terrestrial life was terminated, but his legacy of terror lived on in exaggerated form in Southern newspapers, whose editors never missed a chance to "fire the Southern heart." The Harper's Ferry incident was a boon for KGC recruiters in Texas, and sympathetic newspaper editors were a useful tool.[33]

On October 4, 1859, William Walker silently slipped away from Berwick's Bay in Louisiana in the dark of night with "two or three hundred men from Texas, Alabama and elsewhere" aboard the steamer Philadelphia, headed once again, for Nicaragua. It would be Walker's third, final, and fatal, attempt at conquering a part of Central America with hopes of making it a slave state. His ultimate failure would only add to the isolation and paranoia felt by Texans sympathetic to "Southern rights," which in turn would help the KGC enlist more recruits. The leaders of the KGC certainly understood the value of a biased news media, and to that end, the Clarksville Standard announced with fanfare on November 5th the coming of a new publication:

> THE WHITE MAN will be published weekly at Jacksboro, Jack County, Texas, by Hamner & Donathan and edited by H. A. Hamner and J. R. Worrall; it will be devoted to the Frontier, the frontiersman and his cause, general news and all such matters as may be interesting and informative to general readers.

> The location of Jacksboro on the immediate Frontier and the center and metropolis of the exciting Indian scenes, which are continually being enacted in this most interesting part of the country, together with its direct connection with the Overland Mail with St. Louis and San Francisco designates Jacksboro as a point concentrating an interest, equaled by few, if any, in the State.

Starting out as an anti-Native American campaign paper, Hamner would soon be joined in this venture by his Indian-killing friend John R. Baylor. In the not-too distant future The White Man would change its focus to that of a pro-secession campaign paper. John R. Baylor had been savaged by the press, so his answer was to start one's own media outlet in order to shape the news and the people's perception of the major issues affecting them – in a manner amenable to the Knights of the Golden Circle.[34]

Almost simultaneously, a strange but prophetic carnival of fantasy was being enacted in Dallas, a nest of KGC members. It is best to let an article from the *Dallas Weekly Herald* set the scene; the article's title – "The Tournament."

> About two thousand persons assembled at the Tournament Grounds. After the preliminaries were duly arranged, some dozen Knights escorted by the

Marshalls of the day, in company with the judges, Col. M. T. Johnson, T. C. Hawpe, and Frank Wigginton, rode in fine style down the long line of carriages filled with elegant and beautiful women, rows of horse-men, of hundreds of footmen, to the position occupied by Col. Jno. M. Crockett, the orator elect, who addressed them in a short but appropriate speech inciting them as the representatives of ancient Chivalry in modern times, to the performance of noble and valorous deeds, and pointed to the array of beauty there assembled as incentives to fulfill their plighted work in defense of truth and beauty wherever found.

This was the sort of speech that would be given in towns all over Texas in less than two years, as men were sent off to war to fight for the perceived truth of the Constitution and the Bible as it pertained to the support of slavery, and to protect the beauty of Southern women from the heathen barbarians unleashed by the North. The orator-elect in the 1859 Dallas event, Colonel John M. Crockett, would be one of those leading the Knights to the battle-fields as the first Lieutenant Governor of the Confederate State of Texas. The article continued:

At the close, the Knights rode to the starting point, and at the call of the *Herald,* the Knight of the Old Dominion, (J. D. Kerfoot,) with his lance proudly grounded, couched and well-adjusted, shot forward like an arrow, and took the ring amidst the shouts of the hundreds assembled. Next the Knight of the Prairie (Crill Miller,) dashed forward and succeeded in getting it; next the Knight of Dallas (Mat Moore,) ... likewise took it; then more others whose titles I have forgotten, but who road well and gallantly – The Knight of Tarrant (J. F. Smith,) was very successful.... the Knight of the Prairie, Mr. Miller, was declared the successful Knight.

In a way, the actions of the make-believe Knights on the prairie that day partially explain the allure for Southerners of the Knights of the Golden Circle. Crill Miller, the so-called "Knight of the Prairie," was a slave-owner and member of the KGC. Sir Walter Scott's novel, Ivanhoe, with its tales of chivalry and the bravery of knighthood, had made quite an impression on the plantation class. Joseph O. Shelby, closely associated with one of the five founders of the KGC (his childhood friend, John Hunt Morgan), was known to frequently quote from Scott's book. But there was another reason that this strange carnival of chivalry was held in such a small community as Dallas; the town was one of only six "encampments" of the Masonic Order of the Knights Templar (KT), in the entire State of Texas. The Dallas Knights Commandery No. 6 was formed in 1855 with the assistance of known KGC members John J. Good and John H. Reagan. By 1859 the Knights Templar in Texas had been thoroughly infiltrated by known KGC members. Officers of the Grand Commandery of Texas of the Knights Templar included Samuel Mather, a known KGC member and long-time KT; probable KGC members J.J. McBride of Leon County and C.M. Winkler of Navarro County, known for its KGC castle founded by John B. Jones, who joined the KT Galveston encampment (San Felipe de Austin No. 1) in 1861. Frances Louis Barziza, brother of known KGC member D.U. Barziza, and son of uber-KGC leader and Knight of the Columbian Star member Philip Ignatius Barziza, was elected to the penultimate position of Deputy Grand Commander of the Grand Commandery of Texas, to serve in 1859. Frances L. Barziza had served as Grand Commander at the 1858 KT meeting of the Grand Commandery of Texas, and Grand Commander of Barziza No. 5, the Knights Templar encampment at Wheelock in Robertson County in 1857; "P. J." [sic] Barziza would captain the local KGC Castle at Wallisville, east of Houston, in Chambers County.[35]

As 1859 progressed, the nominal national leader of the KGC, George W.L. Bickley, settled into the Order's new headquarters in Baltimore. By June, he was selling bonds to raise money for the KGC, payable in 1865 at 10 percent interest. The instruments were signed by R.C. Tyler, secretary and George Bickley, commander. On October 1st, a New York correspondent for a Wisconsin newspaper reported that Bickley had been in town for more than a month and "Over four millions dollars, hard cash, are said to be deposited in Wall street"[sic] for the KGC to use in the colonization of Mexico. By December 6th, it was reported by another New York correspondent that Bickley's "expedition to Mexico now numbers nineteen thousand men, and he is provided with ample means." In December, Bickley accompanied his old friend Henry Clay Pate, of Kansas border ruffian fame, to the Cooper Institute in New York. Pate was there to lecture about his experiences with John Brown, the recently executed abolitionist. "General" Bickley introduced the speaker to the crowd, "in the highest terms," and spoke of Pate as someone "he had known for years." This was an entirely credible statement as both men had lived at Petersburgh, Virginia and both started their publishing careers in 1851 at Cincinnati, Ohio – the place where some believe the KGC was founded in 1854. Bickley would greatly enlarge KGC membership in a few months when he expanded upon its operation in Texas. With the last few days of the year 1859 ticking away, the Texas Democratic Party held a mass meeting, on December 20th at Buaas Hall in Austin. Several guest speakers were there to address the crowd and to praise Sam Houston, for whom they voted, and endorsed for a possible run for the Presidency of the United States. All were in favor of preserving the Union – against secession. The speech of Judge E.D. Townes in particular, had much been anticipated; he concluded "by a glance at the Mexican Protectorate, and the glorious march of our empire westward under such a leader." The Judge was implying that a Houston presidency would assure that a large part of Mexico would come under the direct control of the United States, as Houston had previously proposed. This outcome would have suited the KGC just fine; and perhaps to that end, the last speaker was a known KGC promoter and recruiter. His name was George Henry Sweet, who "declared he had been a Democrat all his life: that he had given none but Democratic votes." George Sweet had been elected one of two Secretaries for this meeting of the Democratic Party; J. M. Smith, another known KGC member, was one of the meeting's Vice Presidents. Continuing, Sweet told the crowd "he was so unfortunate as to have been born North of Mason's and Dixon's line; and would, therefore, he supposed, come in the cate-gory of those he had heard so bitterly denounced in the House of Representatives, since he came to the city." Sweet was a New Yorker who, like John A. Quitman, had moved South and adopted Southern ways; he had married a San Antonio woman just two months previously. A veteran of the Mexican War, George Sweet concluded his speech by saying that although he was a personal friend of Stephen Douglas, a northern man who would also run for President as a Democrat, he would vote for Sam Houston for President. With that the meeting adjourned until December 22nd. It is not known for certain whether or not Elkanah Bracken Greer was present at these meetings; although he was a Democrat, he was an extreme Southern Rights Democrat, like his fellow citizen of Marshall, Texas and business partner Louis T. Wigfall, who had been denounced as a "fire-eating Nullifier" by one of the speakers at this rally. Perhaps, if he had not attended, he read the Austin Southern Intelligencer account of what had been said. It could not have made him happy, as he had become sometime earlier in the year the Grand Commander of the Military Order of the Knights of the Golden Circle in Texas. Greer had the right pedigree: he had served in the Mexican War under the command of Jefferson Davis, who in turn was under the command of General John A. Quitman: all three of these men residing in Mississippi at the time of that war. Something was bothering Elkanah Greer at the end of 1859; he was already fomenting in his mind the draft of a circular expressing his dissatisfaction with

George W. L. Bickley's leadership of the KGC: George Bickley was no John Quitman. That circular would be hot off the presses in the next month and distributed far and wide. The coming year promised to be another turbulent one for the people of Texas.[36]

Chapter 8

Black Republicans, Abolitionists, and Indians

On Monday, January 2nd of the new year 1860, the *Houston Weekly Telegraph* editorial staff opined, "Good by to 1859, and all the fifties with it. Good bye to all the evil that has been done with-in them. Let it be buried in darkness and oblivion. [sic]" There was more evil lurking in the darkness ahead in 1860, and for many Texans, 1860 would be the last year of "the good times." The *Telegraph* betrayed its bias as to the definition of "the evil" it contemplated, as it continued: "Good bye to all the oppression of tyrants, all the token faith of rulers, all the ingratitude of Republics." Edward Hopkins Cushing, KGC member and editor of this Houston newspaper was very much in favor of secession and would play a key role in the coming year in the drive toward building a rationale for taking Texas out of the Union. Perhaps in this small op-ed piece published so early in the year, he was already saying his goodbye to the United States. In the same edition of his newspaper, it was noted that yet another "independent uniform company" was formed in the north Texas town of Sherman, "for the purpose of Drills, etc. It is called the Sherman Light Artillery and numbers 60 men." This marked the beginning of the KGC Castle that was known to exist in that Red River community. Organizing drill companies was a KGC specialty.[1]

KGC leader Hardin Richard Runnels had said his goodbye to the office of the Governor of the State just weeks before, in his final message to the state legislature. After reviewing his efforts at militarizing the frontier against real and imagined Indian depredations, paying homage to the sanctity of the Virginia and

Kentucky resolutions as supporting secession, and revisiting the still-sore subject of anti-slavery, abolition "agitation" in Kansas, Runnels finished with the following remarks:

> It is the existence of agitation which requires of us, action to counteract its baleful influences. We have asked, time and again, that the agitation of all mischievous questions, calculated to endanger our domestic polity, or our peace and security, as equal members of the confederacy, should cease. Our prayers have not been granted, and now shall we submit with-out the utterance of a murmur or complaint--without even offering a reason to combat the false dogmas of anti-slavery propagandism, however insidious and covert its form, or hidden object? My own answer, first, last and forever – is unconditionally,

> No! Silence at this juncture, in view of the peculiar political position of Texas, may be misconstrued. Equality and security in the Union or independence outside of it, should be the motto of every Southern State.[2]

Runnels would further prosecute the KGC agenda that year with the help of KGC military leader Elkanah Bracken Greer. The KGC began mailing a circular letter from Greer, dated January 26, 1860, to "the K.G.C. of Tennessee, Mississippi, Louisiana, and Alabama," in which Greer, as "Commander-In-Chief, and President of the Texas Board of War" urged his fellow knights to initiate an invasion of Mexico. Greer was concerned that the United States Congress would establish a protectorate over Mexico, rendering it impossible for the KGC to undertake the invasion and conquest of Mexico for their own private purposes. In his circular Greer under-cut George W.L. Bickley as Commander by noting his "apparent lethargy" in organizing and furthering the organization's agenda. Greer called upon the other four southern states to send delegates to a meeting in New Orleans on an undisclosed day during March of the unfolding year to discuss what was needed to make the movement a success. Greer knew Bickley all too well as he had spent much of his time in 1858 assisting an ailing Quitman by setting up KGC Castles across Texas and Louisiana. More than likely he resented Bickley for his lack of military service in the Mexican War, as that service was the most common shared endeavor between KGC members and especially their leaders. George Bickley was no John Quitman.[3]

The actions of Greer certainly lit a fire under George Bickley, who promised to meet Greer in New Orleans sometime in the first week of February; Greer wrote a relative on February 8th that Bickley missed the meeting by one day, arriving after Greer left New Orleans. Bickley did check into the St. Louis Hotel in New Orleans on January 27th, but when he left is not known exactly. However, someone who soon became proposed as a replacement for Bickley did show up, checking into the St. Charles Hotel on February 2; he gave his name as B.F. Greenough from New York. Also checking into the same hotel on the same day was J. A. Seddon of Virginia, the eventual Secretary of War for the Confederate States of America. Bickley missed this meeting but did follow up with a letter to Greer, the contents of which are unknown, but it reassured Greer for a while. Bickley was busy; he had spent a great deal of his time the previous year in organizing the KGC's Maryland operations from its new headquarters in Baltimore. The remainder of his time that year had mostly been spent in New York, meeting with potential financial backers and political leaders. It is possible that B. F. Greenough was one of those financial sources; James A. Seddon was a likely KGC member. In late October, the *New York Herald* had attempted to tie "a prominent member of the mysterious 'K.G.C.'" to a known abolitionist and insinuated that the KGC had been instrumental in John Brown's raid at Harper's Ferry. This prompted a response in rebuttal from Charles Bickley, a relative of and close aide to George W. L. Bickley, in a card to the editor of the *Herald*. This is one of the earliest public references to Charles Bickley, who would soon become a resident of Texas and play an important role in the development of the KGC there. Charles Bickley was identified as being with a group of KGC, "at the Galt House, on their way to New Orleans waiting to sail to Mexico" in Louisville, Kentucky in late January. Some reports would misidentify him as General Bickley's son, his brother or his nephew; but the evidence shows that his real name was Charles L. Bickley and that he was born in 1835, in Virginia, of unknown parentage. As George W. L. Bickley had been born in 1823 and had no surviving male sibling, it is not likely that Charles L. Bickley was his son, his brother or his nephew; although General Bickley did have a son named Charles Simmons Bickley, born in November 1848, which adds to the confusion. Charles L. Bickley was probably a cousin, as was Joseph Ponsol Bickley of Collin County, Texas; it is likely that Collin County was one of the first places Charles Bickley visited when he came to Texas at an early date. The town of McKinney in Collin County is the first place that the KGC was identified by name in Texas; the editor of the McKinney Messenger warned, "their emissaries are now traveling the State" by late January 1860. In referring to the Messenger report of KGC activity in Texas, the *Dallas Herald* raised the possibility that the

KGC were "proselytizing from other secret organizations;" a somewhat direct allusion to the Masons and their lodges.[4]

In early January, the *Tribune* in New York had carried the rumor "that a detachment of a mysterious military organization, known as the Knights of the Golden Circle, left this port a few days since, for Mexico. Their design is unknown, but their movements are reported to be very mysterious." This report was expanded upon just days later by the *New York Herald*, which stated that "thirty-five hundred men are now in New Orleans ready to embark for Vera Cruz," and:

> They go out as immigrants, and will be received into citizenship by the Juarez, or liberal government, when they will be mustered into service under American officers, such as Generals Ring and Wheat, and will sustain that government until the Senate ratifies the McLane treaty, which they expect will be speedily done. The leaders of these immigrants expect, for the aid they will afford the liberals, to obtain the renewal of the grant for a railroad from Aransas Bay to Mazatlan, in the Gulf of California, and agree to pay for it the sum of ten thousand dollars.... They have assurances that one hundred thousand dollars of the Cuban fund raised some years since will be appropriated to defray the expenses of the expedition, and report says Lord Lyons is of the opinion that they will have no trouble about raising funds in England to complete the railroad enterprise if the McLane treaty is ratified by the Senate.

Aransas Bay is on the Texas Gulf Coast near Corpus Christi. This highly instructive article concluded by saying the "emigrants" from New Orleans were to assist in constructing a railroad, "and at the same time will be recognized as a military organization for their own protection and the protection of the country through which they shall pass." However, a Georgia newspaper printed a warning in an op ed published February 4th stating that other newspapers were deliberately misleading the public about the KGC and were themselves under the control of members of the secret order on which they were supposedly reporting. Many accounts of the KGC's purpose and intent were crafted and fed to the press by "the knowing ones who hoaxed them." It is worth noting in the New York accounts that the late John Quitman's fingerprints were all over this operation, as the Cuban fund alluded to was initiated by Quitman's organization during 1854-55, and that Quitman's protege Chatham Robideau Wheat was to be one of the commanders in charge of the American force in this 1860 operation in Mexico. Lord Lyons is mentioned – he was the British Minister to the United States government in Washington during the Buchanan administration; this implies British involvement in a divisive issue for the American public. The weak link in the chain of this operation was that its success was dependent on passage of what became known as the McLane-Ocampo Treaty.[5]

Meanwhile frustration and discontent were festering in the nation's capital. KGC leader Ben McCulloch had resigned his US Marshalcy effective April 1, 1859, and had become a roving ambassador for the clandestine order. By early 1860, he sent an unusual message to John Marshall in Austin to publish in the *Texas State Gazette* in January, "warning Texas to be prepared for an approaching crisis; not to wait for an overt act, but be ready with the whole South to defend her rights promptly, vigorously, and to the bitter end." Perhaps in response to that broadside, another KGC leader, former Texas Ranger and Sam Houston loyalist J.M. Smith sent a letter to the editor of the *San Antonio Daily Herald* stating, "I myself am not ready for secession or disunion yet, and don't expect to be, so long as the State Governments are allowed to hang up such traitors as old John Brown, or the General Government will do its duty, in demanding and bringing to prompt justice his accomplicies...."[sic] The letter continued, however, and took a darker turn:

> Just so long as the General Government does not interfere with our State Laws, and will execute faithfully all its functions in accordance with the constitution.... Peaceable secession is out of the question, this fact every sensible American who understands our political organization ought to know. It has been my fortune in other days to meet the Indian in his war path and fight him on his own ground... but I candidly confess to you that I am not brave enough to fight Americans North or South, if I can possibly avoid it. Just so sure as this mighty Union, which has been the wonder and admiration of the World, is dissolved, our now smiling, prosperous and beloved land will be drenched in American blood, shed by American hands.

So, the anti-secession faction within the KGC knew that secession would cause war; many rebels would later say that they had no idea that war would be the result. Like Sam Houston, J.M. Smith believed in the Union. On February 13th, Houston sent a letter to his friend Ben McCulloch in Washington, D.C. to say, "there will be stirring times on the Rio Grande ere long. What are you doing? See the President and Secretary of War." Houston was referring to both the hoped-for Mexican Protectorate and the final military operation against Mexican terrorist Juan Cortina and his men, which began on February 1, 1860. On that day, KGC leader John Salmon Ford led his company of Texas Rangers from Brownsville in a joint operation with United States troops under Major Samuel P. Heintzelman; they moved slowly northward along the Rio Grande River searching for Cortina's raiders. On February 4th the combined US and Texan forces did battle with Cortina and his men, killing 29 and wounding 40, before the Mexicans escaped deeper into Mexico. Losses for the Texans were one man killed, and a few slightly wounded, none seriously; Ford returned to Brownsville. He would resume the hunt for Cortinas in Mexico the following month. On February 13th, the same day that Sam Houston had written McCulloch, the Governor also sent an urgent dis-patch to John Floyd, the Secretary of War. To be hand-delivered by Forbes Britton, the assistant adjutant general of Texas, Houston's message was that if the Federal government would not honor its obligation to defend the border between Texas and Mexico, his state could gather 10,000 men to do the job themselves within thirty days.[6]

In Austin, at this early juncture of his latest term as Governor of Texas, Sam Houston was busy organizing his new administration. In January, he had ap-pointed his cousin, KGC leader Thomas Carothers, to serve as Superintendent of the Texas State Penitentiary; about the same time he appointed Ed Burleson, John Conner and W.C. Dalrymple to each raise a company of Rangers for frontier pro-tection. Other, private military companies, many of them vehicles for the further organization of the KGC within the state, continued to form. One such company was formed by citizens of Atascosa County on January 23rd, numbering 60 men. The ongoing problems with Cortina's bandits and the ever-present fear of Indian attacks provided opportunities for Houston's enemies as well as his allies. On Jan-uary 14, 1860 Harris A. Hamner was enlisted as a Captain in the Texas Rangers, enrolled at Jacksboro at that rank with pay for 12 months. He was no longer a Captain in a volunteer organization; he was legitimate law enforcement, but for him it would not be enough. He needed a larger organization to command, and more money. He had the perfect tool for doing so, as editor of his own newspaper, *The White Man*, a white supremacist organ. Other newspapers, especially the *Dallas Herald*, began to reprint his op-ed pieces, like the following one published on Feb-ruary 29, 1860:

> Capt. Hamner, of the White Man, makes an eloquent appeal in behalf of the bleeding frontier.... We give an extract from the remarks of Capt. Hamner. After recounting their sufferings and exposed position, he says: "In view of these facts and in accordance with the wishes of many of our

friends, we call upon our sister counties, Montague, Young, Palo Pinto, Erath, Johnson, Parker, Tarrant, Dallas, Collin, Denton, Wise, Cook and as many others as may sympathize with us, to call, at their earliest convenience, county meetings for the purpose of considering the condition of the frontier, and discussing any ways and means for its relief."

Hamner and Baylor had already run the Texas Reservation Indians out of the state, and through false reports of Indian atrocities, had aided KGC leader Hardin Runnels' militarization of the frontier. However, they were not about to settle for that, for soon *The White Man* would become an advocate for secession. Hamner continued:

Let each county ascertain as definitely as possible, the amount of material they are able and willing to give to a system of defense, and appoint delegates to attend the convention of all counties to be held at the central point, with definite instructions as to the will and disposition of the counties.[7]

Throughout this period the pro-KGC press, led by members such as John Marshall of the *State Gazette*, continued to print editorials in favor of slavery, and against abolition. It was effective in many quarters of the state: The *Richmond Reporter* carried a story in late February of a public meeting in Fort Bend County (near Houston), "in which many of the leading men of Fort Bend participated, which passed resolutions of non-intercourse, and favoring secession if no relief is to be had from abolitionism." The *Marshall Texas Republican* occasionally printed dubious stories of abolitionists "tampering with slaves" like the article in their January 14, 1860, edition, concerning the arrest of a man in Jefferson named Fory R. Arnold, accused of expressing abolition sentiment. This relatively harmless incident would soon be surpassed by ones that were much worse; in fact, of deadly consequence. Until then, newspapers like the *Rusk Enquirer* were content to opine in February that although they agreed with Governor Houston as to the abstract right of secession, they would not "go with him to the extreme that there is no occasion in the Southern States for mutual consultation, and concert of action." Houston wanted to preserve the Union; many in the newspaper business in Texas did not. Then there were the pro-secession "campaign papers" that sprang up in the state: two in particular stand out, besides the White Man – the Corsicana-based *Navarro Express* and the *LaGrange States Rights Democrat*. The editors of both papers were known KGC members; Richard Abbey Van Horn of the *Express*, and Victor M. Thompson of the *Democrat*. Van Horn was a Floridian that had travelled across the country in the newspaper business, finally coming to Texas in 1854 with his brother to begin publication of the Anderson Central Texan. In April 1858, he moved further west to Weatherford where he started the *Frontier News* but sold his interest in that paper six months later, moving back east to central Texas, starting the *Navarro Express* in October 1859. By March 1860, he was printing articles about the KGC, noting the movement of some 30 members of the Order through Corsicana that month, "marching under a banner with the above mysterious letters on it. Their destination and objects were of course, the subjects of curiosity and speculation...." They were very likely headed to the Rio Grande and the border with Mexico. Before long Van Horn began advocating the establishment of a KGC lodge in Corsicana. His contemporary Victor M. Thompson appeared in Texas in early 1860, began publication of the *States Rights Democrat* in the town of LaGrange, situated in the slave-heavy "Black Belt" of the state. Eventually, he and his newspaper were declared the official printer for the KGC of Texas; once the war started in early 1861, he left his Texas paper and returned to Tennessee, mission accomplished.[8]

On February 17, 1860, Colonel Robert E. Lee landed and disembarked from his steamer in the Texas port of Indianola. There he made the acquaintance of Pryor L. Lea, considered by many to have been a member of the KGC. Mr. Lea travelled with Colonel R.E. Lee as far as Victoria, engaging him in conversation. At Victoria, Pryor Lea introduced the Colonel to his brother, Albert Miller Lea, reportedly a spokesman for the KGC. From Victoria Lee made his way to San Antonio on the 19th to take over command of the Military Department of Texas and all the U.S. forces stationed within. On February 24, Albert M. Lea wrote to Governor Houston that Lee "would not touch anything that he would consider vulgar filibustering; but he is not without ambition, and under the sanction of the Govt. might be more willing to aid you to pacificate Mexico...." seeming to say that worst-case, Lee would not interfere with Houston's contemplated invasion of Mexico. On February 25th, a KGC company was announced in Bonham, a Red River Valley town in north Texas, for service on the Rio Grande at the southern end of the state. The notice was published by the Bonham Era, with only the names of the officers listed. The Era was partially owned by Leonard C. De Lisle, the Captain of the KGC company and a local attorney. His 1st Lieutenant, A. M. Gass, was a local jeweler, adventurer and sometime correspondent to the Era. Bon-ham the previous year had been the scene of the disgraceful confrontation between members of the Northern Methodist Episcopal Church conference and members of the KGC led by Samuel A. Roberts, Leonard C. DeLisle and others. In this article announcing their new company, the Bonham Era stated, "In consequence of the distracted state of affairs on the Rio Grande, companies of Rangers are being organized in various counties, throughout the State, to be prepared for State protection, or 'any emergency that may arise.'" Given the difficulties of mass communication across such widely spaced isolated areas, it would seem that Elkanah Greer's message had been received by Texans well in advance of the events of February 1860. On February 20th, Greer wrote Sam Houston that the previous night he had met with Dr. M.D.K. Taylor, the Speaker of the Texas House of Representatives, a hardcore secessionist from Marion County in northeast Texas, who told Greer that

> ...he had a conversation with you... on the Rio Grande subject and that you had "Tellegraphed" [sic] to Washington the true State of Affairs, and that if they delayed action, you would move instantly in the matter...I have the honor to ten-der to you, our Sovereign head, a Regiment of "Mounted Volunteers" which we have already organized east of the "Trinity" river, and are now ready to move at a moment's notice.[9]

While this letter was in transit, Ben McCulloch decided to leave Washington, D.C. for Texas, writing to his mother on February 26th that he was afraid he would miss out on the action on the Mexican border and wanted to get in on the war. Meanwhile Sam Houston replied to Greer, the KGC's supreme military commander in Texas in a letter written February 29th that the State of Texas was bankrupt and could not proceed in the invasion of Mexico without help from Washington and the Buchanan administration. Before Greer could have possibly received this letter, the *Dallas Weekly Herald* reported on February 29th that Greer and KGC leader George W. Chilton of Tyler, Texas were going to Washington, D. C. to offer the services of their "mounted regiment of volunteers," to the President of the United States, to "dismember the Mexican confederacy." The editor of the *Herald* bought into the KGC's dreams of glory, writing,

> The mines of the gold and silver in the Mexican States are literally bursting with the accumulated treasures of ages, ripe and clustering, ready for the daring hero, that will stretch forth his hand to pluck them.

> Let these Texans range on the Mexican frontier, and infuse some of the Anglo-Saxon ideas of progressiveness into the stupid, leaden souls of that

people, – and then the world will witness a change. We hope the President will receive this body of gallant men.[10]

Houston continued to correspond with the Secretary of War in Washington, but it wasn't until February 29th that his envoy, Forbes Britton, arrived in Washington for face-to-face talks with Secretary Floyd, and ultimately, President Buchanan. Buchanan asked Britton if Governor Houston was intending to invade Mexico, to which Britton replied that such action would be unnecessary if the Federal Government would send more regular troops to defend the border with Mexico. Buchanan stalled by passing the buck, saying it was up to Congress to appropriate more funds for such troops. After 3 days of intensified lobbying, Britton reported back to Houston on March 3rd that Secretary of War John Floyd, himself reportedly a KGC member, had privately expressed support for Houston's proposed invasion, saying in so many words that the United States would not stand in the way. This was still not enough support as far as Houston was concerned, so on March 8th, Houston wrote directly by dispatch to President Buchanan that if "the Government has not at its command sufficient troops to afford immediate protection to Texas desired, I herewith tender the services of five thousand Texas volunteers." All Washington need do, wrote Houston, was to "send without delay by steamer or by rail-road conveyances" two thousand percussion rifles, one thousand Sharpe's rifles, three thousand Colt revolvers, and gear for one thousand cavalry. That same day, the Governor sent a circular letter, "To the Citizens of the Frontier," announcing that he had purchased 106 revolvers which would be rationed at the rate of 10 per county to 9 frontier counties. Additionally, he made known that there were about 50 Mississippi rifles and 500 flint muskets, antiquated weaponry, available to those who applied. He left it up to each of the 9 frontier counties to form their own self-defense organizations and register them by filing a $500 bond with the Chief Justice of each county involved. This left the door open for opportunists like Harris A. Hamner, the partner of KGC leader John R. Baylor. "The Executive has now mustered into the service of the State at least 500 men" Houston continued, but noted that the budgeted amount of money to support these 500 men would be exhausted in less than one year. It was a stopgap measure at best, with the KGC hopefully there to fill the demand for 4,500 additional troops needed to back up Houston's bluff to Buchanan.[11]

While Houston continued to maneuver as best as he could, the KGC continued to gain in confidence and stature. The March 8, 1860, edition of San Antonio's *Daily Herald* spoke of "The new and mysterious order of 'Tamborines' recently organized in the South, seems to have already attained an influence and a power of tremendous import – a power extending from Washington city to Mexico – and adequate to settle the destiny of nations." Individual KGC military companies had their own unique names; San Antonio was destined to have as many as four different KGC Castles – their term for "lodge," in place of the traditional Masonic term. In addition, the *Daily Herald* contained a letter from one of the "Tamborines of the State of Texas," identified as "R.L.T., Secretary," from the town of Lockhart in Caldwell County; it spoke of the "League" being organized by R.L.T. "at the different points designated." The anonymous spokesman stated that the organization had "men and means in abundance," and

> There are as yet no tidings from brother B_____ we are looking anxiously for his dispatches from Washington. His first dispatch will be equal to the sounding of Gabriel's horn on that great day when we shall all have to appear at his call. The whole South will unite as one man in the great cause of the "League."

"Brother B" of course was President Buchanan, and "The Tamborines" were the KGC, whose members, including the Governor of Texas, anxiously waited on Presidential approval for their invasion of Mexico, and the aid Houston had requested in the form of arms and equipment. Concurrently, it was reported on March 9th that Charles Bickley, the cousin, nephew or brother of "General" George Bickley was spotted in Montgomery, Alabama with James Ross Howard, a KGC member from New Orleans; the Montgomery Confederation mentioned that KGC members had been traveling through their city, and that "something is in the wind. It is surmised that their destination is Mexico, of which country they desire to take possession." Their true destination at this point may have been the New Orleans meeting called for by Elkanah Greer in his circular letter to discuss George Bickley's future within the organization. Though the exact date for this meeting does not appear in the only copy of Greer's circular known to date, it appears that at least one meeting was set to begin March 14th or 15th. There would be others. The *New Orleans Times-Picayune* noted that Ben McCulloch and Samuel A. Lockridge, both Texas KGC leaders, had checked into the St. Charles Hotel in the city on March 13, 1860. The St. Charles was where the leadership of the Order met for their clandestine meetings; many prominent Texans began to appear at that hotel and the two other principal hotels in the city, before, during, and after the arrival of McCulloch and Lockridge. March 15th saw the arrival of known

Texas KGC members L.C. DeLisle, Amzi T. Bradshaw, W.W. McPhaill, J.W. Davenport, and an unusually large number of Texans at the City Hotel. Almost all these men would assume leadership roles in the Confederacy in Texas once the war started. Two of them, Pryor Lea and John S. Wyche, arrived at the St. Charles just one day before McCulloch and Lockridge. William Henry Stewart checked into the St. Louis Hotel in New Orleans on March 12th; like many higher level KGC members from Texas, he was a lawyer and judge – in his case, in Gonzales County, where the rank-and-file KGC military element was massing at this time. On that same day William Washington Moon, whose career included a stint in the Rangers in Texas and in a Home Guard unit during the war, and his contemporary, Leander Calvin Cunningham, a railroad promoter and attorney from Alleyton, Texas both checked into the other principal hotel, the City Hotel in New Orleans. Both men's careers fit the profile of higher-level KGC. A KGC Castle was known to exist in Alleyton, in Colorado County, Texas. J.G. Coleman, a large slave owner from Smith County, also joined them that day at the City Hotel. Other Texan early arrivals included James E. Shepard of Washington County; Samuel Gabriel Ragsdale, a slave owner from Caldwell County; Robert Reese Neyland, lawyer from Woodville, Texas in Polk County; D. Hardeman, a member of an influential slave-owning family that would include Confederate officers; Frank Lawson, a lawyer from Rusk County, and John Austin Corley, an attorney from Clarksville, Texas in Red River County and a future Confederate officer. The KGC conference would last all month, as people came and went, some to return, probably with news to report from the Mexican border. It is no coincidence that they were in town during the KGC conference.[12]

While some KGC members headed for the New Orleans meeting, others set out for the Mexican/Texas border. Besides the Fannin County company of "rangers" led by L.C. DeLisle, another KGC company assembled in the Rusk County town of Henderson on March 10 where they were presented with a flag made by the ladies' contingent of the KGC. Speaking publicly in favor of this company of KGC were local lawyers and slave-owners Isaac Dans-by and Major Thomas M. Likens, a Mexican War veteran. Both men, as well as James B. Likens, the Major's son, became Confederate officers actively promoting war against the government of the United States. They were the core of the KGC in Rusk County. Another KGC unit under the command of Thomas Troup Gam-mage known as the "Cherokee Greys" received notice on March 3rd that they were to assemble in the Cherokee County town of Rusk on March 10, 1860, "to aid our friends in the protection of American interests." T.T. Gammage later claimed to have been the one who initiated Sam Houston into the KGC; it is possible that their meeting took place in nearby Anderson County at the Osceola Hotel in the county seat of Palestine. Gammage was a wealthy plantation owner, and owned property in Magnolia, Texas, a noted port in Anderson County on the Trinity River. Cotton from the surrounding area was shipped from Magnolia down the river to the Gulf of Mexico to Galveston; no doubt slaves were too, at least occasionally. Whenever Sam Houston wanted to mix among the people of that area, he could be found at the Osceola Hotel in Palestine talking politics with the locals. Anderson County prided it-self as having been settled by "the cream of Southern society," and was the home of one of only six encampments of the Knights Templar in Texas. Another East Texas company of Knights left the Hopkins County town of Sulphur Springs, Texas on March 7th, said to be KGC under the command of Dr. O.S. Davis, according to the Sulphur Springs Monitor. However, others would report that the group was led by Isaiah T. Davis, like Owen S. Davis a slave owner and resident of adjacent Upshur County. Whether the two men were related is not known, but it would not have been unusual for a prominent local citizen like Owen Davis to lead a military procession just as far as the outskirts of town before returning home to attend to business. Along with the men from Hopkins and adjoining Upshur County, these men were joined by a KGC company that left Dallas and another from the Rusk County town of Henderson, Texas, on March 10th. Another smaller company of 15 to 20 KGC left Bowie County on the Red River; passing through Paris, Texas and then Dallas before heading due south to the Rio Grande. Bowie County was home to Hardin Richard Runnels.[13]

Seemingly unaware of the movements of these individual Castles, on March 12th Sam Houston wrote from Austin to Secretary of War John Floyd to say:

> In a New Orleans paper, my eye met a telegraphic dispatch of the 3rd inst. from Washington, stating that the 'President disapproves of the action taken by Governor Houston in calling out volunteers in Texas to defend the frontier.' I can but feel assured that this remark in view of the facts which have transpired since my induction into office certainly justifies and calls for refutation for the reason that I have ordered no troops on the Rio Grande, or destined for that frontier. So far from that being the case, four companies which were on service on the Rio Grande when I came into office, were mustered out of service and two companies were forwarded

under the advice of the Commissioners conferring with Major Heintzelman of the United States Army. They are subject to his orders.

Houston continued by saying in so many words that if he had taken the advice of the citizens of Texas, he would have sent all available state forces into Mexico and would never have withdrawn them "until we should have had 'security of the future.'" He then alluded to the upper echelon KGC, and perhaps the Knights of the Columbian Star in New York's Tammany Hall:

> 'Tis true that since 1857, I have been written to from various parts of the United States urging me to invade Mexico with a view to the establishment of a protectorate and assuring me that men, money, and arms would be placed at my command if I would engage in the enterprise. To these overtures, I made no favorable response, though as an individual I might have cooperated with them, by placing myself beyond the jurisdiction of the United States. Nor was I without an assurance that a large portion of the Mexican population would receive me and cooperate with me in the restoration of order in their country.

Houston may also have made sly reference to the Buchanan Administration itself, as it was inaugurated in early 1857. Many politicians linked to Buchanan's reign were KGC sympathizers, if not members. Houston wrote Floyd in this letter "to assure the President that I will continue or countenance no action with a view to complicate or embarrass the affairs of his administration.... I never have nor will I ever perform an official act that is not intended for my Country's advancement and prosperity aside from all selfishness."[14] This letter does much to explain Houston's complicated relationship with the KGC. Personally, he supported them in their goal of the conquest of Mexico, but officially he rejected their rebellion against the government of the United States, on principle. He was not a secessionist and considered such action to be treasonous. His official stance put him at odds with many of his fellow KGCs.

Two days after the date of this letter, George W. L. Bickley addressed an audience in Montgomery, Alabama on behalf of the KGC, tracing its origin back to 1854 with its mission being "to advance the interests of the Southern States" and secondly, "to Americanize Mexico." He previously claimed that the Knights had a con-tract with the Miramon faction in Mexico, but as the United States had recognized the competing Liberal Party government of Benito Juarez, the KGC now switched sides to support the dominant power. Bickley also claimed that "influential and wealthy citizens" of Mexico were members of his Order. Stumping along with him as additional speakers were KGC proponents from Louisiana and Alabama. Bickley finished his speech by claiming that it would not be too much longer before his troops were assaulting Mexico City. Sometime after the Montgomery speech and probably close to the 15th of March meeting called by Elkanah Greer, George Bickley spoke again at the Carrollton Railroad Depot in New Orleans. The article noted the presence of "Gen. Greer, who is well-known as one of our bravest Volunteer Colonels from Mississippi during the recent war, and who now commands a division of the K.G.C., together with Major Richardson, one of his staff officers" – this being Elkanah Greer of Texas along with Samuel J Richardson, both men residing in Harrison County, the county with the largest population of slaves in the state of Texas at that time. Also seen were "Captain Gay, the wagon-master" staying at the 'Texas Home' while "still many others of character and note are at the St. Charles or quartered with private friends in the city." Captain Gay was probably Gilbert Gay, Captain of the Clinton Castle in Dewitt County, Texas, and a slave owner.[15]

On March 15, Samuel A. Lockridge wrote a letter from the St. Charles Hotel in New Orleans to Samuel P. Heintzelman, in command of the U.S. forces on the Texas border with Mexico. Lockridge was still in attendance at the KGC conference, and at this point, was still believing the assertions of its alleged leader, George W. Bickley, who quickly departed New Orleans on a fundraising mission. Lockridge gave Heintzelman a rare inside look at the KGC, rare indeed for an outsider like Heintzelman. Lockridge had been in contact with some of his friends in the nation's capital but expressed doubt that President Buchanan would back any invasion of Mexico. He did tell Heintzelman that privately, "Companies are forming in all the counties in Texas and all the Southern States to aid Texas if the general government fails...." He neglected to state the motivation that counties in Texas that were hundreds of miles from the border would have for doing such a thing. Apparently, the KGC leadership had thought of that ahead of time and knew that for counties in West Texas where slave ownership was low, the primary concern there was Indian aggression, whether real or potential. The way to organize, drill and equip men for military service and to recruit for the KGC was to manufacture another Indian scare, and they had just the men for that job: John R. Baylor and his partner Harris A. Hamner. On March 20, 1860, a convention of citizens of the frontier counties was held at the town of Weatherford in Parker

County. Delegates were present from Young, Johnson, Jack, Buchanan, Erath, Palo Pinto, and Parker counties. Resolutions were drafted by a committee chaired by KGC leader John R. Baylor. The following resolution was presented March 21st:

> Resolved, that R. B. Hubbard of Smith county, S. Perkey, of Bowie county, S. I. Morgan, of Red River county, B. F. Forney of Lamar county, F. D. McKinney, of Hopkins county, J. W. Throckmorton, of Collin county, C. C. Birkley, of Grayson county, G. A. Everts, of Cook county, J. J. Good and N. H. Parnell, of Dallas county, R. W. Cogins and A. Bradshaw, of Ellis county, Thomas Johns, of Hill county, J. A. McCall, of McLennan county, D. M. Pendergrast, of Limestone county, John Gregg, of Freestone county, C. M. Winkler, of Navarro county, J. E. Cravens and E. H. Horrell, of Anderson county, G. T. Moore, of Nacogdoches county, N. Perry, of Tarrant county, M. D. Ector, of Rusk county, A. J. Hood, of Cherokee county, P. Murrah, Col. Womack and John T. Mills, of Harrison county, be requested to aid us in this movement by soliciting means and money to carry out the object of this meeting, and to report to Capt. A. H. Hamner, of Jack county, from time to time the result of their efforts. [sic][16]

Taking into account some obvious misspellings, (N. H. Darnell, not Parnell; N. Terry, not Perry, and H. A. Hamner, not A. H. Hamner), the above list of names should be taken for what it represented – a roster of the Knights of the True Faith, the second degree, or Financial Degree of the KGC. The names include known KGC members John R. Baylor, John J. Good, Amzi Bradshaw, and others who were to identify as KGC within a few months. Others in the list include at least two future governors of the State of Texas (both disloyal to the United States), several future high-ranking Confederate officers and generals, and politicians who were prominent secessionists. They were important and powerful fund raisers – and they all reported to H. A. Hamner, in his effort to build a private army separate from any government control.[17]

It is worth noting here another name of interest from Hamner's network of fund-raisers - that of E. H. Horrell of Ander-son County. Edward H. Horrell's name is remarkably similar to that of Edward M. Horrell, George W. Bickley's partner in the Ohio-based KGC campaign paper, the Portsmouth, Ohio *Daily Pennant*, predecessor of the short-lived *Plain Dealer*, later published by "E. M. Horrel". Edward H. Horrell of Anderson County, Texas had previously travelled Ohio at an early age when his father, the Reverend Thomas Horrell, was appointed by the

Bishop of Maryland to serve as Presbyter of the Diocese of Ohio in 1836. This Horrell family settled in Cape Girardeau, Missouri, on the Mississippi River not far from its conjunction with the Ohio River, as early as 1823. After moving to St. Louis in 1825, the reverend moved his entire family, including his son Edward H., to Cincinnati, Ohio where they lived in 1831 before moving to Tennessee and returning to St. Louis in 1842. By September 1841, Edward H. Horrell began the practice of law in Missouri, covering several counties including Pulaski County, where he resided. In July 1848 Edward H. Horrell shot and killed Dr. Joseph Dellinger for slandering his wife; the following year Horrell was cleared of all charges. Just months later, his father died on February 22, 1850. Edward H. Horrell inherited his father's six slaves and moved with them and his family to Anderson County, Texas that year. His wife, Elizabeth Florida Mead, had been born in Blountsville, Alabama but her brother Marcus Portius Mead had gone to Texas as early as 1837, soon thereafter settling in Anderson County. Sometime in 1845 Elizabeth Mead and Edward H. Horrell were married in Anderson County, Texas even while Edward resided in Missouri. From Missouri Edward Horrell could have easily travelled by boat to both Portsmouth, Ohio and East Texas, via the Mississippi River to either the Ohio River to Portsmouth or the Red River to East Texas. George Bickley's Ohio partner, "Edward M. Horrell" was said to have joined the Confederate army in Alabama, where he supposedly died in 1864; Edward H. Horrell of Texas apparently never served in the Confederate armed forces and was declared to have died on October 11, 1866, at an undisclosed place. Through his in-laws he did have ties to Alabama. Were they the same person, this Edward M. Horrell and Edward H. Horrell? If they were, this would imply an early tie between George W. Bickley's operation in Ohio and people in Anderson County, Texas as early as 1855. Edward H. Horrell sold his house in Palestine, Anderson County in 1857, said to be "the most desirable residence in the place," and began living in the Osceola Hotel, where Sam Houston would stay whenever he was in town. This might have been more convenient for Horrell if he was travel-ling extensively during this time from Texas to Ohio. Besides Governor Houston, many other KGC members would drop by the Osceola Hotel from time-to-time: Louis T. Wigfall, A. T. Rainey, M. D. Ector, and others as yet unidentified.[18]

On the same day that John R. Baylor's committee issued its resolutions, Governor Houston issued a proclamation that effectively ordered the KGC filibusters gathered at Gonzales to cease and desist. By the time Ben McCulloch arrived in Gonzales from New Orleans, a copy of a letter from Houston was posted at city hall, advising all that any invasion of Mexico was "without authority from the government of the United States or the State of Texas." Houston's decision to back away from the planned invasion may have been influenced by the refusal of Colonel Robert E. Lee to engage the U.S. troops under his command in such a venture; or perhaps Houston was concerned by the *New York Herald* article that appeared on March 21st, implicating him as being responsible for the invasion. "War Between Mexico and Texas – Gov. Houston Heads the Movement," read the article's sub header, which although sympathetic to the cause, implicated him in a major violation of international law. The New Orleans correspondent to the *Herald* cited the failure of the United States government "to do its duty long since to Texas, through the fanatical opposition of the free soil black republican party in Congress," and further:

> In the meanwhile the 'black and brutal' progress of Wm. H. Seward's free negro policy dragged the unoffending people of Texas into the Kansas difficulty. On account of 'bleeding Kansas,' the black republican party withheld the necessary military supplies for the Texas frontier, and the savages were allowed to kill, burn and destroy with impunity.

> The same baneful influence is now at work, paralyzing the arm of the executive, and at last, Texas is compelled to give herself that protection which was guaranteed her by the com-pact of annexation. This free negro policy promises to be finally finished by the election of a black republican President, upon the distinct issue of 'No more slave States.' Thus will have been violated every single article of contract by the United States with Texas, and that too at the demands of the free negro party, led on by Wm. H. Seward.

The unnamed New Orleans correspondent very concisely summarized the manifesto of the KGC leaders there meeting at that moment. According to them, Black Republicans from the Northern states were undermining the security of Texas by leaving it unprotected from Indian attacks, and vulnerable to violent abolitionists like John Brown and others like him in nearby Kansas. This was all in violation of the contract for the annexation of the Republic of Texas by the United States, for as the article said, "Texas was not conquered or purchased, or 'created,' or admitted into the Union as the other States. Texas came into the confederacy upon specific terms of contract, having won her own independence after seceding from the Mexican republic...." *The New York Herald* continued, noting that in this contract of annexation, whereby Texas became a state within the

United States, "Texas made several stipulations, amongst others, the following: Texas to retain the eminent right of domain and her territorial limits intact. Texas to have the right of creating from her territory two or more slave States. The frontiers of Texas to be defended against the incursions of savage Indians, and equally savage Mexican murderers." [sic] So there it was: all the wedge issues that the attorneys within the KGC leadership had crafted to fabricate their rationale for Texas to break away from the United States by seceding, as it once had done from the Republic of Mexico, another anti-slavery union. In the minds of KGC political strategists, the contract between the United States and Texas was null and void; but the people of Texas needed more convincing.[19]

The meeting of top-level KGC in New Orleans continued during these developments, with the *Times-Picayune* and the *Daily Crescent* noting the arrivals of Texans at the principal hotels in town. Wednesday, March 21st saw the arrivals of George W. Guess from Dallas, a known KGC member, along with James Gilaspie, a veteran of the Texas Revolution, the Mexican War, and ultimately the coming Civil War; both men stayed at the St. Charles Hotel. Also checking in at the City Hotel that day was Byron Crandall Rhome, the son of Texas politician and slave-owner Peter Grempe Rhome. Peter Rhome was originally from New York but married his second wife in Georgia before moving to Texas; he would represent Cherokee County as a delegate to the Texas Secession Convention. On Friday, March 23rd, former Texas Governor and arch-KGC leader Hardin Richard Runnels checked into the City Hotel with his brother Howell Washington Runnels; both men were slaveowners and residents of Bowie County, Texas. Joining them that day at their hotel were Alfred Pace, one of the Fannin County KGC, and "J. C. Walker of Guadalupe County." There were 23 slaves held in Guadalupe County under the name "J.G. Walker". John George Walker was a Mexican War veteran, having served as 1st Lieutenant in KGC co-founder Persifor F. Smith's Mounted Rifle regiment. Less than two years prior, Walker had married Sophie M. Baylor in New Orleans – she was the niece of John R. Baylor and George W. Baylor. Walker would win fame in the coming Civil War as commander of Walker's Texas Brigade, a division that had been raised and trained by KGC member Henry McCulloch, Ben McCulloch's brother. However, in 1860, this John George Walker was stationed at Fort Union in New Mexico and did not resign from the U.S. Army until July 1861. Could he have returned to New Orleans on leave? He did have a cousin who was also named John George Walker living in Texas in 1860 who joined the Confederate forces at an earlier date. For some reason, the *Houston*

Weekly Telegraph referred to him as Captain J.C. Walker on at least one occasion. This John G. Walker did raise a company of men for Terry's Texas Rangers., an organization with numerous KGC members among its officer's ranks.[20]

In late March, various Texas KGC members made trips to New Orleans to participate in the ongoing discussions: Samuel Sampson, one of the leaders of the Charles Bickley Castle in San Antonio; George Sweet, originally from New York, but now based in San Antonio; Horace Cone, a Houston lawyer with family ties in New York, currently employed as counsel for the Texas and New Orleans Rail-road, who would co-lead the House of Representatives for the Confederate State of Texas; and John Bailey Anderson, a slave owner originally from Western Kentucky who had relocated to Fannin County in 1859, where he would eventually raise three companies of Texas Confederate soldiers. While the leadership met, the foot soldiers of the KGC continued their journeys towards the Rio Grande; newspapers attempted to follow the progress of these anonymous bands, as shown in a March 28 letter from a correspondent in Waco to the *Dallas Herald*: "Nothing is said about the K.G.C. and the Tambourines, but nothing definite is known about them, as much as the uninitiated would discover, I am one of that number, and am therefore left to conjecture their purposes [sic]." By this time, Ben McCulloch and Elkanah Greer had left the convention in New Orleans in pursuit of other matters. Greer's hometown newspaper, the Marshall, Texas Harrison Flag reported his return on March 23rd stating "From his brief remarks, to us, we are inclined to think the Knights of the Golden Circle have no cause for discouraging apprehensions. Mexico is destined to be Americanized, and that soon." After a brief respite, he was soon on the road again, this time headed for Galveston and the State Democratic Party convention. It was an important meeting, for in Galveston they would choose delegates to represent the Democracy of Texas at the party's national convention later that year at Charlestown, South Carolina. It was there in Charleston that the KGC would make good on its threat to destroy the Democratic Party. It was essential that they sent loyal KGC as delegates in order to accomplish their goal. Some KGC began their travel to Galveston earlier than Greer. On March 13th, Leonard C. DeLisle was spotted in Houston "en route to Galveston to attend the convention." He had left in February from Bonham in North Texas with his company of KGC, headed for the Mexican border, but left them under the control of his 1st Lieutenant so that he could hob-nob with the political element of the Democratic Party. When DeLisle arrived in Galveston on April 2nd, he found other prominent KGC leaders already there in preparation for the start of the convention. These included E. H. Cushing, editor of the *Houston Telegraph*, Francis R. Lubbock, former Lieutenant Governor of Texas during the Runnels administration, T. N. Waul, and Hardin Richard Runnels, who left the KGC convention in New Orleans for this event. The following morning, April 5th, the Democratic Convention of Texas assembled, with Ben McCulloch and other non-delegates in attendance. Before any delegates would be seated, however, they had to be vetted by the Committee on Credentials. Among the 18 members of the Committee on Credentials were Elkanah Greer and James E. Harrison, both late of the KGC convention in New Orleans. Others on this gatekeeping committee included J.D. Pitts, Dr. Charles C. Ganahl of Kerr County, and Charles R. Pryor, editor of the *Dallas Herald*. Pryor would do much in the following months to aid the KGC in its recruiting drive in the state. For now, he was busy, in alliance with Elkanah Greer and other KGC, in deciding who could sit at the convention to deter-mine the ideological platform the Texas branch of the party would advance at the upcoming national Democratic Convention in Charleston. John Marshall, KGC member and editor of the secessionist mouthpiece Austin-based *State Gazette* attended as Chairman of the State Central Committee and called the delegates to order.[21]

After the convention appointed a Sergeant-at Arms upon motion by Hamilton Prioleau Bee, upon a motion advanced by T.N. Waul, the Committee on a Platform and Resolutions was organized, which was announced the following morning. The Committee on Platform held one representative from each Judicial District; and by district number, was comprised of the following men: 1. J.T. Harcourt, of Colorado County; 2. J.H. Duggan, Guadalupe County; 3. A.S. Broaddus, Burleson County; 4. Dr. Charles Ganahl, Kerr County; 5. W.A. Leonard, Jasper County; 6. B.F. Williams, Upshur County; 7. R.M. Powell, Montgomery County; 8. Leonard C. DeLisle, Fannin County; 9. F.F. Foscue, Cherokee County; 10. F.S. Stockdale, Calhoun County; 11. Judge J.F. Crosby, El Paso County; 13. J.W. Durant, Leon County; 14. W.W. Dunlap, Goliad County; 15. R.S. Pitts, Tyler County; 16. R. Ward, Tarrant County; 17. M.V.B. Sparks, Lampasas County; 19. W.H. Parsons, McLennan County; F.R. Worrell, Jack County. For some reason, no Judicial Districts numbered 12 or 18 were reported. Most, if not all, these men were prominent secessionists; Broaddus, Ganahl, Foscue, and Stockdale served as delegates to the Secession Convention, Parsons was the fire-breathing editor of a secessionist newspaper, Worrell was H. A. Hamner's original partner in the *White Man*, and L. C. DeLisle was a known KGC member. Perhaps they all were members. In any event, the final crucial step for the state convention was the election of delegates to the National Democratic Party Convention to be held in late April. John Marshall announced that nominations were to be made for the regular delegates and their alternates, four each from the Eastern Congressional District of the State, with four alternates, and an equal number from the Western Congressional District. According to John Marshall's newspaper, the *Texas State Gazette*,

> The following nominations were then made for the four-regular delegates from the Eastern Congressional District, to wit: H.R. Runnels, Gen. T. Chambers, Gen. E. Greer, F.S. Foscue, Mat Ward, R.B. Hubbard, R.C. Pryor, W.H. Tucker, F.B. Sexton and L.T. Wigfall....

> Messrs Runnels, Hubbard and Foscue having received two-thirds of all the votes, were declared duly elected. There remained but one more to be elected, and after some discussion, it was moved that Gen Greer, having received a majority should be elected by acclamation. To this the other candidates readily agreed, and withdrew their names, when Gen Greer was unanimously elected [sic].

So, the way was cleared for Elkanah Greer, to ensure that the Commander of the Military Knights of the KGC of Texas would represent his state at the National Democratic Party Convention. The delegates for the Western Congressional District that were summarily elected were Francis R. Lubbock, Guy M. Bryan, Fletcher S. Stockdale, and Joseph F. Crosby. As one historian later put it, "Most of these men were prominent political figures in the state, leaders in the secession movement, and later staunch supporters of the Confederacy." This is an understatement: it is known that Greer was Grand Commander of the KGC military in Texas, and that Hardin R. Runnels was a Knight of the Columbian Star; Francis R. Lubbock, his former Lieutenant Governor, was the brother of two known KGC members, John B. Lubbock and Thomas S. Lubbock. F.R. Lubbock became the second Governor of the Confederate State of Texas. Fletcher Stockdale helped draft the ordinance of secession for Texas to clear the path for the state to join the Confederacy, so that he could serve as Lieutenant Governor of the Confederate State of Texas from 1863 to 1865. Guy M. Bryan was one of the leaders of the convention and a slaveowner in Galveston. It is highly likely that all eight of the men who represented Texas at the Democratic National Convention in 1860 were KGC members. They would make good on the threat that John Marshall had made public, that of destroying the old Democratic Party by dividing it. With the right people in place, the Texas State Democratic Convention began to wind down. Before adjourning, several people, including KGC member and newspaperman Victor W. Thompson, presented their credentials as delegates and were seated. John D. Pitts submitted proxies for the counties of Henderson and Williamson, who sent no delegates, and J. A. Quintero was then elected as Third Assistant Secretary to the convention. Jose Agustin Quintero was Cuban by birth but Texan by choice. Involved in the Narcisso Lopez intrigues, which ultimately involved KGC co-founder John Quitman, Quintero was forced to flee Cuba for good. Having previously studied law in the United States, he returned and carefully cultivated a friendly relationship with John Quitman, with whom he corresponded in 1855. Becoming friends with Mirabeau B. Lamar, he served as clerk in the Texas House of Representatives in 1857. Eventually he became a secret agent in Mexico for the Confederate government; he too, was a likely KGC member.[22]

Perhaps cheered and emboldened by the support he had witnessed for the KGC at the state political convention, Ben McCulloch went to Austin; apparently not finding Governor Houston there, he wrote a letter to him on April 6, begging the old warrior to assume command of the KGC expedition into Mexico, but Houston would not budge. The press continued to give free publicity to the KGC, with the Little Rock Old-Line Democrat reporting that George Bickley was staying in New Orleans at the St. Louis Hotel, that Greer and Samuel J. Richardson of Texas were at the City Hotel, and "still many others are at the St. Charles."

> The K.G.C. or "Knights of the Golden Circle," was organized in 1854, more to cultivate the martial spirit of our people than anything else; since then it has steadily grown, until now it numbers over 30,000 members, who are scattered over the Southern States, and holding within its charmed circle many of our most influential men and best soldiers. No organization of its kind has in this country ever combined so much talent with such immense financial resources, and under the present aspect of political affairs, we do not deem it too much to say that the whole nation may soon become deeply interested in the ultimate labors of the K.G.C.
>
> It is generally understood that the K.G.C. are preparing to operate in the broad field which civil war has opened in Mexico to American enterprise and industry.[23]

This article was actually a re-run of an earlier article published in the New Orleans Courier; by April this was old news in New Orleans, but not in Little

Rock. The *Daily Gazette & Comet* of Baton Rouge on the day McCulloch wrote his latest letter to Houston, carried an earlier article from a Baltimore newspaper describing the KGC as having as its sole purpose, "the invasion of Mexico and assists in the establishment of a new government." The article noted that "nearly one thousand signatures" were on the muster roll from Baltimore for the invasion, and "some of whom are of very respectable families." Many of the hopeful invaders were unemployed, but were "being drilled by experienced officers, who have done service in the United States army, and the membership are quite sanguine in leaving this port in two or three weeks, unmolested by the Government." In Mississippi on the day following the Baton Rouge article, the Yazoo City newspaper carried an earlier article from the Vicksburg Sun that the KGC "are en rapport with the Juarez Government. In going, therefore, into Mexico even in a military body of ten thousand men, fully equipped for war, they will go under the invitation of the Government which we have recognized....It is the design of the K.G.C. to occupy and annex Mexico à la Texas." Although the information in these articles was stale by the time they were published, it kept hope alive for men like Ben McCulloch and kept other KGC members on the move – in spite of the internal problems that had surfaced within the organization's leadership. The first known leak to the press of this problem appeared in the *Macon Telegraph*: "New Orleans, April 3rd. – General Bickley, Chief of the Knights of the Golden Circle, has been denounced in New Orleans as an imposter, and his expedition a humbug." On that day, the late KGC founder John Anthony Quitman's son was in town – was he there to confront the pretender to his father's throne? On April 6th, readers in New Orleans were made aware of further allegations of fraud made against "General" George Bickley. The accusation was made by Joseph Davis Howell, the brother-in-law of Jefferson Davis, and a veteran of John Quitman's failed 1855 expedition against Cuba. Howell was joined in these allegations by W.H. Rainey, a noted publisher. It was then reported that by April 7, Bickley was expelled from the convention by dissatisfied members from Louisiana and Alabama who subsequently proposed "Col. Greenough" as their leader. Benjamin Franklin Greenough was a well-known inventor who had made two previous trips to New Orleans in the previous three months and may have still been in town during the attempted coup. Greenough had resided in Cincinnati as had Bickley before closing his Phosgene Gas Lamps business there in 1856. That increases the likelihood that Greenough and Bickley were well-acquainted. What is more significant was the dangerous liquid fire technology Greenough had developed. Perhaps the nascent

Confederate government personified by the KGC had tried to negotiate with Greenough for its development as a weapon. Greenough did receive a U.S. patent in 1843 for modes of using volatile oils for illuminations, and Bickley had an interest in patents as a one-time Officer of The American Patent Company. The Houston *Tri-Weekly Telegraph* carried a story during the war that in 1849 Abraham Lincoln had attempted to interest Congress in the development of Greenough's liquid fire "as a means of attack and defence." As described by the *Telegraph*, it was a flame-throwing technology. Greenough's wife later claimed that she had "prevailed upon her husband not to sell the explosive to anyone." With that being the case, it would explain why "Col. Greenough" disappeared from the picture. For whatever reason the Texas KGC supported Bickley as its nominal leader. In any event, the crisis gave the Texas KGC an opportunity to exert their dominance. There was a surge of visits from Texas KGC to New Orleans between April 3 to April 9: known members Benjamin F. Terry, soon to form Terry's Texas Rangers; George W. Guess back for a return visit; Hardin R. Runnels, editor John Marshall, and probable KGC members John C. French, James Glass, W.H. Duke, William Thomas, Henry Rosenberg and many others. One day in particular – April 9 – saw the arrival of Elkanah Greer, Ben McCulloch, Tom Ochiltree and J. F. Crosby at the St. Charles Hotel. Bickley responded by issuing General Order No. 546 from Mobile, Alabama calling for a national convention of the secret order in Raleigh, North Carolina on May 7, 1860. This certainly bought Bickley more time, and it avoided some conflicts of schedule for delegates to the Democratic National Convention to begin on April 23rd in Charleston. Bickley did have the framework of a national organization to support him, though. In his circular to "Fellow Soldiers of the American Legion, K.G.C.," Bickley alleged that "A studied attempt has been made to break up our Organization, and turn it from the noble purposes for which it was organized, into a disgraceful Filibuster concern which could only end in defeat and ruin to all concerned." While wrapping himself in the KGC flag in order to convey his legitimacy as its leader, he named other leaders of the Order that he alleged were equally insulted by the insurgents within. General "E. Greer, of Texas" was mentioned, and in further accounting for the size of the armed forces recruited to-date by his organization, he stated that General Greer had 3,500 armed men in Texas and Arkansas. All told, "the military department" at that time supposedly numbered about 16,000 – of which General Elkanah Greer's command was the largest enumerated. The Military Degree being the lowest of the three-tiered organization, Bickley then described the Second Degree:

The second department of the Organization is purely financial, and embraces such a class of citizens as can assist in raising means for the K.G.C. It is thus organized: A Central Financial Bureau at New Orleans; State Central Committees in each Southern State, and then in every important place sub-committees. No K.G.C. has the right, or is authorized to accept monies that may be tendered as a loan or donation, except he is one of said committee or is authorized by them to do so.

He went on to say that procedure was for any money collected to be sent to the sub-committee, and from there to the State Committee, and ultimately to the bank at New Orleans. At that moment the financial department was of major importance to Bick-ley, so he only mentioned the Third Degree briefly and that its mission was "the direction and control of the whole Order – to make its laws and counsel the commander-in-chief." He closed by requesting each company or part of a company to send one delegate to the May 7 meeting in Raleigh, "to complete the perfect organization of said American Legion...." More details would be forthcoming at the meeting. He signed the document as "President American Legion" and not as "General Bickley". Perhaps he realized his charade as a military commander was over: now he preferred an executive title. At KGC headquarters at the Maltby House in Baltimore, Robert Charles Tyler, the Commander of the Maryland regiment, answered a query letter of April 10 by blaming the recent discord on an "attempt of Walker, Sockridge and others in N.O., to break up the organization...." By Sockridge it was meant Lockridge, the mistake an error of transcription from cursive writing by the printer's typesetter. Samuel A. Lockridge was indeed still at the Saint Charles Hotel in New Orleans, still corresponding with Major Heintzelman back in Texas. But who was Walker? Was he John George Walker of Texas who had married into the Baylor family? He may have been in New Orleans during the debate over Bickley's future; or it may have been his cousin with the same name. Whatever the case, by April 12, Major Samuel Heintzelman noticed an increased number of KGC operatives on the Texas/Mexico border. They began arriving in late March in small groups by water and by land from different parts of the country. "It is said that there will soon be 2000 of them here," he wrote in his journal. That same day Lockridge penned a letter from the Saint Charles Hotel to Heintzelman saying that he had been conned by the Knights of the Golden Circle into believing that their invasion of Mexico had the support of President Buchanan. It was apparent to him now that this was not true. Still, more men kept coming to South Texas, and more were reported on the way. In St.

Joseph, Missouri the newspapers reported that "several hundred Knights of the Golden Circle from Kansas and Nebraska, had arrived" and would soon start from there to Mexico. On the 13th, Heintzelman noted in his journal, "There is a good deal of talk about the KGCs. The town is filling with them. They have straggled into Matamoros already & be-having badly. They will give us trouble." Matamoros was across the Rio Grande located in Mexico, so some of the KGC crossed the border near present-day Brownsville, Texas in order to enter that Mexican city.[24]

Texas Governor Sam Houston had been mocked in some quarters for his inaction, as in a letter to the editor published by the *Dallas Weekly Herald* on April 11 that stated, "Gen. Houston can't get Mexico himself, and seems determined to let no one else have it. Thank Heaven, he can't help it, and he may as well bay at the moon, as to issue his bleats against the K.G.C., or anybody else." The abuse continued unabated:

> He has grown wonderfully tenacious of the rights of the frontier now that Reagan and Wigfall are making Herculean efforts to send them assistance. The Mexican policy and the Feeding system both fell dead and hang like a millstone around the old General's neck: until, now, he stoops to pick the crumbs that fall from Wigfall's table....

> The general sentiment I have heard expressed is, that the Old Hero is rapidly declining, and his influence gone.

John Reagan and Louis Wigfall were the United States Senators representing Texas in Washington. The press continued to relate false reports of Indian attacks on the frontier. One such story mistakenly claimed that six families had been killed by Indians in McLennan and Bosque counties. A large company of volunteers from Waco were called to search for the phantom marauders only to discover after riding thirty miles that the whole thing was a hoax. As Houston had earlier said, the lies were being told in order to manipulate citizens into joining armed bands. The Governor tried to increase ranger patrols of the frontier by commissioning Colonel Middleton Tate Johnson to raise a regiment for that purpose. Captain J. M. Smith of Waco, himself a KGC, was made Johnson's Senior Captain. Unfortunately, this too, made it easier for the KGC to recruit members. It was apparent to U.S. soldiers stationed in Texas; one officer wrote to his superior on April 25, "I am told that most of the Rangers, the old set, have left, and their places are being taken by the Knights of the Golden Circle. I do not know how true it is." James Pike, a one-time member of a Ranger company in Texas, was accosted by a

KGC recruiter some-time in the spring of 1860 near Fort Belknap. The man so-liciting him was only known to him as Captain Davis, who Pike described as "a ready talker, and well calculated to seduce the unwary into his schemes." According to Pike, Captain Davis enjoyed a high success rate as a KGC recruiter among the Texas Rangers. This Captain Davis was probably James Francis Davis, a lawyer and the chief jus-tice of McLennan County who later was appointed an Enrolling Officer for the Confederacy. Captain Davis settled on the Tomas de La Vega land grant east of Waco and along the Brazos River in 1851; Fort Belknap was located further north on the Brazos River. J.F. Davis, as he was known, was Captain of a group of "patter-rollers" (slave catching patrols) in Beat Number 3 of McLennan County in 1853. Many of these patrols later morphed into KGC companies. Captain Davis' company became known as the Lone Star Guards, and by May 1, 1861 had eighty-one rank and file members. Later that year his company was absorbed into the Confederate army and became Company E of the Fourth Texas Infantry. Eventually the Fourth Texas Infantry became part of the famous Texas Brigade under the command of General John Bell Hood. The Texas Brigade distinguished itself in battle and had very high casualties; many of the companies like Captain Davis' Lone Star Guards were riddled with KGC members. Like many KGC officers, Captain Davis had the luxury of resigning his commission before his company went into battle. His 1st Lieutenant, Erasmus D. Ryan, became Captain of Company E of the Fourth Infantry. Davis then joined a Home Guard company. One of his neighbors within the Tomas de La Vega land grant was J. W. Sedberry, a plantation owner and leading secessionist who by October 1861 had formed a company of 55 men for Beat Number 8 in McLennnan County; Davis became a private in this company and soon became its Captain. On March 17, 1864, he enlisted in Company E of the 1st Regiment of the 2nd Brigade of Texas State Troops; in less than three weeks he was promoted to Colonel and commander of the regiment of militia. He survived the war and returned to the practice of law. It is highly likely that James Francis Davis was the mysterious Captain Davis encountered by James Pike in the early spring of 1860.[25]

Governor Houston could not control the flow of KGC within his state, nor could he influence Middleton T. Johnson's flailing efforts at capturing Indians. Texas newspapers continued to report the arrival and departure of mysterious groups of strangers; the State Capitol seemed to attract them like a magnet. Some continued to refer to them as "the mysterious order of 'The Tambourines', said to have "obtained strongholds" in San Antonio and Austin. Newspapers were becoming more critical of Houston's actions, and no doubt he felt the pressure and some frustration. On or about April 14th, two men from Jack County visited Austin to meet with Governor Houston to claim an allotment of weapons for Captain Harris A. Hamner's Jack County Rangers. By January 14, 1860, Hamner already had 86 rank and file members of this company. In the meeting with the two men, when Houston saw Hamner's name on the company's muster role, according to the *Dallas Herald*, which had criticized Houston recently,

> Houston flew into a violent rage, and denounced the whole affair as an expedition against the Reserve Indians, and called them dastards (cowards! [sic] Said they dare not meet the warrior on the field – were murderers of women and children, &c, &c. - that no white people had been murdered by the Indians until after the Reserve Indians were driven off, and that the missing horses had strayed off, or were stolen by white people. He refused the print, but reconsidered and granted ten pistols, struck the name of Hamner off the roll, and made the second officer the first....[26]

Houston then sent a letter dated April 14, 1860 to the Chief Justice of Jack County, with the instructions that he had "ordered Mr. H. A. Hamner to put the detachment in command of the 1st sergeant until the Executive receives assurances as will admit of his being recognized." Continuing, Houston wrote, "The arms for Jack County will be delivered to the men who have none. You will relieve Mr. Hamner from his bond until he is recognized. The first sergeant, Mr. George Vanderburg, will in the meantime be held responsible for the arms, and will command the detachment until further orders." [27] The *Dallas Herald* continued its negative coverage of the Governor, calling his actions toward Hamner "vindictive" and noting that George Vanderburg subsequently refused to serve as Captain in Hamner's place. Reportedly, Hamner was again elected Captain of the Jack County Rangers and confirmed by a test vote of local citizens. Not willing to let the story go at that, the *Herald* editorialized:

> Such high-handed measures of vindictive feeling against a private citizen will elicit nothing but sincere condemnation from all parties, and have excited the deepest indignation on the Frontier. We are pleased that the people have sustained Hamner, a man who has been unremitting in his efforts to protect the country. Such a course on the part of the Governor, will be visited upon his own head with crushing effect.

Keeping in mind that the Weatherford convention chaired by John R. Baylor on March 21st had formed a regional funding organization to support Hamner beyond the reach of any government, and that Hamner was not a "private citizen" but a public servant, it would seem that it was Hamner that had a conflict of interest. Hamner's private funding sources were secessionists, and Houston was aware of what was really going on there. Soon Hamner's newspaper, *The White Man*, would turn away from publishing anti-Native American bombast and instead concentrate on promoting secession.[28]

The April 20 *New York Times* carried an article quoting Charles Bickley as Aid-de-Camp to Commander-in-Chief George Bickley and the author of a "card in defence of his principal." Charles Bickley declared that his mentor and superior, George Bickley would take no notice of his expulsion from the convention in New Orleans, and in fact promised a new and improved KGC, purged of any "disreputable elements." They would both attend the upcoming May 7 convention in Raleigh. Of much more interest in the mean-time was the National Democratic Party Convention in Charleston, which commenced on April 23 at high noon.[29]

As the three hundred and three delegates from thirty-two states began to arrive in Charleston, they divided into two separate camps. Delegates from Alabama, Mississippi, Texas, Virginia, and North Carolina stayed together at the Charleston Hotel, the city's largest. Here they met with the leader of the southern delegation that opposed the nomination of Stephen Douglas, the Democratic Party frontrunner for the President of the United States. Led by William Lowndes Yancy of Alabama, the strategy of this group was two-fold: the "demolition of the party" followed by the breakup of the Union. However, the delegates weren't the only ones to attend the convention: local residents of Charlestown packed the gallery and vociferously responded to the different debates taking place in front of them. Other spectators, including Ben McCullough had come to witness what would be the beginning of the breakup of the United States.[30]

On the first day of the convention, South Carolinian secessionist leader Barnwell Rhett met with candidate Stephen Douglas' representative to inform him of what the radical southerners headed by Yancey wanted out of a candidate. To support the candidate, the southerners required Douglas to explicitly endorse the Dred Scott decision to protect slave ownership in the territories, although the issue had already been decided in Kansas Territory. For the candidate to do so likely guaranteed his defeat in the November Presidential Election. This was a nonstarter for Douglas. Barnwell Rhett was a long-time advocate of secession and was closely allied with William L. Yancey, a politician with a well-earned reputation as a skillful manipulator. Yancey had determined in advance to adopt the more moderate language of Mississippi Senator Jefferson Davis, which called for a possible future Congressional slave code if needed. In truth, Yancey was in accord with his friend Barnwell Rhett, who favored immediate secession. Yancey surmised that if he attempted to make Senator Davis' proposal a part of the Democratic Party platform, it might induce Northern Democrats to split with the Southern Democrats; if not immediately, then over the longer term as Yancey and others sought to broaden Congressional approval of the proposed slave code. It was a gradualist strategy worst-case; if, instead, it resulted in an immediate rupture within the party, all the better for advancing the case for secession. One of Yancey's previous accomplishments had been in co-founding The League of United Southerners in 1858 with secessionist Edmund Ruffin, one of the five founders of The Sacred Circle. Over time some would allege that Yancey and Ruffin's League of United Southerners had been merged into the KGC after the League had been exposed by the press.[31]

On April 27, the fifth day of the Charleston Convention, the platform committee presented the Majority Report, crafted with Jefferson Davis' ideas within William L. Yancey's strategy. The Minority Report represented the interests of the Douglas faction, which favored "squatter sovereignty," the doctrine that the territory's settlers decide the slavery issue themselves, as they had in Kansas. The separate proposals were debated openly, with Yancey presenting the case for the Majority Report, which stated the National Democratic Party platform would advocate that slaveowner's rights should be federally protected in the territories of the United States. The platform committee was dominated by Southern interests because two Northern contingents, those from California and Oregon, had defected and joined in support of the Southerners' proposal. In the open debate, Yancey told the convention that Northern Democrats should defend the institution of slavery as a positive societal good through their actions. He then turned to the Southern delegates to forgo party loyalty in favor of preserving the institution of slavery by demanding that northern interests guarantee its protection. He knew this was not even remotely likely. When the competing platform proposals were put to the vote on April 30, the Minority Report carried the day by a vote of 165-138. Yancy's strategy had worked. One by one, the radical southern delegations had their spokesman deliver his "protest" or denunciation of the platform, followed by a walk-out of the entire State delegation. Alabama was the first, followed by Mississippi, Louisiana, South Carolina, Florida, Texas, and Arkansas, in that order. Guy M. Bryan, Chairman of the Texas delegation, ended his protest speech by saying, "In consideration of the foregoing facts, we cannot remain in the Convention. We consequently respectfully withdraw, leaving no one authorized to cast the vote of the State of Texas." With that, to a man, the Texas delegation comprised of Guy M. Bryan, Francis R. Lubbock, F.S. Stockdale, Elkanah Greer, Hardin R. Runnels, William Ochiltree, M.V. Covey, William H. Parsons, R. Ward and J.F. Crosby got up and walked out. So did Ben McCulloch.[32]

Rather than being treated like traitors, the members of what became known as the "Seceding Convention" were treated as heroes by the local populace of Charleston. Now revolution was possible, because the South had stood up to the hated Yankees and was preparing to defend its institutions. "We wish to meet the Black Republicans with their abominable doctrines boldly" declared the spokesman for the Louisiana delegation, "we must fight our own battle." The immediate effect of the walkout on the Democratic Party was to prevent the Convention from voting to confirm Stephen Douglas as the candidate. What was left of the Convention had to adjourn, with the intention of meeting again in June at Baltimore to take care of unfinished business; but the Party had been broken. Its remaining delegates knew they had no chance now of winning the Presidential Election, which is exactly what the KGC and their allied plotters wanted. The election of a "Black Republican" President would force the slave-owning South to secede. At this point, they thought that the Republican candidate would be William Seward. The Seceding Convention held separate meetings from the Convention, and over the next few days decided to have their own convention in June, in Richmond, Virginia, the future capital of the Confederacy. They would designate that meeting as the Constitutional Convention.[33]

Back in Texas, most people were unaware of the significance of what had taken place in Charleston. Many were focused on the perceived threat of Cortinas and his band of Mexican terrorists on the Rio Grande border. Major Heintzelman and KGC leader John Salmon Ford had inflicted heavy casualties on Cortinas, who lost at least 150 men killed to the combined US/Texan forces loss of 15 men killed. Cortinas' men began to desert him. However, according to Heintzelman's personal journal, the Texas Rangers under Ford deliberately circulated rumors about Cortinas being back on the river again, "to keep up the disturbances on the frontier." Duff Green, the irrepressible pro-slavery Wall Street magnate, was appointed by President Buchanan to travel to Texas and assess the situation. Green reported back that the Texans were stirring up just as much trouble on the border as the Mexicans. Heintzelman had lost trust in John S. Ford, and Robert E. Lee declined an offer from Sam Houston to accept the Rangers into Federal service. Ford left the frontier on May 10 to rejoin his command in Goliad; some hoped he would lead the KGC invasion of Mexico. In his travels, he encountered some of his men still carrying their state-issued weapons and laughing about how they had fooled Governor Houston once again. Ford did nothing to stop his men from stealing those weapons;[34] and why would he? The KGC needed arms.

The Convention of Knights of the Golden Circle began in Raleigh, North Carolina on May 7 and lasted until May 11; the most significant outcome of this meeting for historical purposes being George W. Bickley's "Address to the Citizens of the Southern States." This lengthy manifesto was produced for publication "by order of the Convention of K.G.C." but did not appear in many newspapers until early September. The published version does not include any of the proceedings from the first two days of the convention. The majority of what did get published is the rationale the KGC wanted to present to the public: "The Knights of the Golden Circle constitute a powerful military organization, as a nucleus around which to hang such political considerations as will, if well managed, lead to the disenthrallment of the cotton States from the oppressive majority of the manufacturing and commercial interests of the North." They also claimed as a goal the formation of a "Defensive Colony" that would attract the law-abiding "good citizens" of Mexico as a haven "from the anarchy and civil wars which have so devastated that country since 1824" since Mexican independence from Spain. However, later in his address, Bickley mocked those freedom fighters for an independent Mexico as "imitative monkeys" and their movement as "ignorant Mexico". After stating "The people of Mexico are indolent" his discourse became even more caustic:

> They are treacherous, because they are ignorant, and recognize their mental inferiority when in contact with the Anglo-American or British mind; they are thieves, only because honesty is not productive of social and public respectability. They are licentious, because virtue has no permanent recognition.[35]

He made it clear that the KGC was a white supremacist organization. It is likely that Bickley was denigrating the mestizo class of Mexico, who are generally thought to have been 75% Native American and 25% European. This is consistent with the actions of the KGC in Texas towards the Native Americans in their State. Bickley, or the person or persons who actually wrote the address, took pains to address the Native American situation in Texas while extolling the virtues of the KGC in that regard:

> It would guarantee peace and order to the Texan frontier; and the develop-ment of the valley of the Rio Grande and our Arizona possessions, and greatly enhance the necessity and value of the Southern Pacific railroad. It would develop ship-building, manufacture and mining in the South, and more equally distribute the population of the country. It would employ all classes and enrich the industrious and sober. [sic]

The previous statement also revealed that the KGC had designs on Arizona and its rich mines. A southern route for a trans-continental railroad would by ne-cessity traverse the entire State of Texas and cross Arizona near its mines before ultimately reaching the Pacific. Elkanah Greer and Louis T. Wigfall were both share-holders in the Southern Pacific Railroad, just one of several railways that were competing for transcontinental access. Not related to today's Southern Pa-cific, it was originally called the Walker Pacific Railroad company and was pur-chased by a group of which Louis T. Wigfall was President and Greer a share-holder. Later it became part of the Texas Pacific railway, which eventually linked up with the Southern Pacific after the war. Many KGC were rail-road speculators, favoring a Southern route for the transcontinental railway rather than the North-ern route proposed by their rivals.[36]

The KGC address also sought to convey a simplified under-standing of its hierarchical structure and its various functions. The history of the Order was given thusly:

> The organization of the K.G.C. is simple, yet we believe well adapted to the ends in view. It was originated at Lexington, Kentucky, on the fourth day of July 1854, by five gentlemen who came together on a call made by Gen. George Bickley, the President of the American Legion K.G.C. Only two of the five organizing members have survived to the pre-sent time. A clause in the fourth article of the obligation states, 'I will never desert the order or its aims as long as five brothers can be found who remain true to its work....

The founding members are believed by this author to have been those five men who comprised John A. Quitman and his inner circle as previously discussed; by 1860, Quitman, Persifor F. Smith and Felix Huston were dead, consistent with Bickley's story. Although the above statement giving an exact date of the Fourth of July is likely an exaggeration for effect (Independence Day), joining the KGC was in fact a lifetime oath. The obligation of a member of the Order did not cease until death. The organization's structure was further explained:

> It is divided into three prominent divisions, and those divisions are again divided into classes, while again classes are divided into departments. There is the first division, which is absolutely a Military Degree, appealing strongly to the chivalry and martial pride of our people. It is divided into two classes – denominated the Foreign and Home Guards.

The address goes on to describe the Foreign Guard as the filibuster force used to invade Mexico; what wasn't stated were the other countries that would be invaded after Mexico was established as a base of operations. The Home Guard was to be something akin to secret police, although it was not described that way in this ad-dress. It would include those over age and of poor health, but also "ministers, lawyers, judges, officials, merchants" in sympathy with the Order and willing to help it achieve its goals. "In this Home Guard there are many of the first men of the South, and a large number of ladies of wealth and respectability – for Southern ladies are admitted to the first and second degree, but not to the third." In other words, the Home Guard was not intended to ever see the front lines of combat, and comprised a protected, privileged class of society.

The second division was also divided into the Foreign and Home Corps classes, and were described in the address in this manner:

> This is the commercial and financial division; the 'Foreign Corps' becomes suttlers, commercial agents, paymasters, post-masters, clerks, physicians, ministers, teachers, editors, hunters, negotiators, &c., &c. The 'Home Corps' assist by their advice, and exertions and contributions in getting money, arms, ammunition, clothing, and other necessary material, and in forwarding the same to the army, and in assisting to direct public sentiment in proper channels, and in sending on recruits as fast as needed.

This meant that the Order would have complete control of all aspects of society: who the preferred (or mandated) businesses were and how that was determined; control over the economy and communications; and importantly, control over the media (newspapers) and the news that was allowed to be reported. The third degree or division was also divided into two classes, those being the Foreign Council and the Home Council, as described:

> This is the political or governing division. The 'Home Council' is one of pure advisement, and takes no active steps. It is unknown to the public or the first division of the K.G.C., and is intended to guard us against infractions of the law. Like other 'Home' classes it enjoys advantages known only to the order. The Foreign Council is divided into ten departments, representing respectively the interests of agriculture, education, manufacture, finance, religion, police, war, navigation, law and foreign relations. Also from the 'Foreign Council' there is selected three classes as a high court of appeals and en-trusted with the making laws for the government of the K.G.C. These classes represent respectively the interests of capital, manufacturing and mining interests, and the interests of commerce and agriculture. [sic]

The address claimed that the KGC army "is composed of four divisions of four thousand men each," or sixteen thousand. The only "division" that realistically approached that number at this time was the Texas-Arkansas division built by Elkanah Greer, assisted by Samuel J. Richardson, Ben McCulloch, John J. Good and others. It is widely believed that they had 3,500 men, most, but not all of them armed and ready to go. The KGC address quoted a card that had been published by Samuel J. Richardson in a Marshall, Texas newspaper stating that he and General Greer had reviewed the allegations made against Bickley at New Orleans and had cleared him of any wrongdoing. Despite that, on the third day of the KGC convention in Virginia, George Bickley handed in his resignation as commander-in-chief of the military department, and it was accepted. Finally, the charade was over, and the actions of the convention lent more credibility to the KGC as a military organization. The convention subsequently unanimously elected Bickley to the position of President of the American Legion, KGC. Bickley was to be advised by a Board consisting of military leaders; one would presume them to have been fighting men with actual combat experience. Wrapping up their meeting on this last day, resolutions were passed, the Order was decentralized, national headquarters for the order was relocated from Baltimore to Knoxville, Tennessee, and the following closing remarks were made:

> That we have made the right issue, the results of the Charleston and Baltimore Conventions will abundantly show, and that the Southern Governors

will have use for us within the next six months, is confidently expected. If so the K.G.C. may find its Mexico in the District of Columbia. Now, men of the South, will you help us or not? The K.G.C. have presented the only practical solution of the slave question ever offered to the American people.[37]

So, in six months the KGC might invade Washington, D.C.? That would place the threatened event to take place sometime in mid-January 1861 or early February of 1861. As something akin to this did happen in early February 1861, it suggests that plans had already been made by the spring of 1860 for an insurrection. The National Democratic Convention had broken up just days before this KGC convention in Virginia, which suggests that the destruction of the old Democratic Party had been part of the grand plan, as John Marshall of Texas had revealed back in 1859. So far, the plan was working, but there was unfinished business that could pose a threat to its execution. The Baltimore Convention mentioned in the KGC address was supposed to be an attempt to reorganize the broken National Democratic Party beginning on June 19, 1860. Those Southern States that had seceded from the Charleston Convention were to meet instead at Richmond, Virginia on June 12, a week before the National Convention. In the intervening time between the KGC Convention in Raleigh, North Carolina and the "Seceding Convention," which was technically a rump convention of a faction meeting in nearby Richmond, the men of the Texas KGC were traveling. Many of them appeared in Washington, D.C. during this time. John J. Good, who had left Dallas sometime after his KGC military company, the Dallas Light Artillery had received their first shipment of cannons, six-shooters and swords on May 2, reportedly dropped off a notice for his company on May 8th for drills in Dallas the following day. The next time he was heard from was in a letter to his wife dated May 22, written in Grand Junction, Tennessee:

> I am getting desperately tired of travelling and wish for some rest but can enjoy none until we reach Washington City.... Several Texans are along and several down right clever New Yorkers who promise to take pleasure in showing me around the city when we get there.

The letter notes that he had come from New Orleans. Grand Junction, Tennessee was just exactly that: the junction of two large railroads, the Memphis and the Charleston Mississippi Railroad lines. Other than the railway stations to the major routes going East/West and North/South, there wasn't much else there.

Three days later he wrote his wife from Washington, D. C., telling her he had met with both Senators from Texas, John H. Reagan and Louis T. Wigfall. The McLane-Ocampo Treaty had been taken up by Congress on May 1, and the issue was still not decided. As Wigfall and Reagan were both KGC members, Good and his Texas travelers had much to discuss with their Senators. In addition to meeting with the political element, Good mentioned meeting with General Hamilton, "Judge Hemphill" (John Hemphill of Texas), and three of the attendees at the failed convention at Charleston: Francis R. Lubbock, Ben McCulloch and Josiah F. Crosby of El Paso, Texas. No doubt they were planning their next moves at the upcoming "seceding convention" in Richmond and the Baltimore Convention one week after.[38]

The next letters Good wrote to his wife trace the KGC pilgrims' progress: on May 27 he was at the National Hotel in Washington with "A large number of Texans" including Francis R. Lubbock and his lady, Josiah F. Crosby, Ben McCulloch and Forbes Britton, Sam Houston's favorite courier in matters concerning Pres-ident Buchanan, his Cabinet, and the McLane Ocampo Treaty. Two days later, Good was staying at the Saint Nicholas in New York along with KGC mastermind Hardin Richard Runnels, Josiah Crosby. F. S. Stockdale, "Judge Crosby and several other Texas acquaintances". No doubt they had come to New York to confer with one of the two surviving founders of the KGC, George N. Sanders, as well as Wall Street sympathizers like Duff Green. Fortunately for the KGC and its plans, on May 31 the Congress of the United States refused to pass the McLane-Ocampo Treaty. This left the door open for an extra-legal, non-government organization to make its moves on Mexico. 39

In North Texas, suspicions were growing towards new residents or travelers from the northern states. In the Collin County town of McKinney, a known location of a KGC castle, some former residents of New York were arrested and flogged for buying property that had been stolen by slaves belonging to Isaac Graves. The men, known only as "old Barnes," "young Barnes" and "Baxter," stated that they did not know that it was "a violation of the law to trade with negroes". The *Dallas Weekly Herald* referred to the men as abolitionists, and carried the following warning from their Collin County correspondent:

> Abolitionists that come here and undertake to carry on trade with the negroes of the country, may expect to get the benefit of a leather strap, and it in the hands of those are skilled in using it.

Collin County did not have an exceptionally large slave population in 1860; officially there were 933 slaves out of a population of 9,264. The county was included in the cultural complex known locally as "The Corners," which consisted of the contiguous counties of Collin, Fannin, Grayson and Hunt; there were known KGC castles in each one of those counties. Their existence was common knowledge by early June 1860, as shown in the correspondence of Collin County resident and Unionist Charles B. Moore. One of his relatives wrote to him that a friend, Dudley Tarpley "says he supposes it to be a revival of the Order of the Lone Star to which he belonged, & was killed off by K. Nothingism." This confirms that the KGC was in fact a reformation of the Order of the Lone Star; John Quitman played a key role in the birth of both organizations. Another friend was quoted in the same letter to Charles Moore as saying that the KGC "are associated together to operate in, or on, Mexico; but deny being filibusters." For many they served as a self-defense force against rebellious slaves. The fear of slave revolt among Texans would spawn an orgy of violence in less than two months of Charles Moore receiving that letter.[40]

While some Texas KGC members prepared to attend the rump convention of Southern Democrats at Richmond, others planned for the meeting of the Masonic Grand Lodge of Texas at the town of La Grange; both meetings set to occur on June 12. John Jay Good would attend neither; he had somehow wrangled an invitation to attend West Point Military Academy beginning June 1, 1860. Here he would be drilled in the use of artillery by General Winfield Scott. This would prove useful to Good and the KGC, as his military company, the Dallas Light Artillery, had already received two small cannons in May 1860. At West Point, he would train in Siege Artillery Tactics until June 20. When the Civil War started in less than a year, he would be ready to fight and kill his enemies thanks to the training he received at their military academy.[41]

Officially known as the Constitutional Democratic Convention at Richmond, those Southern extremist delegates that had broken from the National Democratic Convention in Charleston now assembled at Metropolitan Hall on June 11. Francis R. Lubbock of Texas served as temporary chairman the first day. He began by saying to some applause, "We have met here today, as we did there, to carry out our principles, whatever may be the result. I trust we have come here for no compromises of the Constitution." After the applause died down, he continued: "If we cannot succeed in sustaining those principles, we must create – no, we will not 'create' a new Democratic party, but we will simply declare ourselves the true

Democratic party, and we will unfurl our banner, and go to the country upon true Democratic principles." More applause followed; then it was time to formally accept the delegates. A stir was caused in the crowd when a delegation from New York made itself known and asked to be seated. Thaddeus P. Mott, the chairman of the New York contingent, explained that the National Democratic Association of New York had appointed them as representatives for the Richmond Convention, so that they might have their say in the election of the Presidential candidate chosen by this body of Southerners. In addition to Mott, the other delegates appointed from New York included Colonel Harvey Baldwin, Isaac Lawrence, James B. Bensel and James Villiers. At last, the delegates were all seated, and those from Texas were Guy M. Bryan, F. S. Stockdale, Hardin Richard Runnels, Josiah F. Crosby and Francis R. Lubbock. The New Yorkers were seated, but not counted as delegates. However, when the Committee on Permanent Organization was formed, Thaddeus Mott was appointed to that committee of ten, which included J.F. Crosby of Texas. New York was not represented on the Committee on Credentials, an 8-man body that included Texan F.S. Stockdale. It is not surprising that some New Yorkers would align with Southern Democrats; the Order of the Lone Star had been very active in New York, and the KGC's Third Degree, the highest, political tier of the Order, was called the Knights of the Columbian Star, a designation borrowed directly from New York's Tammany Hall, where the Order of the Lone Star had sometimes met. After the formation of committees, the Richmond Convention adjourned until the following day.[42]

On the second day of the convention, June 12, F.R. Lubbock called the meeting to order; after the obligatory prayer and some minor business matters, the Committee on Organization presented its plan of organization via its Chairman, Andrew F. Calhoun of South Carolina, the son of John Calhoun. John Irwin of Alabama was made permanent President of the Convention, and Hardin R. Runnels one of its Vice Presidents. Francis Lubbock then gave a brief speech thanking the delegates "for the distinguished compliment conveyed in calling me to assist in the organization of this intelligent and important body." He then ceded the chair to John Irwin, who gave a much fiercer speech, reaching its crescendo with " The serpent of Squatter Sovereignty must be strangled." After the applause and the conclusion of his speech, the convention adjourned until June 21 in order to give time for some of the delegates to attend the Baltimore Convention on June 18.[43]

While the high-level KGC and their supporters worked the convention circuit, people were fighting hostile Indians in Texas; sometimes those fighters protecting Texans were the friendly Native Americans from the reservation that had relocated from Texas to the other side of the Red River. Baylor and Hamner, for all their bluster and fund-raising, were not much of a factor in this effort. An Austin newspaper reported that Governor Houston had received a letter from Fort Arbuckle, in Indian Territory, that a war party of Reserve Indians had intercepted a party of hostile Indians intent on raiding Texas, and "overtook, killed and scalped the whole party." The hostile natives were later said to be wild Kiowa tribesmen, allies of the hostile Comanches, not the Comanches that lived on the reservation. "The Reserve Indians are determined to offer all the proofs in their power," the report continued, "that they are not engaged in the raids upon Texas, or the allies of those who are." Still, there was a report from KGC member and Ranger Captain John M. Smith that a white man had been killed by some of the Reserve Indians, and if Smith found this to be true, he would "march the boys against the Reserve Indians and exterminate every last one of them." Smith had been operating out of Fort Belknap, the site of KGC Captain Davis's successful recruiting drive that Spring, as reported by former Ranger James Pike, who was there at the time.[44]

Also, during this time, the Republican Party held its national convention in Chicago from May 16 to 18, 1860, selecting Abraham Lincoln as its candidate for the Presidency. Lincoln had made waves with Southern extremists as early as 1858 when he debated Stephen Douglas, who was now one of three candidates of a fractured Democratic Party. Lincoln had accused Douglas of attempting to condition the American citizenry to the domination of what many called "The Slave Power." As described by contemporary sources, this amorphous "Slave Power" was in many ways similar to the KGC's proposed ruling class of The Knights of the Columbian Star, its Third Degree. John Elliott Cairnes, an early economist defined a slave society in the early days of the Civil War as composed of three distinct classes, "and of these the Slave Power is the political representative." It was this terminology Lincoln had used in his debate with Douglas, which no doubt concerned members of the KGC's Third Degree, because they were supposed to remain unidentified, and unidentifiable to the general public. Although Southern extremists had heretofore focused their scare tactics and hateful dialogue on William H. Seward as the possible Republican Presidential candidate, they now turned those upon Lincoln and his Vice-Presidential candidate, Hannibal Hamlin. The ridiculous extent that the Southern press would go to in this propaganda campaign is best illustrated verbatim by this May 1860 article in the *Richmond Whig*, which incorporated verses from the Book of Genesis in the Bible:

> JUST LIKE 'EM. – The Black Republicans in nominating a candidate for Vice President remained true to their 'nigger' instincts. Hannibal was a leader of Africans, and Ham (without the 'lin') was the ancestor of the black race. (Gen. 9:23.)

> The candidate for the President is Abra-HAM-LIN-coln – more Ham. The Republican Abraham reviles the institution of slavery. How unlike Abraham of old, who was a slaveholder. (Gen. 24:2, 9) [sic][45]

Things were equally tense in Northern Texas as spring turned to summer. Back in Collin County a vigilance committee was formed at a public meeting held May 31 in the town of Plano. The catalyst for this measure was the alleged "matter relative to the conduct, and certain language, which had been used by C.N. Drake, and S.A. Winslow, of Collin, with and to a certain Negro man, Dick, belonging to W.P. Martin of Collin county, which had a tendency to mar the safety and... peace of the neighborhood, and incite the slaves in our community to rebellion." After meeting half an hour, the special committee appointed to deliberate on this matter presented its resolutions. The resolutions gave Mr. Drake two days to leave the county and never return to the State of Texas; Mr. Winslow was allowed one month to do the same. Mr. Martin, the slaveowner, was instructed to give his slave Dick fifty lashes with a whip, "well laid on," and if he failed to do so, members of the vigilance committee would do so in his place. The men of the committee listed their names; they should be considered as probable members of the local KGC Castle that was reported to exist as early as five months prior to this incident. Mr. J.C. Forman, a local slaveowner, was then appointed to select twelve men including himself, "to wait upon Mr. Martin" who was allowed to select the following "gentlemen" as a de facto slave patrol: J.C. Forman, Daniel Klepper, M.L. Huffman, Robert Rowland, Parson Wilkins, William Blalack [sic], James C. Fain, B.F. Mathews, J.A. Fain, G.W. Mathews, William Hughes, and Sanford Beck. There were many Unionists in Collin County, but the town of Plano, with its slave owning population, later voted overwhelmingly for secession, while Collin County as a whole voted against it.[46]

John J. Good, of neighboring Dallas County, may have rejoined the crowd that had accompanied him around the nation's capital. Ben McCulloch was there when the members of the "seceding convention" reappeared in Baltimore on June

19 to rejoin the National Democratic Convention; they were not met with open arms by the loyalist faction of their party. South Carolina didn't bother to attend. The entire delegations from the states of Alabama and Louisiana were excluded from attendance, as were half of the delegates from Georgia and Arkansas. All the previous delegation from Texas was accepted, however, as were those from Delaware and Mississippi. This wasn't good enough for the delegates from Virginia, who took offense and walked out of the convention again, in a show of solidarity. When the Texas delegation followed suit, Ben McCulloch walked out with them; John Jay Good probably did, too. He did not return home to Dallas until sometime in July.[47]

In so doing, John Jay Good missed the statewide gatherings of the Masonic associations that took place in Texas in the month of June. Many other KGC members did not miss them, and their attendance shows the extent to which the Order had infiltrated the Masonic lodges by that time. When the Grand Lodge of Texas met at the town of La Grange on June 10, its roster of Grand Officers included at least two KGC members: John B. Jones as Grand Lecturer for the Middle District of Texas, and Peter W. Gray as Deputy District Grand Master of the 7th District. Those were statewide offices for delineated areas; both positions put these men in place to make many contacts on behalf of the KGC, as travel was necessary, and influence accrued to the position. Both were good for recruiting purposes. At the individual lodge level in 1860 one finds KGC members imbedded: for instance, Holland Lodge, Number 1, in Houston, included known members Thomas S. Lubbock, Peter W. Gray, and William R. Baker, a native New Yorker and railroad executive who married into the Runnels family; and probable members Jacob De Cordova, Henry Sampson, A.M. Gentry, Francis R. Lubbock, and Otto Nathusius, a known member. In Harmony Lodge, Number 6 in Galveston, known KGC members P.C. Tucker, Francis L. Barziza and E.B. Nichols resided; in Austin Lodge Number 12, in the city of Austin, known KGC member Ernst Raven was one of the lodge officers, and Thomas Green was a Master Mason. Along with those known members in Austin were probable KGC members Xavier B. De Bray, a lodge officer, Past Masters B.F. Carter and John Hancock, as well as Master Masons W.A. Pitts and H. Wilke. In Gonzales Lodge Number 30, in Gonzales County, J. W. Lemmond was a Master Mason in 1860, as well as Captain of the Gonzales KGC Castle. Palestine Lodge Number 31 contained known KGC member John H. Reagan, a Past Master. Known KGC member Ben Shropshire was a member of Lafayette Lodge Number 34, at La Grange; W. P. Saufley was Past Master at Jefferson Lodge Number 38 in the port city of Jefferson, on the Red River. Alamo Lodge Number 44, at San Antonio was a Masonic lodge particularly well-stocked with KGC: John M. Carolan was Past Master, with Master Masons W.R. Cowan, William Edgar, Charles DeMontel, Asa Mitchell, and J.R. Sweet. At Dallas in Tannehill Lodge Number 52 were known KGC members George W. Guess, its Worshipful Master in 1860, and Master Mason John Jay Good; other likely KGC members at the Dallas lodge include A.D. Rice, E.C. Browder, T.C. Hawpe, Past Masters John M. Crockett, J. C. McCoy and newsman Samuel B. Pryor, the precipitator of a major slave revolt scare that was to begin the following month. Waco Lodge Number 92 included known KGC Captain James F. Davis and J.M. Smith. Colorado Lodge Number 96 included Master Mason M.B. Highsmith, also Captain of the KGC Castle at Salado in Bell County. Also in Bell County was Masonic Lodge Number 166, the Belton Lodge, led by W.S. Rather, its Worshipful Master, who also served as Captain of the KGC Castle at Blair; among Rather's brother Masons in the Belton lodge were likely KGC members X.B. Saunders, H.E. Bradford, J.W. Embree and E.S.C. Robertson. At the Corsicana lodge, Number 174 were present known KGC members C.M. Winkler and R.Q. Mills, both of them lodge officers and Past Master John B. Jones, credited with founding the KGC Castle in that town. Probable members of the KGC who were members of this Masonic lodge were W.W. McPhail and J.W. Townsend. Bright Star Lodge Number 221 in Sulphur Springs held known KGC member O.S. Davis, and likely member H.H. Farrar, who became a major troublemaker for Union authorities after the war. Unfortunately for the Masons at the Jacksboro Lodge, Harris A. Hamner, John R. Baylor's partner in crime and the publisher of the secessionist organ, *The White Man*, was a member of their lodge in 1860. In addition to these individual lodge members were the proxies they sent in their place to the State convention at La Grange; these included known KGC member Samuel Mather of the Williamson County Castle, a long-time, high-ranking Mason who served as proxy for the San Gabriel Lodge Number 89 and Mt. Horeb Lodge Number 137; as well as George W. Guess of Dallas, proxy for Honey Grove Lodge Number 164 in Fannin County, which included KGC member John Bailey Anderson.[48]

The Masonic organization that was most closely mimicked by the KGC in Texas was the Order of the Knights Templar. A Texas KGC medallion in the author's possession is based on the Masonic Knights Templar medallion overlaid with other Masonic symbols, but according to the Grand Masonic Lodge of Texas, is not a Masonic medallion. On June 22, 1860, the Knights Templar of Texas had their statewide meeting in Annual Conclave of The Grand Commandery in Huntsville, just north of Houston, and firmly in the Black Belt. Among the 14 State officers in attendance, three were known KGC members: Edward Clark as Grand Generalissimo, E.H. Cushing as Grand Junior Warden, and J.W. Davenport as Grand Sword Bearer. It should be assumed that there were other KGC members among the fourteen officers of the Knights Templar in Texas; those three are the ones for which proof exists. Many of the known KGC members of the Grand Masonic Lodge were also Knights Templar, but it appears that to be a "KT" one had to earn the right to become an initiate. The KT's had a different mission and membership in some ways; it was a designation at or near the pinnacle of Masonry. Unlike the Blue Lodges of Masonry, who could accept those of other monotheistic faiths as members, the Knights Templar was a Christian order. The KT's like the KGC, was also a military order, "having drill competitions, inspections, and in their use of the language of chivalry in their rituals." The KT members also considered themselves distinct and held themselves aloof from the "mainstream" Masonic order. For at least two years, the KTs in Texas had debated whether their order should be completely separated from the rest of the Masons. At the 1858 Grand Encampment, with Grand Generalissimo Francis L. Barziza acting as Grand Commander, the following was officially stated: "In the opinion of the Grand Commandery of Texas, the Order of Templar Masonry exists on a different foundation from that of the several organizations of Free Masonry or Royal Arch Masonry". Was the position of Barziza, and the Texas Knights, influenced by the advent and surge to prominence of the KGC in Texas by 1858?[49]

The Barziza family certainly had a great deal of influence within the KGC, as their patriarch, Count Philip Ignatius Barziza was a Knight of the Columbian Star, the highest echelon of the organization. They were also strongly represented within the leadership and membership of the Knights Templar in Texas; one of the six encampments in the state were named in honor of their family – Barziza Number 5, in Robertson County. A four-man committee of Texas Knights Templars was appointed in 1859 to consider a resolution "relative to the disbanding of the Grand Encampment of the United States." This committee consisted of J. J. McBride, John N. Reed, James Wrigley and James Sorley. Their report to the Grand Commandery of Texas reiterated its earlier position that "the Order of Templar Masonry exists on a different foundation from that of the several organizations of Free Masonry or Royal Arch Masonry" and that "the dissolution of one General Grand body does not thereby preclude the existence or continuance of a united head or governing body for Templary in the United States...." In spite of this apparent schism within the Knights Templar, the recommendation was for the Texas Knights to defer to the Grand Encampment of the United States. Once that resolution was recorded, officers for the Texas Grand Commandery were elected for the coming year 1860. When they met on June 22, 1860, in Huntsville, only 5 of the 6 Commanderies in the state were present: those from Galveston, Houston, Palestine, Austin and Wheelock in attendance, with the Dallas Knights absent. Perhaps the Dallas Knights were still on the road with John Jay Good and his entourage on behalf of the KGC. Among the membership rosters recorded, the Galveston Encampment in 1860 included known KGC members N.B. Yard and E.B. Nichols, and probable members Arthur T. Lynn, the serving British consul, as well as P. C. Tucker and James Sorley. The Houston Commandery's 1860 members included several known KGC: Peter W. Gray, Thomas Carothers, Thomas S. Lubbock and Edward A. Stevens. Named after Scotsman A.S. Ruthven, the Houston group also contained probable KGC members A.M. Gentry and A.P. Manly. Palestine Number 2 featured known KGC John H. Reagan and A.T. Rainey, both serving as officers in 1860. Also, among the membership were Nate M. Burford and John C. McCoy, both men from Dallas and likely KGC. John Gregg was also part of the Palestine Commandery which included W.B. Ochiltree. Colorado Number 4, held at Austin, included known KGC members Ed Clark, E.S.C. Robertson, Ernst Raven, G.B. Erath, and Samuel Mather. Barziza Number 5, held at Wheelock in Robertson County, included known KGC Philip I. Barziza, C.M. Winkler and D. M. Pendergast. Francis L. Barziza was listed as Past Commander of the Wheelock encampment; he had moved from Wheelock to Galveston in 1859 and opened a law office in the town that served as the capital of the Texas slave trade. There, he involved himself in the legal aspects of slave transactions. F.L. Barziza had become more active in the "blue lodge" in Galveston after stepping away from the Templars. These men, through their membership in the Templar Order, constituted an effective communication network for the KGC, as the location of each of the six Templar Commanderies was located outside of a 100-mile radius of each other so as to minimize overlap. In this way, the commandery in Austin could service both the towns of Waco and San Antonio; the Galveston commandery could service most of the Gulf Coast, while its neighbor, Houston, just 50 miles or so to the north, could service the Black Belt/plantation country north of Houston and east of Austin/San Antonio; the area more than

100 miles north of Houston was covered by the encampments in Dallas, Palestine, and Wheelock. The KTs had emissaries traveling between each commandery who in addition to performing their duties required by the Masonic knightly order, could have spoken for that other knightly and quasi-Masonic order known as the KGC. The message they carried and the way they bore it in Texas during the summer of 1860, was drawn from their perception of the medieval Knights Templar, as elucidated by the Masonic scholar Rob Morris in August of 1858:

> When they go forth to battle they arm themselves without with steel, within with faith, but do not bedeck themselves with ornaments of gold, for they wish to excite fear in the enemy rather than the desire of booty.
>
> For the same reason they prefer horses that are strong and swift, and not those elegantly marked and caparisoned, as desiring rather to inspire terror than admiration. [sic]

Terror was to be visited upon the people of Texas in just a few short days of the Masonic Templars meeting. Just who was responsible for instilling the terror is still subject to some debate, but what is known for certain is that the events that began in July 1860 would be of great benefit to the expansion of the Knights of the Golden Circle in Texas.[50]

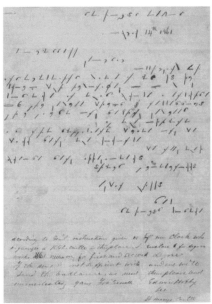

An unidentified KGC member
from Marshall, Texas giving
a secret sign and wearing a cockade

Source: Southern Methodist University

A letter in KGC code
Source: Texas State Library and Archives

A group of Knights Templar. The masonic
Templar order is the Masonic order most similar to the KGC.
Many Texas KGC leaders were Templars as well.

Ebeneezer Bacon Nichols
Leading Texas Mason and banker for the K.G.C.
Source: Texas Grand Masonic Lodge

Samuel Mather
Leading Texas Mason and leader of a KGC Castle in Gabriel Mills,
Williamson County, Texas near Austin.
Source: Texas Grand Masonic Lodge

Peter W. Gray
An important Knight Templar and politician of San Antonio,
said by newspaperman John Newcomb to be a KGC member.
Source: Texas Grand Masonic Lodge

Clinton C. Winkler
An important Texas Mason and one of 61 signers of the notorious
Call For a State Convention, which is believed to confirm his KGC membership.
Source: Texas Grand Masonic Lodge.

KGC flag. Eleven stars for eleven states.

One of several exposes of the KGC written by alleged former members.

Initiation Rituals of the Knights of the Golden Circle.
Source: *An Authentic Exposition of the 'K. G. C.'*

Texas KGC watch fob. According to the Texas Grand Masonic Lodge,
it incorporates Texas Masonic symbols but is not a Masonic relic.
Original owner was a leading citizen of Sherman, Texas.
Source: The author's private collection

Updated KGC seal
George W. Bickley took over as the public face of the KGC in 1858
after the death of John Anthony Quitman.

Chapter 9

"Indians and Abolitionists Combined!"

By the end of June 1860, the KGC had successfully infiltrated the Masonic Order in Texas, including the Knights Templar encampments across the state, enmeshing their organization within the predominate social network of their day. Coupled with their presence in the mass media of the time, the newspaper publishing business, and their influence and participation in the political process in Texas, the Order had reason to be optimistic as their host nation marked its 84th anniversary of independence from Great Britain. Soon they would be ready to declare their independence from the host. The Summer of 1860 would be a hot time in more ways than one.

On July 8, a series of unexplained fires swept across North Texas, almost simultaneously. More than one dozen fires were subsequently reported in communities within a seventy-five-mile radius of Dallas in a twenty-four-hour period. This inaugurated a chaotic period marked by murder and mass hysteria that became known nationally as "the Texas Troubles." It coincidentally, or per-haps conveniently, occurred just months before a divisive Presidential Election. The aftermath of what is also referred to as the Texas slave panic of 1860 would be a major recruitment bonanza for the Knights of the Golden Circle, who proposed to serve as a self-defense organization for slave owners as well as the general public. KGC leaders played the major role of promoting the hysteria and panic through their social network and control of much of the news media.[1]

The initial blaze started in what was then the small town of Dallas, where the official population was comprised of 581 white residents and 97 slaves. The enslaved population was slightly more concentrated in the City of Dallas than in the surrounding County of Dallas, with 14% of the city's population being slaves versus 12% of the county's population; overall the slave population had been growing faster than the white population, which was always a concern for the white population. The 1,074 slaves in the entire county were held by 228 owners. In the owners' minds this bred suspicions of a rebellious spirit dwelling just below the surface of its docile servant population. When a fire of unknown origin decimated most of the business district of the City of Dallas on July 8th, events were set in motion to confirm those suspicions.[2]

What the nervous citizens of North Texas failed to consider was the source of the initial reports of the alleged slave conspiracy. The man most responsible for starting the wave of panic across the region was Charles Pryor, the 28-year old editor of the *Dallas Herald*, a newspaper openly hostile to Governor Sam Houston and sympathetic to John R. Baylor and H.A. Hamner's white supremacist campaigns and secession promotion. Charles Pryor was the brother of Samuel B. Pryor, the one-time Mayor of Dallas, Past Master of Tannehill Masonic Lodge No. 52 in Dallas, and Generalissimo of Dallas No. 6 encampment of the Knights Templar. The publisher of the *Herald*, John W. Swindells, was both Charles Pryor's boss, a brother Mason of Samuel B. Pryor as a member of Tannehill Lodge in Dallas, and along with KGC members John J. Good and John H. Reagan, one of the founders of the Dallas Commandery No. 6 of the Knights Templar. On July 9 Charles Pryor wrote to his friend and editor of the *Houston Telegraph*, E. H. Cushing, that the fire had destroyed much of the premises and equipment used for publishing the *Herald*, but Pryor seemed optimistic that everything would be made right within a short period of time. There was no mention of arson being suspected by anyone in his initial letter. Mr. Swindells wrote similar letters to Charles DeMorse, editor-publisher of the Clarksville, *Texas Northern Standard* the following day, and betrayed no suspicion of foul play. Yet later that same day of July 9, Charles Pryor wrote a letter to John Marshall, who was not only the editor of the Austin *Texas State Gazette*, the mouthpiece for Texas secessionists, but also the Chairman of the State Democratic Party and a known KGC member. In this letter Pryor wrote to Marshall about the Dallas fire, he stated, "It is not known whether it was the work of an incendiary or not." They would soon change the narrative.[3]

People in Dallas were already suspicious, no doubt in part because of the "slave tampering" stories recently reported in their neighboring counties. Several of these reports involved people associated with known KGC members. Alfred Pace of Fannin County was the source of one such story that had been reported by John Marshall's *Texas State Gazette* just one day before the fires began:

We learn from the Quitman *Herald*, that the several murders committed lately in Fannin County by negroes are supposed to have been caused by Abolitionists tampering with the negroes. A negro woman belonging to Mr. Alfred Pace, lately murdered a little son of her master. She was tried before a committee after the adjournment of the District Court in that place and hanged.

Alfred Pace had been in New Orleans during the KGC convention there, checking into his hotel the same day as KGC leader Hardin R. Runnels on March 23. He was also among the men involved in the orchestrated confrontation by the KGC of members of the Northern Methodist congregation in Fannin County in 1859. The story of Alfred Pace and his murderous slave came on the heels of the earlier stories of "slave tampering" in Collin County, situated in between Dallas and Fannin counties. With the stage set for further reports of outrages, on July 12 a fire was reported at the Dallas County farm of Crill Miller. As one early resident of Dallas would later say, "Crill Miller...took the part of a detective and worked up the case." Under pressure of interrogation by his owner, one of Miller's slaves claimed that three white men set fire to Miller's house and barn; not satisfied with this story, Crill Miller and a vigilance committee (local KGC) threatened the slave with death if he didn't specifically identify someone responsible. The slave, a child named Bruce, then confessed that he had been paid by another slave named Spence to set the fires. This coerced confession led to the mass interrogation of the slaves of Dallas County, and eventually, the whipping of all of them, one-by-one.[4]

It must be remembered that Crill Miller had been declared the "winning Knight" in a rather strange medieval-style "jousting" tournament held in Dallas and reported by the *Herald* on November 2, 1859; he had chosen the title of "Knight of the Prairie" as his nom de guerre for that chivalric event. If he wasn't already a KGC member in 1860, he would be by the time the war started in a few months. Crill Miller is not found on the original roster of the Dallas Light Artillery, compiled on March 12, 1859; led by KGC leader John J. Good, the original company included Captain Good, Samuel B. Pryor as 1st Lieutenant, John M. Crockett as 2nd Lieutenant, and as enlisted men, John W. Swindells and Charles R. Pryor. A subsequent roster of the Dallas Light Artillery compiled on February 22, 1861, about two months before the beginning of the war, indicates Crill Miller as 2nd Lieutenant; known KGC member George W Guess is also included as an enlisted man. As the Dallas Light Infantry is considered to have been one of the KGC companies formed in Dallas County, it is likely that all of the men mentioned above were members of the KGC castle in Dallas. Some historians have suspected that the KGC may have staged some of the alleged fires reported to have been the work of "abolitionists" and rogue slaves. However, most believe today that there was a more scientifically plausible reason for the near-simultaneous fires in different towns in Texas: the weather and unstable fire-starting technology. Some reports state that the temperature in Dallas on July 8 was near 110 degrees Fahrenheit. It is a known fact that many stores in North Texas had stock on hand of phosphorous matches, which could spontaneously ignite in unusually hot conditions.[5] None of that necessarily mattered to the KGC; they saw the fires as an opportunity to further their agenda.

So, on July 15, Charles R. Pryor sent an alarming letter to fellow KGC member and Captain of the Bonham Castle, Leonard DeLisle, who was also the editor of the Bonham Era. DeLisle printed the contents of the letter in a special "extra" edition of the Era on July 17, which read:

> I write in haste that you may prepare your people for the most alarming state of affairs that has ever occurred in Texas. On the 8th July the town of Dallas was fired, and the whole business portion entirely consumed, every store in town was destroyed. The next day the dwelling house of J. J. Eakens was burned; after that the residence of E.P. Nicholson was fired but discovered in time to arrest the flames. On Thursday, the premises of Crill Miller, with large supply of oats, grain, etc., were totally consumed.

> This led to the arrest of some negroes and white men. A most diabolical plan was then discovered to devastate this entire portion of Northern Texas, extending even to the Red River counties. [sic]

E.P. Nicholson, whose home nearly burned, was a Dallas attorney, who along with his law partner Justus Wesley Ferris and their wives, checked into the City Hotel in New Orleans during the KGC convention there, on March 19. Like Crill

Miller, E.P. Nicholson became a 2nd Lieutenant in Captain Good's Dallas Light Artillery Company; he was also a slave owner. Therefore, it is the belief of the author that Nicholson was also a KGC member at the time of his "near escape" from the supposed slave revolt of the Summer of 1860. John J. Eakins [sic] was also an original member of Captain John Good's Company, enlisted in 1859.[6]

Charles R. Pryor's strange and frightening letter continued, blaming the plot on friends of two "Abolition preachers, Blunt and McKinney, who were expelled from the country last year":

> The whole plan is systematically conceived, and most ingeniously contrived. It makes the blood run cold to hear the de-tails. This whole country was to be laid waste with fire, destroying all the ammunition, provisions, arms, etc., to get the country in a state of helplessness, and then on Election day in August to make a general insurrection, aided and assisted by emissaries from the North, and persons friendly to them in our midst.

Supposedly the region was divided into districts by the conspirators, with each headed by one white man who supervised the rebellious slaves within. Pryor wrote DeLisle, "A regular invasion, and a real war. You and all Bonham are in as much danger as we are. Be on your guard, and make these facts known by issuing extras to be sent in every direction." DeLisle did that very thing, as one such extra was reprinted on July 28 by the Marshall Texas Republican, located in Harrison County, the county with the largest population of slaves in the state. In addition to his letters to John Marshall and Leonard C. DeLisle, Pryor sent a third letter to E. H. Cushing of the Houston Telegraph on July 21 with even more frightening details of the alleged plot: prominent white citizens had been targeted for assassination; they were to be shot whenever they tried to escape their burning homes. Water wells were to be poisoned to eliminate members of the general population. Pryor now told of a widespread plot that included a large portion of the slaves, who were to have their pick of the white women once their husbands and fathers were killed. This story so terrified slave owners that it was told and retold by their descendants for years, as evidenced by this account 80 years later told by a woman:

> When some Northern Abolitionists came to Dallas during the War and instigated an insurrection among the Negroes, which was to involve the burning of Dallas and the seizing of white property, it was one of Uncle Crill's

young slaves who ran all the way from his place to ours to bring the warning. He gave all details of the plan, which included killing the men who remained at home and taking the women.

According to his story, the darkies had been urged to choose the rooms in the houses they would occupy, as well as the white women with whom they would occupy them. [sic]

The story played not only on the fears of another John Brown-style attack, but also on the older, much deeper fears of the events that occurred in Haiti, with its resulting tales of murder, rape and slaughter of slave owners and their families.[7]

Among the strange and interesting coincidences occurring at the time that the Texas slave panic had its beginning, was the return to North Texas of the KGC members who had left for the failed invasion of Mexico in March. They were held in derision by some, with the *Texas State Gazette* quoting the Bonham Era on July 7th:

The K.G.C.'s in Texas don't seem to know where to find the Mexican Elephant. The Era says that Messrss Cobb and Smith, who left Bonham in the spring for the scene of action on the Rio Grande, have returned. We have seen several who have given up the ghost. [sic]

While being mocked locally, the K.G.C.'s national leader, President George W. Bickley was being portrayed as a fool and charlatan in the national media. On July 18, he posted "an open Letter to the Knights of the Golden Circle" in Washington which was picked up by the *Richmond Daily Whig*, the *Boston Evening Transcript* and the *Philadelphia Inquirer* the following day. Other, more southern newspapers like the *Macon Weekly Telegraph* would re-run the story later under the heading, "Weak in the Upper Story," implying that George Bickley was insane. Of the "Open Letter" to the KGC, it was said by the Macon paper that

It is full of bombastic moonshine about mutability and mutation, analyticism and syntheticism, pyramids and sphynxes. Solomon and Hiram, Uleg-Beg and Genghis Khan, and a great many other persons and things, from Mizraim to Morse, from the Red Sea to Red River.

The *Philadelphia Inquirer* chimed in, saying

When Europe gets into syntheticism, then look out! We shall next hear of her being in apogee. NIMROD, ASHUR, FOHI, MIZRAIM, ATHOTES and MEMNON then receive honorable mention by President Bickley, who unqualifiedly affirms their analyticism. He then passes to ULEG-BEG, GENGHIS KAHN, PSAMMETICUS, FILMORE, PIERCE and BU-CHANAN, but leaves us in distressing doubt whether these worthies are to be regarded as analytic or synthetic, or which it would be right for them to have been. [sic]

Some of what appears to be gibberish was in fact reference to Masonic mysticism, much of which can be attributed to the writings of Albert Pike, then the highest-ranking Mason in the Southern Scottish Rite. What was downplayed or missed outright in the mockery of Bickley's message was his "urgent call" for the Knights "to repair to their encampment, in Texas, by the 15th of September." He had ordered another invasion of Mexico by the KGC, "urging Virginians to take the lead" to achieve the organization's object, "the speedy Americanization of Mexico," and further:

> This truth must be apparent to every thinking man; with Mexico Americanized and Southernized, our area of territory would be nearly equal to that of the North, including the Southern Territories of Arizona, New Mexico, and California; our population would be equal to hers; besides we should possess advantages of climate, soil, productions and geographical position of a very marked character: with this addition to either our system, the Union, or to a Southern Confederacy, we should possess every element of national wealth and power; we shall have in our hands the Cotton, Tobacco, Sugar, Coffee, Rice, Corn and Tea lands of the continent, and the world's great store-house of mineral wealth. [sic]

Bickley was talking about creating an agricultural monopoly in the Americas, North and South; while maintaining political hegemony either in the United States or without it as an independent nation with the mineral wealth – gold and silver from the mines of Mexico, Arizona and California – to back a viable currency on the world market. Possession of California would provide this Southern Confederacy with a Pacific port that would be much more difficult for the "Black Republicans" of the North to blockade; per-haps making disruption of the South's international commerce an impossibility. It does not take too much imagination to consider that Bickley did not develop these long-range plans all by himself. In line with this way of thinking, he was merely the public face, or spokesman for this monopolistic movement. Slave labor was essential for production of these commodities in a most cost-effective manner, so that they could crush any price competition by control of the world market for these items; at least that was their theory. Some of the high-ranking KGC in Texas took this idea very seriously, in spite of the mysticism attached to it by Bickley's delivery, as can be judged by their subsequent actions. By the time of Bickley's resignation as "General" at the KGC convention earlier that year, the KGC was already "forming under a different basis in Texas & other states" according to sometime member Samuel A. Lockridge, who also wrote to Major Heintzelman from the KGC convention in New Orleans that "some of the first men in our country" were among the KGC membership.[8]

Bickley may have hoped that the Virginia KGC would take the lead in an invasion of Mexico from a base in Texas in recognition of the difficulties caused by the Texas slave panic of 1860; but curiously, that panic did not begin in earnest until nearly a week after his release of the "Open Letter" directing the invasion. Either he had foreknowledge of the upcoming crisis, or it was just a lucky coincidence that the fictional slave uprising happened at a time and place fortuitous for the KGC. In any event, the KGC in Texas became preoccupied with the perceived rebellion at home. On July 17, the day before Bickley's declaration, a lynching of a suspected "abolitionist" occurred in Tarrant County, the county immediately to the West of Dallas County, where the "revolt" was first reported. The unfortunate victim was a native of Maine named William Crawford. He had been working in and around the town of Fort Worth and had made the mistake of conversing with some of the slaves, which along with his Yankee accent, aroused suspicion. A slave belonging to Nathaniel "Nat" Terry, one of the largest slave-owners in the county, stated under interrogation that Crawford had sold him a gun and encouraged him to run away from his owner. Tarrant County, Texas was sparsely populated at the time with 5,170 whites and only 730 slaves, but Nat Terry owned thirty-six of those slaves, after losing eighty more slaves due to foreclosure after failing in business in Alabama. He had bought land in Tarrant County in 1854 from Middleton T. Johnson, probably the largest permanent slaveowner in Tarrant County, who was now in command of Sam Houston's failing effort to find Indians alleged to be threatening Texas' frontier citizens. Fort Worth was a frontier town, as there wasn't much settlement West of it. Nat Terry was an avowed secessionist and had formerly served as Lieutenant Governor of Alabama; so, his word carried weight. He was also desperately frightened of losing any more of his human property, as that was the major source of any slaveowner's wealth. So, based on the testimony of a terrified slave owned by Terry, William Crawford was lynched early the morning of July 17. Anthony Bewley was rumored to have been an associate of Mr. Crawford. Mr. Bewley, it must be remembered, was the only full-time resident minister of the Northern Methodist Church left in North Texas. He had been present at the KGC's confrontation of his church's regional conference in Bonham in 1859. Now, Anthony Bewley decided it was time for him and his family to leave Texas on July 17. They fled across the Red River into Indian Territory, where they hid for eleven days. Newspapers like the KGC-friendly *Navarro Express* incorrectly reported that "a preacher by the name of Buley [sic] was hung at Veal's Station" that day, Veal's Station being a small settlement to the West of Fort Worth. That was the place that Crawford had been hung, and where Bewley would ultimately meet his fate. The *Express* additionally reported on the same day that a man named William Steaton was also lynched July 17, "at Sugg's Mill, in Anderson county," as reported by a resident of the nearby town of Palestine. The Knights Templar had one of its six encampments in Texas at Palestine, and that town and its surrounding area in Anderson County would be the site of more lynching during the panic. Steaton had apparently been talking to slaves and was accused of "attempting to incite a negro to fire the mill."[9]

Bewley was in hiding with his family when the vigilance committee in Dallas handed down their sentence to suspected ringleaders of the slave uprising on July 23. Before the final decision was made known to the public, County Sheriff T. C. Hawpe had ex-pressed concern to Nat Burford, the District Judge, that the committee would vote to hang all of the slaves in the entire county. Upon receiving further input from an unnamed slave owner, it was decided that three slaves would be hung, as it would be too expensive to hang the entire slave population; to placate the smaller slave owners who had less to lose, a charade would be publicly staged. It was thought that if a "rich man's negro" was implicated, but then exonerated and his life spared, that "the meeting will not then turn around and vote to hang the poor man's negro." The ruse succeeded, with a concession to the militant faction that every slave in the county would be whipped. The following day the three slaves were hung at 4:00 before a large crowd of spectators. Among the condemned, Sam Smith was said to be a "slave preacher," something considered dangerous by some slave owners as Christianity could imply the equality of all men. Another of the three, "Old Cato," was considered to be a troublesome slave, although his owners, the Overton family, thought very highly of him; and the third man to be executed was Patrick Jennings, who was also popular with many of the white citizens and their children. Jennings had been accused of setting fire to Peak's Drug Store, and supposedly had bragged about it. It was Old Cato who had implicated the other two men who were to hang with him. After their bodies were left hanging for a while, they were taken down and buried in what is now downtown Dallas, in an area thought to be near the Texas School Depository building, later the site of President John F. Kennedy's assassination more than 100 years later.[10]

As later reported by the Marshall *Texas Republican*, Nat Terry of Tarrant County sent a letter on July 24 to Mr. D. B. Martin of Rusk stating that they had evidence of "an extensive plan for an insurrection, instigated by abolition emissaries." At some point thereafter, secret meetings were held between vigilance committees in Tarrant County and the town of Sherman in Grayson County, where a KGC castle is known to have formed earlier in the year. It is likely that Nat Terry was the anchor of a KGC Castle in Fort Worth, along with other men from Tarrant County who would play prominent roles in the continuing pursuit of Anthony Bewley. By late July vigilance committees had been organized in the towns of Anderson, Hempstead, Brenham, Paris, and others; those towns named being in the counties of Grimes, Waller, Washington and Lamar counties, respectively. The Paris vigilance committee had been organized at a mass meeting held there on July 28th to hunt down anyone suspected of Abolitionist tendencies. The *Waco Democrat* published a letter from Judge Burford of Dallas which said that "Under the lash the negroes have admitted that they had in their possession deadly poisons, to be administered to their master's families in food," and in that dire circumstance, the tortured slaves had also implicated "nearly all the negroes of Ellis and adjoining counties." Judge Burford was in Waxahachie, Ellis County, which adjoins Dallas County when he wrote this letter, and of course Tarrant and Grayson counties are near to Dallas County. It is highly likely that Judge Burford or others like him was carrying information for and coordinating with vigilance committees in different counties close to Dallas. So it was that vigilance committees in Tarrant and Grayson counties jointly offered a $1,000 reward for the capture of Anthony Bewley and his return to Fort Worth. Two men from the Grayson County town of Sherman – A. G. Brayman and Joe Johnson – were to lead a party of at least eight men and as many others as they could enlist to pursue Bewley, who had left Indian Territory for Arkansas on July 28th.[11]

While the search for Bewley began, vigilance committees continued to organize across the state and attend to their deadly business. At Columbus, in Colorado County, a runaway slave from Galveston was shot and killed by Alex Dunlavy in late July after he noticed the runaway was armed. Before he died, the slave supposedly told Mr. Dunlavy that there were a dozen armed slaves hiding nearby. On

August 2, the La Grange newspaper in Fayette County reported the lynching of two men suspected of Abolitionist and incendiary activity. Both Colorado County and Fayette County were located in the Black Belt of Texas and had relatively large slave populations in excess of 3,100 each. The Sulphur Springs Moni-tor reported on August 4 that a plot to burn the town of Sulphur Springs had been revealed by the confession of some slaves, who no doubt were whipped into confessing. A night patrol was then instituted at the nearby town of Tarrant. On Sunday, August 5, two white men were reportedly lynched at Tennessee Colony, a settlement near the town of Palestine in Anderson County. The men were cousins; their names, Antney Wyric and Alford Cable. It was said that some of the slaves had been found with guns and poison, and under the lash, had implicated the two men as their suppliers. Wyric and Cable had lived in the area for about three or four years and were tradesmen; Wyrick had a prior conviction for selling alcohol to slaves. Also, on August 5 it was reported that a slave was hung at Science Hill in Henderson County, only about fifteen miles from Tennessee Colony. At approximately the same time it was re-ported the vigilance committee in Ellis County had hung a young man in Waxahachie for "giving strychnine to slaves to put in wells." He had worked in a store, leaving one to wonder, if this story were true, had he innocently sold the strychnine to the slaves, thinking they were going to use it to kill rats on their owners' farms? Many of the stories told during this time were later found to be untrue; rumors ran rampant. For instance: the *Alamo Express* of San Antonio reported that a mapmaker named Parker, who had visited their city, was lynched in East Texas sometime in August for "tampering with negroes;" one week later it retracted the story, saying its source was a letter written in Matagorda on August 6. Matagorda was a town on the Gulf Coast, far from East Texas, but its citizens were obviously nervous; slaves outnumbered the white residents of that county by 2,107 to 1,347. An armed patrol was established in Matagorda by the middle of August.[12]

The evidence Nat Terry wrote about in his letter of July 24 of proof of an abolitionist conspiracy was the document exchanged in Fort Worth on August 10. That day, Paul Isbell, a well-known slave trader in Tarrant County, along with his next-door neighbor George Grant, described as "also a rich farmer," met on the public square with Nat Terry and a man known as Captain Daggett. Ephraim Mer-rill Daggett brought ten slaves with him when he moved from East Texas to Tar-rant County in 1852; he became known as "the father of Fort Worth." A Mexican War veteran, he was considered a war hero as well as one of the largest landowners

in the area. He had his fingers in just about every venture in Fort Worth, so naturally he became involved with the KGC and its anti-abolition crusade. He was
likely a second-degree member of the KGC, as he financially sponsored the development of Tarrant County including the promotion of railroad transportation
through the county. Soon the four men went together to the County Clerk's office,
where Isbell swore under oath that he and Grant had found a letter on the prairie
near their homes at an undetermined time. As both men were slave owners, and
as a slave trader, Paul Isbell sometimes had as many as 200 slaves on hand for sale,
it was deemed that their residences would be a most likely target for abolitionists.
This letter was withheld from the public and was not generally released for publication until after Bewley's death. Although Mr. Isbell swore on the affidavit that
the copy he made of the letter was "a true and correct copy of the original...ex-
cepting that some of the spelling has been corrected," the letter's author was "Wm.
H. Bailey" but was somehow attributed to Anthony Bewley, the Methodist minister. Copies of the letter had been secretly sent only to "confidential men in the
various counties involved in the threatened dangers, to be communicated to a
number of good men to put them on their guard." The letter was used repeatedly
to bolster the claim of an abolitionist conspiracy behind the fires in North Texas.
It would not be published by John Marshall's paper until September 22, but on
August 11, John Marshall did his best to keep the story alive by printing in his
paper, the *Texas State Gazette*, the following item sent from someone in Denton:

> The negroes are confessing to a knowledge of the burning in this section,
> and that they were put up to setting the fires by white men.

> The signs of the times point to the fact that Northern Texas is to be made
> a second Kansas, but they will have a happy time of it we hope, for we
> intend to hang the last one of them.

One of the earliest reports of the mysterious fires that began on July 9 as
being the work of "an incendiary" came from Otis G. Welch, an attorney known
as "the Father of Denton" for his work in laying out the city and naming its streets.
Although originally from Maine, he had been an early settler of Denton County
and later became a Confederate officer commanding troops in Indian Territory.
Quite possibly Mr. Welch was the source of this anonymous report in the *State
Gazette*, as he seemed to be a willing participant in distributing news to feed the
panic.[13]

The Native American tribes across the Red River in Indian Territory re-mained a convenient bugaboo for elements of the KGC. On August 16, A. M. Gass of Fannin County, the 1st Lieutenant of L.C. De Lisle's KGC company, was ordered by Colonel Middleton T. Johnson to bring the remainder of the Fannin County company to help his Rangers hunt down some Indians. Supposedly there were one hundred Kickapoo warriors camped at the junction of the Red and Wichita rivers, preparing to invade Texas. Mr. Gass was now serving as 1st Lieu-tenant of Wood's Company of Texas Rangers; but as Major Heintzelman of the U.S. forces had been told just months earlier, most of the "old set" of Rangers had been replaced by Knights of the Golden Circle. Once again M.T. Johnson's men went on their fool's errand in search of non-existent hostile Indian invaders. Near the end of September Lieutenant Gass wrote the Clarksville Standard, "so we went down, scoured the country and could not find any Indians. We found some troops that said there were no Indians there and had not been." As Anthony Bewley had been hiding in Indian Territory, one wonders if the $1,000 reward money was at least part of the reason so many troops were scouring the area. Bewley had still not been found by the end of August.[14]

Anthony Bewley and his family had reached Benton County, Arkansas at an unknown time in late August and had stopped at the small settlement of Elm Spring for a few days. Before long a group of men led by a Southern Methodist minister confronted Bewley and his party and ordered them to leave. They com-plied and headed further North towards Missouri. Not long after their departure, the bounty hunters from Texas arrived in Elm Spring, hot on their heels. Accord-ing to a local man, the Texans spoke of a $1,000 reward for his capture and claimed Bewley "had been the cause of burning five or six towns, but no one who knows him believes it; but I expect they will hang him. They intend to drive all Northern Methodists from Texas." Bewley knew that he was targeted for lynching but had no idea how close behind him his would-be killers were at this time. For the re-mainder of his flight through Arkansas, his party was harassed and threatened by a group of men from that state. Finally, before turning back, his tormentors told him that they would allow him to flee to Illinois or Indiana, but if he went to Kansas, they would know it and come and get him. This sounded like a KGC member's thought process; there were many KGC members in Arkansas, some of whom were elements of Elkanah Greer's KGC regiment. Bewley and his party were headed into Missouri, which would not be any better than Arkansas, as it was the home of many of the former Border Ruffians who fought in the Kansas troubles of the 1850s.[15]

After six weeks of travel from their home in Johnson County, Texas, the Bewley party finally reached southern Missouri. Unfortunately, Reverend Bewley let his guard down and was captured by his pursuers on September 3 near the town of Cassville. The bounty hunters then brought him back to Fayetteville, Arkansas on September 4, and placed him on a stagecoach back to North Texas, very likely under guard, on September 8. Bewley reached Sherman, Texas on September 10, where he was held overnight. The editor of the Sherman Patriot saw Bewley at the hotel that night and published some unkind comments in his newspaper five days later. Be-tween the time of Bewley's arrival in Sherman on the 10th and his subsequent arrival in Fort Worth on the night of September 13, his whereabouts are unknown, although it is interesting to note that KGC member John Bailey Anderson of Fannin County was later paid $200 for keeping "Buly" by his county's commissioners. John B. Anderson later served as Sheriff of Fannin County from 1864 to 1867; it is possible that Bewley was held in Fannin County after leaving Sherman before his transit further west to Fort Worth. Although the reward for Bewley's capture was $1,000, the alleged leaders of his pursuit, A.G. Brayman and John Johnson and three other men were only paid $50 apiece. That implies that others shared in the reward as well.[16]

Before Bewley arrived in Fort Worth, the citizens of Tarrant County had a public meeting on September 11, said to be the largest ever such meeting in the county's history up to that time. Colonel Robert Gilaspie was appointed chairman of the proceedings, and attorney J. C. Terrell was appointed secretary. Terrell read the incriminating letter supposedly found by slaveowners Isbell and Grant out loud to the assembly. The letter spoke of a secret abolitionist organization known as the "mystic red" which intended to employ "desperate characters" to achieve their plans, as described in the letter:

> The only good they will do will be destroying towns, mills, &c, which is our only hope in Texas at present. If we can break Southern merchants and millers, and have their places filled by honest Republicans, Texas will be easy prey if we will only do our duty. All we want for the time being is control of trade. Trade, assisted by preaching and teaching, will soon control public opinion, (public opinion is mighty and will prevail.) Lincoln will certainly be elected; we will then have the Indian Nation, cost what it will.

Squatter sovereignty will prevail there as it has in Kansas. That accomplished, we have but one more step to take, but one more struggle to make, that is, free Texas.

This letter, dated July 3, 1860, was signed by Wm. H. Bailey, and addressed to "Dear Sir." Anthony Bewley's name did not appear on the version of the letter that was copied and sent abroad to the "confidential men in the various counties involved." It is not necessary to reproduce the entire letter now, although it was read aloud to the people of Tarrant County; they were also told by the committee members that "the incendiary fires, crimes, and Negro insurrections in Texas were known by the abolitionists in Lowell, Massachusetts, three weeks before the news of these events were heralded in Texas papers". Although no evidence of this was provided at the meetings, it was also alleged that the Black Republicans had "enrolled over a hundred picked men to repair to North Texas in the fall." Based on this uncorroborated evidence, seven resolutions were passed by the committee after adoption by the citizens. The first resolution was that "the citizens of Tarrant County considered all persons connected with the crimes 'as having placed themselves beyond the pale of the law's protection'," meaning, the accused would be subjected to summary judgment – lynching without benefit of trial. Resolution two "provided for the organization of discreet men to operate secretly and compile the names of all 'Black Republicans abolitionists or higher law men of every class,' and make two lists in every county." The first list would contain the names of anyone suspected, but the second list would be designated the "Black List" identifying those who were subject to immediate lynching when apprehended. Anthony Bewley was added to the list, but not by public acclamation. Resolution three stated, "There should be no abatement or exemption from entire extermination of the Black List." Resolution four said in effect that those supporting the prior resolution calling for total extermination of the Black List would thus be worthy of citizenship – which also could be interpreted to mean that anyone disagreeing would no longer have the rights of a citizen. The final resolution required the Tarrant County vigilance committee to "correspond with the others in the state in order that a state convention might assemble to take into consideration what further was to be done." There is no record that a state convention of vigilance committees ever occurred, but there is evidence in print that the Texas State Convention of the KGC occurred just five months later in San Antonio; the proceedings were printed by Victor W. Thompson at the offices of his newspaper,

The States Rights Democrat at La Grange in Fayette County. The State KGC Convention must have been coordinated by the "organization of discreet men" who were operating in secret. As then Texas resident and newspaper publisher James Pearson Newcombe later wrote, the KGC "furnished the vigilance hanging committees, and to them belong the credit of the murders and arsons committed during the secession times."[17]

While Reverend Anthony Bewley was in transit to meet his fate in Tarrant County, one of the KGC's heroes met his own end on September 12. The famous filibuster and self-proclaimed President of Nicaragua, William Walker, was executed by firing squad in Honduras after an attempted invasion of that country. This was no doubt a concern and disappointment to many of the KGC upper echelon in Texas, as they had lent monetary support as well as personnel to his efforts at Central American conquest. Now they could add Walker's perceived martyrdom to their list of grievances against the United States government, who they accused of joining with Great Britain in undermining Walker. KGC members such as C.R. Wheat, Samuel A. Lockridge and others had served with Walker on his previous campaigns but were absent from this one. Walker and his men surrendered to British troops hoping for a trial by British tribunal, but instead were turned over to a Honduran general. Walker, now age thirty-seven, had once "beheld greater conquests, more power, a new South controlling a Nicaragua canal, a network of busy railroads, great squadrons of merchant vessels, himself emperor of Central America." At dawn his captors led him out to the beach, where after facing a firing squad of twenty-three soldiers, it was said, "although each shot took effect, Walker was not dead. So, a sergeant stooped, and with a pistol killed the man who would have made him one of an empire of slaves." Walker's fate would not be known to the general public in Texas until weeks later.[18]

Accounts of Anthony Bewley's lynching differ and were no doubt politicized by the bitterness of the conflict between North and South. One very pro-Tarrant County account states that he was implicated by the testimony of a slave named Ned Purvis, owned by the Purvis family at West Belknap. Supposedly Bewley was sworn under oath and confessed that he was the recipient of William Bailey's letter of instructions for abolitionist terror. It was only then that he was hung on the night of September 13 in front of a crowd of "hundreds" of men, on the same tree limb that had suspended William Crawford on July 17, a few miles west of town. An account of the incident cited by the *Methodist Quarterly Review* in 1863 quoted a Fayetteville newspaper, the Arkansian which stated that Bewley made no confession before he was hung, as he realized that they were going to hang him one way or the other. A more recent investigation concluded that Bewley arrived in Fort Worth late in the evening of September 13, was given a meal and allowed to rest. At 11:00 that night he was wakened from his sleep, taken to a tree about three hundred yards west of the intersection of White Settlement and Jacksboro Roads and was hanged there at the same location as William Crawford. One of the first newspapers to break the story was the *White Man*, published by secession-ists H. A. Hamner and John R. Baylor, who could not resist gloating over Bewley's fate in their September 15 edition. Hamner must have been there to witness it, as the *Dallas Herald* didn't cover the story until October 10. The Marshall *Texas Republican* in the October 17 edition quoted the *White Man* as saying Bewley "had been prowling about the country all summer"; three days later the *Texas Republican* quoted a letter from Otis G. Welch of Denton, who had played a role in the in-cendiary scare from the beginning. Welch may have been within the group of "hundreds" that witnessed the lynching, too, as Denton is just north of Fort Worth. However, the Unionists in Texas were not convinced, as the copies of the incriminating letter that were published did not mention Anthony Bewley by name. One loyal newspaper editor in particular, A. B. Norton of the Austin South-ern Intelligencer, had mocked the purported evidence as early as September 5, asking "who is William H. Bailey?" No one could answer him - except, of course, the *White Man*, who published their answer which was taken up by many of the pro-secession papers in the state. According to Hamner's White Man, the words "Rev. Wm. Buley" were written on the back of the original letter, but were never included on any of the copies distributed, nor on the broadside printed and dis-tributed statewide by Bell County secessionists (and likely KGC) John Henry Brown, A. J. Embree and E. S. C. Robertson. What makes Hamner's story even more unlikely is the fact that the victim's name was Anthony Bewley, not William Buley.[19]

During Bewley's pursuit, capture and eventual hanging, the KGC-friendly press kept up a relentless salvo of foreboding, fear and righteous anger. An edito-rial in the *Texas Republican* spoke of the resentment engendered by the fearful prop-aganda and rumors:

> The South has been devoted to the Union, but that spirit, under these con-tinual assaults, is rapidly dying out. Men now speak of disunion not as a mere possibility, but as a 'consummation devoutly to be wished.' Sectional hatred is increasing. Should Lincoln be elected, it will cumulate. The Union

will not survive the shock for it will be taken throughout the entire South, as a formal declaration of hostilities; an endorsement of Black Republicanism with all its enormities.

The election was still two months away when this editorial was published, but it left no doubt as to where its author stood on the question of who was at fault for all the misery being inflicted on Texas. If its author could have blamed the ongoing drought in Texas on the Lincoln campaign, as well as the alleged "Black Republican" abolitionist inspired arson, he would have done it. Others, including KGC members disguising their identities, used the *Texas Republican* as a forum for spreading fear and dread of Lincoln as President, should he win:

> We live in critical times and are now upon the eve of a great Presidential election, which in all probability will decide the fate of this great Republic. And we are free to confess, for we do most sincerely believe, that all the excitement which has been produced of late by Abolitionists among us has been done to paralyse the South and to prevent a full vote in November next. All that men can devise every exertion and every act – no matter how unscrupulous it may be will be brought to bear upon this election. If they can elect Lincoln, it is all they desire. Let us ask what will be the consequences if he is elected.

> One of the very first acts of his administration, will be to repeal the "Fugitive slave law," and then to deny the right of Congress to protect slavery anywhere. On all our border States the effect will be terrible.

> The running of our slaves, flooding our country with Abolitionists and Plunderers; will produce such a state of bloodshed, anarchy, and confusion, as the mine of man cannot conceive, but such as will bring upon us a civil revolution to a certainty. God forbid that the times of the Inquisition, or the bloody days of the French Revolution should come upon us. To prevent such a terrible catastrophe, we must be governed by experience and discretion. We must watch, demand, and protect our rights and liberties, under all circumstances and at all times [sic]....

19. 18. 8.

Note that instead of a signature, or even a penname, the author instead concluded with a bit of code – "19. 18. 8.". The KGC could, and often did, communicate by mail in code. Numbers were often used in place of names and places, and the code itself would be periodically changed to make it more difficult to be de-coded. Combinations of numbers might have different meaning as well. For in-stance, a copy of the ritual for the second, or Financial Degree K.G.C. was found in the State Archives of Texas. At the conclusion of the initiation ceremony for a new member of the Financial Degree, the Captain in charge of the secret initiation was required to give the new initiate the symbolic numbers to be used "If a general war ensues... Name – 18: sign – 25: ans – 26: password – 27: night word of distress – 32: response – 31 and say 5: ...guard sign – 1/2 28:...." It is unknown at this time exactly what "19. 18. 8." symbolized at the time this letter was sent to the editor of the *Texas Republican*.[20]

KGC President George W. Bickley had missed appearing in Texas for his appointed invasion of Mexico on September 15; instead he landed at Galveston on October 10, complete with the standard apologies to pass all around. The KGC soldiers who had travelled from Virginia to South Texas had come and gone by the time Bickley arrived with his "nephew" Charles L. Bickley. Unbeknownst to anyone, Charles Bickley had been in Texas earlier in the year and had secretly mar-ried a Mexican senorita; this would not become public knowledge until his death much later. One could assume that Charles Bickley had already made inroads in Texas: one historian has written that Charles, Dr. George Cupples and Sam Sampson began directing KGC activities from San Antonio "perhaps as early as March 1860." Charles was of much help to President Bickley in the days to come as they began a whirlwind tour of Texas, setting up new KGC Castles in towns as they went. Of course, President Bickley had some explaining to do as to why his second proposed invasion of Mexico had not happened. In so doing, he was able to raise some interesting points, and to speak somewhat realistically. Perhaps he really was acting on input from his military advisors, as had been directed going forward from the KGC Raleigh Conference. Bickley's reasons for failure this time included the depleted condition of the Texas countryside, which was during a long, searing drought that had no doubt depleted many of his financial contributors for such an endeavor, for they were farmers. The drought had also dried up many of the watering holes that would have been necessary for horse-borne supply wagons and cavalry troops. Bickley also spoke of the failure of William Walker's last and fatal expedition to Central America. With the Presidential Election less than one month away, it was imperative that George and Charles Bickley help refocus the attention of their rank-and-file members away from the now settled Bewley mat-ter, which many Texas leaders wanted to keep from spinning out of control. On

October 2, residents of Corsicana awoke to find four men hanging dead in the public square. All four were said to be respectable citizens, all members of the County Court. The editor of the KGC-friendly *Navarro Express*, located in Corsicana, stated "we knew of no conduct of theirs which deserved such a severe penal-ty." Order had to be restored. As best as can be determined considering the large number of false reports, anywhere from 30 to 100 blacks and whites had been killed by the secret vigilante groups. Now was the time for the KGC to capitalize on all the anxiety generated by the triple threat of Indians, Abolitionists, and Black Republicans by expanding and recruiting for the organization in the days leading up to the election.[21]

With or without the presence of the Bickley family, new military companies were forming all over the state. The day before Bickley's arrival in Galveston and Houston, the *Weekly Telegraph* noted the formation of the Davis Guards, at least partially bank-rolled by their 1st Lieutenant and Treasurer, Richard W. Dowling. This was mostly an Irish company, with noncommissioned officers named R.C. Fullond, P.H. Hennessy, Ed McDonnells, Dan Gorman, P. O'Sullivan, T. Hennessy, William Paschal, L. Borkhy and John T. Jorce. This company would prove to be a very brave one during the war and would forever be known as "Dick Dowling and His Forty Irishmen" to generations of Texas schoolboys for their courageous defense at the Battle of Sabine Pass. At this time in 1860, the Knights of the Golden Circle still had many skeptics in Texas; the Corpus Christi Ranchero had said of them, "This morning another party of K.G.C., from the States, arrived here. There must be mismanagement on the part of the leaders, or else a concentration of force would be better understood." The news of the failed September mission to Mexico was still being disseminated in mid-October. A couple of weeks later The Ranchero was still bashing Bickley, quoting the Matamoros, Mexico correspondent of the New Orleans Crescent, who cautioned "all you folks not to be caught in Bickley's new humbug – the Golden Circle. The authorities here do not know hide nor hair of the matter, and it will meet with resistance from all classes. What foundation Gen. Bickley has for his movement is past my comprehension, for I know that he is not authorized to raise men on behalf of the Mexican Government. I think that all engaged in it are on a fool's errand...."[22]

What the unnamed correspondent didn't know was that George Bickley was no longer General Bickley; he had been stripped of that title in Raleigh months ago. He was now President Bickley, who reported to a board of military advisors; they had told him to postpone any movement against Mexico "until the first of

December, at which time we may be more needed at home than abroad." His advisors were now focused on the probable election of Lincoln, and the promised breakup of the United States. This is consistent with the fearful message they had promoted through the press; that if and when Lincoln got elected, all hell was going to break loose. Bickley's title of President may not have amounted to much more than an impressive designation given to a salesman to put on his business card. In fact, it seems that George and Charles Bickley were now commissioned salesmen, earning money from the $1 membership fees they collected from new recruits. George Bickley's real talent lay in making speeches and selling ideas; he had not come to Texas to invade Mexico. Upon landing in Galveston, he gave a brief interview to the *Galveston Weekly News* and left for Austin.[23]

Once in Austin, George Bickley gave his first speech on October 17 to a large crowd in which he attempted to put a positive face on the KGC, disavowing fili-bustering personally as well as for the Order. He tried to position the KGC in the public's mind as "a humanitarian society" that would "'perfect' negro slavery in the South and extend it abroad". He also emphasized that the KGC was not in league with any political party in the country. Much of his speech was vintage Bickley, with his description of the three degrees of Knights and their duties; and he included his old saw about the KGC making "the South strong in or powerful out of the Union." He did add a comparison of the KGC to the Hudson's Bay and East India Companies – "The K.G.C. is precisely such an organization as those, and as they won empires for Great Britain, so may the K.G.C. for a South-ern Confederacy." One of the reporters in attendance could not help but notice an inherent contradiction in Bickley's words: "the speaker began by denying all political objects and purposes; and he patriotically advised election of Brecken-ridge, Douglas, or Bell, if either could defeat Lincoln. – He disavowed disunion objects – and yet he insisted that there are but two parties – a Northern and South-ern party" and that anyone who thought differently than that was not patriotic. Bickley also stressed that if Lincoln was elected President, "resistance would surely follow, and the 'K.G.C.' would become the rallying army for the Southern disun-ionist." When the speaker asked the audience if they had any questions, the first person to rise was retired judge George W. Paschal, an Austin resident who had recently accepted the position of elector for the Union Party. Paschal was a Un-ionist, former newspaper editor and was opposed to Republicans and abolitionists; but he had concerns about the KGC's function as secret police, watching the peo-ple and secretly marking the baggage of travelers who they deemed suspicious.

Bickley did not deny that the KGC spied on citizens, but added, "there ought to have been such an order thirty years ago". George Paschal had asked Bickley whether he and his people would accept the results of the upcoming Presidential Election if Lincoln was the winner; or would they rebel instead? Bickley answered that Governor Pettus of Mississippi and other Southern Governors were members of the KGC, and if they or Sam Houston requested it, "his 'tried sword' would be drawn, to march to the District of Columbia" or anywhere else the Southern Governors required of him. This was all very dramatic, especially considering that Bickley had no real military experience, but others behind the curtain directing him did have the experience, and as it would be revealed shortly, there was a plot afoot.

Although John Marshall of the Austin *Texas State Gazette* was not in attendance, he had heard that Bickley was "frequently and loudly applauded." Marshall defended him in his newspaper as "a man of pure motives and patriotic spirit." As if he did not know, Marshall, himself a KGC member, closed by writing, "We are informed by some of those who were present, that the object of the Association is to foster and protect the institution of slavery against all enemies. He is a fine speaker."[24]

Governor Sam Houston had made a speech in Austin, too, just less than a month before George Bickley. Houston spoke at "The Union Mass Meeting" there on September 22. It was a lengthy speech that began with the old warrior asking forgiveness for his recent ill health; soon he got to the point: "It is said that a crisis is impending. The clamor of disunion is heard in the land." He then began to detail the many fallacies he saw in the rationale for the secession of Texas from the United States. It was not that Houston was anti-slavery or pro-abolition; he in fact owned slaves himself. "It is but natural that we all should desire the defeat of the Black Republican candidates," he continued. "Talk about frightening the North into measures by threats of dissolving the Union! It is child's play and folly. It is all the Black Republican leaders want." Houston knew his audience, and he tried to take the middle ground in order to preserve the place of Texas in the Union. Of his adversaries, the secessionists in the Hardin R. Runnels-Louis Wigfall-Elkanah Greer camp, he began by saying, "we have a new party in our midst. They have deserted the old Democracy, and under the lead of Mr. Yancey, have started what they call a Southern constitutional party." This was direct reference to the events that began at the National Democratic Convention in Charleston, South Carolina earlier that year, in which Runnels and Greer took an active part. "You hear it from the stump, you read it in their papers and in their resolutions," he explained, "that if Mr. Lincoln is elected the Union is to be dissolved. Here is a constitutional party that intends to violate the Constitution because a man is constitutionally elected Pres-ident." Then the Governor began to point fingers: "But who are the teachers of this new-fangled Southern constitutional Democracy? Are they not men like Yancey and Wigfall, who have been always regarded as beyond the pale of national Democracy? Transplants from the South Carolina nursery of disunion. Whenever and wherever the spirit of nullification and disunion has shown itself, they and their coadjutors have been found zealously at work." Houston meant this quite literally; it was not an allusion to the Charleston convention; it was a direct reference to the home state of men like Louis Wigfall, John S. Ford and others who espoused the KGC's cause. The *Palmetto State* maintained an ongoing interest in the secession of Texas: while Houston spoke of them in Austin, Texas KGC leader Ben McCulloch was headed to Columbia, South Carolina to meet with that state's political leaders. Meanwhile the Texas Governor turned to comment on the recent slave panic:

> Here in Texas they convert the misfortunes of people into political capital. Property has been burned in some instances, and here and there a case of insubordination has been found among the negroes.

> Occasionally, a scoundrel has attempted to run a negro off to sell him: and all these things are charged to abolitionism.... Town after town has been reported in ashes, and by the time the report has been found to be false, some new story to keep up the public excitement has been invented.

> The people of the South have been filled with horror by these accounts, and instead of Texas being looked upon as the most inviting spot on earth, they turn from it as from a land accursed.

Governor Houston had publicly stated back in August that many of the stories feeding the incendiary hysteria had been manufactured "for political effect." Typically, the pro-KGC press responded: "old Sam does not believe any more in the rascality of abolitionists than he did in the villainy of the Indians." Houston had finally disbanded Middleton T. Johnson's unsuccessful anti-Indian crusade by early September. Phantom hostile Indians or the story of abolitionists leading a fiery slave revolt that began in Dallas weren't the only rumors out there; by early August it had been reported that "the citizens of Dallas now think their town was fired by two United States soldiers, who, on a former occasion, deserted Camp Colorado and were arrested by citizens of that place...." Camp Colorado was an encampment or temporary settlement for troops of the United States; it was in what was then far West Texas, now central Texas, in current-day Coleman County. Camp Colorado would become a target of the KGC soon enough. On September 22, Houston covered the underlying problem with the secessionist press:

> We all know how every occurrence has been magnified by the disunion press and leaders and scattered abroad, and for no other purpose than to arouse the passions of the people and drive them into the Southern Disunion movement; for if you can make the people believe that the terrible accounts of abolition plots here are true, they will be ready for anything sooner than suffer their continuance. Who are the men that are circulating these reports, and taking the lead in throwing the country into confusion?[25]

Houston knew who those men were; he had intrigued with them previously, and would yet again, so fixated was he on his dream of the conquest of Mexico. He was running out of physical strength and stamina, and his September 22 speech in Austin was his valedictorial. His time had come and gone even while he was still in office. Now George Bickley, Charles Bickley and Virginius Groner had come, and were canvassing the entire state together. Groner was a Virginian who had formerly served in a Ranger company in Texas under John R. Baylor before returning to his home state; he had spent most of his time opening new Castles in Virginia and North Carolina. On October 3 the Democrat Party of Texas had its own "Grand Democratic Mass Meeting" in Dallas; it was advertised that "The most distinguished and valued citizens of the State are invited...."

> Hon. H.R. Runnels, Hon. John Hemphill, Hon. L.T. Wigfall, Hon. John H. Reagan, Hon. Frank Lubbock, Gen. T.N. Waul, Hon. M. D. Graham, Hon. A.T. Rainey, Hon. W.B. Wright, Hon. W.R. Scurry, Hon. G.M. Flournoy, Major John Marshall, E.H. Cushing, Major Nat. Terry, H.R. Latimer, Judge W.S. Oldham, Gen. Wm. Young, Major De Morse, and others, too numerous to mention, from every part of the State, embracing our learned men and most distinguished orators. [sic]

Most if not all, the names listed above as invited speakers for the Dallas mass meeting were either already KGC members or would be soon; some of them like Nat Terry and John Marshall were responsible for spreading the incendiary panic just weeks before. Several were newspaper editors; they were all supporting the Presidential bid of John C. Breckinridge, himself a KGC member and the choice of the break-away Seceding Convention attended by Texas delegates Lubbock and

Runnels. Not long after the Breckinridge forces met in Dallas, John R. Baylor and his brother George W. Baylor appeared in John Marshall's newspaper office in Austin. George W. Baylor had told the U.S. Census taker in 1860 that his profession was "Indian killer." Marshall wrote of their visit:

> We look forward to a bright career for Capt. B.... We regret to learn that the Indians continue to molest our frontier people. The time cannot be distant when a campaign will be made by an outraged people which will obliterate every vestige of the marauding redskins. Several of our citizens called at the Hotel to pay their respects to these gallant gentlemen, and to see the many scalps of the Indians lately killed by them, and other trophies, but Capt. B. and brother had left for San Antonio.

They had left for San Antonio, no doubt to inform and coordinate with KGC leadership the next venture the Baylor brothers and Hamner would spring on the public. It would be announced before the end of the year. Perhaps they sought the counsel of Charles Bickley during their stay in the Alamo City. Major Charles Bickley was Captain of one of the KGC Castles in the city of San Antonio; they called it the Charles Bickley Castle. As for the countryside, it is known that Baylor toured different towns in the State during this time, displaying the scalps of nine Indians allegedly killed in a fight on June 28 at Paint Creek, using these as props for fund raising purposes, with the contributions sent to Weatherford for the benefit of the Hamner-Baylor organization of a private army to defend the frontier.[25]

George Bickley resumed his public speaking tour on October 22, with a speech in the town of Bastrop, county seat of Bastrop County, which was home to 2,417 slaves out of a total population of 7,006. According to a local observer, even skeptics were convinced by Bickley:

> We are informed, that the General met with success in enlisting Knights, and initiating them into the secrets of the 'Mystic Golden Circle.' From what we hear those say who went in, it must be a very good thing; for they seem well pleased with it. It is certainly not a 'Disunion Trick,' gotten up by Southern Fire Eaters; for some of the strongest Union men about town went in, and appear to be well pleased. We expect the General will meet with a full share of success here, from what we learn.

It is after all the hallmark of many a commissioned salesman to stretch the truth, and when the truth of the KGC's real purpose was revealed later, there would be some dissatisfied customers wanting out of the organization. Still, at this juncture, it was all about making the numbers look impressive. Charles Bickley had left the entourage not long before and arrived in San Antonio the same day that George Bickley spoke before the crowd in Bastrop. Charles Bickley, "the Major," called on the editor of the *Alamo Express* where he made it known that the was staying at the City Hotel, and that the KGC still had plans for Mexico. While Charles stayed around San Antonio, George Bickley continued his travels across the State; on October 30 he spoke at the Courthouse in Houston before "a large and curious audience" where he stated that "No movement against Mexico will be made until after the result of the election is known...." It was reported by the Telegraph that Bickley and his speech were well-received, and that "Some forty gentlemen of this city were initiated into the order after the meeting was over...." The Telegraph opined that "a civil war may be thrust upon us" and concluded with "Therefore we bid the K.G.C.'s God speed." During the one-week period from October 28 to November 3, George Bickley reported that he had opened seven new Castles in Texas: one each in Austin, La Grange, Brenham, Chapel Hill, Houston, Navasota and Huntsville, for a total of 208 new members. One month later it was reported that nearly 190 men had joined the Houston castle alone. The leadership of a Castle was subject to change, but at least initially, the leader of the Austin Castle was George W. Harris. George was born in Virginia, served in the U.S. Army briefly before moving to Waco in 1859 where he was a merchant until the beginning of the war. The new Castle at La Grange was under the command of Ben Shropshire, an attorney who with his brother John practiced law in Texas; he also was one of the editors of the La Grange True Issue. Like many KGC, he was a former Know-Nothing or American Party member. Dr. John Lark oversaw the Brenham Castle with twenty-six members; George W. Chapell ran the Chapell Hill Castle, located about fifty-seven miles northwest of Houston; the town was named for one of his relatives. William C. Edwards, a Mexican American war veteran, former member of the State Legislature and editor of the True Southron was tapped to run the new Houston Castle. John L. Lloyd oversaw the small seven-man castle in Navasota and Thomas Carothers, the Superintendent of the Texas State Prison located in Huntsville and a cousin of Governor Sam Houston, was in charge of the forty-eight members of the Huntsville Castle. Sometime during this seven-day run, George Bickley and Virginius Groner had a conference with Governor Houston; it is unknown what they dis-cussed.[26]

About the time that George Bickley was concluding the first week of his speaking and recruiting drive on November 3, an unknown, confidential inform-ant infiltrated a KGC "Council of War" in Texas. Sometime just before or after the Presidential Election, the informant passed information to the Inspector Gen-eral of the U.S. Army of a KGC plot to seize Washington D.C. and inaugurate KGC member John Breckinridge as President of the United States. Something was afoot; on November 5, a Massachusetts newspaper reported that printed ma-terial had been distributed in rural New Jersey warning, "General Bickley marching upon Washington" – among other dire predictions – "in *New York Herald* style". Something along those lines had been implied in the KGC address in Raleigh, when it was said, "The Knights of the Golden Circle may find its Mexico in the District of Columbia." Although no arrests are known to have been made, the threat was taken seriously. The subterranean plot may explain a curious exchange between known Texas KGC leader John H. Reagan, then representing Texas in the U.S. Congress in Washington, and Oran Milo Roberts, a Texas State Supreme Court judge and a probable KGC member, by letter on November 1, 1860:

> Your reference to the Knights of the Golden Circle, and the supposition that the organization may have in view some plan of action on behalf of the South, and implied disapproval of any secret movement for such a pur-pose meets my unqualified approval.

> A secret movement, for such a purpose, could not but prove disastrous in the extreme to the cause of the South....

O.M. Roberts was related to known KGC leader George W. Chilton by mar-riage and was a prominent secessionist. Although Judge Roberts wasn't in favor of this conspiracy, he was to play a major role in the conspiracy behind the seces-sion of Texas from the Union in less than three months. Up until secession, Judge Roberts was corresponding with known KGC members like Richard B. Hubbard and John H. Reagan and would meet with other KGC in a closed-door meeting immediately after the National Election held on November 6.[27]

Abraham Lincoln's name wasn't even allowed on the ballot in Texas and other Southern states; basically Texans had three choices, two of them Democrats: either the KGC candidate, John C. Breckinridge, Stephen Douglas, the Northern Democrats choice, or John Bell of the Constitutional Union Party. The final tally in Texas shows that 75% of the vote, equal to 47,454 ballots went for Breckinridge; only 18 people in the entire State voted for Douglas. Abraham Lincoln won the

Presidency with the smallest percentage of the popular vote in American history. Lincoln did get enough Electoral College votes to win even if all other votes cast against him had been given to a single candidate. Historians have argued that the events of the Charleston Convention, which split the Democratic Party and insured Lincoln's victory, was the result of bad luck, or irrational behavior. However, as previously discussed, this author found evidence of a KGC plan to destroy the Democratic Party as early as 1859 to which John Marshall of Texas was connected. In addition, a recent analysis of the 1860 Presidential Election using modern techniques of election counter-factionals and applied spatial voting theory, shows that Breckinridge never had a reasonable chance of winning, and that support for his candidacy was "only reasonable if the intention were to elect Lincoln." Jefferson Davis and known KGC member Robert Toombs of Georgia at one point met with Breckinridge to encourage him to accept the nomination of the "seceding convention." Davis convinced Breckinridge that the other Democratic candidates would accept a "fusion strategy" to get behind a single party candidate. As the authors of the 2005 study conclude, "If Davis meant, however, to ensure Lincoln's victory by convincing Breckinridge to enter the race by disingenuously concocting a fusion scenario, then his gambit was quite shrewd." By so doing, Jefferson Davis ensured that he would become President of his own country, the Confederate States of America – a very shrewd strategy indeed. The summary statement of the 2005 analysis is quite interesting in retrospect:

> In summary, our series of counterfactual analyses demonstrates that a successful Breckinridge candidacy was never a realistic possibility. We find that the failure to select a candidate in Charleston combined with Breckinridge's entrance into the race increased the likelihood of a Lincoln victory. We believe that this should have been an inescapable conclusion for party leaders, like Davis, who had spent years developing a keen sensitivity to the positions of state electorates, representatives, and senators on the slavery issue. [28]

In other words, Jefferson Davis and other KGC leaders cynically fixed the election so that they could shepherd the rank and file towards secession and the creation of The Golden Circle, a slave empire that would span the Southern United States, Mexico, Central America and the Caribbean. John Bell, one of the losing candidates, wrote,

I repeat, the Breckinridge movement must have been made designedly to elect Lincoln. This design, you will remark, I impute to the few arch leaders, not to the rank & file of the delegates from Va. N.C. Tenn. & Mo. These latter are dupes, but not altogether innocent. The malignancy of some of them led them to prefer the election of Lincoln, with all its possible evil consequences, to the election of Douglas.

It would take a while for the election results to be known in Texas because of the limitations of distance and the communication technology of the day. In the meantime, George Bickley renewed his travels across Texas in the service of promoting KGC membership. On November 7, he was in Marshall and left the following day for the riverboat town and port of Jefferson. Armed groups of men continued to form in scattered portions of the State; Bickley was not the only one organizing. On November 8, it was reported by the Corpus Christi Ranchero "on almost positive authority" that there was "a large body of armed men, mostly from other counties" in the northern part of the Nueces River Basin. It was still not known if Lincoln had been elected. Citizens in the Black Belt community of Brazoria County, the fifth-largest in terms of slave population, scheduled a public meeting for November 24, "in the event of Lincoln's election to consult on the course to be pursued to sustain our rights in the confederacy." At the same time in Corsicana there was an unnamed group moving "to organize a company to be armed with Hall's breech-loading gun." West of Corsicana in Bosque County, veteran Ranger J. B. "Buck" Barry had organized a small company the previous month; another had been raised in Erath County under John Lowe, and yet another in Jack County by secessionist Harris A. Hamner.[29]

The following day after these reports, on November 9, the *Navarro Express* in Corsicana printed notice of "A Grand Buffalo Hunt." The front-page notice proposed in large letters that the Ranger companies in the State - like the ones just forming – "ALL FRIENDLY TO THE CAUSE OF THE FRONTIER – AND OPPOSED TO THE [author: in still larger letters] 'RESERVE INDIANS' will hold themselves in readiness to take a grand buffalo hunt during the present winter." The emphasis on opposition to the Reservation Indians, who no longer resided in the State of Texas, but had been moved across the Red River into Indian Territory the previous year, reveals that this expedition was no ordinary buffalo hunt. It was also plain to see that H.A. Hamner and John R. Baylor were behind it all, as the notice continued:

All persons in the State desirous of joining the party will address 'Buffalo' Weatherford, Parker county, Texas; so that he or they can, by circular, be apprised of the time of starting, as well as what kind of equipage will be necessary – what amount of ammunition will be required – the length of time that will probably be consumed, and all other information necessary. 'Secret Circulars' will be forwarded to all true men desiring to join the hunt. None genuine unless printed at the 'White Man' office, bearing facsimiles of 'BUFFALO.' – *White Man.* [sic]

Baylor and Hamner were the publishers of the *White Man.* So, this was what Baylor, Hamner, and their state-wide network of KGC funding sources had been raising money towards. It was interesting timing since Lincoln had just been elected; it was another way to militarize and mobilize the frontier portion of Texas in preparation for secession and its consequences. Before the "Grand Buffalo Hunt" could get underway, one of the Baylor brothers had a meeting to attend in Austin. Immediately after word was received of the election results by the power brokers in Texas, Judge Oran M. Roberts, KGC member John S. Ford, State Treasurer C.H. Randolph, Attorney General George Flournoy, KGC member George W. Baylor and William P. Rogers "and others" met in Flournoy's office to discuss their reaction to the election of a "Black Republican" as President. Judge Roberts took charge and presented three possible courses of action for this "council of war" to reach a decision that would affect the entire State. As Roberts saw it, they could demand that Governor Houston call a special session of the legislature; or they could attempt to elect a new Governor in 1861 that would be more sympathetic to secession, or they could convince the common people of Texas through a grass-roots movement to demand a secession convention. The council assembled agreed on the third option and embarked on a campaign of mass public meetings throughout the State. Less than a week later, John S. Ford called for a pro-secession meeting in Austin held at the Travis County courthouse; John R. Baylor was one of the featured speakers to the crowd of several hundred, who passed resolutions demanding a special session of the legislature on a call from Governor Houston. Baylor's speech and those of the others had their desired affect; the KGC was controlling and delivering the message.

The behind-the-scenes work towards the "Grand Buffalo Hunt" got underway, but many Texans were not fooled as to its real purpose. John Newcomb, the publisher of the San Antonio *Alamo Express*, had this to say about the "buffalo hunt":

Before the call for a convention was made, there were a few rash men who premeditated forcing Texas out of the Union, without resorting to the humbug of conventions. Capt. John Baylor, a bad man, with a murderous reputation, raised three to four hundred men, in the northern counties, with the avowed object of making a descent on San Antonio and capturing the large supplies of Government commissaries, ordnance, arms &c., guarding which was a small U.S. force. The citizens of San Antonio flew to arms to repel the invasion, and Gen. Twiggs was forced to make a show of resistance, by ordering in reinforcements from the frontier posts, but before they reached the city, the 'Knights of the Golden Circle' petitioned Gen. Twiggs to countermand the order.... The old traitor took this excuse and did countermand his order. But Baylor subsided, not caring to try his luck against the wide-awake San Antonians.

For the time being the attack on the Federal Arsenal at San Antonio was put on hold, to be revisited when Ben McCulloch got back in town. McCulloch was still in South Carolina meeting with secession leaders from that State; he would prove to be a much cooler head in action than John R. Baylor.[30]

The results of the Presidential Election were certainly known in Waco by November 15. A group, probably the KGC organization built there by Captain James F. Davis, had a torchlight parade that night in which an effigy of Lincoln was ridden on a rail through town by two compliant slaves. The Lone Star flag was raised over several buildings, the crowds of people were said to be heartened by "the determined stand taken by the Cotton-growing States" and two companies of military were already organized and ready for action. One of the first mass-meetings held as proscribed by O.M. Roberts, John S. Ford, George W. Baylor and the others who met in Austin, was in the KGC stronghold of Dallas on Saturday, November 17. Perhaps it was the residency there of KGC leader John J. Good that encouraged the fast start, or the presence of the Knights Templar encampment. Slave-panic promoter Charles Pryor's newspaper, the *Dallas Herald*, proudly and intimately detailed the proceedings, described as "a large crowd...the most intense feeling pervaded the entire company. The long-dreaded news of the election of Abraham Lincoln seemed to have prepared the public mind for a free and calm discussion of the importance of that object." Speakers included Judge Nat Burford, Colonel John Taylor Coit, Colonel J. M. Crockett and Nathaniel H. Darnell, who "was grandly eloquent in speaking of the coming glories of the Lone Star Republic." Crockett and Darnell were original members of John J. Good's

KGC company, formed on March 12, 1859; John T. Coit would form his own companies, which more than likely were KGC units, outside of Dallas. On a motion of Judge Burford, a committee was appointed to draft resolutions which would be sent to Austin; among the committee members W.H. Hoard, J.N. Smith, R.W. Lunday, John M. Crockett, and George Beeler were added the names of Judge Burford, T.J. Nash and John J. Good. Robert W. Lunday was also an original member of John Good's company. The first resolution reached by the committee was "That his Excellency Governor Houston be, and he is hereby most respectfully asked to convene the State Legislature...." The third resolution called for Texas to secede from the Union. The resolutions were unanimously approved; then the crowd called for John Taylor Coit to speak, which he did, "with all the vim of a true and gallant Son of the Old Palmetto State...in a patriotic, eloquent, and thrilling address, which was well received and appreciated by the audience." Sam Houston had warned people about those Sons of the Palmetto State (South Carolina) in his mass meeting speech in Austin on September 22; so here was another such prodigal son conducting a KGC forum in Dallas. After Coit finished, on motion by Robert W. Lunday, the meeting was adjourned. This meeting in Dallas, early on in the process designed by those men in Austin, was a blueprint for many others to follow.[31]

The same day as the Dallas mass meeting, another meeting was held in Tyler, Texas "to organize a military company, or companies throughout the county; and also, to make arrangements for a county mass meeting at an early day." Tyler was the residence of O.M. Robert's brother-in-law George W. Chilton, who had organized the nucleus of the KGC in his town as early as February; now, with passions running high, it was time for the Order to reveal itself and expand its membership. November 17, it was also reported that George Bickley and Virginius Groner had been in Marshall for several days, and that "the order was quite numerous in this county already." Of course, it was; Marshall was the home of KGC Commander Elkanah Greer and his business partner Louis T. Wigfall. At least one Castle had been in place in Marshall since 1858, if not sooner. George Bickley soon left the State of Texas in charge of his relative, Charles Bickley; it was reported by the Indianola Courier that "the general headquarters of the order... are now located in San Antonio, to which point are to be directed all letters asking for information." The Indianola paper also reported that the KGC Castle in La Grange was "steadily increasing in numbers and popularity. It now has 60 members, among whom the most respectable and enterprising of our citizens may be numbered." Thomas S.

Cook would shortly be revealed as the organizer of the La Grange Castle; he was the former editor of the La Grange True Issue. He was not the only KGC revealing himself; on November 22, 1860, sixty-one members of the KGC in Texas revealed themselves in a published "Call for a State Convention." The earliest version of this notice, which would be republished by other newspapers later, first appeared in the Clarksville Standard. Nineteenth century historian Hubert Howe Bancroft published an oft-quoted account of this event, stating that all of the "sixty" names posted in support of the "Call for a State Convention" were KGC members; there were actually sixty-one names, and many of them were known members of the KGC. The rest of them certainly by their actions and associations should be considered KGC as well. Among the readily recognizable names are known KGC members Henry E. McCulloch, John J. Good, A.T. Rainey, D.M. Pendergast, John Gregg, W.S. Oldham, Roger Q. Mills, C.M. Winkler, George W. White, John R. Baylor, George W. Baylor, Thomas Green, George W. Guess, Ed Clark, W.M. Hardeman, and a host of others.[31] These were not all of the KGC members in the State, however.

For San Antonio resident Charles Anderson, "the outbreak of the Rebellion," or the American Civil War, started on November 24. On that day, a public meeting had been set for Breckinridge voters to be held at the Alamo, "to take action for the secession of the State." Charles Anderson had been invited to speak for the Union, as he was a well-known loyalist in Bexar County; his brother Robert Anderson was commanding the U.S. troops soon to be stationed at Fort Sumter. Charles Anderson agreed to appear as a speaker for the Unionists of Bexar County at the mass meeting on November 24. As he described the affair in his own words,

> It was the design and under the management of the K.G.C., and its intended proceedings were perhaps the most 'cut and dried affair' ever known amongst the shams of politics. The Rev. Dr. Boring, a celebrated and very able divine of the Methodist Episcopal Church, South, was to open the services by a wise, sober, and pious argument of the questions, constitutional, political, and military. Colonel Wilcox, an ex-member of Congress from Mississippi, and soon a candidate for the same office in the new Confederacy, and an eloquent stumper, was to follow with the usual fire-eating exhortations, threats, and promises. Then a Mr. Upson, a San Antonio lawyer, from Buffalo, N. Y., was to conclude the grand first act of the dread drama... in Southern pro-slavery gushes, as was so usual, wherever, as too often, a Yankee did southernize himself in politics.

John Allen Wilcox was a high-ranking and influential KGC member in San Antonio; he would help draft the Ordinance of Secession for the State of Texas. He was a member of the San Antonio Castle, one of the largest in the State in terms of membership, with over 100 members. By the beginning of the next year, there would be three different castles in San Antonio, and a fourth would be added by the end of the summer. There were many KGC residing in the San Antonio area; the city was the largest in Texas at the time, with an official population of 8,235. Christopher Columbus Upson was the San Antonio lawyer whom Charles Anderson referred to, and he was born in New York – as was the original leader and one of the five founders of the KGC, John Anthony Quitman. As San Antonio resident James P. Newcomb would later write of the KGC, "Many of the secession leaders were either apostate sons of New England or foreigners. Gen. Waul [author: Thomas Neville Waul of Texas] is an Englishman but claims to be a South Carolinian." Like many KGC members, Upson enjoyed a position of privilege during the war to come, functioning as a voluntary aide with the rank of Colonel, while acting as a special treasury agent for the Confederacy; strictly a non-combat role. He did not have to get his hands dirty unless he wanted it so.[32]

The Reverend Dr. Jessee Boring was on the dais to preach the Gospel according to the KGC. When he had finished, it was Charles Anderson's turn to mount the stage. Anderson, a native of Kentucky and a slave owner even then, was still in favor of the Union and gave a stirring speech in its favor. An observer of the event later wrote, "Anderson replied, and took the assembled multitude by storm. They were perfectly astonished at the oratory and logic, and when he was through with his reply, they cheered him, and the band played 'Yankee Doodle' and 'The Star Spangled Banner'...." The final part of Anderson's speech is given below:

> Must the true, permanent, and invaluable interests of the Southern people – their lands, their slaves, their property, personal and public, their peace, their patriotism, all, all be forever thus made a sacrifice to mere politicians, for the sole benefit of merest politicians? Will our Southern statesmen (for we have yet a few statesmen left us) thus always continue to de-vote all their faculties and energies to the single end of propagating the faith of slavery for its diffusion as a political institution, and in the soils and climates, where neither 'King Cotton' nor 'Queen Sugar' can ever reign or reside?

As soon as Anderson finished, it was said by an observer that "if the vote could have been taken then, there would not have been fifty votes for secession in the town." Seeing the changing emotions of the mob, KGC leader John A. Wilcox "ascended the platform, and told the people, that they had been deceived in this man Anderson,"

> ...that they thought him an ordinary Texas farmer, while on the contrary he was one of the sharpest politicians and best stump speakers in the whole country; that he was a friend of Wendall Phillips, Garrison, and other Abolitionists.

When Anderson vehemently denied the charges and called Wilcox a liar while trying to get at him on the platform, it was said, "There were twenty pistols drawn in a second" according to an observer. Anderson wrote, "but for the brave and disinterested violent interference of Mr. Story, the head of the K.G.C.s, in actually dragging me out of a fight, doubtless there would have been, from this my folly, much bloodshed and many deaths.... For his K.G.C.s, on the ground, appeared to me the majority." He also noted that the KGC members were all "doubly armed" while the Unionists "so far as I know, were all unarmed." That was the last time Anderson spoke in Texas as a Unionist; eventually he escaped the State and joined the Union army. And what of Mr. Story, "the head of the K.G.C.s"? He was William R. Storey, a respected citizen of San Antonio who applied early in the war for a Captain's position in the Commissary Department, another non-combat position. His application to Jefferson Davis was signed by "citizens, and members of the State & National Legislatures" including known KGC members John S. Ford, Asa Mitchell, Samuel A. Maverick, A.J. Rice, C.H. Randolph, the State Treasurer; William Henry Parsons, the noted fire-eater and member of the Texas delegation to the 1860 National Democratic Convention in Charleston; R.W. Brahan, N.H. Darnell and many others. KGC members were pledged to always lookout for their brother Knights.[33]

Ben McCulloch was still in South Carolina, otherwise he would have lent his name to the "Call for a State Convention" alongside his brother Henry. On November 28, he penned a letter from Columbia to John Marshall at the *Texas State Gazette*, which led off with "Don't let our gallant State be behind all her sisters of the South in resisting Black Republican aggression." McCulloch continued by writing that South Carolina "would be out of the Union by the first of January next." Of major concern to the "Distinguished Ranger" as Marshall designated him, was the possibility that President Lincoln would "remove the federal arms from the arsenals of the State." He was obviously signaling that he intended to seize the Federal Arsenal in San Antonio, as John R. Baylor had sought to do just days earlier under the guise of his bogus "Buffalo Hunt." The general tone of McCulloch's letter was aggressively adversarial:

> Will Southern men, will Texians, submit to these insults from our coequals in a government established by our forefathers for all their children alike? Never! Never! Can we have any hope in the sense of justice on the part of such people? No! Then let us act together in one common cause, and we will avoid bloodshed and war. If we submit now, will we not be goaded into resistance by the continued aggressions of these people?

There would be hell to pay when he got home. In the meantime, things were progressing in his home State. On November 29, Charles Bickley sent an update to the *Houston Telegraph* with summaries of recent communications with various KGC castles around Texas. Among those contacts listed were J.B. Lubbock of Bastrop, one of the brothers of Francis R. Lubbock; David C. Jones of Owensville in Robertson County; Ned P. Clifford of Navasota, Grimes County; George W. Harris of Austin, Travis County; Thomas S. Cook of La Grange, Fayette County; and Samuel Mather, also a high-ranking Mason in Gabriel Mills, Williamson County. In addition, notice was given George Bickley that "letters have been forwarded to you at Marshall". Notice was also given to "Report to Headquarters" for James Guest of Boonville, Brazos County; Thomas B. Haynes of Independence, Washington County; and John L. Winston of Caldwell, Burleson County, as well as "other Commandants of K.G.C. Castles, who have not reported to Headquarters will please do so immediately."[34]

On November 30, Virginius Groner, back in Virginia with the title of Commander, 1st Virginia Regiment, KGC, sent a letter to Mississippi Governor J.J. Pettus, offering the services of twenty-thousand men if needed to defend his State in case of its secession from the United States. George Bickley had already exposed Governor Pettus as a member of the KGC, but the membership of what had once been a secret Order were becoming publicly defiant and bold. In Texas, this defiance was often displayed with flags and symbols. In Dallas, it was reported that many of their citizens were "wearing the cockade of our national colors, blue ribbon with a golden star. Some wear cockades of red." Described as "a knot of blue ribbons with a military button at the center, pinned to the left side" of one's hat, the cockade was a symbol of solidarity with rebellious Southerners in States like South Carolina, where the blue cockade was the mark of a member of the Minute Men – and some, like Horace Greeley of the *New York Tribune*, believed "Minute Men" to be another name for a KGC company. In the Texas Gulf Coast port city of Indianola, the Courier had noticed, "a number of blue cockades, surmounted by metalic [sic] five-pointed stars, worn on the hats or coats, of many of our citizens. The cockade is the badge common to the citizens of the Southern States. The star is peculiar to Texians." The Courier hoped that this combination of symbols would be adopted throughout the State, "by those favoring resistance by State action to the principles of the Black Republican party." Also peculiar to Texas was the raising of the Lone Star flag, the old flag from the days of the Republic of Texas before it became a member of the United States. Once the news of Lincoln's election got around, the Lone Star flag was reported flying in Galveston, as well as "every steeple east, and many are in favor of the Lone Star Republic once more." Clearly, many Texans were under the impression that when their State seceded, they would go it alone as an independent republic once more. The idea of joining a confederacy of slave-owning States was not yet on their minds.[35]

Resistance to the legitimate government of the United States was on the minds of Texas KGC leaders and their propagandists. The *Navarro Express* had been promoting the formation of uniformed military companies across the State since late November. On December 3, their offices were visited by William T. Patton of Flowerdale in neighboring Freestone County, now "orderly sergeant in a new company organized in that neighborhood called the Prairie Wake Ups". W. T. Patton was showing off the new uniform of his company, consisting of "a frock coat and pants made of homemade jeans, with red and white worsted stripes on the breast". William T. Patton was associated with both the Fairfield and Corsicana KGC Castles, so his presence in Navarro County that day was to help John B. Jones and others organize their Corsicana Castle. In this same edition of the *Navarro Express*, the editor reported that a military company had been formed in Navarro County and was to meet, probably for the first time on Saturday December 15. There were "already seventy-five names on the roll and additions every day, and doubtless many will join after the organization of the company." The editor wasn't finished, though: he was concerned that Navarro County was not pulling its weight:

> Our county is behind all her sisters in this matter, and we think it time they
> were waking up. Freestone has five military companies already fixed out to

fight, and Navarro with as large a voting population, has yet only resolved to have one. Come up on the day aboved [sic] named, organize and go to work making preparations....

Not every editor in Texas was as gung-ho about supporting a secret organization that propounded the creation of a police state. The Marshall *Texas Republican* took a step back from its unquestioning support of the KGC in early December. While saying, "We believe in Southern organizations" but hoped that "whatever is done, shall be done openly and with the knowledge of our entire people. In other words, we do not believe in secret organizations, and particularly secret military and political organizations. We regard them as dangerous in a republic." Poor fool; the writer apparently really believed that the Republic of Texas was returning. It was a little too late for that to happen.[36]

Down in the Black Belt of Texas, the KGC was vigorously pursuing its agenda. On December 8, the citizens of Colorado County organized a Secession Club, and formed a committee to interrogate their county's current State Congressmen, Senator C.C. Herbert and Representative Samuel J. Redgate, as to their views on secession. The primary mover behind the secession club was former Secretary of State Thomas Scott Anderson, who served under Governor Hardin Richard Runnels, a known KGC member; T. Scott Anderson had joined the Order of the Lone Star earlier which virtually guarantees his KGC membership. The committee members were William J. Herbert, E. P. Whitfield, John C. Upton, and Howel A. Tatum, a known KGC organizer associated with the Columbus, Alleyton, Eagle Lake and Wharton Castles, while serving as Captain of the Columbus Castle in Colorado County. The interrogation of their politicians was a litmus test; Senator Claiborne C. Herbert had no problem passing that test; he was a plantation owner with forty-seven slaves and voted to convene the Secession Convention. He was also identified as being one of the "respectable citizens" enlisted in one of the unnamed "military companies" in Colorado County in December 1860 – meaning he was a KGC member. Representative Samuel Joseph Redgate had a more difficult time; he was one of a few State representatives who defied the majority and opposed secession. His second term of office from 1860 to 1861 would be his last although he did stay in Texas until after the war.[37]

As it was in Texas in the summer of 1860, Kansas was locked in the grip of a severe heat wave and drought. As the nation drew closer to war within itself, some of the old tensions flared up again; one of Abolitionist/terrorist John

Brown's former associates, a Kansas Jayhawker named James Montgomery, became actively involved in terrorizing the pro-slavery population of Kansas again. Fearing attacks from pro-slavery forces from Texas, Montgomery went back East to raise money for guns and ammunition. Returning home to Linn County, Kansas on September 8, 1860, Montgomery found his neighbors greatly excited about the lynching of alleged abolitionists in Texas that had begun with the burning of Dallas earlier that summer. Refugees from North Texas, as many as sixty or seventy at a time, had arrived at Leavenworth around mid-October, bringing tales of terrible persecution and slaughter of free-state men. These refugees were reported to be from the Texas counties of Grayson, Collin, Denton, Tarrant and Johnson, "which they represent to be the worst afflicted part of Texas." Rumors were circulating of a plot by pro-slavery men to invade Kansas and extend the slaughter that began in North Texas. On November 12, one of Montgomery's associates known as Charles R. Jennison, lynched a man named Russell Hinds who was accused of kidnap-ping an escaped slave and returning him to his owner. Montgomery did not take part in the action but was outspoken and approved of the killing. Montgomery personally witnessed another killing of a pro-slavery man a day or so later, and in a few more days, he and his men did capture and hang another pro-slavery man named Sam Scott. James Montgomery believed that the execution of John Brown had encouraged his old enemies to revive the "Blue Lodges" and systematically exterminate all the anti-slavery forces in Linn County; he claimed that he had "incontestable evidence" to prove it. Consequently, the press in Missouri began to exaggerate reports about the threat of Montgomery and his men; soon the rumor was that Montgomery could raise twenty-thousand men to invade Missouri to perpetrate mass murder.

By December 12, Charles Pryor of the *Dallas Herald* had seized on this story for his own purposes, in an apparent attempt to reprise his success in stirring the panicky, fearful citizens of North Texas again. In this latest alarm, he wrote, "Montgomery is to be guided into Texas by certain abolitionist preachers, expelled from this State...to avenge the injuries inflicted on them by citizens of this State." He then concluded that "since their plans were made known in the Bewley letter, we need not be surprised at any enormity that may be attempted by them." Pryor's immediate recommendation was for the County of Dallas to arm and equip a company of men for immediate protection. In the meantime, U.S. troops had been sent to arrest Montgomery in Kansas; by the time they reached his camp on December 6, Montgomery and his men had disbanded and vanished. That wouldn't be the end of the story for Charles Pryor, though; he would do his best to keep the people paranoid. The *Navarro Express* also continued to do its part; it not only suggested that Navarro County organize against this newest threat to the frontier, but that all of the military companies being formed in the State should join Baylor and Hamner's Grand Buffalo Hunt, now slated to begin in January.[38]

By December 15, the KGC in Austin was running advertisements in the *Texas State Gazette* publicly announcing their meetings. In that same edition of the *Gazette*, John Marshall and his staff reported that Reverend Jesse Boring had sent them a copy of the speech he had given in San Antonio at the mass meeting there on November 24. The *Gazette* described the KGC-approved Gospel of Boring as "a splendid argument...in which he demonstrated the necessity for prompt resistance on the part of Texas to Black Republican rule. We intend to publish it. We rejoice that all classes of our citizens are devoting themselves to the defense of their country." Other religious figures were joining in: the *Navarro Express* published the fund-raising schedule of Reverend R.E. Sanders, who was to tour communities in Ellis, Navarro, Freestone, Limestone and Hill counties, "on behalf of the suffering people living on the frontier. Contributions of men and means for their protection earnestly solicited." Hamner had started another story in the White Man about marauding Indians killing whole families on the frontier. The area West of Fort Worth, and outside Jacksboro where this latest outrage was reported to have taken place, was so remote that it was difficult to confirm these stories. Soon Charles Pryor pounced, in great big letters in the December 16 edition of the *Dallas Herald*:

EXCITING NEWS.

900 Indians reported on Red River.

The Whole Frontier Threatened.

Indians and Abolitionists Combined!

The thrilling and scary story had come in Tuesday evening as the *Herald* was set to go to press, from Joe A. Carroll, "a well-known and reliable gentleman" of Denton County, with a letter from "Capt. W.L. Fletcher" to back up the story. The letters were sent to the publisher of the *Herald*, Mr. Swindell, the Knight Templar and member of John J. Good's KGC company, the Dallas Light Artillery. The report from Mr. Carroll was that the Indians were now only fifty miles away from Denton, having driven the terrified citizens of the western counties before them like frightened sheep. Carroll pleaded, "in God's name send us men, arms and ammunition.... Do send us all the assistance you can." Captain Fletcher's accompanying letter was no less dramatic:

> The Indians, in large bodies are collecting at the mouth of Farmers Creek on Red River, and dancing war dances, and we are informed that they are dancing over the Scalps that was taken in Jack and Parker.

> The Shawnees, Caddoes, Kickapoos, and other tribes are together, and they have taken large droves of horses American that they have stolen, and that is not all, they are stealing daily from our citizens [sic]....we are all well assured that this is a move of the Abolitionists and Indians together to overcome Texas. Come to our rescue and that in haste....

> Lt. Balor [sic] and Hamner are there tell them to come.

The public waited for further news of the impending disaster. Conveniently, and likely encouraged by the perceived threat to North Texas of the Kansas Abolitionist forces, on December 15, the men of Dallas County met and organized the Dallas Minute Men, consisting of 75 privates and seven officers; the officers being J. M. Crockett, Captain; J. C. McCoy, 1st Lieutenant; A.A. Johnson; 2nd Lieutenant; E.C. Browder, second 2nd Lieutenant; William Traughber; 1st sergeant; John H. Bingham, 2nd sergeant; and N.H. Darnell, ensign. Just about all the men in Dallas were in more than one military company; Nathaniel H. Darnell had formed his own company of Rangers as well. One could imagine that the men were doing about all they could do to respond to all the reported threats. John J. Good's still extant Dallas Light Artillery company was equipped with cannon and small arms; now known as "General John J. Good," he was to address the people of Dallas on Saturday, December 22, "upon the great question now distracting the public mind." The ladies were invited to attend also.[39]

Organization against threats real and imagined continued in other parts of the State as well. On December 20, in the Colorado County town of Columbus, the citizens were addressed at their courthouse by KGC Captain and newspaperman George H. Sweet and Major Charles Bickley. Captain Sweet addressed the political issues of the day, much as General John Good would do in Dallas, and Charles Bickley spoke of "the principles of the Order of the Knights of the Golden Circle." Captain Sweet impressed the reporter for The Citizen with his oratory skills, and his "thrilling speech" in which he stressed "the necessity of immediate action upon the part of the South." Bickley covered the standard material about the origins of the Order and its goals, and The Citizen was moved to write, "indeed all good Southern men are already K.G.C's in principle." If the KGC was successful in attaining its goals, opined *The Citizen*, it would be "the accomplishment of great good. The principles of the Order very naturally suggest a connexion with Gen. Houston's Protectorate over Mexico." [sic] The editor also made known that Charles Bickley had visited with him and had succeeded in establishing a Castle in Columbus, "numbering some ten or a dozen members." By the end of February, the Columbus Castle, captained by Howel A. Tatum, reported twenty members. By that time there were three other Castles in that same county in the towns of Oakland, Eagle Lake and Alleyton with another forty-two members. The captains of those Castles were Lawrence E. LeTulle, Isaac J. Frazar (sometimes written as Fraquor, Frazer, Frazier or Frazor) and Jonathan K. Hanks, respectively. Dr. Isaac James Frazar practiced medicine in Eagle Lake, and with his father founded the Wharton County community of Frazarville in 1857. The Wharton Castle eventually became one of the largest Castles in the State, with 100 members.[40]

On December 17, the Secession Convention of South Carolina had begun, and unlike the National Democratic Convention that had met earlier in the year, this convention was closed to the public; attendance was by invitation only. Robert Barnwell Rhett, the owner and editor of the *Charleston Mercury* had been campaigning for years for this event. Now that the destruction of the United States was underway, he celebrated it as a personal triumph. As the Secession Convention began, he had visions of himself as the president of what he called "a great Slaveholding Confederacy" that would become an empire, as he described it:

> We will expand, as our growth and civilization shall demand – over Mexico
> – over the isles of the sea – over the far-off Southern tropics – until we
> shall establish a great Confederation of Republics – the greatest, freest and
> most useful the world has ever seen.

Although he was describing The Golden Circle perfectly, which suggests that he was a member of the Order, he was in for major disappointment. Once the convention began, he found that the professional politicians had no use for him other than as a propagandist. Robert Bunch, the British Consul in Charleston kept the British Empire posted on the progress of the secessionists in South Carolina, and described the conventioneers thusly to Lord Lyons back in Britain:

> Their great aim is to be recognized by Great Britain. They try to bluster
> about England wanting cotton and being obliged to get it from them (that

is, from a Southern Confederacy, for no one, I suppose, is ass enough to think that South Carolina will form an independent empire for any great length of time) ....I always tell them not to reckon too much upon their monopoly, as the English are a determined and not a particularly stupid people, and if they are put to it, will certainly grow plenty of cotton in India or elsewhere and leave them out.

There was an important lesson for the secessionists in Texas in those words from Bunch to Lord Lyons, but none of them were listening. After hearing South Carolina's new Governor Francis W. Pickens give a speech in which he declared that his state's citizens expected their government to "become strongly military in character," Bunch wrote, on December 19, his interpretation: "Slavery can only be maintained at the point of the sword." The Knights of the Columbian Star knew that and had taken steps towards that in the design of their new society. The political leadership caste of the KGC were prepared to enforce a military dictatorship to create and maintain their empire for slavery. Elkanah Greer, the Commander-in-Chief and President of the Texas Board of War for the KGC, was married to the sister of South Carolina Governor Francis Pickens' wife. As Ben McCulloch had been in South Carolina for almost two months through October until he was reported in Georgia in late November, the close relationship between the Texas KGC and the secession movement in South Carolina is apparent. The Palmetto State became the first state to formally secede on December 20, when their ordinance of secession was signed. A copy of the South Carolina secession document would not be published for public consumption until Christmas Day. As Ben McCulloch had earlier predicted, South Carolina was out of the Union before the first of January.[41]

Readers of the *Dallas Herald* got their own KGC Christmas gift of a sort; the December 26 issue featured an update titled, "Those 900 Indians!" It began by thanking the more than ninety men from Dallas County that had ridden many miles west to rescue the poor citizens of the frontier in Jack and Parker counties. Other communities near Dallas, the towns of Mesquite and Trinity Mills had also sent "companies of gallant men, who were eager to meet the enemy and to chastise them properly." The news was that they were all returning home now, "after learning that there was no need of their service." There were no hostile Indians "dancing over the Scalps" of their alleged victims; in fact, no victims were mentioned. The article continued:

While on the subject, we would caution our friends on the frontier to use the utmost prudence in calling upon neighboring counties for assistance. Always be sure that there is real danger and then call with all your might, and it will assuredly be answered. This little expedition has been attended with considerable expense and trouble; and is well calculated to restrain the ardor of men who are ever prompt to render assistance to their fellow-citizens.

This was certainly one way for society to "become strongly military in character;" to have the average person believe that they were constantly under threat and needed to gather in armed assembly. On December 27, the newest threat from the forefront of the secession movement in South Carolina was that Major Robert Anderson, the commander of the United States garrison, had moved his men under cover of darkness from an indefensible position at Fort Moultrie to Fort Sumter. This put his force of eighty-five men in a position commanding the entrance to Charleston Harbor. It indicated to the secession leaders in Charleston that Major Ander-son intended to make a stand in defense of the Federal Arsenal at Charleston. Oddly enough, Texas KGC member Louis T. Wigfall, a former resident of South Carolina would play a lead role in the outcome of the events yet to unfold at Fort Sumner; Robert Anderson was the brother of San Antonio resident Charles Anderson.

For the time being, at least for the Christmas season, members of the KGC in Texas cheerfully looked to the future. One of them, Thomas S. Cook, named by Charles Bickley as the contact for the La Grange Castle, had instead by December 27, "gone to Northern Texas with a view of making it his home." Apparently, Mr. Cook wasn't concerned about any threats of violence in North Texas; no fear of rebellious slaves or marauding Indians and Abolitionists for him. Cook was described as "with huge mustaches, blue cockade, golden circle, with all manner of Southern fixins displayed about him," and it was cheerfully said that his return as editor of the *La Grange True Issue* was desired "as soon as possible". The KGC leadership in Texas were brimming with confidence and looking ahead to the new year and a glorious future.[42]

Chapter Ten

The KGC Takes Over in Texas

New Year's Day, 1861, the KGC was on the march in Texas. Forty men under the leadership of Captain John Karner, accompanied by Captain William T. Patton of the Fairfield KGC Castle, passed through Navarro County on their way to join the Grand Buffalo Hunt led by John R. Baylor. The KGC's western expedition took its name from the "buffalo hunt" led by Kansas abolitionist Jim Lane in 1856. Soon to join the KGC's "buffalo hunt," John Karner was an old hero of the Texas Revolution. Born in Bavaria in 1817, he came to Texas in 1835, served under Captain Henry Teel, and ultimately witnessed the surrender of Santa Anna to Sam Houston at the Battle of San Jacinto. He became a large landowner by 1860 with over 7,400 acres of land in Freestone County alone; previous year's tax records indicated additional land holdings in Limestone, Navarro, Falls and Leon counties in Texas. More importantly, he owned 9 slaves in Freestone County at Fairfield and 7 more slaves in Henderson County. He was an experienced Indian fighter, having been a member of a Minute Men company patrolling the land between the Trinity and Brazos rivers after the Texas War for Independence. Now he was marching with the KGC supposedly to fight Indians once more. One of the men he was marching with, Captain William T. Patton, was a 25-year old fellow resident of Freestone County who was increasing in importance to the KGC and would soon be authorized to raise Castles in Navarro, Freestone, Henderson, Leon and Grimes counties. On this particular journey in January Captain Patton was described by the *Navarro Express* as "armed with one of Colt's six shooting rifles, pistols, &c." The other men were described as "well-armed" and all were headed for the rendezvous point with John Baylor at Lost Valley in Jack County.

By January 15 they were "to leave for the 'buffalo rouge,' alias Indian 'stamping ground'" from the rendezvous point according to the *Express*, which voiced support for this as an opportunity for all "who wish to avenge the murder of women and children". It was further noted by the *Express* that another company was to form in Navarro County by January 8 to join this crusade for vengeance against enemies real or imagined.[1]

On January 2, Texas Senator Louis T. Wigfall telegraphed South Carolina Congressman Milledge Bonham at Charleston in-structing him to cut off supplies to the Federal garrison at Fort Sumter, "and take Sumter as soon as possible." Exactly how and why Wigfall felt he could dictate such actions to the South Carolina Congressman are not known; Fort Sumter would remain as it was, unscathed, until April. What prompted Wigfall's suggestion was the resignation of John Floyd on December 29 from his post as U.S. Secretary of War, the same day he had ordered seventy-eight cannon to be shipped to the Texas port of Galveston. Wigfall had been in communication with Floyd, a known KGC member, keeping him abreast of developments in South Carolina; after Floyd's departure Wigfall would aid Ben McCulloch in the acquisition of arms for Texas. The day Wigfall sent his telegraph advocating the seizure of Fort Sumter, the Governor of Georgia ordered 125 Georgia Volunteers to seize Fort Pulaski near Savannah. The following day, January 3, the empty fort was occupied by the secessionists. Alabama's governor gave similar orders that same day to occupy Forts Morgan and Gaines. The situation was different in Texas, however. There, Governor Houston still held out some hope that Texas might vote to stay in the Union. He had convened the State Legislature to meet in extra session on January 21, hoping to forestall the State Secession Convention which was scheduled to meet just one week afterwards in Austin. Nomination of delegates to the Secession Convention was to be completed by January 8. By that time one of the Austin newspapers wrote of their city, "Orders of knighthood have been established, and eagles, stars and garters are being constantly worn upon our streets. Considerable sensation is being produced by the wearers as they enter different crowds." No Federal installations had been seized in Texas – yet. The armed groups of men needed for such a venture were already being organized by the KGC; some of them were massing for the so-called "Grand Buffalo Hunt." Others in North Texas, particularly Harris A. Hamner, already knew in January that they were going to corner the Federal troops at Camp Cooper in the following month, at the same time as the Federal Arsenal in San Antonio would be raided by the KGC.[2]

On January 8, the day for completion of nominations for secession convention delegates, Major Charles Bickley issued "a call from Headquarters of the Texas State Division of K.G.C." for a convention, "of delegates from the various Castles of the State assembled at Braden Hall, in the city of San Antonio, Friday, Feb. 22." Braden Hall was the site of regular meetings of the San Antonio KGC, according to one of their members, New York-born Morgan Wolfe Merrick who arrived in Texas in 1850. He described Braden Hall as being in the upper story of the Braden Hotel on Carcel Street (later renamed Market Street) in between Yturri and Cochran streets. Multiple sources describe the Braden as a first-rate facility, with an extensive livery stable and feed store attached; next door was a smaller building, a former bakery used by the KGC as an armory. It was the first hotel built in San Antonio; its owner, Edward Braden, was a German immigrant, one-time Texas Ranger and Indian fighter who joined the Alamo Rifles, a known KGC company also known as Captain Prescott's Company of Knights, headed by William Prescott. This company was later commanded by KGC member Captain Samuel W. McAllister with Edward Braden as 1st Lieutenant. Captain McAllister was designated Captain of the Charles Bickley Castle in San Antonio at the time of the KGC convention. Therefore, it is a certainty, that Edward Braden was a KGC member also, judging from his associations and the role he played with the Order.[3]

The hoped-for KGC Castle at Corsicana in Navarro County was formed sometime during the week of January 6 to 12 as announced by the *Navarro Express.* The *Express* would subsequently announce that John B. Jones, a high-ranking Mason within the Grand Lodge of Texas was the Captain of the Corsicana Castle. In fact, the *Express* was "happy to announce that this organization has now a castle at this place" and described the KGC as "a truly Southern institution, the only object and every energy of which is devoted to the advancement of Southern interest." The Corsicana newspaper encouraged enlistment, adding

> At this time, especially, when concert of action is essential to the maintenance of Southern liberty, does such an institution become profitable and valuable. Many may object on account of it secresy [sic], but the K.G.C. has no secrets that can call a blush to the face of any honest man.

The only newspaper produced within the county was overtly positioning this secret organization dedicated to secession, the advancement of slavery and hostile action against Latin American countries as an "institution"; many who read this diatribe were naive young men looking for adventure and a way to enhance their status within society. The *Express* also appealed to greed by speaking of the Order as "profitable and valuable," a reference to the acres of land in the new empire promised to new initiates. Some of them would later realize that they had been lied to by the partisan press as well as the leadership of the KGC as to the organization's true intentions. However, at this point the Federal Government wasn't totally convinced that the KGC really existed. On January 9, a committee in the House of Representatives was formed "To inquire whether any secret organization hostile to the United States exists in the District of Columbia" and whether any Federal employees were active within it. This committee would meet and question potential witnesses right up to the time that the KGC began their march to take over the Federal arsenal in San Antonio. By then, of course, the committee findings were superfluous. The Order was already on the move in Texas, as shown by a letter sent by probable Collin County KGC members Eli Witt and S. S. Lyons to "Colonel" John Taylor Coit on January 9. A Princeton University law graduate and son of Yale-educated John Calkins Coit, John T. Coit had been the final speaker at the Dallas secessionist rally on November 17; now he was being approached for a leadership role so that he might set an example for the slave-owning faction in Collin County. The letter began by informing Colonel Coit: "The young ladies of McKinney are preparing a Secession Flag, to be raised prior to the day of Election, and are desirous that you should address them upon the subject of Secession. [sic]" So John T. Coit was to attend a pro-secession rally in McKinney, the county seat on February 22; but the real purpose of the exercise was revealed in the next sentence: "A dinner will be prepared by them, and they probably will present the Flag to a Union man with the request that he will hoist it." The flag raising ceremony was a set-up; the purpose was to publicly put a Unionist on the spot. If he knuckled under and raised the flag of secession, he would compromise his principles; if instead he stayed true to his principles and refused to raise the secession flag, he would publicly identify himself as "an enemy of the Southern people," which prior experience shows was a dangerous position to take in North Texas and Collin County specifically. Most of the rest of the letter to Coit was a rant against Unionists in North Texas, but it concluded with this chilling message:

> As soon as you receive the invitation from *headquarters*, and the time is ascertained for you to address those chivalrous young ladies, we will be glad if you will inform us, and we will accompany you, or be present, if nothing happens to prevent:

With the hopes that you will respond to the call, that you 'will lead the blind by a way which they know not, and in paths with they have not known', and that you will acquit yourself of the duty assigned to you. [italics added]

The term "chivalrous young ladies" bespoke of pretentions to royalty, feudalism and militant knights; it was a term often used to refer to pro-slavery Southerners. The quotation cited in the second paragraph above is from the book of Isaiah 42:16. John Taylor Coit was a religious man; his father John Calkins Coit was a Presbyterian minister in South Carolina. It must be remembered that KGC members frequently quoted passages from the Bible to justify their actions in support of maintaining slavery, as they considered it "ordained by God"; John T. Coit's Yale-educated father, although a minister, was described as "a violent champion of the Southern Cause." In this instance, the set-up of a Unionist was being directed by "headquarters" – no doubt KGC headquarters in San Antonio. This incident involving Coit would have tragic consequences for the Collin County community, as the Unionist in question was the duly elected Sheriff of the county, James L. Read. Once the State of Texas formally seceded there would be hell to pay for Unionists like Sheriff Read and his supporters.[4]

Some of the earlier adherents to this chivalrous Order of American knights known as the KGC were beginning to doubt the sincerity of their leaders. On January 20, one such disillusioned KGC wrote an anonymous letter from Sherman, Texas to the editors of the *Louisville Journal* stating, "I wish to call the attention of the people of the United States to the singular fact, that thousands of young men were induced to become members of that organization for one particular purpose (and one only), and which purpose has since proved to be false, or at least, a minor one. This I can prove by papers in my possession." The "one particular reason" this anonymous knight referred to was the failed attempts at invading and conquering Mexico. The letter continued:

About one year ago the papers necessary to the establishment of an encampment of the K.G.C. were forwarded to this place, and were placed in my hands. I no longer feel under any obligation to keep the oath I took when initiated, because the true object of the organization was not in the ritual. The object stated there was simply the peaceful "colonization of Mexico." I was elected captain of this encampment, and assisted in the initiation of some twenty members.

We awaited orders from headquarters, expecting every day to take up the line of march for the Rio Grande. No such orders came.... the real object of the association was the dismemberment of our Union, a treasonable effort to overthrow the Federal Government. I have therefore washed my hands of the whole affair, and pronounce it a low-down, dirty concern, deserving the utter contempt of every true patriot and lover of his country. Out of the twenty-four members of my company, but two favor secession.

It is interesting that the writer of this letter used the term "encampment" in reference to the Sherman Castle; that term is used to describe the local organizations of the Masonic Knights Templar. "Orders from headquarters" are mentioned again, implying some central directorate at work, albeit ineffectively. The writer was not the only one who felt misled and betrayed by the new direction the organization seemed to have taken. Sherman, Texas had in fact seen the organization of its KGC company, the Sherman Light Artillery, as announced by the *Daily Telegraph* on January 2, 1860. Sherman was in one of the counties of the *The Corners*, a reference used by local residents to describe the contiguous counties of Grayson, Collin, Fannin, and Hunt; Sherman was in Grayson County, directly west of Fannin County. There was at least one Castle in each of these four counties; but it is possible that the Castles in these counties were under the jurisdiction of, or subservient to, a ruling caste located at McKinney, the county seat of Collin County. The Collin County Castle was rumored to be quite large in terms of membership. However, of the four counties in "The Corners," the one with the largest slave population was Fannin County, with 1,464 slaves, to 933 in Collin, 1,194 in Grayson and 517 in Hunt County. The Red River counties of Fannin and Grayson had more plantations, as direct access to a river was ideal for supporting a slave-based agricultural economy. Still, the anonymous letter seemed to suggest that even the KGC members in such a county were against secession but in favor of the expansion of slavery through territorial conquest. Another knight with those sentiments was Fannin County KGC officer A. M. Gass, who publicly announced in the Standard that he was leaving Texas. Before the war started, this former 1st Lieutenant of Captain L. C. DeLisle's Bonham KGC company left Texas for good for the free State of California. He settled in San Diego, became a Republican, married, raised a family and continued the profession he once practiced in Bonham, that of a jeweler. He had once mounted an expedition from Fannin County to Pike's Peak in Colorado, searching for gold; no doubt the lure of Mexican gold had compelled him to join the KGC originally. He renounced his KGC membership and lived a happy and prosperous life away from the Democrats and secessionists in Texas. He would not be the last to change his mind and his affiliations. The only problem such men faced was the threat of death for their disloyalty to the Order, as expressed in a document titled, "Obligations of the Knights of the Golden Circle" found in the papers of Dallas County KGC member George W. Guess. Mr. Guess was described as "an influential attorney in Dallas" and the "presiding officer of Tannehill Lodge," the Masonic Lodge in Dallas, from 1860-1862. The document, in the form of an oath of obligation, is not in his handwriting. Among other things, the affiant was required to "swear that you will forever abjure all allegiance to the government of the United State [sic] or any other enemy we may have either foreign or at home." Additionally,

> ...that you will not give aid or comfort to the government of the USA or any other enemy either directly or indirectly and you further swear that you will aid and assist the government of the CSA to overthrow and destroy the government of the USA by all means in your power both in and out of the army. [sic]

This oath of obligation seems to have been implemented at the point that the KGC became a part of the Confederate States of America armed forces - which suggests the Order remained intact throughout the Civil War – at least in Texas. But the obligation made one thing clear: betrayal of any inside information meant a death sentence, as spelled out in the final paragraph of this document:

> So these and all of these you solemnly swear binding yourself under the no less penalty of being taken by your brethren and being hanged by the neck until you are dead, dead, dead and your bones to bleach upon the plains as unworthy of being buried if you should be so vile as to reval these obligations so help you God [sic]

Members of the KGC in Texas took a pledge of secrecy that applied to them for the rest of their lives. One such member of one of the Castles in San Antonio, an Englishman named R. H. Williams, described the KGC's secret police organization as "a Texan Mafia". There was a code of silence, and it was enforced; Mr. Williams's manuscript of his experiences as a KGC member were published only after his death in England. In it, he wrote of witnessing many "deeds of ruthless murder" by the San Antonio Vigilance Committee, run by KGC member Asa

Mitchell, who Williams remained in fear of for the rest of Mitchell's life, which ended less than six months from the termination of the war.[5]

Just East of Fannin County, on January 21, some citizens, many of whom were no doubt KGC, met at the Lamar County Courthouse to form a Secession Club. These men represented a minority in Lamar County, the county seat of which was Paris, but they were a vocal minority in a county with a population of 2,833 slaves and a total population of 10,136; twenty percent of the households owned slaves. Attorney B.F. Forney seemed to be the driving force behind the organization of the meeting, which object he explained to the crowd, "should be to favor the secession of the Southern States from the Federal Union and the formation of a Southern Confederacy ...in liberating the South from the aggression of the Northern fanatics". Officers were elected, with H. L. Williams as President, and thirteen Vice Presidents, several of whom can be identified as businessmen with storefronts on the town square; Dr. P. W. Birmingham, grocer T. J. Saufley, Dr. Lafayette Yates, stable-keeper Turner Edmondson and others. More importantly were the real rabble rousers, the guest speakers there to advocate secession. These men were attorney W.J. Bonner, Esq.; Dr. T.B. Pettus; William B. Wright, one of the best criminal attorneys in the area, and R.H. Bennet. William B. Wright was conspicuously in New Orleans during the KGC convention, checking into the City Hotel there February 19 and February 22, making it more likely he was a member of the order. Noticeably absent, or at least not mentioned in the newspaper account of the event, was Captain Milton Webb, organizer of the first military company Lamar County produced for Civil War service. Webb had organized his militia on the 29th of the previous December with 83 men initially mustered; they were now ready to assist the KGC leadership in achieving their goal of separating Texas from the United States. Webb would offer their service to the Secession Convention in Austin, which began on January 28.[6]

On Monday afternoon at 2:00 on January 28 the Secession Convention began with a prayer given by Episcopal Bishop Dr. Alexander Gregg; after his benediction the delegates began to organize by selecting as its President, Judge O.M. Roberts. Every county in Texas had elected two delegates from their county as representatives for the Convention, who were now in attendance. According to Hubert Howe Bancroft, "The election was held January 8th, polls being opened by the knights of the golden circle whenever judges, loyal to the union, refused to obey the call." Many of the delegates thus chosen with the help of the KGC were in fact KGC members and among the sixty-one names in the Order's published "Call for a State Convention". Even the convention's doorkeeper, Wilson Randle, was KGC; he had been present in New Orleans during the KGC Convention there the previous March. Now the delegates in Austin had selected Judge O.M. Roberts to lead them, who in his acceptance speech stated the following:

> The crisis upon us involves not only the right of self-government, but the maintenance of a great principle in the law of nations – the immemorial recognition of the institution of slavery wherever it is not locally prohibited – and also the true theory of our general government as an association of sovereignties, and not a blended mass of people in one social compact.

After making clear the reason for the Secession Convention that Roberts and his fellow KGC members had first publicly advocated on December 3, 1860, Convention Secretaries were elected. Next was the appointment of five men to examine the credentials of any would-be delegates. Those important gate-keeping gentle-men were William T. Scott, M.D. Graham, Nathaniel Terry, A.P. Wiley and Thomas Jefferson Devine. Nathaniel Terry was the driving force behind the apprehension of and lynching of Reverend Anthony Bewley in Tarrant County, which he now represented as that county's delegate; T.J. Devine was also a powerful KGC member in San Antonio and would be one of the few people in the United States arrested for treason after the war that he was now helping to inaugurate. Soon the Convention adjourned until 7:30 that evening. Just before they reconvened, M.D.K. Taylor, Speaker of the House and confidant of Elkanah Greer the then-military leader of the KGC in Texas, escorted the Reverend Dr. George Carter to the Speaker's stand "to deliver an address on the issues of the day." Speaker Taylor introduced the Reverend Carter to the audience; his address was not solely religious, but rather concerned the "Impending political crisis." A journalist in attendance wrote that his speech "held the vast assembly of intelligent gentlemen who composed the convention completely spell bound by the force of its convincing logic and eloquence."

> I cannot do less than to say, that it was a most complete and perfectly successful vindication of the present position of the South, constitutionally, politically, practically, religiously and morally. During the delivery of the address, the Hall was densely crowded with spectators.... During the utterance of some periods by the speaker, the effect upon the hearer was almost like an electric shock, holding him spell-bound for a moment and then making the old Capitol tremble by the force of the applause. I cannot convey

to our readers any just conception of the speakers power over the minds of those who listened....[7]

The speaker, George Washington Carter, was an ordained Methodist minister, as had been the late Anthony Bewley; however, Reverend Bewley's brand of the Methodist faith was not appreciated by the KGC. Men like Nathaniel Terry didn't want that brand of Methodism talked about in their State; certainly not at their Secession Convention. Charles Anderson had already met Nat Terry's brand of Methodist preacher in the confrontation he'd had earlier in San Antonio with KGC leader John A. Wilcox; in that incident the particular minister of the Southerner's god was the Reverend Dr. Jesse Boring. The good Reverend Boring's speech was reprinted in full by the *San Antonio Weekly Herald*, which also rhapsodized over Reverend Carter's address to the Secession Convention. Anderson later wrote of his experiences of this time in Texas, and specifically:

> ...the 'Knights of the Golden Circle.' It was to this band of mostly mere villainous desperadoes that the success of rebellion in Texas was mainly due – indeed, it may be said wholly due, unless we must except, as another great coadjutant influence to the same end – in another association of a widely different character. This was the Methodist Episcopal Church, South. This church had, as you may recollect, its origin in a schism based solely in pro-slavery zeal.

Anderson made his belief in the role of the Methodist Church even more plain, writing, "...the Methodist Episcopal Church, South, became an organized, separated religious body, and a vast power for evil, as well as for good, in our country. In Texas, certainly, and I believe throughout the Southern States, it was almost unanimous for a dissolution of the Union." The Reverend George Washington Carter soon prioritized his beliefs by resigning his position as president of the Methodist Soule University in Chappell Hill, Texas and returned to his native Virginia. There he became a Colonel in the armed forces and received permission to return to Texas and organize Confederate troops for the killing that was to take place; but that was months still in the future. The Confederacy was still in its formative process during the Texas Secession Convention. By the start of the Texas convention, the States of South Carolina, Mississippi, Alabama, Florida, Georgia and Louisiana had already seceded. The plan for Texas worked out between the secessionists led by O.M. Roberts, the KGC and Governor Houston's pro-Union faction, was for the delegates of the Secession Convention to vote to pass or reject an Ordinance of Secession; if it was passed by the Convention delegates from each county then the voting public of Texas would have final approval in a State-wide referendum on February 23. Popular vote would be the ultimate determinant of whether Texas remained in the United States.

The second day of the Secession Convention, January 29, delegate John A. Wharton proclaimed and so moved that "it is the deliberate sense of this Convention that the state of Texas should separately secede." On Friday, February 1 with Governor Houston present, the convention voted to approve the Ordinance of Secession by a vote of 166 for and 8 against. Some of those voting against secession, like James W. Throckmorton of Collin County, were slave owners themselves living in counties with KGC Castles; a vote against secession did not necessarily mean they were not KGC members. The author believes J.W. Throckmorton was in fact a KGC member, as had been his ally, Governor Sam Houston. Throckmorton was one of the financiers of Baylor and Hamner's private army which was now prowling West Texas on the "buffalo hunt." This dispute within the KGC had manifested itself in the previously mentioned defections of A.M. Gass in Fannin County, and the unnamed member in nearby Sherman, Texas.[8]

There was also friction between two of the KGC Castles in San Antonio during the Secession Convention held in nearby Austin. The San Antonio Guards, a designated KGC company, invited the Alamo Rifles to join them in a flag-raising ceremony, in which the United States flag would be removed and replaced by a Texas State flag. The Alamo Rifles declined the invitation by meeting and passing resolutions which were published by the *Tri-Weekly Alamo Express* on February 4. The second resolution stated "We bow with all deference to the sovereignty of the State, and will...as much as any men in defence of her honor, her rights, and her cause – but we will never participate in a rejoicing of the fall of the stars and stripes, and until the State has seceded through her proper channel – the people – we acknowledge no other thing." This did not settle the dispute between these different Castles in San Antonio. On February 5, Major W.J. Clarke, a high-ranking KGC leader in San Antonio, addressed the Alamo Rifles after their "drill and business" were finished that evening. William John Clarke was born in North Carolina where he had been state comptroller from 1850 to 1855; a Mexican War veteran, in 1857 he moved his family to San Antonio and became President of the San Antonio and Mexican Gulf Railroad. He was also an attorney in the firm of Clarke, Cooke & Company. Among his co-directors of the railroad were KGC members Samuel A. Maverick, Asa Mitchell and R.W. Brahan. On October 6, 1859, Clarke and fellow KGC members Asa Mitchell, Samuel A. Maverick and George H. Sweet had registered displeasure with General Twiggs of the United States army stationed in San Antonio as to the ability of the army to protect their fellow citizens against Indian depredations. The solution reached at that time was for a committee of five men – O. D. Cooke, Judge Hewitt, J. L. Trueheart, Asa Mitchell and Sol. Childress – be appointed to raise money to equip, maintain and outfit two companies of armed men. This may have marked the beginning of two of the KGC Castles in San Antonio. Yale-educated Samuel Maverick was Chairman of that committee and George H. Sweet, who had toured the area with Charles Bickley in setting up Castles in 1860, was Secretary of the San Antonio committee in 1859. Now, in February 1861, one of those Castles needed reassurance. The Secession Convention had adjourned on February 4 to await the results of the popular vote; but in reality, a portion of that body was still operating in secret, styling themselves The Committee on Public Safety. The members of this secret committee were called "commissioners". So, on February 5, Major William J. Clarke gave this speech to the anxious members of the Alamo Rifles:

> I love the Alamo Rifles – I love every man in San Antonio – I come before you merely as a disinterested individual, without any authority for doing so, but merely to tell you what your duty is in these stirring times. The K.G.C. love you, they are sworn to protect you and the rest of the city – they are for the South and Texas – they have been misrepresented – they love you and expect you to stand by them when they kick up a muss – the people of Texas [10,000 voters] have declared themselves out of the Union – you must ratify their action at the ballot-box – you will be expected to back some unknown, and till now unheard of commissioners if they demand the government property – we must submit to our rulers – I, for one, 'come weal or come woe,' will die by the people of Texas, 'from whom I have received nothing but kindness.' Mr. Rifles, I again assure you, you are a ghlorious set of fellows and I love you. Adieu! [sic]

Of course, Clarke was lying to the rank-and-file membership; he did have the authority to direct them; he was Captain of the San Antonio Castle Number 1 and he would be one of the main participants in the upcoming KGC Texas State Convention held in San Antonio on February 22, the day before the citizens were allowed to vote on the Ordinance of Secession. In this February 5 speech, he implied that the vote had already been decided. Perhaps it had been – without any input from the public. As James P. Newcomb, the editor of the *Tri-Weekly Alamo*

Express reported in this account of the meeting between the two stated, "Some of our bull headed fellows could neither make head nor tail out of his remarks. They are and will remain in the dark until further developments as to who our rulers are and who those commissioners are." In fact, those heretofore unknown commissioners were plotting with Ben McCulloch to "kick up a muss" by demanding the government property possessed by the U.S. military stationed in San Antonio.[9]

Who those commissioners were had been decided on February 3: Yale alumnus Samuel Augustus Maverick, also a direct descendant of Samuel Maverick, the first slaveowner in Massachusetts; Thomas J. Devine, Philip N. Luckett and James H. Rogers were to negotiate the surrender of Federal property from the U.S. military forces to the KGC, the State of Texas and other "citizen groups" aiding in the seizure. Samuel Maverick and Thomas J. Devine were known KGC members; it should not be too much of a stretch to suspect that both Philip N. Luckett and James H. Rogers were members as well. Their appointment was finalized by the Chairman of the Committee of Public Safety, John C. Robertson, an attorney from Smith County, an East Texas county with a large KGC presence dominated by George W. Chilton. The Committee of Public Safety was appointed on January 30 by the Secession Convention delegates to carry out the military logistics of the seizure of Federal property. All fifteen of the original Committee had prior military experience; several – A. T. Rainey, John Alexander Green, John S. Ford and John A. Wilcox – were known KGC members, and sever-al others including Robertson, Luckett, James H. Rogers and John Henry Brown were probably members. Thursday, January 31, the Convention met in "secret session" and added three more men to the Committee of Public Safety; those being Francis W. Latham of Cameron County (John S. Ford's home), KGC member William S. Oldham of Washington County, and probable member Charles Ganahl of Kerr County. The following day was the day for the signing of the Ordinance of Secession by the convention delegates. Before that momentous occasion, the delegates were treated to a speech on the convention floor from General John McQueen of South Carolina, who was in attendance as a commissioner from the newly seceded state. Of course, McQueen was there to lobby in favor of the secession of Texas. After completing other business, the convention adjourned until 7:30 that night. When they reconvened Nat Terry introduced a resolution to the Committee on Public Safety that it appoint five military commissioners "whose appointment shall continue as long as the emergency lasts, or they shall be superseded by the appointment of others, who then elected shall constitute a permanent military board with full discretionary powers on all subjects rightfully appertaining to military affairs." Obviously, he hoped to be one of the five military junta leaders. This resolution was referred to the Committee on Public Safety for further consideration, as was an offer of service to the convention by John J. Good's KGC company, the Dallas Light Artillery. Another likely KGC company, the Tyler Dragoons of Smith County commanded by James P. Douglas, had offered their services to the convention the previous day. Later these two companies would merge during the war. These things considered, the next order of business was the signing of the Ordinance by the delegates, which was done by the end of that day, February 1. The convention had passed the resolution to take effect March 2 if approved by the voting public on February 23. On February 3, the Committee appointed Ben McCulloch as the military officer to lead the takeover of Federal assets in Texas. The letter of instruction signed by John C. Robertson additionally stipulated that McCulloch, "hold yourself in readiness to raise men and munitions of war, whenever called on by the Commissioners to San Antonio, and to be governed as directed by the secret instructions, given said Commissioners concerning said command, and you will station yourself at the residence of Henry McCulloch, and await the communications of said Commissioners, or the Committee of Public Safety." They were getting ready to "kick up a muss" as their associate William J. Clarke had said.[10]

The military companies of the KGC were tailor-made for the assignment at hand given Ben McCulloch. They were already assembled, drilled, armed and understood the mission. Unlike John R. Baylor's men who were still in West Texas on their "buffalo hunt," they were at hand. Both of the McCulloch brothers, Ben and younger brother Henry Eustace McCulloch, hurriedly retired to Henry's ranch, known as "Ranger's Home," eight miles north of Seguin in Guadalupe County. At least one KGC Castle was in Seguin, with 35 men under the command of Captain Stephen Wright. Nearby Comal County had a Castle with 30 men under the command of Captain T.J. Thomas; other Castles including two from San Antonio, one from Pleasanton in Atascosa County organized by E.B. Thomas, another from DeWitt County under the redoubtable William Scurry and one from the Medina County town of Castroville to be called upon. Besides this, Henry McCulloch was the serving U.S. Marshal for the East Texas District, appointed for a four-year term by President Buchanan; as a former Texas Ranger, he had extensive contacts to be drawn upon. On the 5th and 6th of February Henry sent letters to Thomas C. Frost, Robert B. Halley, J.B. Barry, Harris A. Hamner and David C. Cowan instructing them to raise companies of 100 men each. This action was not authorized by the State, as it would have been if these men were being mustered as Texas Rangers. As U.S. Army Major John T. Sprague would report in a few months, "The Ranger of the present day, however, is but an imitator of those brave and resolute men, the pioneers of Texas, now extinct. Within the State there is a secret association, known as the 'K.G.Cs.'" Major Sprague was present at the takeover of Texas by the so-called Texas Rangers, who were in reality in the service of the KGC.[11]

Although the main body of the Secession Convention went into recess after February 4, the Committee of Public Safety continued to operate as a de facto military government of the State of Texas. The composition of the original membership of the Committee had changed over time; KGC member John A. Wilcox resigned from the committee on February 2, probably so that he could take part in the military occupation of San Antonio; his place was taken the same day by Thomas J. Devine, another KGC member. Two days later, KGC member Thomas S. Lubbock was added to the Committee; eventually J.J. Diamond from Cooke County was added also. That day in the evening session, seven delegates from Texas were selected to represent the State at a convention of the seceding states to be held in Montgomery, Alabama from February 4 to March 16: those delegates being John H. Reagan, Louis T. Wigfall, Thomas N. Waul, John Gregg, W.S. Oldham, William B. Ochiltree and John Hemphill. However, none of the Texas delegates would be present in Montgomery during the first ten days of the Convention of seceding States. For that period of time, the convention consisted of delegates from the States of Alabama, Florida, Georgia, Louisiana, Mississippi and South Carolina. By the time the first delegate from Texas arrived on February 15, the six seceding States had already chosen Jefferson Davis as President of the Confederacy by unanimous vote on February 9; Alexander H. Stephens had been chosen as Vice-President on Monday, February 11. John Gregg delivered a copy of the ordinance of session for the State of Texas and was given a seat on the floor of the First Confederate Congress in session on Friday February 15. Because the Texas secession ordinance did not take effect until March 2, the Texas delegates made it known that they would not vote on any Convention resolutions until that time but would attend the meetings. Apparently, the rest of the Texas delegation was straggling in, as Thomas N. Waul did not arrive until Monday February 19. By that time, a lot had happened in Texas. Coincidentally, Charles Bickley had issued General Order No. 31 from KGC Headquarters in San Antonio on February 1, notifying all that the General Headquarters would move to Montgomery, Alabama on

March 1, 1861. At that time any applications to establish new Castles in Texas would be directed to Dr. George Cupples in San Antonio. Dr. Cupples, Charles Bickley and Samuel Sampson had been jointly responsible for the operation of KGC headquarters in San Antonio. Samuel Sampson was a member of the small but growing Jewish community in San Antonio; he was also a slave owner. His presence as a KGC leader demonstrates that at least in Texas, one's religion was not a bar to membership in this secret Order; the same could be said of the Masonic Order, which only stipulated monotheism as a requirement. The KGC always tried to be at the center of the action, and so it temporarily moved its headquarters to Montgomery, soon to become the temporary capital of the Confederacy.[12]

While the Montgomery Convention met, the KGC in Texas began to make its moves: on Wednesday, February 6, a small expedition of 16 armed horsemen left Dallas. Their objective was to become part of a military force that would take over the United States garrison at Camp Cooper in West Texas. At that time, the garrison at Camp Cooper numbered 270 armed regular troops. The horsemen from Dallas were under the command of Captain Robert B. Ward, formerly a sergeant in the U.S. 2nd Cavalry stationed at Camp Cooper; Ward had served under Captain Earl Van Dorn at Camp Colorado before transferring to Camp Cooper in 1856 under 1st Lieutenant Richard W. Johnson. The officers of the 2nd Cavalry had been hand-picked by Jefferson Davis when he served as Secretary of War; Van Dorn would soon command Confederate troops from Texas. Now known as Captain R. Ward, the former U.S. Army sergeant was a known member of the KGC in Texas and had prior knowledge of Camp Cooper's layout and the lay of the land around it. He was "the inside man;" in fact, John P. Newcomb, editor of the San Antonio-based *Alamo Express* described Ward as "the eminent K.G.C." and declared that it was he that helped to bring the "order of the Knights" to prominence in San Antonio, hosting their early meetings at his boardinghouse, The City Hotel, before they moved into The Braden Hotel. Newsome also asserted that Ward had been "body guard to his Knightship Bickley" – an apparent reference to George W. L. Bickley, the alleged founder and de facto chief salesman of the Order. Ward was born in Tennessee and lived in New York for a time, two places where he might have made George W. Bickley's acquaintance at an earlier time. Newsome described Ward's role with the KGC as "the right man in the right place." Ward had completed his term of service with the U.S. Second Cavalry at Camp Cooper in late February 1860. Now he was guiding the KGC in an attack on his former base that surely was planned in his home city of San Antonio, at KGC headquarters. It was a long journey of about 275 miles from San Antonio to Dallas, where Ward began his crusade. Ward told the *Dallas Herald* that his group covered 40 miles on the first day they left Dallas; they had written previously to another "citizen group" in the Dallas County town of Lancaster to join them in Weatherford in Parker County west of Fort Worth 70 miles further. The Lancaster group, under the command of KGC Captain Crill Miller, described by Ward as "two little squads of patriots" met them there in the pouring rain with 20 more armed men.[13]

Marching further to Fort Belknap, Ward's company of KGC were met by another company of 25 more men from Fort Worth under Captain Ashley Newton Denton. Here they were also met by "Mr. Farier" who in all probability was Franklin L. Farrar of nearby Ellis County. Farrar became Captain of Company F of Nathaniel H. Darnell's Regiment of Texas Volunteers. The KGC is known to have provided the core of the first Confederate troops organized in Texas. Ward had been "hosted" by Emory W. Rogers in Waxahachie, the seat of Ellis County; Rogers was considered the founder of Waxahachie and was probably the leader of the KGC Castle known to exist in that town. Both Frank Farrar and Emory Rogers owned slaves in Ellis County, so it is likely they knew one another well. They and their men traveled more than 100 miles to participate in this expedition. Rogers would join the expedition to Camp Cooper with his own company of men in a few days. Before Rogers could get there, Captain Ward and his ever-growing group of KGC paramilitary men met up with the infamous Captain Harris A. Hamner at Weatherford, who initially had only 3 men with him. Not wishing to appear inadequate, Hamner immediately left Weatherford to go even further west to Palo Pinto County in search of more men. When he returned to Weatherford Hamner brought 30 more men under the command of Captains Jerome B. McCown and C.C. Slaughter. This is especially interesting as E. W. Rogers later noted that Captain McCown and his company were from Austin County, just 30 miles east of Houston near the Gulf Coast in South Texas; what were they doing more than 300 miles from home, up in far Northwest Texas? McCown, like Frank Farrar, was a Mexican War veteran; like Henry McCulloch, McCown had been a Captain in the 1st Regiment of Texas Mounted Rifle Volunteers. Like Henry McCulloch's brother Ben, McCown had also fought Indians in Texas as Captain of a Ranger company. Jerome McCown's company later became the seed of the 5th Texas

Mounted Volunteers and ultimately the 5th Texas Cavalry in the Confederate military. Christopher Columbus Slaughter, leader of the Palo Pinto Rangers, was a major cattleman whose father George W. Slaughter had sided with John R. Baylor and Harris A. Hamner's successful campaign against the Brazos River Indian Reservation. Once again Slaughter was under Hamner's command. It is reasonable to consider these men as KGC, by virtue of their participation in what was a centrally coordinated effort that required them to travel a great distance. In his account of this expedition to Camp Cooper Captain E. W. Rogers stated to the *Navarro Express* that his company was organized on January 28 and was mustered into service at Belknap on February 9. Writing from Camp Cooper, Rogers stated, "On reception of the news of the ordinance of secession by the convention, I left my station and proceeded directly to this post, with some citizen troops from Lancaster, Dallas, Fort Worth, and a few from Collin County." The Committee of Public Safety was the centrally coordinating body for the secret movements of the KGC; many of its members were KGC, and in sending combat veterans like Frank Farrar and Jerome McCown to aid in the takeover of Camp Cooper, they were not leaving anything to chance. In addition to his ample combat experience, McCown had served two terms in the Texas House of Representatives and chaired the Military Affairs Committee in 1855. He was well-connected politically across the State. These were not ordinary "citizen troops."[14]

While the KGC was gathering in Northwest Texas for the assault on Camp Cooper, the Commissioners for the Committee of Public Safety sent notice to Ben McCulloch "to call out and collect such numbers of the volunteer force or 'minute men,' as you may deem necessary for securing and protecting the public property at San Antonio." This express dispatch dated February 8 gave the green light to Ben McCulloch to proceed with the takeover of the Federal Arsenal in San Antonio. It was to be the grand prize that the KGC would win for the future Confederate State of Texas, as it supplied all the United States troops in the Department of Texas under the command of General David E. Twiggs. Colonel McCulloch's response was received by the Commissioners just two days later, informing the Committee that "he expected to be at or near Seguin on the thirteenth or fourteenth, with whatever force he could raise." While all this was secretly taking place, the Committee was negotiating with General Twiggs for the voluntary surrender of the Arsenal and all other "public property" owned by the U.S. military stationed in Texas. All of these things – the "Grand Buffalo Hunt" led by KGC leader John R. Baylor; the massing of troops in Northwest Texas for the assault on Camp

Cooper; the massing of troops in South Central Texas by Ben McCulloch for his assault on the Arsenal at San Antonio, and the negotiations with U.S. Army General David Twiggs were all occurring simultaneously over great distances. In effect, Baylor's men, said to number some 400 armed horsemen, were protecting the Western flank of the KGC's force soon to be engaged in removing the very Federal forces that had been protecting the Western frontier now occupied by John R. Baylor and his men. As the Commissioners had written to their Chairman on February 8,

> The conclusion we have arrived at is this: That we must obtain possession of that which now belongs to Texas by right of force, or such a display of force as will compel a compliance with our demands, and that without an hour's unnecessary delay. In all these movements, celerity, secrecy and strength, should be our motto.

Considering the scarcity of telegraph lines or any other form of long-distance communication capability in Texas at this time, this was truly an impressive accomplishment. Also impressive is the fact that the journeys undertaken by the KGC in this campaign covered hundreds of miles, all of it on horseback or on foot. This took planning and preparation. On Tuesday February 12, groups of men from Caldwell County began to gather in the area around the town of Seguin in neighboring Guadalupe County. The following morning, they marched "in fine style" into the town square, where they were met by John Ireland, the former Mayor of Seguin and one of Guadalupe County's delegates to the Secession Convention. It was noted that a number of these "volunteers" from Caldwell County were past their prime but were game for a fight if necessary. They were then regaled by "Edgar Rogan, Esq., a knight of the quill" who gave a "short and stirring speech." The following morning, "The K.G.C.'s under Capt. Herron" left Seguin as a group for an unknown destination. Later that same day another group of "volunteers" – designated by the Southern Confederacy as "The Guadaloupe volunteers or Invincibles, we don't know which"[sic] left Seguin for parts unknown.[15]

In the far northwestern part of the State, on February 14 it was noticed by U.S. Army Captain Stephen Decatur Carpenter, the post commander at Camp Cooper, that strange men were mixing among the cattle herded around their base, no doubt foraging for rations from the supply meant for the Federal troops. Captain Carpenter, who oddly enough was also a slave owner, wrote his commanding officer that day that "a force is concentrating about this post for the purpose of attacking us, and of taking possession of the public property" and that they were "coming in by small parties." More than 300 miles away in South Central Texas, forces under Ben McCulloch were assembling that same night for the assault on the Arsenal at San Antonio in the wee hours of the morning of the 15th, as reported by a correspondent for the Seguin Southern Confederacy, who was there:

> On Thursday evening, the 14th inst., most of the companies from this place, the K.G.C.'s commanded by Capt. Herron, or as the Brownsville correspondent, of the New Orleans Delta, during the Cortena war, designated him, 'the fighting parson,' and the 'Guadalupe Irregulars,' as some wag was pleased to call them, left Seguin for 'Young's Pasture,' about five miles above town. The Guadalupe 'Irregulars' chose Thomas N. Minter, Captain, in the place of H. E. McCulloch, resigned; and Wm. Suffold was chosen 1st Lieutenant, in the place of T. N. Minter, promoted. Dr. J. W. Fennell was chosen Surgeon of Capt. Minter's company. [sic]

The KGC "fighting parson" was Andrew Herron of Guadalupe County, a 55-year old minister who owned twenty-three slaves living in eight different "slave houses." In addition, his 25-year old son Andrew C. Herron apparently owned another 15 slaves in the county also under the name of Andrew Herron. The Reverend Andrew Herron was on the Board of Trustees of Guadalupe High School in 1853, the year he and his brother built the lovely Parson Andrew Herron house on West Court Street. In 1860, he lived near Dr. J. W. Fennell, a medical doctor who owned four slaves. Thomas N. Minter was a 45-year old farmer; too old to fight, he became a Captain in the Quartermaster department stationed at Hempstead, Texas. William Saffold (not Suffold) was a 31-year old farmer who also lived in Seguin, with eighty slaves held in the county. Henry Eustace McCulloch had resigned from his KGC company on February 8, as he had been notified by the Committee on February 5 to prepare himself for a much larger undertaking. He was to take command of the forces employed by the secessionists to take possession of the U.S. military posts on the northwestern frontier, from Fort Chadbourne to the Red River, the border with Indian Territory (now Oklahoma). His brother Ben had assumed command of the middle third of the State, between Fort McIntosh and Fort Duncan up to Fort Chadbourne, and John S. Ford was responsible for the southernmost district from the lower Rio Grande River at Brownsville to Fort McIntosh. All three of these men in command were KGC members. It is natural that Ben McCulloch would draw heavily upon the ranks of the secret Order for this mission. The travelling correspondent for the Seguin newspaper continued his report on the gathering of the troops for the San Antonio assault:

> About four miles beyond the Cibolo... the Guadalupe companies and the Caldwell companies, stopped for dinner. From this place several of the troops were sent to the Salado to stop all communications with the city. The Salado was reached about an hour...where the troops were soon engaged in active preparations for physical comfort. Troops continued coming in until midnight, and as large squads would come up, they were greeted with lusty cheers.... Some time after night, a company from Gonzales got in, and by midnight our numbers had swelled to some five hundred men.

The records from the KGC Texas State Convention that was to commence in one week from this event show that the Seguin Castle in Guadalupe County was led by Captain Stephen Wright, with 35 men; Wright was an Englishman, the editor of the *Guadalupe Times* and the past Worshipful Master of the Guadalupe Masonic Lodge Number 109, located in Seguin. Among Wright's fellow Masons in the Seguin lodge were KGC members Ben and Henry McCulloch, J.W. Fennell, Nat Benton and probable KGC member John Ireland, who represented Guadalupe County at the Secession Convention. This close familiarity in more than one secret association together is why the McCulloch brothers felt comfortable with these particular men. Not all the Castles across the State of Texas would be represented at the KGC convention the following week as some of them were busy taking possession of Federal property. It is likely that there was more than one Castle in Guadalupe County. There were two different Castles from Gonzales County at the convention – the Brown Castle headed by T.W. Lemmonds and the Belmont Castle Captained by J.J. Ramsay, with 36 men between them. At least one of the unnamed Castles in Caldwell County was apparently led by William R. Cowan of Lockhart, who would attend the State Convention of the KGC.[16]

Ben McCulloch had assembled his forces just five miles north of San Antonio on Salado Creek, drawing men from seven "citizen volunteer" companies as well as from seven identified KGC companies. Those seven acknowledged KGC units were the San Antonio Castle under the command of John A. Wilcox; the Charles Bickley Castle from San Antonio under the command of Trevanion T. Teel; the Pleasanton Castle from Atascosa County, commanded by James Walker, an Englishman and recruited from Lavaca County; the New Braunfels Castle, from nearby Comal County, commanded by Theophelus J. Thomas; the Seguin Castle, commanded by Reverend Andrew Herron; the Castroville Castle from Medina County, commanded by James Paul, and a company from DeWitt County under the command of William Scurry. They were ordered by McCulloch to begin their march on the Federal Arsenal at San Antonio by one o'clock in the early morning hours of February 15, a Saturday. Like the assault on Camp Cooper, which was still underway at this hour, the KGC may have employed an inside man – 2nd Lieutenant Joseph F. Minter of the 2nd U.S. Cavalry. He had served at Camp Cooper before transferring to Fort Mason, under the command of Robert E. Lee. Just weeks before the assault, in December 1860, Joseph Minter had been designated the Regimental Quartermaster of the U.S. 2nd Cavalry, which would have given him access to the Arsenal in San Antonio, a city he had lived in since 1850. Thomas N. Minter, perhaps related to Joseph F. Minter, resided in nearby Guadalupe County where he kept seven slaves. Upon Henry McCulloch's resignation as Captain of the "Guadalupe Irregulars" Thomas N. Minter took his place as Captain of this KGC company, in time for the capture of the Arsenal. McCulloch's brother Ben ordered that one hundred of the five hundred assembled would march into San Antonio "under cover of darkness, and take commanding positions." Of this vanguard of one hundred, twenty of these men "were taken from Capt. Minter's company". When the war was over and Joseph F. Minter asked for a Presidential pardon, he stated that he resigned from the U.S. Second Cavalry "on or *about* the 31st March 1861" [italics added] and that he had joined the Confederate forces in Texas at San Antonio with the initial rank of Captain. Born in Virginia, he had lived in Texas since December 1838. He would not be the only member of his regiment to betray his country; promotions were difficult to come by in the 2nd U.S. Cavalry, and the conditions of service in Texas were often miserable. Coincidentally (or not), both Thomas N. Minter and Joseph F. Minter wound up in non-combat positions as quartermaster officers in the Confederacy; Thomas N. Minter as a commissary officer in Texas with the rank of Captain appointed by Major Sackfield Maclin, another turncoat from the U.S. Second Cavalry in Texas, and Joseph F. Minter as a Major and the Chief Quartermaster of the Trans-Mississippi Department based in Shreveport. Sackfield Maclin had been one of the original organizers of the protective society known as the "Blue Lodge" in Kansas, the earliest manifestation of the KGC as a paramilitary organization. He had been the paymaster for the U.S. Second Cavalry but became involved in the negotiations with The Committee of Public Safety for the surrender of U.S. forces in Texas, on behalf of General Twiggs, the commanding officer of all forces in the Department.

Some say Twiggs had signaled the Committee and its KGC members early on that he would surrender without a fight, as his personal sympathies lay with the South and the cause of slavery. In fact, Governor Houston had sent General Twiggs a dispatch on January 20 warning him "that an effort will be made by an unauthorized mob to take forcibly and appropriate the public stores and property to uses of their own, assuming to act on behalf of the State." Twiggs did nothing to prepare for what ensued.[17]

Before the rest of McCulloch's forces entered the city of San Antonio, some of the local KGC had been at work early that morning. According to San Antonio newspaperman James P. Newcomb:

> The Alamo, comprising the Quarter Master's Department, had been captured early in the morning, by a man by the name of Edgar, a clerk in the department, at the head of some city "Knights," there being no one to oppose them. The agreement between Twiggs and the commissioners was, that the posts be surrendered and the troops march out of the State by way of the coast, with all the honors of war.

The official report shows that Captain William M. Edgar led the Alamo City Guards in the takeover of the Quartermaster Department, which effectively put the KGC in possession of the ammunition and supplies meant for the U.S. troops who were soon surrounded. Despite weeks of rumors and threats against the Arsenal in San Antonio, both General Twiggs and Lieutenant Joseph Minter had not posted any guards to protect the Quartermaster Department. When the rest of McCulloch's men marched into the city, they were met by The Alamo Rifles, another KGC company under the command of William Prescott. Various KGC took turns commanding the men along the way; William Saffold, one of the largest slaveowners in Seguin, had served in that capacity as Lieutenant of Captain Thomas N. Minter's company, but once in the city, command was passed to "Lieutenant Yeager" [sic]. William Overall Yager was a graduate of the Virginia Military Academy in 1852; after graduation he studied law at the University of Virginia from 1853-1854. In 1855 he went to Kansas – the same year the KGC had appeared there. For a time, he served as a clerk in the Kansas Senate before being appointed the first ever Probate Judge for Shawnee County, from 1855-1856. It was there that he allied with the pro-slavery faction in incorporating the towns of Neosho and Lavinia and the Tecumseh Lyceum and Library Association. Yager lived in the town of Tecumseh, whose development had been encouraged by John

Wilkins Whitfield, at the time serving in the U.S. Congress representing Kansas Territory. The pro-slavery forces had intended for Tecumseh to become the State capitol, but the anti-slavery forces eventually won, and made Topeka the capitol instead. Tecumseh subsequently withered on the vine as pro-slavery settlers left the State. J.W. Whitfield was said to be the largest slave owner in Kansas and would soon relocate to Texas and rise within the chain of command of the military forces there. Yager also appeared in Texas not long before the Civil War began and would also rise in the military establishment in Texas, by virtue of his service as Ben McCulloch's second-in-command for the assault on the Arsenal. According to the correspondent for the *Southern Confederacy*, "Lieutenant Tribble commanded the K.G.C. detachment," this being Alexander Tribble of Seguin, who would attend the State Convention of the KGC. Others, who had obviously been tipped off by the KGC that the assault was in progress, were on hand to lend their support, according to the report from Seguin:

> The press of Lockhart was represented by the editor, as was the Union Democrat of this place. The legal profession was pretty unanimously represented. All save one from Seguin, Reagan, two Cowens and McWright, from Lockhart: Parker, Stewart, Harwood and Evans from Gonzales, with perhaps others; and Mr. Harris of Comall. We saw one old gentleman from Gonzales, pass through Seguin, with a gun on his shoulder, in his sixty-seventh year, and we saw many who looked as though they were approximating a hundred.
>
> The war feeling is fully aroused, and if necessary, four fifths of the population in this and some of the adjoining counties, would shoulder their arms, and march forward to fight. [sic]

"Reagan" was likely Morris R. Reagan, the brother of KGC member John H. Reagan who had resigned his position as United States Congressman from Texas and had gone home to Palestine in Anderson County. A delegate to the Montgomery Convention in session from February 4 to March 16, John Reagan didn't get to Alabama until after the Arsenal raid. His brother Morris Reagan was one of the signers of the KGC's call for the Secession Convention and lived in southern Travis County. When Morris Reagan gave a speech in Austin in early November, George W. Bickley, Charles Bickley and Virginus Groner were in the audience. The editor of the pro-Union Austin-based *Southern Intelligencer* was there also and reported that "Gen. Bickley mistook him for 'one of 'em,' and gave the sign, and after the speech, claimed him," lending credence to Morris R. Reagan being a member of the KGC. The attorneys mentioned were likely KGC members, and as best as they can be identified from the 1860 census records from their counties of origin, were Robert McCright (not "McWright"), Champion Cowan, a slaveowner as well as an attorney and W. R. Cowan, a known member of the KGC, all from Lockhart. Also on hand were members of the New Braunfels Castle, organized by Theophelus J. Thomas, a twenty-five-year-old school teacher in Comal County who was born in Georgia but raised in Matagorda County, Texas. However, members of this KGC "company of twenty-five or thirty from Comal county" elected to be led into San Antonio by Dr. Ferdinand Lindheimer, the nearly sixty-year old editor of the *New Braunfels Zeitung*. Also reported to be included in this group was "Dr. Bracht" who must have been New Braunfels resident Felix Bracht, of whom it was said, "where there is to be a battle for the South and her institutions, the Dr. will be sure to be on hand." Comal County was heavily settled by German immigrants, and this would be problematic for Captain Thomas of the New Braunfels KGC Castle in the near future. Many German immigrant residents of Texas were anti-slavery; others were pro-Union, but some may have joined the KGC strictly to participate in the hoped-for conquest of Mexico. Lindheimer himself had been at the Battle of San Jacinto, where Texas won its independence from Mexico. Bracht's brother Viktor had allied himself with New York investors in a proposed railroad venture in Mexico, which might have influenced his loyalty to the KGC and its Mexican ambitions.[18]

The four attorneys from Gonzales County present for the early morning assault mentioned by the Southern Confederacy were H.S. Parker, William H. Stewart, T.M. Harwood and M.L. Evans. William H. Stewart owned five slaves and was soon recommended by Captain John Cotlett Key to serve as Acting Quartermaster, eventually attaining the rank of Major in the Commissary Department, a position favored by many KGC. Captain Key was also a lawyer and a neighbor of H.S. Parker in Gonzales. J.C.G. Key was one of the Captains in charge of Colonel Jones' battalion of Rangers from Gonzales under the overall command of Ben McCulloch on this mission to take over the Arsenal. The other Captain in charge of Jones' battalion was Travis Hill Ashby. As for the other attorneys from Gonzales that were a part of this mission, T.M. Harwood owned eight slaves; there were no slaves under M.L. Evans' name, but there were six slaves in Gonzales County owned by J.E. Evans. Sometimes the oldest son of a plantation class family was expected to take a lead role in family matters, especially when they were in line to inherit the family's wealth. "Mr. Harris of Comall" was one such case. Comal County was majority German and bordered Hays County where the Reverend Buckner Harris served the Methodist Church South congregants in the town of San Marcos. He was the 27-year old son of Judge Buckner Harris, a wealthy planter of nearby Gonzales County who kept 36 slaves there in 1860. The Buckner Harris family moved from Georgia to DeWitt County, Texas in 1846 and had 46 slaves there in 1850. Grandson of Revolutionary War General Buckner Harris of Virginia, the young itinerant preacher would soon be recommended by KGC members for the position of Regimental Chaplain for the 6th Texas Infantry of the Confederate States. Being on the vanguard of the creation of what they hoped would be The Golden Circle had its benefits in rank and position. So here Reverend Harris was part of a hostile movement against the U.S. military force at San Antonio, joining in with another minister of the South, Reverend Andrew Herron.[19]

Another such scion of a wealthy planter family who participated in the KGC-led assault on San Antonio was George Thomas McGehee. The oldest son of Thomas Gilmer McGehee, George was raised on the family farm on the San Marcos River where his father had sixteen slaves in 1860. One of their neighbors in the lush valley between the Blanco and San Marcos rivers that formed a plantation district was Clement Reed Johns. Described as "a lifelong Democrat and a Mason who never joined a church," the 43-year old Mr. Johns owned seven slaves in 1860 which he kept in Hays County; he also kept a house in Travis County in Austin with his wife and two young children. He was serving as the State Comptroller and often clashed with Governor Sam Houston; Johns also was one of the sixty-one signers of the call for a Secession Convention. Those men signing were said to be KGC members. Curiously, there was a Clement R. Johns, Jr., age 23, who also lived in Travis County and may have been the owner of the six slaves held there under the name "C.R. Johns". As the correspondent for the *Southern Confederacy* noted in his published report of the men in the Arsenal assault, "We believe there was but one representative from Hays county – Mr. George McGehee – and one from Travis – Clement R. Johns, Jr.; but it was only because there had been no call upon those counties for volunteers."[sic] Regardless, it is safe to say that all of these slaveowners were certainly supporters of the KGC and most likely members as well. Some political figures served as common soldiers in the assault on the Arsenal. A report of the incident provided by the *San Antonio Herald*, probably witnessed by its publisher John Davis Logan, a KGC member himself, reported the following public figures as among "the command... of some six hundred men, the real bone and sinew of the country;"

> among these of our acquaintances, we were pleased to meet with such men as Hon. Thomas H. Duggan, State Senator from the Guadalupe District, Hon. Wm. H. Stewart, member of the Legislature from Gonzales, John Ireland and W. E. Goodrich, Esqs., of Seguin, also, Judge Douglass, Chief Justice of Guadalupe county, and Dr. Smith, of Lockhart.[20]

Three of the Commissioners – Thomas J. Devine, Samuel A. Maverick and Phillip N. Luckett, stated in their official report to J. C. Robertson, Chairman of the Committee of Public Safety that when McCulloch marched his force into San Antonio that "he was joined by about one hundred and fifty K.G.C.s, and about the same number of citizens who were not members of the order, and about the same number from the Medina, Atascosa, and the country west" of the city. The KGC were said to be well-armed. This gave McCulloch numerical superiority over the Federal troops in the Arsenal at the rate of approximately 1,100 to 160 by 8 A.M. that Saturday morning, February 16. Of the final total of McCulloch's forces, it was said that 80 percent of them were KGC. General Twiggs surrendered later that day and his troops were marched out of the city, to a location to await transportation by sea out of the State. The "volunteers" from Seguin began drifting home the next day. In the meantime, the U.S. troops stationed elsewhere throughout the State had no idea as to what had occurred in San Antonio, as stated by Lieutenant Zenas R. Bliss of the 8th U.S. Infantry, stationed in far West Texas. "Fort Davis was then called 470 miles from San Antonio," he later wrote, "and Fort Quitman was about 140 miles still further West, and Fort Bliss at El Paso was nearly, if not quite, 750 miles from San Antonio, and 60 miles West of Quitman." Mail delivery from San Antonio to those outposts had been restricted and was probably being monitored. Although General Twiggs reached an agreement on February 18 to surrender all U.S. forces in Texas, Lieutenant Bliss remained at Fort Quitman until April 5, totally unaware. Meanwhile, the commander of U.S. forces surrounded at Camp Cooper, far North of but not so far West as Fort Davis, realized on his own that something was up, writing to a superior on February 16, "we are to be attacked, for the purpose of the pillage and plunder of the Federal property intrusted [sic] to our protection." In this dispatch Lieutenant Carpenter offered to sacrifice his life and that of all his troops in defense of Camp Cooper, writing, "each would rather lay his corpse to molder upon the plain he defends than to drag it hence to be the laugh and scorn of every honest lover of his country's glory." By this time the KGC-led force of some 230 men had been greatly augmented by the arrival of State Troops under the command of Colonel William C. Dalrymple. Within this regiment of Mounted Rangers were six companies, some commissioned by Governor Houston to raise as many as 70 men each. The exact size of the combined force of Texans is not known, but it was about 350 Rangers and 230 KGC that surrounded a Federal garrison of 270 men. Camp Cooper was not set up as a defensive position to begin with, a fact noted by Captain S.D. Carpenter, the post commander. Colonel Dalrymple sent a dispatch to Carpenter assuring him that he was in command of Texas State Troops and that Carpenter had twenty-four hours to surrender Camp Cooper "with all arms, munitions, and property of every description." From Williamson County (near Austin) Colonel Dalrymple had been commissioned a Captain by previous Governor and known KGC member Hardin Richard Runnels. Houston had re-commissioned him as Aide to the Governor with the rank of Colonel to bring some semblance of control to what he had described as a "mob" to General Twiggs. Captain Carpenter, realizing the nature of his situation, responded to Colonel Dalrymple on February 19 in the affirmative, and Camp Cooper was taken over by the Texans on February 21. That same day, February 21 witnessed the occupation of Brazos Santiago, an island at the mouth of the Rio Grande River by Colonel John S. Ford and his command of fellow KGC officers. Among Ford's officers were Hugh McLeod as lieutenant colonel, and eventually Benjamin F. Terry as major and Captain John Littleton – all known KGC as was Ford. No doubt others within his force of 500 men were members of the Order, too. Some of these men would join another KGC expedition to Virginia in a few months led by Thomas S. Lubbock – specifically Ben Terry, Dan A. Connor, J. Mayrant Smith, Dr. J.F. Matchet and Dr. Victor Friedeman. General Sidney Sherman described Ford's men as "planters, merchants and clerks, who would not be willing to do garrison duty, but on the contrary would be anxious to return." It was rumored that the Union commander was considering a counterattack; he was stubbornly resisting General Twiggs' order to surrender. Ford's forces were soon augmented; E.B. Nichols arranged for additional companies of armed men to reinforce Ford's men. Nichols went back to Galveston on February 28; from there he was able to rally 300 more men from Galveston, Houston, Liberty County, and Fort Bend County. These men were already armed and assembled and were not State troops, so they must be considered KGC – especially considering the identities of their commanders.

Most of them are already known to have been members of the Order, and due to circum-stance the others should be, too. They were: Henry Van Buren, Galveston Artillery; Nahor Briggs Yard, Galveston Rifles; William H. Redwood, Lone Star Rifles; Samuel Boyer Davis, Lone Star Coast Guards; William Edwards, Milam Rifles; Fred H. Odlum, Davis Guards, and Daniel A. Conner, Fort Bend Rifles. Once these reinforcements were in place, the U.S. troops eventually surrendered and gave up their weapons. Among the arms confiscated by the Texans were 21 artillery pieces, badly needed for the war that would commence in a couple of months. Fort Sumter had still not been attacked at this point, and Lincoln was not yet the sitting President. The KGC Texas State Convention was to begin in San Antonio on February 22, one day before the general public was to vote on the Ordinance of Secession.[21]

One of the men working behind the scenes to aid the military Knights in their takeover of Texas was Master Mason Ebenezar Bacon Nichols of Galveston. He had been the Grand High Priest of the Royal Arch Masons in Texas from 1851 to 1853. In January 1855 he was one of the original members who founded the Grand Encampment of Texas for the Knights Templar, the Masonic faction most closely resembling the Knights of the Golden Circle in Texas. That first year he is listed as the Grand Captain General of the Grand Commandery, KT; the following year he was a member of the subordinate encampment at Houston along with known KGC members Peter W. Gray, Thomas Carothers and Edward Alexander Stevens. Known as A.S. Ruthven No. 2, its namesake Archibald St. Clair Ruthven was also a member. Born in Scotland in 1818, Ruthven was an established merchant in New York City at an early age. In 1840 he left New York for Houston where he quickly established himself as a successful importer on the Texas coast. By 1855, he was living in Galveston and working as a cotton buyer for the New York firm of Nelson, Clements & Company. That year he also helped found the Grand Encampment of Texas of the Templar Knights, along with E.B. Nichols and others, and served as the KT's first Grand Commander for the State. He also was active with the Knights Templar of the Invisible Friends Commandery No. 1 in New Orleans. By 1861, KT encampment Ruthven No. 2 included as members the aforementioned KGC as well as known KGC members Thomas S. Lubbock and John B. Jones. However, Ruthven and Nichols were listed that year on the roster as members of San Felipe de Austin No. 1 KT commandery in Galveston. They had become involved in the secession of Texas, with Ruthven as a blockade runner, and Nichols as the Texas KGC's banker. In the thirteen years from 1848 to 1859, Nichols had served nine years as the Grand Treasurer of the Grand Masonic Lodge of Texas. He was now most certainly a high-ranking KGC in a non-military role, at least a Knight of The True Faith, the "financial degree" and second highest of the three tiers of the organization. By 1861, he was a "commission merchant" and cotton broker in Galveston, the premier slave-trading center in Texas. Commission merchants were often those men involved in the slave trade as the term was a more socially acceptable one than "slave trader." Born in New York, Nichols had fought Indians as a member of the Texas Rifles and, by 1860, was a Director as was James Sorley of the Galveston and Tyler Railroad. In 1861, Nichols owned twelve slaves. The Secession Convention had appointed him a Commissioner to act as receiving agent for all federal property captured, which meant he was part of the secretive cabal that was running the State. He had also been charged by the Convention to procure the money, supplies, and transportation for John S. Ford's military expedition from Galveston to the mouth of the Rio Grande River. Nichols found most of what he needed from his contacts in New Orleans and accompanied Ford and McLeod on their mission. John S. Ford mentioned the existence of a secret fund that was used during the secession crisis in Texas to encourage the mutiny of U.S. Army officers; the money was held in Citizens Bank of New Orleans and disbursed by E.B. Nichols. This demonstrates without any doubt the strong connection between high-ranking members of the Masonic Order in Texas and the KGC. One would not see either of these New Yorkers, Ruthven or Nichols, at the KGC Texas State Convention; they were busy with other matters behind the scenes. The conduct of the KGC's convention in Texas would fall mostly under the direction of another native New Yorker, Charles Arden Russell.[22]

Charles A. Russell had been accidentally born in Waterloo, Canada in 1822 when his family had crossed the river from their native New York for temporary business reasons. After his birth his family returned to their home in the town of Erie, which was later renamed Newstead, New York. His father died when Charles was barely fourteen years of age. After working in Buffalo for a few years he went west to Michigan when just seventeen. At age eighteen, he enlisted in the United States Army for five years and served in an artillery battalion. When his unit was transferred to Corpus Christi, Texas during the Mexican War, Charles decided to stay in Texas after meeting his wife-to-be Miss Emeline Camilla Brightman in the nearby town of Goliad. They married in 1847, living in Goliad County where Charles assumed different positions as a public official. In 1852, he was employed to survey the new town of Helena in Karnes County and soon moved his family to the new town, buying a lot on the San Antonio River. By 1855, he was admitted to the bar and specialized in land law. In addition, he became the first clerk of the San Antonio River Baptist Association and began trading land certificates. With his excess earnings he began to buy slaves. At about this time he began a long friendship with John Littleton, a KGC member; soon Charles Russell joined the Order as well. When Littleton resigned his position as a delegate to the Secession Convention so that he could raise soldiers for John S. Ford, Charles A. Russell took his place in the second session. Before that happened, some of his friends talked him into attending the K.G.C. Texas State Convention in San Antonio, beginning February 22.[23]

On Friday the first day of the State K.G.C. convention, Charles Russell took a seat in Braden Hall and watched as it was organized. The first order of business was to elect by acclamation the officers of the convention itself, which was then announced:

> ...by acclamation, Col. John A. Wilcox, of San Antonio, President; Col. G.W. Chilton, of Tyler, Vice President; W.R. Cowan, Esq., of Lockhart, and Victor W. Thompson, of La Grange, Secretaries; Dr. J.E. Park, of Seguin, Sergeant-at-Arms, and E.B. Thomas of Atascosa, Inside Sentinel.

At this point, Charles Russell was a virtual unknown, although his friends had strongly urged him to attend. He would soon distinguish himself. As he told his wife in a letter, "I felt as though I was small potatoes. But it so turned out, and I hardly know [how] I got into it, that I controlled the whole action of the Convention and did almost everything that was done there." Because of his "grasp of military management" he ultimately "was elected by a unanimous vote as the secretarial and detail executive of the order – he was elected 'Adjutant-General for the State of Texas.'" – of the KGC. The other convention officers elected were well-known: The Castles from Lockhart, Seguin, La Grange, and Atascosa had taken part in the successful takeover of the Federal Arsenal in San Antonio, as had John A. Wilcox. Victor W. Thompson was the publisher of the Texas KGC's campaign paper, the *La Grange States Rights Democrat*. George W. Chilton had been a statewide leader of the Order since its earliest days in Texas. Dr. John E. Park only owned one slave in Seguin but would serve as a Confederate surgeon in heavy combat. Elijah B. Thomas was Captain of the Pleasanton Castle in Atascosa County.[24]

Next, Trevanion Theodore Teel conducted the rollcall of "delegates entitled to seats in the Convention," and these men answered, as later published by the *States Rights Democrat*:

John A. Wilcox and A. Mitchell, representing San Antonio Castle; G.W. Chilton, Tyler Castle; W.R. Cowan, Lockhart Castle; Victor M. Thompson, La Grange Castle; Lieut. R.W. White, Blair (Belton) Castle; W.P. Patton, Fairfield and Corsicana Castles; J.T. Kilgore, Yorktown Castle; H.A. Tatum, Columbus, Alleyton, Eagle Lake and Wharton Castles; Gilbert Gay, Clinton Castle; P. Clark and D.S. Page, Beeville Castle; A. Tribble and J.E. Park, Seguin Castle; T.T. Teel and E.A. Stevens, Chas. Bickley Castle; E.B. Thomas, Pleasanton Castle; W. B. Cone, Philharmonic Castle; P.J. Barziza, Wallisville and Galveston Castles; C.A. Russell, Helena Castle; Chas. Bickley, Concrete, Bastrop, Gonzales and Castroville Castles, W.L.L. Davidson, Hondo Castle; and E. Trimble, George Bickley Castle. [sic]

Printed documents of this era are rife with misspellings, often due of the inability of the person manually setting type for the printer to read someone else's cursive writing. This document, although published by a "sitting member" of the Convention, Victor W. Thompson, is no exception. For instance, "W.P. Patton" was William T. Patton, and this error was not subsequently repeated in the rest of the document; "P.J. Barziza" was actually Phillip Ignatius Barziza, the grand old man of the Barziza clan. His initials were often mistaken for "P.J." because of the way he wrote the capital letter "I". He was a member of Italian nobility, with English noble blood in his veins as well. Upon emigrating from Italy, he lived for a time in Virginia, where no less than former President of the United States Thomas Jefferson had been his lawyer. Perhaps for those reasons alone he was accorded the highest rank – the third tier of the Order, as a Knight of the Columbian Star. This most secret of designations within the KGC was only revealed in a letter Barziza sent to Charles A. Russell – which means Russell was also a Knight of the Columbian Star. One could only identify as a third tier member to another of the same level. Phillip Barziza's youngest son, Decimus et Ultimus Barziza, known as D. U. Barziza for obvious reasons, was also a known KGC member who had helped organize Castles in Booneville, Brazos County; Independence, Washington County and the town of Caldwell in Burleson County. He also had intended to organize a Castle in Milam County, but it is unknown as to whether he succeeded. The author believes Barziza's other sons, especially Francis L. Barziza, the eldest son and a leader in the Knights Templar in Texas, were also members of the KGC.

None of those Castles organized by D.U. were represented at the Convention, nor were numerous others known to exist in North Texas and Northeast Texas. No one from Bonham, Dallas, Fort Worth, Greenville, Sherman, Waxahachie, or even Marshall were allowed on the floor. This Convention was an exclusive affair for only the most influential. Victor W. Thompson, one of the sitting delegates, did later report in the *States Rights Democrat* that "The services of the order in the State – comprising 8000 members – will be tendered at the Convention." Others present in San Antonio at the time of the KGC Convention would echo that number as reliable.[25]

After rollcall at the Convention different committees were created to assess the situation and make plans for the new empire that would result once Texas seceded from the Union. A Committee of Good Order was appointed by "the Chair" who one might assume was Convention President John A. Wilcox. This committee consisted of "Capt. H.A. Tatum, P. Clark, Esq., Lt. A. Tribble, Capt. W.B. Cone and Capt. P.J. Barziza." Almost as an after-thought, Charles Bickley was added to the committee on a motion from the floor. "Major" Bickley then read a letter from his relative George W.L. Bickley, the national President of the Order and it was referred to the committee just created. Of the members of the committee, Howal A. Tatum was a well-known artist and planter who owned and occasionally traded slaves in Colorado County; all that is known of Patterson Clark is that he was a member of the Beeville Castle led by Charles Carrol Jones, and apparently a lawyer. Captain C.C. Jones was not present at the Convention – he was a Justice of the Peace in Bee County – but fellow Beeville Castle member Dr. Daniel S. Page was in attendance. The Beeville Castle reported fifty members, half of whom were foot soldiers. Alexander Tribble of the Seguin Castle had been the Lieutenant that had helped command "the K.G.C. detachment" during the march from Seguin to capture the Arsenal in San Antonio. William Baker Cone was a member of the Philharmonic Castle in Wilson County, which was led by Captain E.J. Pitts and reported thirty-three members. Captain Pitts wasn't present either.[26]

It must be noted that on the first day of the Convention, some men who had not been granted seats as delegates were allowed to take seats as alternates, meaning, they too, were members, and most of them were familiar figures within the Order. Those men were Powhatan Jordan, Robert B. Ward, A.J. Rice, William J. Clarke, Dr. George Cupples, Samuel W. McAllister, John M. Smith, and George Henry Sweet. Powhatan Jordan was a graduate from a military academy in Virginia who became a doctor after graduating from Columbian University in Washington, D.C. as an M.D. He served as a surgeon under John Salmon Ford during the Comanche expedition in 1858 after moving to San Antonio. Robert B. Ward was the former sergeant in the U.S. Second Cavalry and had been the KGC's inside man for the takeover of Camp Cooper. He owned a boarding house in San Antonio. A.J. Rice was just who he said he was: A.J. Rice. He went by that name for all of his life, although his first name was Andrew. He owned twelve slaves in Victoria County in 1860 but lived in Bexar County. He was no joke; after the war started, he joined Asa Mitchell's Company of Minute Men in San Antonio, which in reality was the secret police organization for the vigilance committee of Bexar County. He became a man to be feared. Asa Mitchell was one of the seated delegates at this Convention, representing San Antonio Castle as was Convention President John A. Wilcox. It was the largest Castle listed in terms of membership, with 115 horse soldiers and 30 foot soldiers. William J. Clarke was the Captain of the San Antonio Number 1 Castle; he was an attorney and a Director of the San Antonio and Mexican Gulf Railroad, along with KGC members Samuel A. Maverick and Asa Mitchell. The name of the railroad itself sounds like a KGC pipe dream, but by the time of the Convention its line to Victoria was complete. It was intended to be extended to connect San Antonio to a port on the Gulf of Mexico. Another one of the alternates, Dr. George Cupples had been appointed by George Bickley to effectively run the Texas State Headquarters of the KGC at San Antonio whenever he and Charles Bickley were away. A native of Scotland, Dr. Cupples was considered the best surgeon in San Antonio. Alternate Samuel W. McAllister was a jack-of-all trades businessman in San Antonio and serving as the Captain of the Charles Bickley Castle at the moment; he had previously been a City Alderman for Ward Number 3 in San Antonio. Powhatan Jordan would soon be working with McAllister in the clean-up operations necessary to confiscate all remaining U.S. property in the State. John M. Smith was a well-regarded, seasoned Texas Ranger and had been a Captain under Middleton T. Johnson's failed Indian expedition; he was against secession and was trusted by Sam Houston. The Governor's cousin, Thomas "Carruthers"[sic], was reported to the Convention as being the Captain of the Huntsville Castle in Walker County, with twelve members. Last among the invitees listed was George Henry Sweet, like Charles Russell a native New Yorker who married a Texas girl. George sometimes accompanied Charles Bickley to speaking engagements around the State. He was a Mexican War veteran as well as an editor of the *San Antonio Herald*.[27]

After the alternates were seated, a motion was made to create a committee on Secret Business of the Order. The members of this ominous sounding committee were some of the most radical and militant the KGC would produce in Texas: George W. Chilton, Asa Mitchell and Captain William T. Patton. Following this a motion was made to form the Committee on Military Affairs, consisting of Howal A. Tatum, who had spearheaded the formation of four Castles in his county and served as the Captain of the Columbus Castle; Edward Trimble, the Captain of the George Bickley Castle in San Antonio and Charles A. Russell, the new Adjutant General of the Order in Texas. After Charles Bickley read a "circular letter from Headquarters" the Finance Committee was formed, consisting of William R. Cowan, William B. Cone and Dr. Cupples. Then the Convention adjourned for the weekend, to meet again at 9 o'clock Monday morning. Until then, KGC members were free to work the polling places in their counties on Saturday the 23 as voters were given the chance to vote to approve or reject the Ordinance of Secession.

J.T. Sprague, one of the officers in the U.S. 8th Infantry, was witness to election day in Texas that Saturday: "The people were called upon to cast a vote clearly written out – for secession, against secession. The polls were guarded with care, and the bold man who dared to vote in the negative *was marked*, in the common parlance of the day." In some counties, the voting experience was markedly different. In Ellis County, where there was at least one KGC Castle, it was reported that in Waxahachie the KGC marched en masse to the polling place to cast their vote, no doubt to intimidate other voters. Even so, 172 people voted against secession in that county versus 527 who voted in favor of seceding from the United States. Further North in the State, Collin County Unionist Charles B. Moore recorded his voting experience in the Lamar County town of Paris on what he described as a blustery and rainy morning:

> To Paris in a buggy with Aleck Mehane to vote against Secession. Mutch excitement.[sic] The secession flag with 13 stars hoisted on a high pole. The Disunionists came into town with their flag at the head of the procession but the Union procession was 2 or 3 times as long & had two Union flags. Secession was voted down by 87 votes in town.

Henry S. Moore brought in the returns.... The secessionists admit the county has gone for Union.

The next entry in Charles Moore's diary the day after the election states, "The probability now is that all North Texas has voted against Secession but I think Texas has most likely voted herself out of the Union."[sic] He was correct: when the votes were officially counted on March 4 by a three-man committee including Nat Terry, one of the most ardent secessionists in the State, the overall tally was 46,129 votes for secession and 14,697 votes against. Both Collin County, where Charles B. Moore resided, and Lamar County, where he voted on February 14 were carried by the anti-secession vote. Fannin County, adjacent and in-between Collin and Lamar counties also voted against secession. This is interesting because there were KGC Castles in Collin, Fannin and Grayson County, just north of Collin County, which had organized a Castle there in January 1860. Grayson County rejected secession as well. Other counties with known KGC Castles also had very close votes; Colorado County had 584 votes for secession and 330 votes against. Texas was the only State of the original Confederacy that allowed its citizens to vote for or against secession. Out of a total of 154 counties, 122 had voted, and out of those voting it should be noted that Texans were not voting to join the Confederacy; only to secede from the Union. Some voters, and others like Sam Houston, held out hope for a return to the old days of an independent Republic of Texas but it was not to be. Charles Anderson, one of the few men in San Antonio to take a public stand against the secession movement, had this to say about the election of February 23:

> And thus was consummated one of the meanest and yet most successful treasons... of all history.... Of its successes, the *first was, that it carried the so-called election*.... Without this brilliant *coup-de-main* (the first victory of Rebellion), the majority would have surely been, in Texas, *for the union cause*. As it was, only forty-two thousand votes (less than half the total votes of the State), was polled, of which thirteen thousand votes were given by the now confounded and dismayed Unionists.

San Antonio newspaper editor James P. Newcomb was also present and a witness to the election and its results. He attributed the outcome to "The shortness of the time, precluded the possibility of a fair expression of the people, and after developments brought to light the fact that many of the reported secession majorities that were reported, were false."[sic] With someone like Nat Terry appointed by the Secession Convention to count the votes, it would be easy to suspect the final voting tally. Others have noticed extremely one-sided results reported by some counties where the KGC was active, leading them to speculate voter intimidation by the secret society. For instance, in Webb County on the border with Mexico, there were no votes against secession; the same is true for Zapata County, also a border community. In Karnes County, home to Charles A. Russell, there was only one vote recorded against secession versus 153 votes in favor. Marion County in deep East Texas and Fort Bend County in the Gulf Coast Black Belt, also recorded zero votes against secession. J.P. Newcomb summed it up thusly:

> The Capital, San Antonio, and several western towns and counties, gave Union majorities. But while we claim a great majority of the people as Union in sentiment, we cannot escape the humiliating fact, that they stood by with folded arms and allowed the conspirators to presume their opinions, and commit them, soul and body, to the work of treason... War was not thought of. Had the people of Texas believed that civil war would be the inevitable result of secession, they would have recoiled from it. But step, by step, they were led gently, but swiftly down into the depths of treason....[28]

All four of the men quoted above as witnesses to the election, soon left Texas for a safer environment, as their lives were endangered by their opinions. At this point, though, John R. Baylor was still on his diversionary search for Native American sanguinary conquest. It was not going well. On Sunday, February 24, part of his force of "buffalo hunters" arrived at Camp Cooper, having exhausted their horses and with sickness among the men. They had left "Camp Rendezvous" on January 26 as part of an expedition of 250 men but had returned with no Indian scalps to show for it. From February 24 onward, more of Baylor's men began returning to other frontier outposts like Fort Chadbourne, "in detachments, having had a long hard campaign into Indian country." Most of them were out of food and "almost destitute of clothes". The mission was failing in terms of actually making contact with any Indians, but it had been a successful way of organizing a large group of armed men with warfare on their minds and maneuvering them around the Western frontier of Texas. While Baylor continued to meander the frontier, on this particular Sunday members of the Committee of Public Safety were in session in Galveston making plans to take possession of a U.S. naval vessel, the Henry Dodge, with a crew of twelve men, guns and ammunition. The entire crew was said to be disloyal to the Union, and a deal was struck whereby they would surrender their vessel to the Texans. Also that day the committee made arrangements to confiscate a load of railroad iron, with the help of Mr. A.M. Gentry, President of the Texas and New Orleans Railroad Company. These things accomplished, the committee adjourned, leaving three of their number, James J. Diamond, A.T. Rainey and James R. Armstrong to prepare for the military defense of Galveston.[29]

The following day, Monday, February 25, the K.G.C. State Convention reconvened for its second day of official meetings in San Antonio. Charles Bickley read the resolutions reached by the Committee on Good Order, the first of them calling for the election of officers to the Military and Financial department of the Texas K.G.C. to complete the State organization. That done, they proposed to formally offer the services of the Texas Division of KGC to the State government, "for offensive and defensive measures, as the case may be." Elucidating some administrative matters, the Committee of Good Order then formally expressed its "thanks in behalf of the K.G.C. of the State of Texas, to the editors of the *San Antonio Herald, Houston Telegraph, Galveston News,* and other papers throughout the State, for the kindly interest they take in our Order, and the complimentary manner in which they always speak of the same." Indeed, the KGC could not have induced the secession of Texas without favorable coverage from the press, such as this piece written by the *San Antonio Herald* that ran on the front page of the *Dallas Herald* just a few days before the secession election titled, "Order of the Knights of the Golden Circle – Its objects, Aim and Principles":

The K.G.C. is a Southern Institution – the counteracting power of the "Emigrant Aid" and "Wide Awake" Societies of the North. It is a lawful company, based upon "Christian principles," looking to the winning of Empire for the South. – It recognizes and propagates slavery as a divine institution, wisely established by Jehovah himself and fraught with all the elements of social, moral and political good to the negro, and conducive to the best interests of our country. It inculcates the doctrines of "Manifest Destiny" and teaches that the Star of Empire is Southward. It would show an outlet for the free negro population of the Southern States. It would gain control of the Gulf of Mexico and the vast trade thereof. It would keep lands peculiarly adapted to our system of labor out of the hands of the Abolition majority of the North. It would cultivate the chivalric spirit of our people and tie them together in a bond of brotherhood. It would give peace and protection to society and help elevate and ennoble our race. It would protect the weak and punish the bad. It would revive in our midst the days of chivalry and at the same time furnish the South with a complete and effective military system.

Of course, they were really talking about the reestablishment of the monarchy they or their ancestors had once lived under as a British Colony or as citizens of European countries abroad, with the plantation class as royalty served by knights, knaves, and slaves. The tribute from the *Herald* went on painting its lovely picture of a slaveowner's paradise and then went into the standard fare of how the organization was structured, what the fees were to be paid, how to organize a Castle, etc. This grand, free advertisement had appeared in Dallas just 3 days before citizens were to vote on the Order of Secession.

The next resolution was for the KGC convention proceedings, except for those "as may relate to matters of a strictly private character, be published for circulation throughout the State." Accordingly, the proceedings were published, but at the time of the re-search and writing for this book, not a single copy of them could be found in the State of Texas. The only surviving copy of these printed proceedings was found in an archive in New York City. After the war all the copies in Texas must have been destroyed. In concluding its report, The Committee on Good Order appointed three men to prepare "an address to the people of Texas, in behalf of our Order" [sic], those men being George W. Chilton, John A. Wilcox and William B. Cone.

Next to report was the Committee on General Military Affairs, chaired by Charles A. Russell. This report was quite extensive. It began by referring to the rumor brought to the convention by committee member Howal Tatum of a "servile insurrection" looming in the near future. On this basis this committee's report began:

> That for the purpose of making the K.G.C. effectual as a home police, as well as the general welfare and expansion of the Order, they recommend a full and complete military organization of the Home Department; and inasmuch as many citizens, well qualified to do the interior work of the Castle very effectively, would prefer not to occupy a conspicuous military position, they recommend that the military organization of the Order be separate and distinct from the Castle organization.

So it became the stated policy that resulted in a Castle being identified by one name, but the military company associated with that Castle identified by a different name. Obviously, there would be people serving the KGC in more than one role, and as a part of two separately named organizations. This had already occurred in Texas to some extent. Additional regulations relating to this Home Department

were specified: there would be one Marshal of the State to be the commander of
the Order in Texas; he would only be subject to the orders transmitted from the
President of the Ameri-can Legion, at this point George W.L. Bickley. Further,
Texas would be divided into three Brigade Divisions, each under the command of
a Brigadier General appointed by the KGC Convention. Each Brigade Division
would be subdivided into at least three Regimental Divisions, each with a Colonel,
Lieutenant Colonel and two Majors. The State Adjutant General – Charles A. Russell – would have the rank of Colonel, would have custody of all the general records of the Order and orders issued by the Marshal of the State. He was to remain
in residence at Headquarters, which at this point was still in San Antonio. There
would be an Adjutant General in each Brigade Division with the rank of Major.
With matters of the functioning hierarchy established, the committee then turned
to a discussion of how the police state would be established. The police force
would be drawn from the military force of each Castle, with officers separate from
the Castle officers, "provided that any of the military officers may at the same time
fill an office in the Castle, at the discretion of the Castle." This was necessary
because the KGC would be spread very thin; most Castles didn't have more than
30 to 100 members at this point. General Regulations 6 and 8 are the most perti-
nent as to what the police state saw as its role in this new society they envisioned.
Regulation 6 stated "It shall be the duty of the military company in each Castle to
aid and assist the civil authorities in bringing to justice all offenders against the
laws of the State of Texas in relation to slaves and free persons of color; and it
shall be the duty of said Military company to act as a police company under the
laws of the State." Regulation 8 ties the KGC directly to the creation of vigilance
committees and committees of safety. Each Castle was required to appoint such a
committee,

> consisting of members of the 2d. degree, whose duty it shall be to consider
> and decide on the propriety and necessity of instituting legal proceedings
> against each such persons, white or black, as there shall be reason to suspect
> of having violated the laws enacted for the protection of the slave institu-
> tion.

This clarifies who was to benefit the most from the KGC's secret police organization. The second degree members were known as the Knights of the True
Faith, who were primarily the Financial Degree and were expected to help regulate
the business side of things; for a slave state, slavery, and matters connected to

slavery, were important business. It should be remembered that although credita-
ble sources put total KGC membership in Texas at this point as 8,000 members,
that not all of those members were Knights of the Iron Hand, the Military degree.
With the secret police structure and procedures established, the Committee
wrapped up its presentation with Charles A. Russell appointing another committee
charged with carving the State into the proposed Districts. These men were Howal
A. Tatum, John E. Park. W.L.L. Davidson, Victor W. Thompson, William J. Clark
[Clarke], Phillip Barziza, George W. Chilton and Charles Bickley.[30]

After a few moments the Committee on Division returned with their deci-
sions, consisting of three Brigades of three Regiments each, with specific counties
in Texas relegated to a Regiment. For instance, the First Brigade, First Regiment
consisted of the counties of Cameron, Hidalgo, Starr, Zapata, Webb, Dimmitt,
LaSalle, McMullen, Duval, Encinal, Nueces, San Patricio, Live Oak, Bee, Karnes,
DeWitt, Goliad, Victoria, Refugio and Calhoun. Many of these counties were
sparsely settled and on or close to the border with Mexico. There were over 150
counties in the State, so it is not necessary to enumerate each Regiment at this
time. Before the commanders of these Brigades were appointed, the Committee
on Uniforms and Equipments reported to the assembled body. Although the Convention had impressive plans for the outfitting consisting of different uniforms
for different ranks, some of the KGC companies in existence already had their
own uniforms. It is questionable as to whether they ever appropriated the money
to convert their uniforms to the standards proposed by this committee. One sus-
pects not. John B. Stone, Alexander Tribble and "Mathiew Taylor" [sic] were the
creative force for the proposed designs. Then on motion, the Convention adjourned until 8 o'clock that night. When they returned, they unanimously elected
Dr. George Cupples to the position of Surgeon General for the Texas KGC. Captain Trevanion T. Teel then announced that all delegates' treasurers' reports were
due for submission to the Finance Committee by 9 o'clock the following morning.
Then the Convention adjourned for the day.

That following morning, Tuesday, February 26, the first order of business
that we know of, as it was published in the proceedings began at 10 a.m. with
Colonel George W. Chilton in the Chair in place of John A. Wilcox. A detachment
of Union infantry of thirty-two men had unexpectedly arrived in San Antonio
from an interior post, obviously unaware of the coup that had taken place. They
were immediately surrounded by two hundred armed Texans and forced to surrender unconditionally. Possibly this hostile force of armed men were KGC under

the command of John Wilcox, necessitating his absence from the Convention. The roll was called at the Convention and the answers reveal that of the delegates present on the first day, several were not present this third day of the meeting. Those men not accounted for in the roll call besides John A. Wilcox were George H. Sweet, Powhatan Jordan, Robert B. Ward, John M. Smith, Samuel W. McAllister, and A. J. Rice. Taking their place were newcomers James Wilkinson of Bell County, John B. Stone, and Mathew Taylor, the latter two having served the previous day. Also newly accounted for were A.T. Brown and J.T. Mathew. A.T. Brown was a Prussian German immigrant who arrived in Galveston in 1842. After a trip to New York, he returned to Galveston via New Orleans and by 1860 owned ten slaves in Gonzales County, Texas, making him a member of the plantation class. His colleague's real name was James T. Mathieu, although it was often recorded as J.T. Mathew or Matthews or Matthieu. He was a British citizen, born at Port-of-Spain on the isle of Trinidad in 1821. By 1850, he owned seven slaves in Gonzales County. All the others in attendance the first day of the Convention were present in this third session. Dr. Cupples then addressed the delegates with a report from the Finance Committee that is of historic significance. The report compiled by Cupples, William B. Cone and William R. Cowan is a tabular statement of "the number of men for Service, and of the Funds on hand, as also of other available re-sources...prepared from the scanty data furnished by twenty-eight Castles." This by no means provided information on all the Castles present, or all in existence within the State, but it does list the Castles by name, the counties of their location and the names of their Captains. According to Victor W. Thompson, one of the Secretaries of the Convention, there were forty Castles represented at the Convention; it should be inferred that the fact that only twenty-eight submitted reports of their resources was due to many of the other Castles being involved in military activity across the State, taking over and occupying forts and military facilities. Others, those from Northeast Texas, were still on John R. Baylor's Grand Buffalo Hunt, which had not completely terminated yet. Still, the tabular report is a wealth of information that shows that prominent men sometimes served as Captains within the KGC. Two of the Castles submitting their reports indicated that they did not have a Captain. Those were the Wharton Castle in Wharton County, one of the largest in the State with 100 horsemen listed as available, equipped with 100 "rifles or guns" and 20 Colt pistols. The other Castle with no one at the helm was the Hondo Castle in Medina County with twelve horsemen equipped with twelve guns and five Colt pistols. The largest Castle listed in terms of membership was the Huntsville Castle in Walker County, the home of Governor Sam Houston. With 150 members, the Huntsville Castle was managed by Houston's cousin, KGC Captain Thomas Carothers. Only 12 of the 150 members were listed as soldiers. William Lott Davidson was representing the Hondo Castle at the Convention; he was born in Mississippi in 1838 but was raised on a plantation near San Antonio on the Medina River. His father, Alexander Hamilton Davidson was a delegate to the Secession Convention from Colorado County where he kept nineteen slaves. A graduate of Davidson College in North Carolina, an institution named for his great-uncle, William Lott Davidson returned to Texas and became a Texas Ranger, serving under filibustering Rangers William R. Henry and James H. Callahan, infamous for leading the Callahan Expedition in 1855, described as a glorified slave hunting foray into Mexico.[31]

Of the twenty-eight Castles reporting their assets, it should be noted that most of these were located in counties near San Antonio, and the area East from there across the Black Belt of the State. The smallest Castle reporting, the Eagle Lake Castle of Colorado County with its Captain listed as "I.J. Frazer" had only five members. Isaac J. Frazier owned twenty-one slaves in Colorado County. There were three other Castles in the same county, however; those being the Alleyton Castle with fifteen men under Captain J.K. Hanks, the Columbus Castle under Howal A. Tatum with twenty men and the Oakland Castle with eight men under Captain Lawrence E. LeTulle. All the Colorado County Castles had been formed with the help of Howal Tatum; some of the smaller ones like the Oakland Castle under Lawrence E. LeTulle may have been family affairs. Lawrence LeTulle and his family were rice planters originally from Virginia and his brother Victor D. LeTulle, a merchant, was an officer in one of the early companies formed at Oakland. The roster of the Oakland Guards included an enlisted man registered as "T. W. LeTulle". Jonathan K. Hanks of the Columbus Castle was a Mexican War veteran and slave owner. The Wallisville Castle in Chambers County near Galveston had twenty-five men led by Captain Phillip I. Barziza, who served a dual role as a Knight of the Columbian Star and as a recruiter for other Castles. Bell County had two Castles that reported – the Salado Castle and the Blair Castle – although there may have been at least one more from that county. Henry E. Bradford, E. H. P. Bristowe, James F. Hardin "and others" in Bell County had requested permission from Governor Houston to form a militia company in late November of the previous year – just after Lincoln's election. In turning them down, Houston wrote, "I infer that you propose to organize a volunteer corps subject to a more stringent discipline and drill.... you can organize under the act approved February 15th, 1858, incorporating Military Companies." Many of the most likely KGC companies were organized under the 1858 Act, which when passed incorporated pre-existing "uniformed companies" into Ranger companies. The Salado Castle with its force of forty-six men were led by "M. Highsmith" who was in fact Malcijah Benjamin Highsmith, a former Texas Ranger who had participated in the Texas Revolution as an eight-year-old boy. He was also a veteran of the Mexican War, serving under his father Samuel Highsmith. His background had much in common with other Texas KGC warrior-leaders. The Blair Castle of Bell County, with its seventy would-be-warriors, were led by Captain "W.S. Rauther" who was actually William Samuel Rather, the Worshipful Master of the Belton Lodge No. 166 of the Masonic Order. Several other KGC and probable KGC were members of his lodge in Bell County; most notably Henry E. Bradford, E.S.C. Robertson and J.W. Embree. Robertson and Embree had done much to promote the Texas Slave Panic of 1860. In addition to maintaining a large Castle, William S. Rather was also a successful merchant and a substantial cotton planter.[32]

DeWitt County had three Castles that reported to the convention. John O. McGee was Captain of the Concrete Castle, named for the town of the same name, which hosted Concrete College, one of the most popular boarding schools in Texas. By 1861 the town of Concrete was considered an educational center. With only sixteen members listed, the Concrete Castle was still the best-funded one of all the twenty-eight Castles reporting. The other two Castles in DeWitt County were the Clinton Castle with thirty members under Captain Andrew J. Hodge and the Yorktown Castle with fifty-six members under Captain Joel S. Miles. Hodge was a slave owner and a doctor who chose a fighting man's role in the war – at least for a time. Joel S. Miles was an officer in the Coleto Lodge No. 124, located in Yorktown, where his Castle was coincidentally located. Among his fellow members in this Masonic Lodge was known KGC member J. T. Kilgore, Past Master of the lodge and representative of the Yorktown Castle at the State KGC Convention. James Thomas Kilgore of Maryland met his wife Caroline Elizabeth Bookwalter in Ohio where they married in 1850 and moved to Texas. He was a farmer in Dewitt County in 1860. Most of the other Castles – the four in San Antonio/Bexar County, two from Gonzales County, and others – have already been mentioned; but it is worth pointing out some of the more uniquely named Castles that reported. There was the Sweet Home Castle of Lavaca County, with twelve members under Captain John R. Pulliam; the Star of the South Castle in

Uvalde County with fifteen members commanded by Captain C. S. Short; the Castroville Castle in Medina County under the command of James Paul with twenty-seven members, many who were involved in the takeover of U.S. military posts, and the previously mentioned Philharmonic Castle in Wilson County with thirty-three men led by E. J. Pitts, whose identity remains somewhat obscure.[33]

After the presentation of the tabular chart of the twenty-eight Castles, the meeting adjourned until 2 o'clock. When the delegates returned and resumed their meeting, George W. Chilton was again serving as Chairman. Alexander Tribble of Seguin then introduced a resolution that Victor W. Thompson be elected State Printer for "the Texas Division, K.G.C., and that all communications, official or otherwise, affecting the interests of our order, be published in *The States Rights Democrat*, thereby making him the organ of the K.G.C. in the State." Charles A. Russell moved that the resolution be adopted, and so it was, motion carried. Phillip Barziza then moved that the assemblage elect "a Marshal, Brigade and staff officers, and a State Treasurer, and that the Marshal be empowered to appoint all other officers necessary to a complete organization of the several departments." George W. Chilton of Tyler in Smith County was chosen as Marshal of the Texas Division; then the Brigade commanders were elected. For the Eastern Brigade the delegates chose Elkanah Bracken Greer of Marshall in Harrison County, the county with the largest population of slaves. For command of the Middle Brigade, John Salmon Ford, who some thought was the best available military officer in the State, was chosen. Command of the Western Brigade went to John A. Wilcox of San Antonio, and for State Treasurer of the KGC, James Vance, a well-to-do merchant of San Antonio was chosen. After concluding some other business, R.W. White of Bell County made a motion that "the State Printer, publish and distribute in pamphlet form, ten copies of the proceedings of this convention to each Castle, represent-ed herein...." Victor M. Thompson, the newly designated printer for the Texas KGC was to be reimbursed by James Vance, the organization's new Treasurer. Charles A. Russell, the State Adjutant General for the Knights, then recommended that a three-man committee be formed to research and report back "as far as practicable" the number of Castles organized in Texas, the numbers of first and second degree members of each Castle and the name of the person organizing each Castle. This implies that some Castles may have remained somewhat autonomous or independent from the governing body assembled in convention. The necessity of recording only the names of the first and second degree Knights implies that there were a limited number of persons designated as belonging to the

Third Degree and that membership in that degree was not open to new inductees; at least not independently from the State governing body. As best as can be determined, only four persons have been identified as members of the Third Degree in Texas: Hardin Richard Runnels, the former Governor; Ben McCulloch, the master-mind of the takeover of the Arsenal in San Antonio; Phillip Ignatius Barziza, and Charles Arden Russell. The three members who were appointed to the committee to conduct the count of Castles were not recorded in the minutes of the State Convention, although it is likely that Phillip I. Barziza was one of the three and Charles A. Russell was another, due to the subsequent correspondence between the two men. It is recorded in the minutes that on the evening of the third day of the convention, the KGC met in secret session beginning at 8:30 p.m. with John A. Wilcox as Chairman. Eventually they adjourned until 2:00 the following afternoon, perhaps indicating that they met until a very early hour of the morning.

That next day, the fourth and final day of the convention began at 2:00 that afternoon as scheduled, with "Mr. Clark" [sic] introducing a resolution recognizing "General George Bickley as Commander-in-chief of the American Legion of K.G.C." It was unanimously adopted, which seems to contradict the earlier resolutions of the National KGC Convention that met in Virginia the previous year in which George W. Bickley resigned as Commander and assumed the office and title of President of the American Legion, KGC. The second resolution also introduced by "Mr. Clark," which also passed, stated "no further assurances are required of our faith in him to consummate the cherished objects of the organization." Although the minutes state that a quorum was present and that roll was called this fourth and final day of the meeting, no names of the attendees were listed. It is known that both Patterson Clarke of Bee County and Captain William L. Clarke of San Antonio were present the second day of the meeting, but that does not identify the "Mr. Clark" [sic] who submitted the resolutions in favor of George W. Bickley. A couple of different resolutions of gratitude to the officers of the convention and the two host Castles from San Antonio were issued by Dr. Cupples and William L. Davidson, respectively. Davidson's resolution indicates that two of the three Castles in existence in San Antonio at that time routinely met at Braden Hall. Along with the resolutions issued by Dr. Cupples and William Davidson were two more proposed by Charles A. Russell. One of these resolutions was that the Castles within the State of Texas that recognized the officials elected in the State Convention would be considered a part of the national organization. Russell's other resolution was for the appointment of three field officers

of a Financial Bureau, upon the establishment of such bureau to govern the financial affairs of the State organization. Records of those appointments have not been
found. The convention concluded and those remaining on site were then treated
to "able and brilliant speeches" by George W. Chilton and John A. Wilcox as to
the aims of the organization.[34]

Just as the convention in San Antonio was ending Wednesday February 27,
Henry McCulloch was leaving Camp Colorado, which after his consultations with
its commanding officer, Captain E. Kirby Smith of the U.S. 2nd Cavalry, was
abandoned the previous day. E. Kirby Smith soon joined the Confederate armed
forces after surrendering his post and its supplies to the Texans. Henry McCulloch
was headed toward Camp Chadbourne with companies of men under the command of J.B. "Buck" Barry and Robert Bonner Halley, who McCulloch refers to
in his reports as "R.B. Holly". McCulloch didn't actually know R.B. Halley; he had
asked his friend, E.S.C. Robertson of Bell County, "to select a man to raise a company hurriedly...and, if possible, to have them all ready by breakfast next morning."
The fact that Elijah Sterling Clack Robertson was able to accomplish that feat by
introducing McCulloch to fellow Bell County resident R.B. Halley, suggests that
both men were KGC members in that same county. On February 15, Halley's
company had 65 members. Both Halley and Barry, along with Captains Thomas
Claiborne Frost II, Harris A. Hamner and D.C. Cowan had each been instructed
by Henry McCulloch on February 5 and 6 to raise companies of up to 100 men
each. David C. Cowan had joined Frost's company and Harris A. Hamner had
elected instead to join the siege of Camp Cooper, so McCulloch left a portion of
Captain Frost's company in charge of Camp Colorado while he pushed ahead with
Barry and Halley's companies to Camp Chadbourne. Sometime in late February,
the younger McCulloch brother and his command reached their objective and
found it under the command of Captain S.D. Carpenter, who had earlier sur-ren-
dered Camp Cooper to the KGC and the State troops under Colonel William Dalrymple. Henry McCulloch reported by letter dated February 28 that Captain Carpenter of the First U.S. Infantry had accepted the same terms of surrender for
Camp Chadbourne as before at Camp Cooper. Carpenter and his men were to
abandon their post and march to San Antonio, "governed in all respects by the
terms agreed upon by the commissioners of the convention, Hon. S.A. Maverick,
T.J. Devine, and P.N. Luckett, and General D.E. Twiggs, of the United States
Army". Although Sam Houston was still Governor of Texas, he was not in con-

trol; as ex-pressed by U.S. Army Major J.T. Sprague when he arrived in San Antonio in early March 1861, "the entire country was governed by a vigilance committee, supported by volunteer troops."[sic] By that statement Sprague meant the Committee for Public Safety and its commissioners, and the military units of the KGC.[35]

On March 1 in San Antonio, William T. Mechling, a disgraced former member of the U.S. 8th Infantry who had been dismissed for stealing, was serving as a Captain in the Texas forces and as Assistant Adjutant-General. In the performance of his duties he inspected several detachments of KGC military units that were to serve as State troops. The following day, he issued a report designating the assignments or posts of these troops in a dispatch to the Commissioners on the Committee for Public Safety. Lieutenant Samuel W. McAllister of Captain Powhatan Jordan's Company was assigned to command one sergeant, one corporal and eighteen privates to guard Fort Davis. Several members of Captain Trevanion T. Teel's company of KGC were given separate posts; 2nd Lieutenant John C. Moody [or Moodie] with one corporal and fifteen privates were sent to Fort Lancaster, 1st Sergeant T. L. Wilson with one corporal and fifteen privates were assigned to Camp Hudson, and Lieutenant B.E. Benton of Seguin was sent to guard Fort Mason with twenty mounted men. Additional men under known KGC members Lieutenant James Paul of Castroville were sent to Camp Verde and more under Lieutenant William C. Adams of Uvalde; thirty-five in total were divided between Fort Duncan and Fort Clarke. This implies that there was more than one Castle in Uvalde County, as Captain C. S. Short reported to the State convention only 15 members in his Star of the South Castle in that county. Captain T.T. Teel and his 1st Lieutenant Jordan W. Bennett were on stand-by with fifteen privates each, waiting for the order to occupy the U.S. bases at Fort Duncan and Fort Clarke. One by one these Federal posts would fall to the KGC and be abandoned by the U.S. military.[36]

The second session of the Secession Convention reconvened on Saturday March 2, the day the KGC military units received their orders to occupy the line of forts on the Western frontier. Charles A. Russell, the newly elected Adjutant General of the Texas KGC, now took his seat at the Secession Convention. He took the place of his friend John Littleton, the Captain of the Helena Castle in Karnes County, who was away at Banquette busily building a Company of "Mounted Rangers" for the Rio Grande Regiment commanded by Colonel John

S. Ford. On that day he wrote his wife a letter from Austin updating her on his progress:

> Our K.G.C. arrangement has placed me in a position of influence in that order where I shall be able to think to direct its action to good and wise purpose. My position is one of advisory character and will not be generally known, so you need say nothing about that. I will probably also occupy some other position in the Organization which will not be secret.

He was not the only high-ranking KGC member who shuttled between the KGC convention in San Antonio and the Secession Convention in Austin. No quorum being present, the Convention adjourned that evening until the following Monday, March 4; on that day the Secession Election votes were officially tallied. Governor Houston then issued an official proclamation that the State of Texas had seceded from the Union. The independence of Texas barely lasted a day, for on Tuesday, the 5th, the convention adopted an ordinance uniting Texas with the Confederate States. Unlike the opportunity given the citizens of Texas to vote for or against secession, no such opportunity was accorded them on the question of joining the Confederacy. The average person had no say in the matter, but they would have to live with the consequences. The Confederate States of America needed Texas for several reasons, one of which was to build an army.[37]

Chapter Eleven

Building an Army and Stifling Dissent

March 4 was the last opportunity for conspirators to prevent Abraham Lincoln from assuming the office of the Presidency; it was Inauguration Day. There had been rumors that Ben McCulloch, along with Texas Congressman Louis T. Wigfall, were part of a plot to kidnap and perhaps murder Lincoln before he could take office. McCulloch had been in Washington D.C. before he hurried home to Texas in early February to plan and execute the successful assault on the Federal Arsenal at San Antonio. Rather than resign his office in the United States Congress as fellow Texan John H. Reagan had done on January 15, Louis Wigfall had remained at his post in Washington, where he was not really wanted, in order to collect information for KGC leadership and the Confederacy. The Texas Congressman was in contact with a Baltimore affiliate of the KGC known as the National Volunteers. An informant learned from a local KGC member that the National Volunteers had been drilling and that Ben McCulloch supposedly surveyed Washington and planned the coup d'état. United States Attorney General Edwin Stanton warned of this reputed plot and defensive measures were taken. Lincoln's planned journey to Washington would take him by train from Cincinnati through Baltimore to Washington for his inauguration. President-elect Lincoln was heavily guarded and quickly hustled through Baltimore at 3 A.M. and on to Washington by 6 A.M. the morning of February 23, much to the derision of the secessionists, who mocked Lincoln's caution as a sign of cowardice.[1]

Ben McCulloch may have helped drill the National Volunteers or helped plan a potential kidnapping of Lincoln by scouting the area, but there is no proof of this; he was far away from Baltimore and in Texas in mid-February and early March. On February 18, he had written to the Chairman of the Committee of Public Safety in San Antonio asking for a new assignment, as he had fulfilled his obligation to capture the Federal Arsenal in that city just 3 days earlier. On February 24, McCulloch had written to Louis Wigfall, who was still in Washington, but the contents of their correspondence is not known. The following day he wrote from San Antonio to John H. Reagan who was at his home in Anderson County, near Palestine, Texas. In this letter McCulloch seems to be reporting to Reagan, who had been out of office since his resignation from Congress on January 15; perhaps Reagan was also a Knight of the Columbian Star as was McCulloch. That Third Degree of the Order was known to be the political degree of the KGC. McCulloch was advising Reagan as to the steps to be taken in forming an army to defend the State of Texas:

> I shall urge the Convention to take prompt action to defend our frontiers. Some of the cavalry regiments would do for that service; the infantry would do for those passes on the Rio Grande; yet such men don't wish to go into service unless it was permanently. This the State cannot offer. One year, if not sooner discharged, is the terms she will offer. It suits volunteers. The arms we get from the Federal Government are not such as will be of much use to the State, particularly in defending her frontiers. We ought to purchase some for that particular service. The Colt pistol and the Morse altered gun are the best, if we can get them.[2]

McCulloch had written Samuel Colt on February 24 preparing the arms manufacturer for a potential order and inquiring as to where the weapons might be shipped. He requested Colt to address his reply to him in Austin, the State Capitol. Before McCulloch received authorization, his fellow KGC member John H. Reagan left Texas to attend the 1st Session of the Provisional Congress of the Confederate States of America in Montgomery, Alabama, taking his seat on March 2. Two days later McCulloch received a directive from Montgomery to raise "provisional forces" in Texas to protect the frontier. These troops were to be "received into the service of the Confederate States" under the provisions of a bill not yet passed that would create the army for the new breakaway republic. This directive was soon countermanded by one from the Secession Convention in Austin dated March 9 authorizing McCulloch to purchase 1,000 Colt revolvers and 1,000 rifles.

This confusion due to the demands of competing authorities was a harbinger of problems to come in the war soon to be inaugurated. Ben McCulloch had the liberty of transferring his assignment to raise volunteer troops in Texas to his brother Henry, already in the field and along the frontier. This freed Ben to pursue the purchase of weapons from Samuel Colt for which he had previously laid the groundwork. Of major concern to the Texas confederacy was the safe delivery of those weapons and the avoidance of their confiscation by their enemy, the Lincoln administration.[3]

Louis T. Wigfall continued his spying activity in Washington for as long as he was allowed, writing the newly elected President of the Confederacy in Montgomery from Washington on March 11, "It is believed here in Black Republican circles that Anderson will be ordered to vacate Fort Sumter in five days. An informal conclusion to this effect was arrived at Saturday night in Cabinet. Anderson telegraphed, it is said, that he had no fuel and but fifteen days provisions." Robert Anderson, the brother of Texas Unionist Charles Anderson of San Antonio, was the commanding officer of the Union forces at Fort Sumter. While Wigfall did his level best to exploit his position in the U.S. Congress to the detriment of the Federal government, former Texas Congressman John H. Reagan actively participated in the Confederate Congress and on March 6 was nominated by Jefferson Davis to be Postmaster-General of the Confederate States of America. Naturally this was approved, and Reagan left the assemblage sometime after March 11 to begin raiding the U.S. Postal Service, relieving that body of its loyal Southern employees. Ben McCulloch had begun his journey from Texas at roughly the same time, boarding a train at Alleyton for Galveston; from there he took a steamboat for New Orleans, arriving March 15. From New Orleans McCulloch resumed his travel by land for Montgomery, at this point both the capital of the Confederacy and the KGC as well. KGC members Samuel Lockridge of Texas and Virginius D. Groner of Virginia had been at Montgomery for several days prior to McCulloch's departure from Texas.[4]

At Montgomery, the formation of the Confederacy continued apace with President Jefferson Davis nominating James Sorley of Texas to the position of collector of customs in Galveston on March 16. Sorley was a native of Scotland and like his fellow Scotsman and Galveston resident Archibald St. Clair Ruthven, Sorley was a very high-ranking Knight Templar. Both men were slave-owners. No doubt Sorley and Ruthven were close as both were leaders in the Templar order and had made their fortunes in the cotton export trade in Texas. Sorley would serve as the first and only customs collector for the Confederacy at Galveston for the entire war. Jefferson Davis made his appointments to official positions based on the appointee's personal loyalty to him as well as their professional competency. Sorley was widely known throughout the South, not only for his high profile work on behalf of the Knights Templar on a national basis as well as in Texas; he was a named principal in one of the largest commission merchant firms in the entire South – Sorley, Smith & Company. Commission merchants were generally involved in the slave trade as well as the cotton business, and as Galveston was the premier slave trading center of Texas, as a slave owner himself, it is very likely that Sorley was involved in the trade through his firm. That, along with his role in bringing the Knight Templars to Texas suggests to the author that Mr. Sorley was a high-ranking member of the Financial Degree of the KGC in Galveston. As early as 1860 the KGC Castle in Galveston was considered by out-of-state KGC members as possessing "strange irregularities" whereby the "work of the order was materially changed by would-be reformers, and all its machinery remodeled to suit the new programme." This may have been in reference to the reformation of the Order "under or upon a different basis" that Samuel Lockridge had reported to Major S.P. Heintzelman by letter from the 1860 KGC Convention in New Orleans. It may also have been a reference to the "irregular" nature of the international cotton trade, and the fact that Texas cotton would still find a market in Northern cities – war or no war.[5]

The same day as Sorley's nomination was put before the Provisional Confederate Congress in Montgomery, President Davis also nominated a long list of officers to be appointed to the Confederate Army. Not very many Texans made the list composed by President Davis; again, his nominations were based on his personal connections, and as a West Point graduate Davis tended to ignore skilled commanders like Ben McCulloch because they had not at-tended the Academy. For the record, the Texans nominated by Davis included Walter H. Stevens as Captain in the Adjutant-Generals Department; Thomas L. Rosser as 1st Lieutenant in the Corps of Artillery as well as 2nd Lieutenants John O'Brien and Felix Robert-son to the artillery. In the infantry the highest-ranking Texans appointed by Davis initially included H.C. McNeill, First Lieutenant and 2nd Lieutenants William B. Ochiltree and John Bradley. The highest-ranking officer Davis recommended to the command of the infantry in this initial round of appointments was Earl Van Dorn. Like Davis, Van Dorn was from Mississippi and a West Point graduate; unfortunately for the men he would command, Van Dorn graduated near the bottom of his class and was notoriously undisciplined. He was a disaster for the Confederacy and for the unfortunate Texans who served beneath him. From the very beginning, there was conflict between Jefferson Davis and the leadership of the Texas KGC; when given the opportunity, the Texans would choose their officers using different criteria. In the beginning at least, the KGC from Texas were liberally represented in the officer's ranks at the head of those units organized in the Lone Star State, and not in the army as designed by Jefferson Davis.[6]

Concurrently with the appointment of James Sorley to his Confederate position in Texas, the legitimate government of the State, as represented by Governor Sam Houston, released a proclamation titled, "To The People of Texas." It began in part with an update of his status: "Worn out with the cares of office, I had retired to the bosom of my family to spend the remnant of my days in peace." Of the Convention that now was effectively in control of Texas, he wrote

> My worst anticipations as to the assumption of power by this Convention has been realized. To enumerate all the usurpations would be impossible, as a great portion of its proceedings have been in secret. This much has been revealed:

> It has elected delegates to the Provisional Council of the Confederate States, at Montgomery, before Texas had withdrawn from the Union, and who on the 2d day of March, annexed Texas to the Confederate States and constituted themselves members of Congress, when it was not officially known by the Convention until 4th of March, that a majority of the people had voted in favor of secession....It has created a Committee of Safety, a portion of whom have assumed the Executive powers of Government....This Committee of Safety has brought danger instead of safety. It has involved the State in an enormous expense for an army where no army was needed, and has left unprotected those who needed protection.

Houston's address went to great pains to paint the picture of what awaited the State of Texas along the new path it had taken – "A government has been fastened upon you, which is to be supported from your pockets, and yet you have not been consulted. You are to be taxed in the shape of tariffs on the necessaries and luxuries of life, which you have hitherto purchased free of duty. You are to have high postage and all else in proportion...." His statements were prophetic; he concluded by declaring that acts of the Secession Convention were "null and void." The Convention had sent George W. Chilton, the newly elected Marshal of the Texas Division of the KGC to visit Governor Houston to determine his intentions, to which Houston had replied with his refusal to recognize the Convention. The Convention required the Governor to take a "test oath" of loyalty to the Confederacy that day, which he refused. The Convention met the same day that Houston released his proclamation and declared that the office of Governor of Texas was "vacant" as of March 16. On the motion of T. J. Chambers, Lieutenant Governor Edward Clark was declared "now the lawful Governor of this State." Edward Clark had signed the Call for a Convention, which virtually assures his KGC credentials. John Ireland then offered a substitute declaration of Governor Clark's ascendancy to the office including a statement regarding Houston's refusal to "take the oath of office as provided by this Convention" and set the date of Clark's inauguration for Monday, March 18. Houston was out; his political career was over. He only had a couple of years left to live.[7]

The day after Confederate Governor Clark was inaugurated three more forts on the Texas frontier – Fort Clark, Fort Inge and Fort Lancaster – were all abandoned; concurrently members of the Texas legislature were administered the new oath of loyalty to the Confederate States. It was already beginning to look like Houston's predictions were going to come true. Sackfield Maclin, the traitorous former U.S. Army officer who was now serving the Confederacy as its Acting Quartermaster General in Texas, wrote to the Convention in Austin on March 16 advising the government of the threat of "Indian depredations," terminology that would be much used during the war to come; reports of these attacks were already "daily reaching these Head Quarters." Colonel John S. Ford also wrote John C. Robertson, Chairman of the Committee of Public Safety on March 20, that since his last report a week earlier, he had learned of "authenticated accounts of Indian depredations" in which "Twenty-seven persons are reported to have been killed, many ranches plundered, and hundreds of head of stock been driven off." With most of the U.S. troops in captivity or soon to be, the frontier of Texas was vulnerable. One of the newspapers in San Antonio had previously written of the removal of U.S. troops as "sham, farce and incipient tragedy" and that the largest city in the State had "settled down into a sullen gloom." Not everyone in Texas was celebrating its secession. Two days later, George W.L. Bickley singled out this newspaper, the *Alamo Express* for condemnation for the crime of "injuring the K.G.C." Bickley's broadside was published by a competing secessionist newspaper in San Antonio, having been submitted by Elisha Andrew Briggs, the secretary of a KGC Castle in Medina County. Briggs was later appointed by the Confederate Governor of Texas to a position of responsibility for recording and reporting claims for livestock stolen from the surrounding ranches. Many of the leaders of the KGC would find ways to profit from the coming calamity; those who protested would be persecuted.[8]

Chaos brings opportunity and those who exploit it for their own gain are known as opportunists. One such person was John Wilkins Whitfield, who previously left his home in Tennessee for the Kansas Territory, where he backed the losing pro-slavery side as a high-ranking member of the "Blue Lodge" faction during the troubles in the 1850s. "Blue Lodge" was the earliest term used for the KGC when it first saw action in 1855 in Kansas. Now Mr. Whitfield saw Texas as a success story in his cause and landed at Galveston on March 17, 1861. The Civilian reported, "General Whitfield has located in Texas, and brings with him the first negroes which were carried to Kansas, and the last to leave it." Whitfield would rise to power in the military and political establishment of his newly adopted state. The KGC looked out for the welfare and progress of its members, one of the special benefits of being among the membership. The day after his arrival in Galveston, the Convention in Austin created the 2nd Mounted Rifles for frontier protection, at least on paper. The next step was the nomination and election of officers to command the new military force. Ben McCulloch was not in attendance and by this time had passed through Mobile on his way to Montgomery. It was up to the Texas Convention delegates to choose the men to make up the command structure. On the night of March 19, the delegate from Bosque County nominated Harris A. Hamner for the position of Colonel; the three other nominees were N.H. Darnell, John S. Ford and F.F. Foscue. On the final ballot, KGC leader John Salmon Ford received 96 votes, Hamner received 14 votes, Darnell received 10 and Foscue received 9; John S. Ford was declared the "duly elected" Colonel of the new frontier regiment. Next was the ballot for Lieutenant Colonel. John A. Wilcox of Bexar County nominated fellow KGC member A.T. Rainey, who immediately withdrew his name. Other known KGC leaders – John J. Good and John R. Baylor – were nominated as well as W.P. Lane and one other. The votes were evenly distributed, so with no candidate receiving a majority of the votes, a second ballot was held. Nat Terry, the KGC leader of Tarrant County, withdrew the name of John J. Good; W.P. Lane's name was withdrawn also. The contest was now between two men, Mr. McFarland and John R. Baylor; Baylor won the second ballot by only 5 votes and was declared Lieutenant Colonel. The final leadership position to be determined by ballot was that of Major. Mr. A.J. Nicholson of Fannin County nominated Harris A. Hamner; A.H. Davidson of Colorado County nominated W.J. Herbert and KGC member Thomas S. Lubbock nominated Edwin Waller, Jr. Waller was the son of the Secession Convention delegate from Austin County and a probable KGC member; he had played a key role in creating a vigilance committee in his county. When KGC leader John Salmon Ford besieged Brazos Santiago, Captain Edwin Waller commanded Company C of the Rio Grande Regiment organized March 10. Therefore, it is highly likely that Waller, too was KGC. When the final votes were tallied at the Convention on March 19, Waller was elected Major of the Frontier Regiment.[9]

While the Confederate State of Texas was beginning to organize and build its troops, the KGC continued its expansion within the State. On March 21, the house organ of the KGC, the *La Grange States Rights Democrat*, noted that their subscription clientele had increased substantially, as "people seem to appreciate our efforts to build up a paper that promulgates sound sentiments, and are flocking to our assistance." For this the editor expressed gratitude to "Capt. P. J. Barziza [sic] and our brethren at the K.G.C." This of course was a reference to Philip Ignatius Barziza, one of the Knights of the Columbian Star. He was still actively canvassing the State, organizing Castles. KGC interests would be favored, just as KGC candidates for official positions, no matter how large or small. On March 20, John Rosenheimer, who like fellow KGC member Samuel Sampson was a member of San Antonio's Jewish community, wrote Edward Clark, the new Governor installed by The Committee. Rosenheimer was an officer of San Antonio Lodge Number 11 of the Independent Order of Odd Fellows, as was Trevanion T. Teel and W.A. Menger. KGC leader Teel had been kicked out of the Masonic Order for some unknown infraction years earlier; Rosenheimer's clothing store was across Alamo Plaza from the Menger Hotel. Rosenheimer now wanted the position of Notary Public for Bexar County, as "the present Notary Public of this County refuse to take the oath of Allegiance to the Confederate States of America." Bexar County KGC leader and Commander of the KGC Western Brigade John A. Wilcox was copied in on the letter. While the KGC expanded in all ways in Texas the protection for the frontier of the State continued to collapse; Fort Chadbourne was abandoned on March 22. That was the day that the State Secession Convention ratified the Confederate Constitution. The following day, Ben McCulloch arrived in the nation's capital, Washington City, and immediately went to the home of the Senator from California, William Gwin. Gwin, a wealthy Southern transplant to California and the state's first U.S. Senator was rumored to be the top KGC leader in his adopted state. Learning of McCulloch's presence in Washington, D.C., Louis Wigfall feared for McCulloch's safety and freedom due to the role he had played in the seizure of Federal property in Texas. Wigfall, who was formally expelled from his position in the United States Senate the same day as McCulloch's arrival, convinced McCulloch to meet him in Alexandria, Virginia the following day. From Alexandria, McCulloch wrote a dispatch to Samuel Colt concerning the arms deal in progress. Wigfall also wrote a letter to Colt in support of McCulloch; both letters were hand-delivered to Colt in Connecticut by Samuel Morse, the inventor of the rifle being bought by McCulloch for the frontier Rangers. A day later, on March 25, the Texas State Secession Convention adjourned, having completed their business.[10]

March 26 revealed Louis Wigfall and Ben McCulloch in Richmond, the city soon to become the seat of Confederate power. Wigfall's daughter noted in her diary that day, "Sumter has not yet been evacuated. I don't believe Jeff Davis will allow them to trifle with him much longer [sic]....". Even so, preparations for war proceeded. By the 28th the first shipment of 250 of McCulloch's pistols had been sent to New Orleans, having shipped just in time from Colt in Hartford through the port of New York. Shipments to locales in the South were soon to be seized or restricted by the U.S. government. Meanwhile, the development of the armed forces in Texas continued. Some companies were already organized and well-armed, ready for action; many of these companies were likely KGC units that had formed months or years earlier. One such company, the Denton Rangers from Denton County in North Texas were associated with Otis G. Welch of that place, a man who had played a major role in spreading the bogus "slave panic" in 1860 that resulted in numerous lynching. Welch wrote Governor Edward Clark on March 24 on behalf of the Denton Rangers "to tender their services to the State or the Confederacy." Welch sent to Clark the muster roll that listed the members of the company, describing them as "good men and true. Many have seen service both in Mexico and on the frontier. The company is well officered." Then he gave the Governor his assessment of the risk of disloyalty among the region's different counties and population:

> Though we carried our county by only 67 for secession yet when the delegates who misrepresented us in the Convention were elected they beat us nearly two to one the people are still coming over and were we to take the

vote today we would more than double our Maj. Denton is all right and I think Wise will and Cook will be but Grayson & Collin almost hopeless in these other Counties will continue to lift the union party until nothing is left but those who really see nothing objectionable in Mr. Lincoln and his doctrine – that accomplished we will know better how to act. [sic]

This ominous conclusion to the letter reveals that the KGC, among whose primary purposes was to provide a secret police force, already had designs on the loyal Unionist population spread across several counties in North Texas. Grayson and Collin counties had voted against secession, so many of their citizens would be subjected to surveillance, harassment, and even death. In about a year this would culminate in a series of mass lynching's. Many of the companies formed in Texas for military service to the State or the Confederacy would find it difficult to obtain proper weapons; but not the KGC. The men of the Order had been privately funded from the beginning. This is why the Denton Rangers were described by Welch as "very well armed" with good horses – "well mounted." They were eager to rain death upon their enemies.[11]

The Unionist population of North Texas were not alone in their situation, however. The German population of Central Texas was also suspect, as early on many Texas Germans had declared their opposition to slavery and secession as well. Thomas Hardeman, a planter and member of a family that had been well-represented at the KGC convention in New Orleans in 1860, also wrote Governor Clark in March 1861. Hardeman already had a company organized at Prairie Lea, a town in Caldwell County, one of those counties with known KGC castles. The initial issue raised in his letter proposed the appointment of John Lampkin to the position of commissary for "the Regiment to be raised in Texas" – KGC leader John S. Ford's regiment. "We are all going to visit the dutch by invitation today," he wrote, indicating that the "dutch" (the Texian term for Germans) in his county would be accounted for and monitored. He closed his letter to Governor Clark by indicating that if "Old Sam" – Sam Houston, the illegally deposed former Governor – "attempts to turn you out send a line to Prairie Lea and you can get a good Company." They too, were already armed and eager, even though the war had not yet begun. The regiment of which Hardeman wrote would be called upon to fulfill one of the dreams writ large by the KGC. Already the groundwork was being laid for this mission. In early March the Secession Convention had sent two Commissioners from Texas to New Mexico and Arizona to gauge support for the Confederacy in that land. Their names were Philemon T. Herbert and Simeon Hart; both men resided in El Paso. P.T. Herbert was one of the delegates from El Paso County to the Texas Secession Convention; Hart, a native New Yorker, was a businessman who had married into a prominent Mexican family of the State of Chihuahua, one of the states in Mexico thought to be in favor of annexation to the United States. Hart had grown rich by supplying flour to the army, becoming the wealthiest man in the area by 1860; he was also a former judge in El Paso County. Previous researchers have thought that there was a KGC Castle in El Paso. The city had contributed one of the dele-gates, Judge Josiah F. Crosby, to the failed 1860 National Democratic Convention in Charleston that had been sab-otaged by the KGC. It is likely that Crosby, Herbert and Hart were also affiliated with, or in Hart's case, were a financing source for the Order in far West Texas. By March 24, 1861, Northern newspapers were reporting that Herbert and Hart had travelled further West "to invite the cooperation of Arizona and New Mexico in the formation of a Southern Confederacy" and that the provisional Governor of Arizona had "responded approvingly."[12]

By March 26 Colonel Earl Van Dorn was in Indianola, a Texas port on the Gulf assessing the situation as to the status of the captured U.S. troops. He wrote the Confederate Secretary of War that he was leaving Indianola that day to attempt to recruit some of those troops held at Green Lake, a camp about twenty miles inland, thinking "I shall have no difficulty in securing many of the troops and officers." By March 30, a confidential informant working for KGC leader John H. Reagan wrote the new Confederate postmaster from Saluria, another Texas Gulf town, that Van Dorn had failed to recruit anyone from the enemy's ranks. The informant, Hugh W. Hawes expressed concern to Reagan that none of the cap- tured troops had departed and related a rumor that Fort Sumter would not be surrendered until all of the Union troops in Texas could be concentrated for an attack on Pensacola. Hawes noted that with so many Texas towns undefended, the 500 or so expelled Union troops gathered at Indianola, supported by several ships then anchored off the Texas coast, could pose a danger. Thomas N. Waul, like Van Dorn and Jefferson Davis all fellow Mississippians, had written the Con- federate President advocating for Van Dorn to assume command of Confederate forces in Texas. Hoping to meet with Colonel Van Dorn, KGC member Waul had gone to San Antonio on April 1 only to find the following day that Van Dorn had returned to Montgomery. Waul expressed concern by dispatch to Jefferson Davis that the Confederate troops in Texas were without a leader.[13]

With McCulloch safely quartered in Richmond, Louis Wigfall and family left that city and arrived in Charleston, South Carolina on April 1 – April Fool's Day. Wigfall wanted to be near the action, and tensions had been rising in the city across the harbor from Fort Sumter. He attached himself to the Commanding General P.T. Beauregard and almost never left his side. Ben McCulloch was still busy shepherding his arms shipments from Connecticut to Texas; on April 2 he wrote Samuel Colt asking for credit for his purchase until he could get the funds from the State of Texas to pay for the shipment upon its arrival in New Orleans. Colt agreed to these terms, so McCulloch made his preparations to leave Richmond April 3 hoping to reach New Orleans by the 7th. While he was in transit Governor Clark in Texas wrote to Jefferson Davis on April 4 and indicated that Texas had 1,700 miles of frontier to protect and that the Confederate government had provided only one regiment to replace the 2,700 U.S. troops that had been taken out of service in the State. The government in Richmond would soon respond but not in the way hoped for by Governor Clark.[14]

On April 6, one of the KGC advocate newspapers, the *Texas State Gazette* of Austin, edited by KGC member John Marshall, published the troop deployments and officer appointments made by Henry E. McCulloch:

> I have appointed Capt. Thomas C. Frost at Camp Colorado; S.G. Davidson or R.B. Hally at Fort Chadbourne; James B. Barry at Camp Cooper; W.H. Duke at Jefferson; Milton Boggess at Henderson; Jas. H. Fry, at Austin, Travis co; T.H. Ashby at Gonzales; William A. Pitts, at Seguin; W.G. Tobin and G.H. Nelson at San Antonio, to raise companies to compose a regiment called out by order of the President of the Confederate States. [sic]

This regiment would become known as the 1st Texas Mounted Rifles. Thomas C. Frost became H.E. McCulloch's second-in-command as Lieutenant Colonel; James Buck Barry, Major; James H. Fry, Captain of Company A; William A. Pitts, Captain, Company B; William G. Tobin, Captain, Company D; Goveneur H. Nelson, Captain, Company E; Sidney G. Davidson, Captain, Company F; Milton M. Boggess, Captain, Company H and Travis Hill Ashby, Captain, Company I. Most if not all of these men were probably KGC, as were both McCulloch brothers. Robert B. Halley had decided to resign after participating in and leading his men in the takeover of one of the frontier forts manned by U.S. troops. Sidney G. Davidson had caught the eye of Henry McCulloch in late February while at Fort Chadbourne who thought young Davidson had a bright future as a leader of men, so he put him in Captain Halley's place and promoted him. Captain Davidson was killed by Indians on June 22, 1861, an early casualty of the war in Texas he had helped start and so eagerly supported. He was among the first of many to come. Dr. Jessee Boring, the fire-eating secessionist preacher who had spoken at the San Antonio rally that featured the beleaguered Charles Anderson as the spokesman for the Unionists, decided he could do more good healing mangled bodies than healing tortured, fearful souls; so he became Assistant Surgeon in Henry McCulloch's regiment.[15]

Ben McCulloch had reached New Orleans a day ahead of schedule on April 6. While there he wrote to Governor Edward Clark of Texas that he would remain in the Louisiana port city until the rest of the shipments of pistols and rifles arrived and he could arrange for their transport to Texas. He also told the Governor that the future shipments would be sent by Adams Express to avoid their confiscation by the enemy, as shipment from the Port of New York was no longer possible due to a crackdown on steam-ships bound for the Gulf of Mexico. Shipments by rail and by river were still possible, however. While McCulloch waited on the shipments from Colt and Morse that Wigfall had helped arrange, the former Texas Congressman was with his family in Charleston, South Carolina. One local woman described in her diary a conversation she'd had with Wigfall's wife about their expectations for life during wartime, "with Yankees in the front and negroes in the rear." Lady Wigfall put a damper on the proceedings when she declared that "slave-owners must expect a servile insurrection, of course." Her way of thinking foretold the creation of a strong police state to watch the people and their slaves and to keep them in line. The KGC's "Home Guard" units would serve in that capacity as well as some others that would be especially created for espionage purposes. The ladies' conversation about these matters on April 8 was interrupted by the sounds of cannon fire, the result of a display by the Confederate forces meant to intimidate the Union troops defending Fort Sumter. The real attack had yet to begin.[16]

The following day the rest of the shipment of Colt pistols arrived in New Orleans, but for the concerned citizens in the Governor's office back in Texas, April 9 was a good-news bad-news sort of day. The news of McCulloch's receipt of 750 more top-notch pistols for reshipment to Texas was good news; the not-so-good news was a requisition from the Confederate Secretary of War in Richmond, Virginia for 3,000 men from Texas to serve in the Confederate Army, either as infantry or in two companies of artillery. This of course would take men out of the State who could have served in frontier defense. It was only the first of several requisitions from Texas and the other Confederate States for "national" service. It would be a game-changer for some of the KGC in Texas. Confidence among its members and sympathizers was high on April 9; Louis Wigfall wrote from Charleston that day to an unnamed Colonel in Texas regarding McCulloch's pistols. He mentioned to the Colonel that the Rangers should receive these new pistols "as part pay. I do not know what the pay of a Ranger is but it must be per month nearly the price of a pistol." Wigfall confessed that he had broken a promise he had made to Ben McCulloch, that he would go to Montgomery on his behalf but instead went to Charleston, where he was given a staff position by General Beauregard. Louis Wigfall eagerly anticipated the coming attack on Fort Sumter and cavalierly referred to the inevitable slaughter that would result from the war to follow: "Would you like to have a lock of Anderson's hair? You can have Doubleday's scalp if you have a fancy." Others expressed their excitement or concern on this day, with Edward C. Wharton writing from the office of the Galveston News to John Tyler, Jr., son of the tenth President and a rabid secessionist, at the urging of Charles Bickley. Wharton referred to Charles Bickley as" the head of the KGC. The major has had much to do with the working of secession in Western Texas and can give you a good deal of news." San Antonio was considered Western Texas in those days, and the city was the sometime home of Charles Bickley. Wharton's report went on to note that "some fifteen hundred" U.S. Troops were still located at Indianola on the Texas coast, supposedly waiting for transport out of the State to a point back North. This had previously been reported by Hugh W. Hawes, a citizen of Indianola to John H. Reagan; and on this same day Hawes wrote to Reagan again on the status of U.S. troops still in the State. Both Wharton's report and Hawes were ultimately passed on to Colonel Earl Van Dorn, who on April 11 was ordered by the Confederate government in Montgomery to proceed to Texas where he would assume command of all Confederate troops in the State.[17]

Two of the top tier KGC leaders in the Texas Order had an interesting exchange on the day Van Dorn received his orders. Philip Ignatius Barziza wrote to Charles A. Russell at Helena, Texas that he was "anxious to be instrumental in carrying on the work of the K.G.C." but that he was frustrated that his efforts to organize Castles in any other counties other than Fort Bend, Liberty, and Polk were restricted. Referring to Russell as "General Russell," Barziza stated that he had already organized castles in Fort Bend and Liberty counties, and that "my success was beyond my utmost expectations." His statement is significant for two reasons: one is the fact that Charles A. Russell had yet to formally enter the Confederate Army or the State military forces, and "General" was the same title given to George W.L. Bickley, the titular head of the national organization. The second fact of note in Barziza's statement is that he had already opened KGC Castles in Fort Bend and Liberty counties, two locations previously unknown to historians. He had exceeded his expectations in those counties, for they both contributed reinforcements for KGC leader John S. Ford's Rio Grande Expedition, answering quickly the call by arriving at Brazos Santiago on March 2, not returning home until March 15. The official records indicate that the Liberty Company, later known as The Liberty Invincibles was led by Kindallis "King" Bryan and Captain Watson Ducat Williams. The company from Fort Bend was led by Captain Daniel A. Connor, a member of the plantation class with 33 slaves. Although large by State standards, Connor's slave holdings were dwarfed by those of Kyle and Terry – William Kyle and Benjamin Franklin Terry, co-owners of the Oakland Plantation in Fort Bend County. They were absentee owners but still mustered 105 slaves just in Fort Bend County. Barziza was writing this letter from his home in Wallisville, in nearby Chambers County asking "to be fully empowered to organize Castles in all of the Counties of 1st Regiment of the Third Brigade of the State of Texas" [sic]. Three KGC Brigade districts were created at the Order's State Convention by a committee of "Messrs. Tatum, Park, Davidson, Thompson, Clark, Barziza, Chilton, and Bickley" on the second day of the Convention. This committee was chaired by Russell. The area desired by Barziza for development purposes included the counties of Galveston, Harris, Chambers, Jefferson, Orange, Hardin, Liberty, Montgomery, Walker, Madison, Polk, Tyler, Jasper and Newton; roughly one-third of the populated area of the State, comprised of counties somewhat centered around the coastal area surrounding the cities of Galveston and Houston. After asking Russell for a recommendation "for any office to Gen. Chilton," Barziza closed his letter with this:

> Should you think proper to give me the authority desired in the premises, you will send me enough Degree Works of the 1st & 2nd degrees to organize five or six Castles, also a set for my Castle at this place, as I have never received them, although I have long since paid for them. (I mean Second Degree Works.) You will send all other papers or books that may be necessary for the proper organizing of Castles. I would respectfully recommend

the name of G. W. Whitting of this place for Act. Adjutant General of the 3rd Brigade. [sic]

It is a certainty then, that George W. Whitting of Galveston was KGC also. Barziza then signed off as "Yours in 57, Philip I. Barziza. Capt. Wallisville Castle, Wallisville, Chambers County, Texas." The term "57" is code for a Knight of the Columbian Star, the highest and most secretive degree of the KGC; by identifying himself as one of that tier, Barziza also identified Charles A. Russell as a Knight of the Columbian Star as well, as no member of that degree was allowed to identify himself as one unto anyone else but another such member of the Third Degree. Clearly Philip Barziza wanted a much larger role for himself in the Order.[18]

Pro-secessionists in Texas were impatient for the conflict to begin; one such man in the town of Tyler was running ads in the Tyler Reporter selling "those fine Kentucky Rifles warranted to kill an Abolitionist at 400 Yards!" Tyler was the home of "General" George W. Chilton who was not only Captain of the Tyler KGC Castle but also the newly elected Marshal of the entire Texas Division of the KGC (replacing Elkanah Greer). Fort Sumter was fired on by Confederate forces in Charleston on April 12, beginning the war for the rest of the country. Not every KGC member was happy to see this, however. Robert B. Ward, the turncoat U.S. soldier who served as the inside man on the KGC's assault on Fort Cooper, changed sides again. He left San Antonio on or about Tuesday, April 9 as noted by James P. Newcomb of the *Tri-Weekly Alamo Express* on Mon-day April 15:

> We have learned that Ward, the eminent K.G.C, whose departure we no-
> ticed last week, found that the K.G.C. did not pay as well as his old avoca-
> tion, and consequently he followed the army to Green Lake, where he again
> enlisted in the service of Uncle Sam. He first applied to the company to
> which he formerly belonged and was rejected, but managed to enlist in one
> where he was not known.... we are impressed with the magnitude of the
> loss sustained by the order of Knights; for it was him who nourished it in
> its infancy...who housed it – who talked for it – who bullied for it – who
> acted as body guard to his Knightship Bickley – in fact Ward was the right
> man in the right place.

Newcomb never missed a chance to stick his finger in the eye of the KGC and their supporters, and his actions would soon bring trouble to him. His writing before and after the war offer much aid in identifying many KGC members in San Antonio, as he would return to publishing another newspaper in that town in peacetime. As usual, Newcomb was right; in this instance, about Ward – his military record held in the National Archives shows that he re-enlisted in the U.S. Army at San Antonio on April 1, 1861 for a five-year term. After he was transferred out of Texas with the rest of the Union forces, Ward was formally accepted into service in Carlisle, Pennsylvania and later became a Captain in Company D of the 11th Pennsylvania Cavalry.[19]

The more virulent of the "Southern patriots" reacted differently. The day after the attack on Fort Sumter the Southern Confederacy in Atlanta in a notice titled, "'Ho! For the Wolf Chase' – The Hunt is Up" announced that "Those who wish to join the 'Sons of the South' will make application at the Armory...." That name – The Sons of The South – was one name used by the KGC during the Kansas Troubles of 1855 and 1856. In Texas the Sons of The South was organized by KGC leader John Salmon Ford, who referred to it as the Order. Ford stated that one of its central principles was that although the army was created by law, it was subordinate to "the civil authority." Of course, the KGC could be said to be that civil authority. According to Ford, if the army was not subordinate to civil authority, "The will of officers would be the law." Ford then proceeded to define the Order's real mission, identifying its enemies:

> The men who advocate these dangerous principles place themselves upon the platform of Seward and Lincoln. They tacitly admit the higher-law doctrine as true, and they justify the Black Republicans in all their inroads upon the constitution, and their outrages of every character, because they have perpetrated all these enormities as measures dictated by and vindicated by the public good.... There is no doubt but, that those who have withheld their service, and refused their support to the Confederate Government in the dark hours of peril would be pleased to institute other measures of redress. To open wide the floodgates of disorder, confusion, and violence, and to introduce anarchy would be to them a labor of love.

What Ford was really saying was that the Order of the Sons of the South would be a secret organization engaged in hunting deserters and those suspected of being disloyal to the Confederate government. Before the end of the war in Texas they would become in effect an assassination squad. "Ho! For the Wolf Chase!" indeed.[20]

Philip Ignatius Barziza was not the only KGC leader still engaged in organizing new Castles in Texas. Edwin Hobby wrote a letter to KGC leader Charles A.

Russell from St. Mary's, a town in Refugio County on April 14. Although the letter was written in the code used by KGC members, it has been translated. Edwin Hobby, designated in this letter as Secretary of the St. Mary's Castle which had been organized by his brother Alfred Hobby was writing to request more "degree works... necessary for first and second degrees." He was helping "Mr. Clark who organizes a K.G.C. castle at this place". This means that there was more than one castle in Refugio County. Both Alfred and Edwin Hobby mustered out later that month as members of a Home Guard unit in their county commanded by Captain William T. Townsend and Lieutenant William H. Long. Provisions for the Home Guard had been made public by George W. Bickley at the National KGC Conference in Virginia the previous year. The same day as Hobby's coded letter, Ben McCulloch wrote from Montgomery to Texas Governor Edward Clark that he had been assigned to take command "of the Indian Territory, N. of Texas & S. of Kansas" with five regiments – two mounted and three on foot. One of the mounted regiments would come from Texas, one from Arkansas; the infantry would be comprised of two regiments of Indian troops and one from Louisiana. McCulloch had accepted the command, "though I would have preferred going to Va at present." He further informed the Governor that 2,000 of the guns captured by McCulloch in the Arsenal raid at San Antonio were ordered by the government to be shipped North to Dallas, as well as a battery of artillery. Dallas was to be the rendezvous point for that portion of the force recruited from Texas. Two days later, Governor Clark was notified by the Confederate Secretary of War that the new national army needed an additional 5,000 men from Texas to serve the Confederacy. This meant more able-bodied men would be taken from the State and made unavailable for frontier protection.[21]

Tuesday evening, on April 16, Earl Van Dorn made his reentry into Texas by ship at Galveston. Van Dorn had been given authority by Jefferson Davis to take command and organize an expedition to capture the Star of the West and other steamers at anchor off the Texas coast. As soon as he arrived, he notified General Sidney Sherman of the Texas forces of his purpose and his mission and Sherman immediately issued a call for volunteers. Having seen the ability of the KGC to provide volunteers for prior expeditions on short notice, such as the men recruited by E.B. Nichols for reinforcements during the Rio Grande campaign, Van Dorn made good use of them. The evening of the sixteenth the Wigfall Guards, under Captain James McGrath were already assembled at their armory for regular drill and immediately volunteered all forty of their number. Soon about thirty more

men of the Island City Rifles, under Captain Muller, as well as the Galveston Artillery commanded by Captain Henry Van Buren had joined as well. By one account the Davis Guards also joined; both Van Buren's company and the Davis
Guards had been involved in the initial invasion of Brazos Santiago. General Sherman promised Van Dorn a total of 400 men for the expedition if he would just
wait until the following morning when he could contact the companies on the
mainland at Houston, many of which had been involved in the Rio Grande Expedition. Van Dorn decided not to wait and by 3 A.M. the small war party of some
80 men had boarded the Matagorda for transport by sea to Indianola. The Matagorda arrived at Indianola within a few hours and disembarked, the men changing
ships by boarding the steamer Rusk. Utilizing the steamer, Van Dorn and his men
shortly thereafter boarded the Star of the West and took possession from its captain and crew without firing a shot. From that point on the Star of the West belonged to the Confederate government and soon made its way back to Galveston
with Van Dorn aboard, during which time he began to make plans to return to
Indianola and nearby Green Lake, where some 650 U.S. troops were still waiting
for transport out of Texas and back to the Union. Van Dorn had made a favorable
first impression upon the secessionist element within Texas; the Star of the West
had evaded capture at Fort Sumter but had fallen into enemy hands thanks to the
KGC in Texas. Among the names of men from Galveston who participated in the
capture were William Nichols, the son of General E.B. Nichols, and former U.S.
soldier Lieutenant Thomas B. Maclin, who was probably related to Sackfield
Maclin, another turncoat and KGC member.[22]

The bombardment of Fort Sumter, which began the evening of April 12 had
ended on April 14 with the evacuation of the fort by Union troops under their
commander Robert Anderson – but not without some strange behavior by Louis
Wigfall. On or about noon on April 13 the flagstaff at Fort Sumter had been shot
down during the artillery barrage. Upon seeing this the Confederates stopped firing, thinking that someone in the fort had hauled down the colors in preparation
for a surrender. Ever the opportunist, Louis Wigfall rowed across the harbor in a
boat without the knowledge of the commanding officer, General P.T. Beauregard.
He attempted to accept the surrender of Fort Sumter, only to find that the garrison
had no intention to surrender at that point. When the fort raised their flag again,
shelling resumed until Wigfall persuaded Anderson to call for a cease-fire. Eventually Anderson surrendered to the Confederacy, but not to Louis Wigfall. The
question was, upon whose authority did Louis Wigfall presume to act? As a result

of the surrender, on April 15, U.S. President Abraham Lincoln issued a proclamation asking several states to raise 75,000 troops to put down the rebellion. Word
of the surrender of Fort Sumter did not reach San Antonio until April 17. When
it did, Henry McCulloch immediately dashed off a letter to the Confederate Secretary of War reminding him that several hundred Union soldiers were still in
Texas. McCulloch knew that within a few more days he would have six companies
organized and ready for the field, but by April 17 only one had arrived at headquarters in San Antonio. It was immediately mustered into service while McCulloch counted the days before the others arrived. That same day George W. Chilton, the KGC Marshall of the Texas Division, wrote a proclamation from Montgomery, Alabama, the KGC's national headquarters:

> In view of the threatened invasion of Texas by Lincoln's abolition horde,
> and in further view of the fact that the Confederate States of America has
> so many points exposed to at-tack from the enemy, that its army as at pre-
> sent organized, may be inadequate to ample protection;

> I therefore order the Captains of each Castle of K's G. C's. within the State
> of Texas, to meet me at the city of Galveston, on the 1st day of May, A.D.
> 1861, with a complete muster roll of companies. Each Castle will hold itself
> in readiness for immediate orders. It is desired that as many of the field
> officers as can do so, will also be in Galveston at the time appointed.

To this press release George W. Bickley appended his statement, serving notice to the KGC in Kentucky, Virginia, North Carolina, South Carolina, Georgia,
Alabama, Tennessee, Missouri, Arkansas, Louisiana, and Florida to be on their
guard. Also added to Chilton's broadside was one brief order from Major Augustus Larrantree, the KGC commander for Arkansas for that state's companies to
stand at the ready "for further orders."[23]

Others within the State had been eager for battle well before the bombardment of Fort Sumter. Captain Milton Webb of the Red River Valley county of
Lamar had organized the Lamar Cavalry at the town of Paris in December of the
previous year. He had tendered their service to the Secession Convention by letter,
which was received on March 8. He had recruited these men to serve under Colonel John Salmon Ford for frontier defense. However, Colonel Ford indicated he
did not need any more troops. Perhaps Ford was concerned by the fact that many
of Webb's men had no weapons. Webb wrote Governor Clark on April 17 that he
was taking his company to Camp Cooper where they expected to receive some

captured supplies and arms. There they would await orders. By April 1 Webb had signed up 110 men for service from Lamar and Hopkins counties and registered his muster roll at Paris on April 18. Webb financed his company from his own pocket from April 10 until the 25th; on April 20 they became part of Henry McCulloch's 1st Mounted Riflemen and were stationed out West at Fort Belknap. They remained in State service in Northwest Texas for the rest of the war.[24]

Although he had been rebuffed at the Secession Convention in his quest for higher office, the ever-ambitious Captain Harris A. Hamner was out in Weatherford on April 15 signing up more recruits. On April 18, he wrote to Governor Clark, submitting the muster roll of his company by way of George W. Baylor, who became his Lieutenant. He noted in his letter that he had fulfilled his duty assigned him as Enrolling Officer and that his new company was quartered within five miles of Weatherford. Previous scholars have suggested that the KGC provided the core of the first regiments formed in Texas; it follows then that KGC members often functioned as enrolling officers at the beginning of the Civil War, as they were the most committed and ambitious to aid in building the army for the new empire. Governor Clark had divided the State into military districts on April 17, and an "Enrolling Officer" was assigned to each district. When the assigned officers' names were published that month, it is apparent that many were known KGC. For instance, Pryor Lea was the enrolling officer for Refugio, San Patricio, Nueces, Goliad, Bee and Karnes counties; William Edgar was the enrolling officer for Bexar, Wilson, and Comal counties. James Franklin Davis, the famous "Captain Davis" of KGC recruiting fame around Fort Belknap, was the enrolling officer for Milam, Falls, Williamson, Bell, and McLennan counties. Clinton McKamy Winkler, a signer of the Call for a State Convention, was enrolling officer for Limestone, Freestone, Navarro, Hill and Ellis counties. Other military companies appear to have formed around charismatic figures with previous war experience. William C. Young and James W. Throckmorton were those sorts of men, and sometime before April 17 they had organized "volunteers" in North Texas for an assault on the Federal troops garrisoned North of the Red River in Indian Territory. On April 17, they occupied Fort Washita "in force," according to the Union commander reporting the incident, and discovered that the troops guarding it had been ordered to evacuate their post the day before their arrival. Finding that there was no fight to be had at Fort Washita, many of the men, including Throckmorton, returned to their homes; but some of the KGC stayed. The job was not finished. There were two more forts in Indian Territory to conquer.[25]

The advance on Fort Washita had occurred simultaneously with Earl Van Dorn's successful operation to capture the Star of the West. All the while the State was struggling to organize sufficient forces to satisfy the levies of the Confederacy while maintaining frontier defense. On April 20, the Captain of the Comal County Castle, Theophelus J. Thomas, wrote Governor Clark from New Braunfels of the challenges facing him:

> I am willing to believe that all the citizens are willing to respond to any emergency but the great obstacle I have found is the want of arms. The people here are almost destitute of arms and ammunition and had they known or could be satisfied that they could get arms from the Government they would send for them immediately. They are generally poor in this County, can raise and turn out in the field if they would move in the cause at least 200 good fighting men.

Other KGC companies were greatly reduced in numbers as their men joined Confederate military units in a desire to be where the action was going to be. Tignal W. Jones, one of the KGC leaders in Tyler, Texas wrote the Governor on April 21 that upon returning home to this Northeast Texas community he found that only fifteen rank-and-file men remained in his company, the Tyler Dragoons. His company had been organized as cavalry, but at that time the Confederacy had expressed a greater need for infantry or artillery, so many of his men had joined what became the artillery company of Lieutenant James P. Douglass. This company was in existence in January, as the Tyler Dragoons had offered their service to the Secession Convention on the 28 of that month. Jones took a vote among his remaining men as to whether they should disband the Tyler Dragoons, and a majority voted to disband and enter the infantry service. Jones was supportive of Douglass, calling him "a very worthy young man and efficient officer" and informed the Governor that the new company commanded by Douglass would stand in place of the Tyler Dragoons. He also mentioned to the Governor the existence of another new infantry company in Tyler commanded by a "Mr. Yarborough."[sic] This group became Captain Harvey Yarbrough's Company of 107 men from Smith and Wood counties. Tignal Jones also complained of "the impossibility of our getting horses...the failure of the Legislature to make any arrangement for arming the Cavalry volunteers confined in the State," and the probability "that infantry and Artillery Companies will alone be called for (if a call is made at all)." Captain Jones then resigned and stated he would not reenter the service unless there was an actual invasion of Texas. This letter of Tignal Jones is a perfect example of how and why many of the KGC companies reformed under different leadership and were deployed under new names. This process was being repeated across the State. On April 22, Daniel McDowell Short wrote the Governor from Nacogdoches that he was concerned that his company would be "crowded out" of Colonel John S. Ford's regiment and asked Clark to consider his force for Confederate service. It is likely that Short's company was KGC; Short represented Shelby County in the Secession Convention. He wanted to be a part of Ford's organization; Colonel Ford was a high-level KGC military leader, and his regiment has the distinction of having more KGC leaders absorbed into it than any other in the State of Texas. Failing to find a place with Ford's regiment, D.M. Short and his company became Company E of KGC leader Elkaneh Greer's cavalry, soon to be organized. The absorption of these companies would not be the end for the Order; its members had taken a lifetime pledge to aid and support their fellow members. It was mainly the First Degree members that became actively engaged in combat. Many of the Second and Third Degree members of the KGC remained at home or worked secretly behind the lines performing other functions.[26]

Colonel Van Dorn had returned to San Antonio and informed Henry McCulloch of his plans to arrest the remaining members of the U.S. Army still in Texas. McCulloch was still getting his force of six companies together when Van Dorn left headquarters at San Antonio on April 21, leaving KGC member Sackfield Maclin in charge of commanding the troops in and around the State's largest city. Van Dorn then left for Indianola by Victoria and McCulloch was ordered to follow by forced march with his complete force. While Van Dorn was on the road, the KGC in the form of the Alamo Rifles under the command of John A. Wilcox, commander of the KGC Western Brigade, arrested the fourteen Federal soldiers and officers remaining in San Antonio on the morning of April 23. Other officers of the Alamo Rifles included William Prescott, Captain; 1st Lieutenant Pasquale Leo Buquor, a former Texas Ranger and veteran of the Mexican War; John Earl, 2nd Lieutenant; and Alexander M. Ruiz, 3rd Lieutenant. Noncommissioned officers and enlisted men of note included Gustav Peltzer, Edward P. Alsbury, John B. Baccus, Jr., James R. Marmion, George Menger and Oscar Menger, both Menger Hotel family; and T.G. Newcomb, apparently the brother of the embattled Unionist and journalist James P. Newcomb. The captured Union officers were taken before Major Sackfield Maclin for a rather terse verbal encounter between Maclin and his former comrades. The terms offered the captured officers were that they could submit to being held as prisoners of war or sign a parole document stating they would not take up arms or serve in the field against the Confederate government. Upon signing their paroles, they would be allowed to leave Texas if they wished. Asking for 24 hours to consider their options, the U.S. soldiers met the following day and signed their paroles. By that time, April 24, Colonel Van Dorn reached the rendezvous point at the town of Victoria, where he had instructed his "volunteer" companies to gather before proceeding to Indianola. Who were these troops that massed at Victoria from April 23 to April 24?[27]

The paramilitary groups organized into companies, by company commander and county of origin, were listed by Colonel Van Dorn in his report of his successful campaign to capture the U.S. troops who surrendered at Indianola on April 25. No doubt the companies utilized by Van Dorn were privately financed KGC companies. Some of the men in those companies had participated in earlier anti-United States government operations, like Ben McCulloch's capture of the Federal Arsenal at San Antonio, John Salmon Ford's Rio Grande Campaign, and Van Dorn's audacious capture of the Star of the West. As listed by Van Dorn,

> The companies which reported at Victoria on the 23d and 24th of April were – Captain Herbert's company, Colorado; Captain Scarborough (Davis Guards), De Witt; Captain McDowell, Lockhart; Captain A.C. Horton, Matagorda; Captain W.R. Friend, De Witt Rifles; Captain Hampton, Victoria; Captain Upton, Colorado; Captain Holt, Fort Bend; Captains Jones and Harris, Colonel De Witt's command, Gonzales; Captain Williams, Lavaca County; Captain Fulkrod, Goliad; Captain Kyle, Hays County; Captain Stapp, Indianola; Captain Searcy, Colorado; Captain Phillips, Lavaca Town; Captain Finlay, Lavaca Town; Captain Pearson, Matagorda; Captain C. S. Olden, Texana; Captain Barkley, Fayette; Captain Gordon, Matagorda County. [sic]

Despite a few misspellings and other errors, as one of the goals of the author of this book is to identify as many of the 8,000 plus KGC members in Texas as possible, the full identities of the above officers should be determined as nearly as possible. William J. Herbert organized the first militia in his county, the Colorado Guards, and had secured adequate weaponry for it in March 1859. When the militia was disbanded, the Colorado Guards reorganized; by March 1860 his Lieutenants were John Samuel Shropshire and Howal A. Tatum. John Shropshire's brother Ben was a known KGC member as was H. A. Tatum. Herbert had been nominated for, but lost in the voting, the chance to serve as Major in John Salmon Ford's 2nd Texas Regiment; there were many KGC members in Ford's officer corps. Captain Andrew Jackson Scarborough's Davis Guards, not to be confused with the Davis Guards from Houston under Captain Frederick H. Odlum and Lieutenant Richard "Dick" Dowling, were based out of the town of Concrete in DeWitt County, a known location of at least one KGC Castle. John O. McGee was Captain of the Concrete Castle; Scarborough must have over-seen the Castle's affiliated company, as had been outlined at the K.G.C. Texas State Convention. They were a company that already had their own uniforms at the beginning of the war, suggesting that they were privately financed as were KGC companies generally. J. B. Holland was their 1st Lieutenant; when the Captain was unavailable, he would have commanded the company, which by the beginning of the war listed 119 rank and file members. Although they were "poorly armed," the record indicates that they were "ready & willing to go anywhere for action" as were most extremists at the beginning of the war. Samuel J. P. McDowell, Captain of the Lockhart Volunteers, was 37 years old, the son of Irish immigrants. He married Cate Shropshire, who was no doubt related to fellow KGC member Ben Shropshire, the Captain of a Castle in Fayette County. McDowell had been a member of the notorious Callahan Expedition in 1855, an illegal slave hunting foray into Mexico that resulted in the burning of the town of Piedras Negras and created an international incident. An expose of the KGC published by a former member in 1861 stated that the Order had evolved "From a small and insignificant band of kidnappers and fillibusters" and that "the Knights have, by no means, forgotten their original pet idea of slave stealing." Captain McDowell was one of those slave-stealing Knights. Albert Clinton Horton of Matagorda was one of the wealthiest men in the State and a large slaveowner who owned at least two plantations. Born in 1798, he was too old to do any real fighting so was probably the financial backer of his paramilitary group. He had served as the State's first Lieutenant Governor in 1846. Having a small private army at one's disposal made sense to a man who owned 150 slaves and needed to keep them under control. Captain William R. Friend of the DeWitt Rifles studied law at Princeton University and practiced law in Alabama until moving to Clinton in DeWitt County in 1857. His home in Clinton shared a location with the Clinton KGC Castle captained by A. J. Hodge. His 1st Lieutenant was James K. White and one of his company's Sergeants, Gilbert Gay, had attended the K.G.C. Texas State Convention, making it more likely that Friend's company drew heavily from that organization. Captain George James Hampton was sheriff of Victoria County from 1858 until August of 1861. He also had formed a company of Texas Rangers to battle Juan Cortina in 1859 where-upon he became acquainted with John Littleton, another Ranger turned KGC. In April 1861, his company was known as the Victoria Blues but later they changed the company name to the Victoria Invincibles before joining the Fourth Texas Mounted Volunteers.[28]

Captain John Cunningham Upton managed his mother's plantation in Fayette County and found time for military pursuits. No doubt he saw the KGC as an organization that could protect his family's investments in the plantation economy. He oversaw one of the companies listed as being from Colorado County, adjacent to Fayette County which had at least two KGC Castles; Colorado County had at least four. His company in Colorado County became the nucleus of Company B of the 5th Texas Infantry, which in turn became part of Hood's Brigade. He would die in battle at the second battle of Manassas. He and his brother William Felton Upton would both rise to the rank of Lieutenant Colonel before the war ended. John T. Holt had formed his company, known as the Fort Bend Rifles, as a mounted rifle company on January 14, 1860 at Richmond, Texas in Fort Bend County. Dan Connor of Fort Bend had taken 30 members of the Fort Bend Rifles to reinforce Colonel John S. Ford for the assault on Brazos San-tiago earlier in the year; apparently Captain Holt was not involved in that escapade but he, or at least his company, mustered at Victoria for the assault on Indianola. John T. Holt's company eventually became the core of Company H of Terry's Texas Rangers, the 8th Cavalry in Confederate service. Knight of the Columbian Star Philip Ignatius Barziza established a Castle in Fort Bend County, as earlier noted. "Captains Jones and Harris, Colonel DeWitt's command, Gonzales" were Isham G. Jones, Captain of the Gonzales Rifles and his 1st Lieutenant W.H.A. Harris. Not much is known about these men; Colonel DeWitt was probably Chris-topher Columbus DeWitt, a slaveowner and "zealous secessionist." He was the son of Green DeWitt, an early settler of Gonzales; Jones and Harris had a private in their company by the same name as C.C. DeWitt's father, so they were probably related. "Colonel" DeWitt was a little old for military service, so he likely was the financial sponsor of this company. Gonzales County had at least two Castles; one under Captain T.W. Lemmond and the other commanded by J.J. Ramsay. "Cap-tain Williams, Lavaca County" was Joseph C. Williams who served as 1st Lieuten-ant in a company that later formed in Halletsville, Lavaca County. Ouachita P. Preston was Captain of this later version of this group. This became Company M of Whitfield's Legion, a creation of John Wilkins Whitfield, the KGC transplant from Kansas Territory. Eventually Williams transferred to Company C of the 27 Texas Cavalry, as Whitfield's Legion was also designated and reclaimed his title of Captain. "Captain Fulkrod, Goliad" [sic] was Phillip Fulcrod, whose military records are fragmentary and incomplete. He was appointed a 2nd Lieutenant in the Confederate Army on November 2, 1861, and ordered to duty with a unit of field artillery assigned to the 5th Regiment, commanded by Tom Green, a KGC member by virtue of his signing of the Call for a Convention. Fulcrod spent much of his service as a recruiter, rising to 1st Lieutenant in Captain E. Abat's Horse Artillery company. Eventually he was relieved of that duty by the General Commanding the District of Texas, New Mexico and Arizona in order that he might raise a battalion of military cadets from Houston. He was probably related to Mathias Fulcrod of Goliad County who owned nine slaves in 1860.[29]

"Captain Kyle, Hays County" was Fergus Kyle, one of five sons of Claiborne Kyle who served in the Confederate forces. Fergus and his father were early settlers of Hays County, having moved there from Mississippi in 1844. Both men dabbled in Texas politics, but Claiborne was too old for frontline combat, born in 1800; he served in the Texas House of Representatives during the war. Fergus, after leading his company of "volunteers" to victory in Indianola, joined with others to form Company D in Terry's Texas Rangers, 8 Cavalry. Starting as a private, he was soon elected to 1st Lieutenant and later promoted to Captain. After the war he was an unreconstructed rebel, wearing his Confederate uniform for the rest of his life on special occasions. "Captain Stapp, Indianola" was Darwin Massey Stapp, a veteran of the Texas Revolution who served in the Texas House of Representatives from 1851 to 1854. From 1856 to 1864 he was Collector of Customs at Saluria, where he led his "volunteers," the Indianola Guards in 1861 after serving in the Texas Secession Convention. Eventually Stapp was made a Brigadier General in the 24 Brigade, Texas State Troops, in charge of the defense of Matagorda Bay.[30]

"Captain Searcy, Colorado" was a resident of Lavaca County even though the official record lists him as commanding a company from Colorado County. Officially his name was Albert W. Searcy, an attorney who moved to Texas from Tennessee in 1850. His wife, Mary Louisa Hanna was a member of a slave owning family from Louisiana who inherited property from her mother. Albert Wynn Searcy was 2nd Lieutenant of Oliver C. Searcy's company of 74 men headquartered at Halletsville, Lavaca County in early 1861. His brother Isham Searcy owned nine slaves and was brother-in-law to KGC leader John R. Baylor. When Oliver

C. Searcy's company merged into Company D of John Wilkins Whitfield's 27 Calvary later in the year, Oliver became 1st Lieutenant and Albert became 3rd Lieutenant. He was promoted to 2nd Lieutenant before his death in battle in Tennessee in 1863. "Captain Phillips, Lavaca Town" was Alexander H. Phillips, Jr. the son of a successful lawyer and native New Yorker who moved to Harris County, Texas in 1832. Alex Phillips, Jr. attended Princeton University and graduated with honors, returning to Lavaca, Calhoun County, Texas to practice law. He was a wealthy young man by the time he was thirty years of age. He was the Captain of the Lavaca Guards that threatened the U.S. Troops at Indianola on April 24; his 1st Lieutenant, R. E. Sutton, later took over as Captain when Phillips was promoted to Major in 1863. Alex Phillips, Jr. was killed in Alabama that same year.[31]

"Captain Finlay, Lavaca Town," was George Preston Finlay, an attorney and Mexican War veteran who moved to Lavaca, Calhoun County, Texas from Kentucky in 1853. He served as a state senator from 1860 to 1861; after the Ninth Session of Congress he was elected Captain of an infantry company in Victoria County. After the incident at Indianola he was briefly listed as a private in A.H. Phillips Jr.'s Lavaca Guards. Eventually, his company became Company H of the 6 Texas Infantry. After being released in a prisoner exchange in 1863, he served in KGC member Roger Q. Mill's 10 Texas Infantry at Chickamauga before transferring to a position as judge advocate for the Confederacy. "Captain Pearson, Matagorda"[sic] was Dr. Edward Adolphus Peareson, who had been born in South Carolina and received his medical degree from the Citadel in his home state. After that he studied medicine in Paris, France where he received another diploma. Moving to Victoria in 1846, he soon relocated to Matagorda in 1848 and was the editor-publisher of a newspaper there. He was the county's only doctor. In February 1860, Dr. Peareson was one of the incorporators of the Matagorda Railroad Company. Matagorda County was plantation country: in 1860 it had more slaves than white citizens. Cotton was the big crop, but cane sugar and cattle were major factors in the economy, produced with the help of 2,107 slaves. During the slave panic of the summer of 1860, Dr. Peareson organized a company of men for a slave patrol known as the Matagorda Coast Guards. This was the company he led to Indianola less than a year later. His 1st Lieutenant, James Selkirk, was also one of the incorporators of the Matagorda Railroad Company and a fellow officer of the Matagorda Lodge No. 7, a local Masonic Lodge. Peareson was the Worshipful Master of the Lodge. Eventually the company he created and led became Company D of the 6 Regiment of Texas Volunteers, which was in Confederate service as part of Granbury's Brigade. Dr. Peareson died within months of the end of the war of a lingering illness that began during his military service. He fit the profile of a typical leader of Military Knights in Texas.[32]

"Captain C. S. Olden [sic], Texana" was Clark Lewis Owen, a fearless soldier with lengthy experience and the serving Grand Master of Texas for the International Order of Odd Fellows in 1861. He came to Texas from Kentucky to join in the fight for Texas' independence from Mexico and served again in 1840, fighting the Comanche Indians. He also participated in state-sanctioned filibuster movements against Mexico, as part of both the Somerville Expedition and the Mier Expedition in the 1840s. After this he moved to Texana in Jackson County where he was elected twice to serve in the State Legislature. He led the Texana Guards in the hostile action against the United States at Indianola. Later, his company became the nucleus of Company K in the 2nd Texas Infantry. He was killed leading his men into battle at Shiloh in 1862. "Captain Barkley, Fayette" [sic] was Richard Alexander Barclay, who participated in an ill-fated venture known as the Dawson Expedition of 1842 in which his brother Robert was killed. Richard A. Barclay escaped and made his way back home to Fayette County via New Orleans. In April 1861, Barclay led his small company to Victoria to participate in the capture of U.S. soldiers. Shortly thereafter in June, "Barkley" and his 1st Lieutenant L.W. More led 50 rank and file members into the ranks of the 22nd Brigade of Texas State Troops thereby avoiding Confederate service. Richard A. Barclay died of pneumonia in 1866 while on a cattle drive. Lastly, of the companies and their commanders listed in Van Dorn's General Or-der No. 4, "Captain Gordon, Matagorda County" is a bit of a mystery. *The Official Records of the War of the Rebellion* do not acknowledge his existence, or rather, his participation in the incident at Indianola April 23 and April 24. Also, the reliable Galveston newspaper *The Civilian and Gazette* does not mention "Captain Gordon" in its report of the incident either. The only other known company of any size from Matagorda County in existence at the time was the Caney Rifles captained by Edward S. Rugeley with 64 men. However, there was a Jesse Gordon enrolled as a private in the Caney Rifles. Later in the war Captain Jesse H. Gordon's Company is mentioned in official correspondence from San Antonio as "never having mustered, but the officer in command says there is an order at district headquarters which authorizes the company to report to Colonel Benavides. Only forty men in the company." Apparently, Captain Gordon's Company was an "independent" company of "volunteers" who elected not to show up in Indianola. Perhaps Captain Gordon was too busy tending the 43 slaves he kept on his plantation in Matagorda County. His commanding officer Colonel Santos Benavides was a reliable operative in charge of a mostly Hispanic force that was responsible for policing the border with Mexico. He sometimes utilized KGC members in his regiment, as when known KGC Captain C.C. Jones of the Beeville Castle served as Benavides 2nd Lieutenant. Mat Nolan, who had previously served under KGC leader John Salmon Ford, eventually became Lieutenant Colonel in Benavides' regiment. Benavides had been a slave catcher along the border as well as a sometime smuggler. His experience in these matters allowed him to effectively aid KGC Knight of the Columbian Star Charles A. Russell in his cot-ton smuggling venture, moving Texas cotton across the border so that it could be safely sold in Mexico during the war, avoiding the blockade by sea. Other researchers have suggested that Benavides was probably the Captain of a KGC Castle in one of the border counties, its existence suggested by voting patterns in those counties during the secession election and by his cooperative efforts with Charles A. Russell. As many as fifty prominent Tejano families in the San Antonio area were slave owners. Benavides offered them protection and loss prevention by capturing slaves attempting to escape across the border. Both J.A.G. Navarro and Alexander Ruiz were known KGC members and it is likely there were many other Hispanic members of the Order.[33]

The remaining U.S. Troops stranded at Indianola surrendered on April 25. Van Dorn's operation was considered a great success, so naturally many would-be warriors wanted a share of the glory. It was reported that 500 stand of badly needed arms were captured. Although Henry McCulloch's six companies could not reach the Gulf in time to participate in the confrontation and surrender, they were mentioned in Van Dorn's report – "five companies of cavalry, under Captains Pitts, Tobin, Ashby, Bogges, and Nelson, and the battery of light artillery, under Captain Edgar, from San Antonio...." Captain William M. Edgar was also Captain of the Alamo City Guards; a company affiliated with one of the San Antonio Castles. Captain Travis Hill Ashby had commanded a company of men from Gonzales County that participated in the takeover of the Federal Arsenal in San Antonio February 14 under Ben McCulloch. The newspapers struggled to parcel out the accolades that were already spread thin from overuse. "We fear that we shall never be able to report all the volunteers who responded to the call of Col. Van Dorn, for the capture of the U.S. Troops at Indianola," the Galveston *Civilian* and *Gazette Weekly* stated, but then attempted to give its accounting of their numbers:

> ...three companies from Lavaca county; one from Hallettsville, commanded by Capt. Searcy, numbering about 86 men; Capt. York's company from Rocky Creek, about 60 men. Capt. A.J. Scarborough's company from Brushy, 90 men. From Wharton county the company consisted of about 50 men. The company from Victoria county, under Capt. J.G. Hampton, had about 60 men. The DeWitt company, Capt. W. R. Friend, about 50 men. Jackson company, Capt. C.L. Owen, about 100 men. Fort Bend company, Capt. Holt, about 50 men. Two Goliad companies. Colorado company, Capt. Herbert, 80 men. Lockhart company, under Capt. McDowall, 70 men. Two companies from Gonzales, commanded by Capts. Key and Harris. [sic]

The article mentioned another source on the incident, the *Matagorda Gazette*, reporting that "the two companies from Lavaca were commanded by Capts. Finlay and Phillips" and that the company from Matagorda was commanded by "Capt. Pearson" meaning Captain E. A. Peareson. The presence of "Captain York" and his company from Rocky Creek was not disclosed by Van Dorn in his report, which suggests he may have been a stand-in for the usual company commander. Yorktown had been alluded to as a ready source of men for any emergency by KGC leader William R. Scurry in his April 20 letter to Governor Ed Clark, as well as "Brushy" which was revealed to be a reference to Captain Scarborough. Yorktown, in DeWitt County where William R. Scurry resided, was also the site of a documented KGC Castle. The town had been named for John Allison York, an early settler of Lavaca County and Indian fighter who lost his life in battle with the Native Americans in 1848. His brother James Allison York was wounded in the same battle but escaped. John York left a wife and several children; at least two of his sons resided in DeWitt County in 1860. His brother, James Allison York, stayed in Lavaca County where he had eleven slaves in 1860, giving him $15,000 in personal worth. The third-born child of John Allison York, Jonathan C. York had followed in his father's footsteps by serving in Company C of the Mounted Battalion of Texas Volunteers, fighting Indians from 1854 to 1855. By 1860, he was married with a family and owned six slaves. One of his brothers lived in the same county; John Pettus York, a 23-year old farmer living in the town of Clinton, from where William R. Scurry had written his letter to the Governor. His personal wealth was substantial for a young man, with real estate worth $3,180 and a personal estate of $3,807. Not much else is known about J.P. York, other than he signed up for combat duty just a few months later when he joined Captain Leander M. Rayburn's Company of Texas Volunteers in the 8th Cavalry. As an inexperienced young man, he had no idea at the time that he had sealed his fate, for Rayburn's Company soon became Company E of Terry's Texas Rangers, a reckless group of shock troops peopled by many KGC members. They would soon see action in what became a deadly guerilla war in Central Tennessee that would cost John Pettus York his life. As it concerns the identity of the "Captain York" from Rocky Creek in Lavaca County he could have been any one of those three men, but for this writer's money it was probably James Allison York, the 55-year old former Indian fighter whose plantation was near Rocky Creek in Lavaca County, close by the settlement known as Sweet Home. The Sweet Home Castle was run by Captain John R. Pulliam, who later enlisted in John Salmon Ford's 2nd Mounted Rifles under Captain James Walker. Pulliam started as Walker's Orderly Sergeant and later became an officer. As the Sweet Home Castle listed only 12 horsemen armed with rifles, slave-owner "Ellison" York as he was sometimes known, had to draw from a larger area than Sweet Home to field the 60 men he was reported to have commanded. Perhaps his DeWitt County nephews joined him at Indianola.[34]

In spite of some confusion as to which "volunteer" companies participated in the Indianola raid and under which commander, both Van Dorn's official report and the *Civilian* and *Gazette Weekly* were in accord, generally, as to the composition of Henry McCulloch's late-arriving force. Those six companies were commanded by Captain William A. Pitts (69 men); Captain Travis Hill Ashby (79 men); Captain William G. Tobin (72 men); and according to Van Dorn, companies of undisclosed quantities of men commanded by Captain James H. Fry, Governeur H. Nelson and Captain Milton M. Bogges. KGC Captain William Edgar was also a late arrival with 56 men and 4 artillery pieces. Of McCulloch's captains, four of them (Bogges, Ashby, Fry and Pitts) enlisted before April 17, the day the news of the attack on Fort Sumter reached San Antonio. The 17th was the day that Henry McCulloch knew that a state of war existed between the Confederacy and the United States. McCulloch himself as well as his six captains, all came from counties with at least one KGC Castle. For instance, Milton M. Bogges, an Indian fighter like McCulloch enrolled at Henderson, Rusk County on April 6. Rusk County had contributed KGC members for the first failed attempt to invade Mexico in March

1860, and the existence of the Henderson Castle is documented. Travis Hill Ashby had enrolled in Henry McCulloch's 1st Cavalry on April 15 but as previously stated had commanded men under KGC leader Ben McCulloch in February's raid on the Arsenal. Ashby lived in Gonzales County, which had at least two documented Castles, per-haps as many as three, if the Castle started by A. D. Harris was separate and apart from those led by Captain J.W. Lemmond and Captain John J. Ramsay. In addition, Henry McCulloch had signed "the Call for a Convention" as had his Captain James H. Fry; Captain William A. Pitts father, W.C. Pitts had also signed the public appeal for the secession convention. That they were signatories (or the son of a signer in Captain Pitts' case) on that document greatly increases the likelihood that Captains Fry and Pitts were KGC.[35]

Having the manpower and the weapons to defend the new Confederate State of Texas was of major concern to the general population. The fear of being conquered by the "Black Republican horde" added to the stress many felt as the losing party in the secession election. The secessionists wanted the general populous to rely upon them as the new authority and as bastions of the new society the KGC intended to create. They made sure that their attempts to reach crisis points like Indianola were recorded and transmitted by the press. To that end it was reported that the also-rans of Van Dorn's Indianola caper got their credit, too. These included a "company of volunteers, from Milam county, under Capt. J.C. Rogers" who got as far as LaGrange in Fayette County before they discovered they had missed the whole thing. Also among them was "The Fayette company" that made it as far as Victoria before learning they'd missed out; as well as "The Austin Light Infantry, under Capt. B.F. Carter". Benjamin F. Carter was an attorney in Austin, Travis County and was likely associated with the Austin Castle, as was the Austin City Light Infantry he commanded, with Xavier B. DeBray as his 1st Lieutenant. There were 67 men listed on the company roster as of April 24, 1861. Within a month this company became part of the Tom Green Rifles, and eventually Company B of the 4th Regiment, Texas Volunteer Infantry in John Bell Hood's Brigade. Tom Green had been one of the signers of the Call for a Convention, as well as fellow Travis County residents Sebron Graham Sneed, John T. Pruitt, John Baylor Banks, George W. White, George Flournoy, Morris Reagan, James P. Neal, John Alexander Green (the brother of Tom Green) and Ed Clark – the Governor. As previously noted by historian H. H. Bancroft, all these men should be considered KGC members. George W. White and Morris Reagan were documented as members, and it was George Flournoy who participated in the secret council of war that drafted the Call for a Convention; it was Flournoy that published the call, and his name appears as "G. Flournoy" on the roster of the Austin City Light Infantry on April 24. The Secession Convention added eleven additional names to the original list of 61 men who signed the Call for a Convention, adopting a resolution put forth by George W. Chilton, the Marshall of the Texas Division of the KGC, on March 16, 1861. Among these additional men recommended by the high command of the KGC were Travis County residents Robert J. Townes, A.R. Crozier, and Josephus Murray Steiner. These men should be considered KGC members as well.[36]

This was a very uncertain time for the people of Texas. Anonymous reports were sent to the editors of various newspapers with-in the State to buttress the secession cause, an action which itself portrays the atmosphere of doubt surrounding the future. The implication, although widespread hostilities had not yet commenced, was that there was no going back now. One such anonymous letter from LaGrange to E. H. Cushing of the *Houston Weekly Telegraph* assured its readers that Fayette County would back up its support for secession with armed forces. A public meeting to this end had been called by Joseph L. Gay, "one of our wealthiest planters" urging immediate action as early as the day before the attack on Fort Sumter. By the end of April, the anonymous writer reported, "Larkin Price has a company already formed. The K.G.C. have a company also and there is a company at Winedale. The whole county will be put on a war footing immediately." Readers were also assured that the German-born residents of Fayette County were "enthusiastic" in their support and some had even volunteered for military service. Obviously concerns remained as to the Germans' loyalty to the secession cause; concurrently a Galveston newspaper reported that "some disagreements" were occurring in San Antonio over secession, where the largest city in the State included a large population of German-born and Hispanic residents. These persistent problems were said to have been "exaggerated by rumor." The Telegraph gave more information as to how these problems were to be dealt with in San Antonio: a general meeting was held there for "citizens of all parties and classes" which put everyone on notice that they "would resist the coercive policy of the Republican ad-ministration to the last". Three of the four featured speakers at this declaration were known KGC leaders: Samuel A. Maverick, John A. Wilcox and George H. Sweet. The propaganda press reported that these types of speeches "had a very happy effect upon the Un-ion crowd present." This of course was wishful thinking, and the public indoctrination and suppression of loyal Americans still resident in San Antonio would continue. Similar meetings were held elsewhere in the State. In Dallas, a special public meeting convened for the organization of the "Dallas Home Guards, Company A" which would be armed with weaponry purchased with the Dallas County Treasury surplus revenue. The committee in charge of the proceedings then recommended that similar meetings be held "in every precinct or populous neighborhood in the county." May 3 was set as the day for the first company of Dallas County Home Guards to be formally assembled. Although the Home Guard had been designated as performing a police function by KGC leadership, with so many new military units forming from older KGC units, it would become increasingly difficult to separate the KGC from Texas State forces and/or Confederate forces. However, in many instances it is easy to see the role the KGC leadership fulfilled in building the new society of Confederate Texas; they were in the vanguard of anti-American aggression early in the war especially. Fort Washita in Indian Territory north of the Red River had fallen to such forces on April 17; now on May 5 the remaining two forts in Indian Territory, Arbuckle and Cobb, were seized by men led by KGC operatives. Noted KGC recruiter and military leader William T. Patton revealed his role in securing these forts in a letter dated May 5 to the *Dallas Herald*. Fort Washita had been virtually abandoned after being turned over to the irregular Texas forces, many of whom, like James W. Throckmorton, had returned home. Captain William T. Patton had taken a small detachment two miles north of the Red River on April 25, and on May 3 sent a detachment of 25 men to Fort Washita. The detachment was under the command of Lieutenant Frederick Samuel Bass, a graduate of the Virginia Military Institute and a resident of the KGC stronghold of Marshall, Texas where he taught at a private military academy. Upon reaching Fort Washita that night Lieutenant Bass informed Colonel William C. Young the following morning that they had occupied that place and had sent 20 men to occupy Fort Arbuckle. There they captured six wagonloads of provisions meant for U.S. soldiers. In his dispatch to Colonel Young, Bass stated that Fort Washita was now held by only 5 of his men and asked for reinforcements. When William Patton left Indian Territory on May 3, 600 troops from Texas had crossed the Red River to oppose the estimated 450 U.S. Troops who were then in retreat. Captain Patton stated that another 400 Arkansas troops and as many as 200 Native American troops would soon reinforce the Texans. "The Indian Nations are all right and sound on the slavery question," Patton stated, and "the flag of the Southern Confederacy has been raised at the Capital." More armed "civilians," likely KGC, were heading north into Indian Territory to

block the feared Kansas abolitionists. This continued to be a major fear of the
Texas secessionists, as Colonel Young stated, "if war continues we shall have for-
ays from Kansas, and this northern frontier must be well prepared." Young
painted a fearful picture of the situation for North Texans: "we cannot afford to
send troops to the South" he stated, as there were no railroads in the Northern
part of the State for the rapid deployment of troops, unlike the Gulf coast or more
developed parts of the State: "...up here a foray could be made, immense damage
done, and the parties away, before we could have a defensive force to repel them."
Colonel Young's concern, coupled with the threat of Native American "Indian
depredations" influenced many KGC members to stay closer to home than the
Confederate front lines in order to protect their property and wealth, as well as
their families. Lieutenant Bass eventually was joined by men from Dallas commanded by Captain T. Flynn, another company under Nicholas H. Darnell, another company of 51 men known as the White Rock Mounted Rifles under Captain John H. Daniels, and another from Cedar Springs under the command of
Captain John H. Cochran, the secretary of the Dallas Committee that organized
Home Guard units for Dallas County. Soon it was reported that men from Collin,
Dallas, Grayson, Fannin, Lamar and Hunt counties had assembled a force of about
1500 Texans north of the Red River. Their enthusiasm was in part fueled by a false
report printed May 7 and circulated by men from Marshall, Texas stating "Montgomery, of Kansas, at the head of 2,000 or 3,000 men has taken possession of
Forts Washita and Cobb, on our northern frontier, and threatens the invasion of
our State and the desolation of our country." This fear tactic had been a proven
winner for the KGC during the phony "slave revolt" the previous year – Montgomery was a favorite bugaboo for North Texans. Among the names of the signers of the bogus circular were Frederick S. Bass and Walter P. Lane; both men
would soon raise companies for the war, which had yet to begin for most Texans.
Days after the alarmist circular made its de-but, emissaries from Texas were in
New Orleans "begging for arms" from the Confederate arsenal in Louisiana, using
the false report that the "poorly armed" Texans were facing a large Federal force
across their Northern border in Indian Territory. By the following month, however, Fort Washita was held by just 100 troops under the command of Otis G.
Welch, the KGC leader of Denton, Texas. Apparently, the majority of the public
did not notice the deception. Many of these same men, like William T. Patton, had
mustered out for the absurd "Grand Buffalo Hunt" earlier in the year. Perhaps it
was only absurdity prima facie; in retrospect it appears that the "buffalo hunt" may

have served as a rehearsal for the takeover of the Federal forts across the Red River from Texas in Indian Territory.[37]

As April ended and May began, Colonel Earl Van Dorn was reportedly camped in Victoria with 2,300 men waiting for the arrival of the last Union troops left stranded in Texas. Their quarry had been stationed on the far Western frontier at Fort Bliss, Fort Quitman and Fort Davis, 600 miles away from any word as to what had transpired in the rest of the State. The KGC continued to lend considerable support to Van Dorn by forming what became designated as the Battalion City Volunteers. Composed solely of "civilian" forces from San Antonio, the Battalion City Volunteers were composed of five different companies, most of whom were led by men with ties to the KGC. These companies were known by the Captains that commanded them: Captains Duff, Wilcox, Navarro, Kampmann and Maverick. James Duff had participated in the seizure of the Federal Arsenal in San Antonio and would be at the center of the most heinous suppression of dissent in Texas during the Civil War. Duff would declare martial law in the Hill Country and command the men who perpetrated the notorious "battle of the Nueces" which was in fact the unnecessary slaughter of German dissidents who were attempting to escape Texas into Mexico. Because of his early role in pre-war hostile action against the Federal troops stationed in Texas, and because he was elected Lieutenant Colonel in command of a battalion comprised of KGC members, it is reasonable to consider James Duff as a KGC member as well. Definitive proof of his membership is provided by the fact that he had started as a private in the Alamo Rifles, a known KGC company and quickly rose to the top. He was elected in early May 1861 to the position of command of the Battalion City Volunteers, reporting directly to Confederate Colonel Earl Van Dorn. Reporting directly to Duff was Major John Carolan, another known KGC member elected by the rank-and-file; Captain Wilcox was John A. Wilcox, commander of the Alamo Rifles. The Battalion's Lieutenant and Adjutant was James R. Marmion, an early officer of the Alamo Rifles, elected 2nd Lieutenant in March 1859. Rounding out the Battalion staff were O.D. Cook, Sergeant Major, and John Newton, another member of the Alamo Rifles, now elected Lieu-tenant and Quartermaster. Among the line officers, Captain Wilcox was another known member of the KGC and had commanded the Alamo Rifles in the takeover of Federal facilities in the city in February; now his company was absorbed into the Battalion City Volunteers. The names of two of the other captains, Navarro and Maverick, were connected to known KGC members; "Captain Navarro" was Jose Angel Navarro III (Jose An-gel Navarro the young-er), the brother of KGC member and Castle officer Jose Antonio George Navarro (J.A.G. Navarro); and "Captain Maverick" was the aged Samuel Augustus Maverick, a member of the Committee for Public Safety. Samuel A. Maverick soon became a member of the dreaded Vigilance Committee of San Antonio as lieutenant to Captain Asa Mitchell, another known KGC member, for the duration of the war. "Captain Kampmann" was John Herman Kampmann, a Prussian-born businessman in the construction trade. In addition to building the Lone Star Brewery, Kampmann was contracted by the Menger family to build the famous Menger Hotel in San Antonio; George and Oscar Menger were both mem-bers of the Alamo Rifles. After his company was absorbed into the Third Texas Infantry, John H. Kampmann spent the majority of the war running a factory in LaGrange manufacturing uniforms for the troops.[38]

Van Dorn and his KGC cohorts met the union stragglers near San Lucas Springs, where they were joined by still more KGC eager for a confrontation with the enemy. Captain Trevanion T. Teel, another known KGC operative, had been shadowing the retreating Union soldiers from the time they had crossed by Fort Clark on their way to San Antonio and their ultimate destination of Green Lake near the Gulf Coast. Teel conducted his reconnaissance in force, leading a com-mand of 100 men combined with a battery of six artillery pieces. The footsore Yankee soldiers had started on their journey from Fort Bliss near El Paso, led by Colonel Isaac Van Duzer Reeve and picked up more men from both the Eighth U.S. Infantry and the Sixth U.S. Infantry along the way. Altogether, the Reeve party comprised 320 men, dozens of whom fell ill, got lost or deserted, reducing his effective strength to 270 men. Eventually they camped at Adams Hill, in sight of San Lucas Springs, the night of May 8, having begun their march in early April. The following morning KGC-led forces appeared in large numbers, lined up across from them as if for battle; the incident became known as the so-called Battle of Adam's Hill. Colonel Van Dorn commanded the rebel force, which has been estimated as large as 2,000 well-armed men, comprised of Henry E. McCulloch's six companies, plus a squadron of KGC Middle Brigade leader John S. Ford's troops led by KGC officer John R. Baylor; also KGC Captain William Edgar's battery of light artillery and the Battalion City Volunteers led by James Duff. Cap-tain Teel's force joined these men as well. KGC Western Brigade leader John A. Wilcox and former U.S. Lieutenant James Patrick Major served as aides to Van

Dorn during this incident and along with another KGC collaborator, former Union soldier Joseph F. Minter, were instrumental in convincing the grossly outnumbered and outgunned Union troops to surrender. On May 10 the captives were marched through San Antonio. That day Colonel Van Dorn was able to write from San Antonio to the Confederate Inspector General in Montgomery that "I have the honor to report that I have met the last column of the United States troops in Texas yesterday at noon, on the El Paso road, about thirteen miles from this city, and that Colonel Reeve... surrendered unconditionally." Official correspondence of the event mentions other known KGC leaders as participants; Lieutenant James Paul of the Castroville Castle, Captain John J. Good from Dallas, Captain William Prescott and judges P.N. Luckett and Thomas J. Devine. With Samuel Maverick and the aforementioned judges present, the Committee for Public Safety was in attendance and involved. The day following the public display of the defeated U.S. Army, arrangements were made to confiscate their weapons, which had been estimated at up to 800 stand of arms. In an accounting for the materiale confiscated with the considerable help of the KGC in Texas, it was reckoned that 5,000 stand of arms had been captured from General Twiggs by Ben McCulloch, including 1,000 stand that Twiggs had loaned to citizens of San Antonio; that Van Dorn had captured "upwards of five hundred stand of arms" at Indianola, with another 800 at Adams Hill; and that "several light batteries of artillery at San Antonio more than are necessary for service there" resulted in a need for a redistribution of resources. As a result, the Confederate Secretary of War ordered Van Dorn on May 14 to send a battery of six artillery pieces to Dallas along with 2,000 stand of arms including "Sharp's carbine and rifle, United States rifles, and Colt's pistols, with ammunition for the same." The day after, on May 15, KGC leader Elkanah Greer received orders from Montgomery "to raise a Regt. of Texas mounted men for a special purpose & for service in the Indian Territory". This new regiment would be filled with men Colonel Greer had previously recruited in his former role as military director for the KGC; his new command was to be headquartered at Dallas – weapons for what became the 3rd Texas Cavalry, also known as the South Kansas-Texas Regiment were already being procured from Van Dorn's command in San Antonio. Greer's regiment would serve under the also newly minted Brigadier General Ben McCulloch. Their "special purpose" would be the invasion of Missouri in support of their beleaguered allies in that State.[39]

The KGC had been spread out across the entire State of Texas, from the Red River and beyond into Indian Territory to the North, to the West of San Antonio and the Rio Grande River in the South at precisely the time that KGC Texas State Marshall George W. Chilton had called for their attendance at Galveston on May 1st. Unlike the KGC State Convention held in San Antonio in late February, there are no records of any such meeting taking place on the date assigned. Victor W. Thompson, the editor of the *States Rights Democrat*, the "official printer" and house-organ of the Texas KGC, had left Texas behind for one of his former homes, the State of Tennessee. There at Bethel Springs (near Purdy, Tennessee) on May 1 he joined Company B of the 1st Regiment of Mississippi Cavalry. His partner in the *States Rights Democrat*, J.G. Wheeler, continued to publish the paper until it was suspended in September. The number of newspapers published in Texas would continue to shrink throughout the year. With Thompson no longer available to cover any events in Galveston it still appears that attendance was light at the KGC's scheduled State conference. There was much activity in Galveston and its nearby sister city of Houston in early May; on May 2 a Home Guard company calling itself the Sumter Guards met in Houston and elected officers. Horace Cone, who had been present in New Orleans during the KGC conference there in 1860, was elected Captain; Cone was at least 40 years old and his officers were even older. Algernon P. Thompson, 1st Lieutenant was 43 years old; 3rd Lieutenant Henry Francis Fisher was 56; his other officers, 1st Lieutenant A.N. Jordan and Orderly Sergeant G.A. Jones were of indeterminate age. This was typical of many Home Guard units; they were comprised of the aged and the unfit for battle. Still, one of the goals of Texas KGC leadership was the enrollment of every man in some form of military service, as would be publicly revealed just two weeks later. The same day the Sumter Guards reorganized, the steamship Texas arrived in Galveston from New Orleans bearing Captain Henry Van Buren and his second-in-command, Lieutenant F. W. Malone. These two men commanded the Galveston Artillery Company, which had participated in the initial occupation of Brazos Santiago as part of the Rio Grande Expedition led by KGC Middle Brigade commander John Salmon Ford. They had also participated in the capture of The Star of the West under Colonel Van Dorn. It is likely that they had come back to Galveston for the KGC meeting; if so, they were a day late.[40]

There was a general movement of what look like KGC military companies to the Gulf Coast from across the State of Texas in the first days of May. Although their motivation is not crystal clear it was stated that their target was Virginia. Texas troops were hoping to make their bid for glory by being at what they perceived to be the front lines. The problem with their assumption was that the Confederate government had not requested their presence. Captain Alfred C. McKeen of the Galveston-based Lone Star Rifles was one of the first to suggest this as early as May 3 when the *Civilian and Gazette* reported that his company of 100 men were "ready and anxious to leave for Virginia" as they saw that as "the great battle-field between the North and the South." That same day the Marion Rifles from Jefferson, Texas arrived at New Orleans with the same object in mind. Ultimately under the command of Harvey H. Black, these 111 men were literally the first Texas troops to muster into Confederate service on April 27. On May 4, the Livingston Guards from Polk County landed at Galveston with their company of 80 men where they were joined by another company of 58 men from Polk County calling themselves the Cold Spring Rangers. Bearing in mind that the Polk County companies were composed of private citizens and not authorized military units, it would seem that KGC mastermind Count Philip I. Barziza had made good on his promise to organize Castles in Polk County. Fellow Knight of the Columbian Star Ben McCulloch was in New Orleans when he sent a dispatch May 3 to fellow Texans Louis T. Wigfall and General Thomas N. Waul asking them to ask the Confederate Secretary of War if more volunteer troops from Texas would be accepted into service in Virginia if they paid their own expenses for transportation. General Waul answered back the same day by dispatch that "Secretary will not accept the regiment from Texas." Even if these troops volunteered at no expense to the government, they were not needed. Ben McCulloch then went from New Orleans to Montgomery, the capitol, and long-time KGC leader Hugh McLeod left the Louisiana port city and returned to Galveston on May 5. The day after McLeod's arrival the Wigfall Guards met in Galveston and reorganized their company, electing new officers, placing James McGrath in command as Captain and N.C. White as 1st Lieutenant. That night the Galveston City Guards met and voted to change their name to the Galveston City Grays. They too, elected new officers, placing their trust in Captain Ephraim McLean and his 1st Lieutenant J.S. LeClere; McLean was a member of the plantation class, an owner of 10 slaves in Galveston County in 1861. It appears that this KGC company was attempting to change their image to Confederate gray. It was announced by one of the Galveston newspapers that Texan Charles G. Baylor, brother of KGC members John R. and George W. Baylor, had succeeded in his trip to Belgium to negotiate an arms deal for the Confederate troops in Mississippi, Tennessee, and Kentucky. During the war, it would be alleged that the KGC in other states had an unusually close relationship with the government of Belgium. It has frequently been postulated that the Great European Powers sought the division of the United States as a means of reducing its power and standing on the world stage. The same edition of the Galveston News that commented on Charles Baylor's overseas mission also reported that a British naval squadron had moved into the Gulf, ostensibly to defend British shipping. The Union blockade of Texas ports like Galveston would begin disrupting Confederate shipping later in the year.[41]

It appears as if the Texas KGC was still attempting a state-wide rally of sorts to be held sometime in May. Following up on Grand Marshal George W. Chilton's published announcement in April for a May 1 meeting in Galveston, President George W. Bickley issued a May 1 appeal that was published on May 7 for the Texas Castles to report to either General Chilton at Tyler, or to Colonel Charles A. Russell at Helena in Karnes County – these locations being at geographic extremes from one another. Continuing, Bickley stated, "The president begs the order to respond fully and promptly to the call of Generals Chilton, Ford, Wilcox, and Green, and stand on the *defensive* until our national troubles are over." [italics added] Besides G.W. Chilton, Bickley referred to John Salmon Ford, John A. Wilcox and Thomas Green as the major war leaders for the KGC within Texas, and implied that the KGC was going to stay home in a defensive position rather than take the offensive by traveling to Virginia. However, some Texas KGC leaders had other plans. Beginning May 7, KGC leader Thomas Saltus Lubbock published an appeal to the public in the *Houston Weekly Telegraph* to raise troops in Texas for Virginia. Lubbock ended this rather long-winded screed thusly:

> Come, brothers, come: Meet me in the City of Houston, on the 20th of May, armed with such weapons as you are accustomed to... put in your purse not less than $250, and then as the 'independent Texas Guerilla's,' [sic] we will hasten to Richmond City, Virginia – our next destination, the 'Federal Capitol:' and then, my boys, wherever glory calls.

All interested were to make application to T.S. Lubbock, care of E.H. Cushing, editor of the Houston Telegraph. Meanwhile, Castles across the state continued their business as usual: one of the Corpus Christi Castles ran ads in May stating that regular meetings would be held every Friday evening at 7:30 in the Virginia House. The Castle officers were listed as William I. Moore, Captain; Henry W. Berry, Lieutenant; Simon Jones, Inspector; George Pfeuffer, Guide; Charles E.

Clark, Sergeant; Jacob Ziegler, Treasurer and Thomas E. Hooper, Secretary. Lieutenant Henry Berry was the Mayor of the city. Other known members of the Order in Corpus Christi included George Conklin, John Riggs, Felix Noessel and his brother Otto Noessel. Otto T. Noessel had been a prominent member of the Committee for Public Safety in Corpus Christi and surrounding Nueces County under the direction of Benjamin F. Neal. Days later, an anonymous letter dated May 12 was published in San Antonio giving the status of the KGC Castle in New Braunfels, Comal County and its affiliated military company, the Confederate Guards of Comal. "This company numbers fifty men," the letter stated, "and is composed wholly of the K.G.C. of our place. This company is made up of the leading men in our community, and a more efficient, well-disciplined body of soldiers can rarely be found." The anonymous writer was probably Theophelus J. Thomas, the Captain of the Comal Castle. Thomas had listed only 30 members just months before at the KGC State Convention in San Antonio in February. Although he had previously complained to Governor Clark of difficulty in enlisting volunteers, he had nearly doubled the size of his company since then, the expansion fueled by secession and the attack on Fort Sumter. Whoever the writer really was, he mentioned that his company had offered its service to Colonel Earl Van Dorn, and that two other companies were forming in Comal County but gave no indication that these other companies were KGC. Notice was made in San Antonio on May 13 that two Castles of the KGC would meet that night "at the Castle" – probably Braden Hall, the site of regular meetings and the KGC State Convention. The two Castles had special business to attend to that night: at midnight the KGC broke into the offices of the *Alamo Express* and destroyed its printing press and burned down the building. The *Express* had frequently mocked the KGC and had been previously condemned by its President George W. Bickley for "injuring the K.G.C.". This was the end of the last Unionist newspaper in the State of Texas. The remaining newspapers were threatened, as reported by the Indianola Courier, which reported the demise of the *Alamo Express* and expressed the opinion that the destruction had not come soon enough. The following day, the newly unemployed publisher of the *Express*, James P. Newcomb, was advised by friends to leave town. Newcomb did so and headed for the Rio Grande River and the border with Mexico. It was later determined that the KGC had intended to hang him, and either hang or banish some 150 prominent citizens of San Antonio suspected of disloyalty to the new order. Cooler heads prevailed for the time being, but Newcomb escaped Texas through Mexico and stayed in California until the end of the war. Dissent would not be tolerated.[42]

Neither would political discourse, in the ideal world of the KGC. The KGC's official publisher, the *LaGrange Southern Rights Democrat*, announced on May 16 that there was no longer any need for political parties in Texas:

> We want good and tried men to guide our affairs, and merit should be the only passport to honor and position. There are no parties now in Texas, and the public weal must not be made to yield to personal ambition, and individual aggrandizement.

In other words, the personal life was dead in Texas, if the KGC had its way. The Knights of the Columbian Star would determine which men had the merit for any position in their new society. In the same edition of the *Southern Rights Democrat*, Knight of the Columbian Star and Texas KGC Adjutant General Charles A. Russell posted "An Address to the Knights of the Golden Circle in Texas." Among his opening comments, the native New Yorker stated, "Since the commencement of our organization in Texas, events have rapidly transpired which prove the truth of our principles and a necessity of our existence." He did not stop there with his exaltation of victory:

> But the time has come to shake off the idle day dreams of peace, and prepare for battle. No vain hope can now hover over us. There is no room for hope. No idle words are now needed, but strong arms and willing hearts. War is upon us; our homes and firesides are threatened with invasion. I need not exhort you to arm and prepare for the conflict....But while I am satisfied with your patriotism and your bravery, I am fearful that many may forget amid the absorbing events of the day, the obligation which they owe to the Order of Knighthood in which we claim to be brethren.

I believe that wherever, we may be scattered as individuals we shall be true to the principles upon which our Order is founded, but am fearful we shall not be sufficiently mindful of that part of our obligation which relates to the machinery by which we expect to spread and perpetuate those principles. Upon that I admonish every member to be attentive and vigilant. Use every opportunity that may offer to establish the working machinery of the Order until our Castles shall arise like monuments all over the land.

The leading spokesman for the Texas KGC was reminding the membership that their obligation to their fellow Knights was a lifetime obligation. Russell was also directing them to continue to form new Castles wherever they went; he also suggested that the Confederacy as a country was but a vehicle for the expansion of the Order. He wasn't finished, but continued by acknowledging what he deemed "slander and misrepresentation" of the role the KGC intended to play in the war they had played a major role in starting, was that "That petty jealousies and a spirit of party monopoly would prevent us from taking part in active warfare, unless we could be called into service as a body with our own officers and organization." So again, in concert with the message carried by the publisher and editor of the *Southern Rights Democrat*, there was to be no place for political parties in the new Order, not even the Democrat Party that had been monopolized by members of the Order previous to the beginning of hostilities. Russell then took pains to emphasize that KGC membership would not shrink from participating in violent combat:

> We have taught no such practice. I admonish you to go forth wherever your
> country may call singly or in companies, as circumstances may require. But
> do not let the stirring events of war cause you to forget the principles that
> have been taught you, and do not forget that those with whom your lot may
> be cast, may become, by your teachings and through your instrumentality,
> linked together by the iron hand of a common brotherhood as Knights of
> the true faith. Wherever you may go you may sow the seed that shall bring
> forth fruits of blessing to our country and glory to our Order.

Beneath the flowery language of Russell's address to the membership were recognizable code words known within the Order. The "iron hand" is an obvious reference to the first Degree of the KGC, otherwise known as Knights of the Iron Hand. They were the battlefield soldier element of the KGC that would do all the fighting and dying for the glory of the Order. Not all of those on the front lines of the coming battles were only members of the lowest of the three Degrees: some, by their own choice – like Knight of the Columbian Star Ben McCulloch – would choose to serve as battlefield commanders. In any event, Russell's statement links active military participation to the lower two Degrees of the three total Degrees of the Order, in the statement of the "iron hand" in a "common brotherhood of Knights of the true faith." The second, or middle Degree of the Order were designated as Knights of the True Faith, and their role was one of supply, organization, creation and redistribution of wealth for the common defense and maintenance of the Order. Many Knights of the True Faith, in exchange for their greater financial contribution, would find somewhat safer positions in the armed forces as quartermasters or commissary officers. As this degree incorporated the money-men of the Order, it should be assumed that it would include the blockade runners whose job it was to raise revenue through the international sale of cotton. This valuable commodity would soon become the most important revenue stream for the Confederate State of Texas, so naturally bureaucrats were needed to supervise and regulate that trade. Those positions were also open to Second Degree members. The Second Degree also included the newspaper editors and publishers whose job it would be to spread propaganda meant to cast the Order in the eternal light of chivalry and the honor for The Cause. Provisions for the Home Guard were made at both the First and Second Degree levels. The KGC's way was the only way; and there was no hope of any other way in Texas as long as they were in charge.[43]

As Charles A. Russell had commanded, more KGC companies were integrated into larger defense forces. On May 20 General Sidney Sherman, a native of Massachusetts who had been appointed commandant of Galveston by the Secession Convention, began the organization of the First Battalion of Galveston Artillery. This new battalion was a consolidation of three different companies, two of which were likely KGC units as they had previously served under John S. Ford, commander of the Middle Brigade of the Texas KGC for the occupation of Brazos Santiago back in February. Those two companies were the Galveston Artillery Company A commanded by Henry Van Buren and the Davis Artillery organized by Samuel Boyer Davis and commanded by Lieutenant Edward Von Harten. In the future reorganizations to come, Samuel Boyer Davis would assume a very powerful position at the center of the Texas Confederacy, while Edward Von Harten would be promoted to Major commanding the 1st Texas Heavy Artillery. As things stood on May 20, Van Buren took over as Captain of the Galveston Artillery after long-time KGC member Hugh McLeod stepped down, A.S. Labuzan was elected 1st Lieutenant and Ed. Malone was elected 2nd Lieutenant. From one of the far tentacles spread by the Texas KGC, one of its leaders, Ben McCulloch wrote the Confederate war department on May 20 from Little Rock, Arkansas reporting a dearth of arms and munitions at that location. General McCulloch concluded that sufficient weaponry might be obtained from Fort Smith, a post further North of Little Rock and at the western edge of the state, bordering Indian Territory. To that end McCulloch left Little Rock for Fort Smith on May 23, accompanied by his aides and Albert Pike, a Confederate Indian Commissioner some have mistakenly credited with taking over the direction of the

KGC upon the death of its true founder, General John Anthony Quitman. It is more likely that Pike was a high-ranking KGC member responsible for helping organize the Order among the Southern Cherokee Tribe. By the summer of 1861, it was acknowledged that the KGC within that tribe was led by Chief Stand Watie, who went on to become the highest ranking Native American officer within the entire Confederacy. Watie was the last Confederate General to surrender. Months after the war was over, one scholar wrote of "the presence in the Cherokee Nation of the KGC and of pro-South [probably Masonic] Blue Lodges" prior to the beginning of hostilities. Soon troops from Texas and Stand Watie's Cherokee Rifles company would join Ben McCulloch and Albert Pike in warfare. Albert Pike was the highest-ranking member of the Southern Scottish Rite of the Masonic Order. This author believes that the KGC was incubated within the Masonic Blue Lodges and used the pre-existing network of Masonic lodges as a vehicle for high-ranking Masons to recruit low-level Masons into the military degree of the KGC.[44]

While General McCulloch spread its tentacles north the Texas KGC also spread its tentacles into the West. KGC leader John R. Baylor, elected Lieutenant Colonel in John S. Ford's regiment of 2nd Texas Cavalry, had arrived in San Antonio on May 7. Serving under Baylor was Captain Harris A. Hamner and Lieutenant George W. Baylor. Hamner and his company of more than 100 "rangers" had left Weatherford for San Antonio on May 2. While in San Antonio raising more companies for Ford's regiment, John R. Baylor participated in a propaganda rally led by KGC Western Brigade commander John A. Wilcox. Held in the Main Plaza of the Alamo City on Saturday night, May 25, citizens were told by the KGC commander of "the necessity of unanimity of sentiment in the South, and of course amongst ourselves, as War actually existed for our subjugation." Wilcox was followed by John R. Baylor who "then addressed the meeting in a very eloquent though colloquial strain which had a very great effect." These speeches were followed by public professions of loyalty to the New Order by "several of our most worthy citizens, who had been opposed to secession but who declared in the most decided manner, that in the war of subjugation, they were good citizens of the Confederate Government...." Of course, they did; it was necessary for their continued survival. In spite of Colonel Earl Van Dorn's bravado, there were still five captured Union soldiers still held in Texas in late May. One of these men, Lieutenant Zenas R. Bliss, would not be sent from Texas until 1862. While he and his comrades were held in San Antonio, he was approached several times by local citizens who while pretending to be loyal Confederates, were secretly biding their time until the inevitable end of the war. They kept their true loyalty to the Union a secret, as union loyalists were watched; spies were assigned to follow such individuals. While loyal citizens cowered before the power of the KGC, men like Baylor sought to expand its new empire. On May 27, Colonel Van Dorn wrote John S. Ford of the necessity of sending Texas troops west to occupy Fort Bliss near El Paso and the border with New Mexico. Two companies of John R. Baylor's men were initially sent to Fort Bliss, both commanded by known KGC members Samuel W. McAllister and Trevanion T. Teel. Baylor would soon use Fort Bliss as the base from which to invade New Mexico and Arizona. Trevanion T. Teel would later write, "The objective aim and design of the campaign was the conquest of California, and as soon as the Confederate army should occupy the territory of New Mexico, an army of advance would be organized, and 'On to San Francisco' would be the watchword...." The aim of the Arizona campaign was to fulfill the long-term goal of the KGC: "If the Confederates succeeded in occupying California, New Mexico, and Arizona, negotiations to secure Chihuahua, Sonora, and Lower California, either by purchase or conquest, would be opened". The intent was to spread the institution of slavery to the Pacific coast, but other opportunities awaited the empire so established: ports on the Pacific Ocean almost impossible to blockade by the U.S. Navy; control of gold and silver mines in California and Arizona, and possession of lands needed for a southern route for a trans-continental railway independent from the United States. Confederate money would be backed up by reserves of precious metals, making its currency viable on the world market and less subject to erosion of its purchasing power due to currency devaluation. The Gulf of Mexico would be linked to the Pacific. If the KGC were to accomplish this, the world would be a very different place.[45]

It is known that certain KGC members, some from outside the state, were training and drilling the new military companies being organized in Texas for Confederate service. In one instance, a "Captain Upshaw" said to be a West Point graduate was reported to be performing "good service in drilling the Washington county troops." Many of these drill instructors were integrated into Confederate or State troops as sergeants or drill instructors; Charles Bickley found such a position in Texas early in the war. Some of these temporary residents of Texas found their way back to their home states once the real combat began. One such individual was John Speed Rudd, a native of Spotsylvania County, Virginia, born in 1831 in the town of Lynchburg. He is listed as a member of the Class of 1851 at Virginia Military Institute, having entered in 1847 and leaving after one year. In

1850, he applied for entry into West Point but left before graduating to join the filibuster William Walker for a year. Nevertheless, in May 1861, he found himself employed as a drilling master in Grimes County, Texas, near the small community of Prairie Plains. A local newspaper published at the county seat of Anderson, Texas reported that he was a graduate of West Point and "one of the lamented Walker's faithful in Nicaragua...." He had enrolled as a private in Captain Procter P. Porter's Company of the 17th Brigade of Texas Troops on May 7, but by the end of the month he had been promoted to 5th Sergeant. Although Captain Porter's Company was soon merged into the 4th Texas Infantry as Company H and Rudd was promoted again to 3rd Sergeant, John Speed Rudd never fought for Texas. He made his way back to his native Virginia where he briefly served as an officer on General Longstreet's staff; so did several other Texas KGC. The vehicle for the transport of many of them from Texas to Virginia was the company of Independent Texas Guerillas organized by Texas KGC leader Thomas S. Lubbock. Included in this group of 40 men or less were fellow KGC members John A. Wharton, Benjamin Franklin Terry and probable member Thomas J. Goree. Lawrence E. LeTulle, Captain of the Oakland KGC Castle in Colorado County also made the trip to Virginia with Lubbock's Guerillas where the local press referred to him as "Mr. La Toole". Others who made the cut for the initial trip were Dr. J. F. Matchet, a surgeon; "Captain" Dan A. Conner, a slave owner and leader of the Fort Bend KGC company in John S. Ford's March 2nd raid on Federal troops at Brazos Santiago; "Colonel" John T. Thatcher, a slave-owner and political figure from the Houston area; "Captains" J. Mayrant Smith, Victor Friedman, and two men, "Aldridge" and another Smith whose identities are not presently known with certainty. It is likely they were all KGC members or were required to join the Order before this journey if they hadn't already. They began their journey from Texas in time for some of them to serve on General Longstreet's staff at the First Battle of Bull Run as scouts while others made camp for more Texas recruits to follow. Among the early KGC arrivals from Texas was a blood relative of President Abraham Lincoln and grandnephew of General Benjamin Lincoln, George Washington's second-in-command during the Revolutionary War. He was Thomas Blodgett Lincoln, born in Philadelphia, Pennsylvania in 1813, descended from Samuel Blodgett, one of the primary developers of what became Washington, District of Columbia. Like Texas Knight of the Columbian Star Philip Ignatius Barziza, Samuel Blodgett had corresponded with Thomas Jefferson. Samuel Blodgett's descendant Thomas Blodgett Lincoln had settled in Rusk County,

Texas soon after the state won its independence from Mexico. When arrested later in Cincinnati, Ohio in the summer of 1861 for treason (attempting to buy weapons for the Confederacy), Thomas Blodgett Lincoln was described as "a prominent citizen of Texas" who had been at Bull Run, also known as the Battle of Manassas, as had Lubbock's Guerillas. This Lincoln was also of royal descent, in the line of King Robert II of Scotland and Elizabeth Stewart. He was soon released and allowed to return to Texas where he stayed until the end of the war. Years after the war, Thomas Blodgett Lincoln was identified as "an agent of New York capitalists" involved in railroad speculation in Texas and "a leading member of the Knights of the Golden Circle". He wasn't the only former New Yorker in the Texas KGC. New York-born Knight of the Columbian Star Charles A. Russell exhorted his fellow Texas Knights in his address published on May 16 to always impress upon their friends, neighbors and acquaintances the im-portance of proper military drill – wherever they went. Other residents of Rusk County in Texas particularly KGC member and Mexican War veteran Major Thomas M. Likens heeded Charles A. Russell's call. Although too old for combat Major Likens served as drill instructor from the very beginning of hostilities. Part of the grand plan of the KGC was to make every man in Texas a servant of the new military society – either as a soldier or support staff.[46]

On June 1, 1861, an editorial was published by unidentified staff of the San Antonio Ledger and Texan, under the direction of A. MacLeod and J. T. Dashiell. Titled, "The Order of K.G.C.," it was a hagiography written by someone who was initially "much opposed to the order on account of the mystery which enveloped its operation, and the secrecy with which they were carried on...." Now, however, the writer claimed to be much pleased with the results wrought by the Texas Knights and those in San Antonio, as stated below:

> The whole course of the K.G.C., in this city and elsewhere, the immense services they have rendered the State and the South, the steadiness with which they press on to their aim, their forbearance, under the most unjustifiable and un-merited obloquy cast on them in many instances by those who but for them would have suffered in their persons or property, or both, the consequences of their own blind opposition to the irresistible will of the people, and the torrent of events; their careful avoidance of even the appearance of abuse of the immense power they wield; their modesty in triumph and the moderation of their whole proceedings have fully satisfied us that but for them, the struggle in which we have been engaged, would in

Western Texas have resulted in sanguinary collisions and civil war inviting invasion from the North.

The conclusion of the above portion of the editorial, which continued beyond this excerpt, is tragically wrong. In a few years, the KGC's President and front-man George W.L. Bickley, took credit (or more appropriately, the blame) for inaugurating "the greatest war in history." A recent reappraisal of the cost of Bickley's great war estimates the death toll including both sides to be 750,000, the midpoint chosen from estimates that range from 650,000 to 850,000. Still, on June 1, 1861 the anonymous author was aware that for practical purposes, the entire Union Army in Texas had been expelled without firing a shot. Contrary to more recent accounts of the capture of the Federal Arsenal in San Antonio on February 16, 1861, this contemporary account stated the following appraisal of the KGC's influence:

> Of the State troops to whom General Twiggs surrendered the government property and the military posts, *four-fifths were K.G.C.*, and without the aid of the order, the Committee of Public Safety could never have taken the steps which resulted in the perfect and signed success of their operations, without so much as the risk of a collision. [italics added]

Recent accounts have mistakenly underestimated the KGC's role in the military maneuvers that expelled the U.S. Army from Texas as being as small as 150 men out of the thousands that participated. The more contemporaneous account from June 1, 1861, suggests the real number of KGC members responsible as being 80 percent of all those who participated, which is consistent with the accounts of other witnesses, such as Charles Anderson, U.S. Major J.T. Sprague and newspaper editor James P. Newcomb, who was quoted by historian Hubert Howe Bancroft in his 19th century account. Other contemporaneous accounts given to U.S. Major Heintzelman stated that the "old" Texas Rangers (State troops) had been replaced by Knights of the Golden Circle well before the events of 1861. It is to this dominant position the KGC had arisen to in Texas that the writer for the Ledger and Texan attempted to speak as he ended his tribute with the following summation:

> The order sits in the high place of the nation, but has never stooped to advance its members to the exclusion of merit wherever it was to be found. The K.G.C. confident in their overwhelming strength, the result of their conscious integrity and patriotism, laugh to scorn the revilings, as they pass

unheeded the threats of their enemies, who, by their very hostility, might be held up as legitimately incurring the charge of disaffection to our glorious cause.[47]

Bearing in mind that the last Unionist newspaper in Texas had been literally destroyed by the KGC just days earlier, one must keep the preceding editorial in perspective. Events would occur in Texas in the months and years ahead that would tarnish the glorious image the KGC had carefully crafted for its organization through the media. While the bravest and most radical members of the secret Order died on far-flung battlefields, the stay-at-home bureaucrats of the political and financial degrees of the KGC would become a nuisance to the average citizen of Texas.

The KGC
and the "Texas Guerrillas"

Although the creation of the "Texas Guerillas" has been briefly discussed heretofore in this book, it is worthy of further discussion. More of its members can be identified and should be discussed. Enhancing the understanding of how this irregular military unit was created highlights the significant role played by the KGC in Texas and in starting the American Civil War.

The Texas Guerillas were the creation of Thomas Saltus Lubbock, the younger brother of Confederate Governor of Texas Francis R. Lubbock. Thomas S. Lubbock was a well-known KGC extremist and promoter. He had a history of bold risk-taking through involvement in the Texas Revolution of 1836, the Santa Fe expedition in 1841 and the Somerville expedition against Mexico in 1842. In 1857 he was elected 1st Lieutenant of the Milam Rifles, a militia unit that may have been an early KGC company. Exactly when T.S. Lubbock joined the secret military order is not known. As his other brother John B. Lubbock was a known KGC member and leader, it is likely that his brother Governor F.R. Lubbock was KGC as well; not just from familial relations but from the various roles F.R. Lubbock is known to have played in the secession of Texas.[1]

T.S. Lubbock first publicly presented the idea of forming the independent Texas Guerillas just weeks after the bombardment of Fort Sumter. Thomas Lubbock's guerilla unit was created to give select members of the secret pro-slavery order a role in the first battle of the war, popularly known as the First Battle of Bull Run, or the Battle of Manassas. The individual guerillas had to pay their own expenses and meet certain privately disclosed requirements. By identifying as many members of Lubbock's band of irregular soldiers one can identify that many more KGC members due to their association with known KGC members in the Texas Guerillas. Since Lubbock's band of men were selected by him for special service in Virginia at the beginning of armed conflict, it is highly likely that the exclusive nature of this service was another way of promoting the secret Order of the Knights of the Golden Circle in Texas.[2]

T.S. Lubbock was a large slave owner by Texas standards, with 31 slaves held in Harris County alone, placing him solidly in the plantation class. He was also a political leader within the State Democratic Party, elected Chairman of a Brecken-ridge and Lane Club in July 1860. After the November Presidential Election, he rallied opposition to newly elected President Lincoln by organizing a committee on resolutions to foment secessionist sentiment in Harris County. He represented Harris County at the Secession Convention which began January 28, 1861, in Aus-tin. He was elected to the Convention's Committee of Public Safety on the 30th, placing him in a leadership role in the secession of the State. By April 1861, he was appointed by the Mayor of Houston to the Committee of Safety and Correspond-ence for the City of Houston, along with fellow KGC members Peter W. Gray, A.J. Rice and E.H. Cushing, the position being that of a vigilante organization. At about the same time, his brother John B. Lubbock was organizing men in Bastrop County, where he had established a KGC Castle, to join the expedition to capture the remaining U.S. troops stranded at Indianola. John B. Lubbock reportedly gave "a short, stirring speech" to send some 50 men against the hapless Federal forces. Perhaps his brother's speech served as inspiration for T.S. Lubbock.[3]

May 7, 1861, the *Houston Weekly Telegraph* carried the first of several ads placed by T.S. Lubbock. The title read in bold letters, "Ho! For Virginia! Glory Calls Us!" The opinion piece began by recounting one-by-one the contributions to the Con-federate forces already in the field made by all the other states in the fledgling slave empire. The impending field of battle was stated to be Virginia, where "our free-dom from black Republican domination is to be won." Lubbock exhorted his fel-low Texans to organize for the coming battle by meeting him in Houston on May 20, fully armed and ready to "hasten to Richmond City Virginia" – with at least $250 in their pockets and the full complement of "saddle trees, and horse equip-ments." Lubbock referred to the proposed organization as "the 'independent Texas Guerillas'." Interested parties were to contact him care of fellow KGC member and newspaper editor E.H. Cushing. He was doing all he could to further the war effort.[4]

Cushing of the Telegraph did his part in generating war propaganda through his newspaper:

> In the war that is before us there will be a good deal of hard fighting to be done. Those who will make up this company will be men who have a character to sustain, and who will not fool away their time or chances when a scrimmage is on hand. The Texas Guerillas will be the terror of the enemy, and the crack regiment of the South.

The name "Texas Guerillas" stuck and was carried in turn by the *Dallas Herald*. Coincidentally perhaps, someone whose actions would cement the Texas Guerillas place in history was making a decision almost simultaneously that would change his life and many others for eternity. Native Georgian James Longstreet resigned his commission in the United States Army on May 9, 1861. He had served for 20 years and risen to the rank of Major. He too, began a pilgrimage to Richmond from his base in the Southwest and his path would soon cross that of T.S. Lubbock. They would serve together at the First Battle of Bull Run.[5]

Captain Lubbock left Texas in early May to confer with associates in Montgomery, Alabama, temporary home of the KGC and the Confederate government. They might have told him that the seat of the Confederate government was destined to move from Montgomery to Richmond, Virginia. From Montgomery he traveled to Pensacola, Florida where an invasion by Federal troops was expected. On Friday, May 24, he left Pensacola and returned to Houston on May 29. Lubbock soon began to realize that many Texans talked of joining his Guerillas but could not come up with the funds necessary for the trip. Therefore, the trip to Virginia had been postponed for June 5. He found that the promised numbers still did not appear, so it was not until the evening of June 10 that his party of some 20 volunteers left Houston by boat for Galveston. Leaving Galveston by sea the following day for Brashear City, Louisiana (today's Morgan City) they soon realized they were sharing the ride with James Longstreet, who was also headed to Richmond to offer his services to Jefferson Davis.[6]

Among the small group of Texas Guerilas getting acquainted with Major Longstreet were Benjamin Franklin Terry, a wealthy slave owner and sugar planter well-known to Captain Lubbock; John Austin Wharton, a prosperous attorney and member of the Secession Convention; Thomas Jewett Goree, an attorney whose law firm had moved from Montgomery to Houston; and several men who had participated in the Rio Grande Campaign led by KGC leader John S. Ford against Union troops. Besides "Colonels" B.F. Terry and J.A. Wharton, the expedition included "Colonel" John Thatcher, a plantation owner and neighbor of B.F. Terry. Thatcher had "a small force" of slaves on Oyster Creek in Fort Bend County and seemed to have a problem with some of them running away, as he posted ads offering rewards for the return of two different male slaves in 1858. A man like him would appreciate the support of the system offered by the KGC. Other than the three Colonels on board the steamer Bell when it landed at New Orleans on June 15 were "Captains" T.S. Lubbock, Dan A. Connor, John Mayrant Smith, "Aldridge," "Freeman" (Dr. Victor Friedeman of Galveston), another "Smith" and "Surgeon Machett" – Dr. J.F. Matchet, a Houston surgeon and professor at the Texas Medical College. "Aldridge" was more than likely A.A. Aldrich, a former County Judge in Houston County and member of the Masonic Lodge in Crockett, Texas. This Aldrich became an officer in Hood's Texas Brigade and served in Virginia. Dan Connor, J. Mayrant Smith, Dr. Friedeman, Dr. Matchet and B.F. Terry had all served active duty during the recent Rio Grande Expedition for Brazos Santiago and had thus made reputations for themselves among the secessionists. J. Mayrant Smith, a land speculator, had married Terry's daughter. He would lead an interesting life. There were several men in Texas during this time that went by the name "J.M. Smith," and at least one man by that name was a known KGC member. It is highly likely that all the Texas Guerillas were members as well. It was a select group.[7]

The mysterious second Mr. Smith with Lubbock's Guerillas was "Colonel" Morgan L. Smith, a native New Yorker turned Texan and neighbor of John A. Wharton, with whom he was traveling. This Mr. Smith had come to Texas in 1838 and started a business selling equipment and supplies to slave owners, particularly those plantation owners in the sugar producing business. Morgan L. Smith, in addition to his supply business, owned and operated Waldeck Plantation in Brazoria County which under his direction became the largest and most efficient producer of sugar in the State of Texas. He held the plantation with its attendant slaves from 1842 until November 1859 when he sold it all for a large amount of money. Months later the new owner reported 212 slaves among the taxable property owned. John A. Wharton also owned a large plantation in Brazoria County – Eagle Island Plantation on Oyster Creek, from which he produced sugar as well as cotton with the labor of 133 slaves.[8]

Lubbock, Terry and Wharton, accompanied by fellow KGC's Louis T. Wigfall, Thomas N. Waul, along with the newly promoted General James Longstreet, had met with President Davis the evening of June 21 and pleaded that he legitimize the Lubbock Guerillas. Thomas Goree, also a member of Lubbock's Guerillas, wrote on June 23 that the President had already "agreed to receive 20 companies from Texas for the war. They ought to be here in a few weeks. In a day or two there will be 4 or 5 Texas Companies here, one from Polk, one from Tyler Co., one from Harrison, and one from Cass." At this point some of the Texans who had travelled to Virginia began to disperse on different assignments. Lawrence E. LeTulle, the Captain of the KGC Castle in Oakland, Texas left the Texas Guerillas and apparently joined a band of Virginia guerillas known as the Moccasin Rangers. The Virginia guerillas eventually were consolidated with other such bands into the 3rd Regiment, Virginia State Line. LeTulle finished the war with Virginia State Line's successor organization, Jackson's Battery of Light Artillery. John A. Wharton left Richmond on June 24 to buy weapons and other supplies to take back to Brazoria County in Texas. On June 30, Wharton and Morgan L. Smith left Brashear City, Louisiana on the schooner Shark for Galveston and ultimately Brazoria. On July 4, the Shark was stopped and boarded by men from a Federal blockade ship. Wharton's cargo comprised of 200 muskets and other supplies for uniforms was confiscated, and the boarding ship's captain gave the handful of passengers an ultimatum: either take an oath to never oppose the United States Government, or face detention in Key West. Colonel Wharton responded that he'd rather go to Key West. When confronted directly, Morgan L. Smith responded in like fashion, adding that "nothing could induce him to take an oath inconsistent with the allegiance due his adopted state." Eventually the Union naval captain relented and released his prisoners. The war had not become as savage and bloody yet as it soon would.[9]

The events that transpired on the Shark raise interesting questions. Morgan L. Smith never joined the Confederacy, although he pledged his loyalty to Texas rather than the United States, to a Federal official. He had actively financed the slave economy in Texas for decades; what was he doing with the Lubbock Guerillas? Plantation society was an exclusive club, so the odds are in favor of him being closely acquainted with the members of Lubbock's Guerillas, other than his friend John A. Wharton. Was he financing the weapons purchases for his friends? This is an interesting question as Morgan L. Smith moved with his family back to New York in 1860 where he stayed during the Civil War; and yet he apparently never suffered any consequences for his actions. There were rumored to be KGC members in New York during the war.[10]

The Lubbock Guerillas went into active service on July 1 and were given rations and forage for their horses, which they had supplied themselves, along with their weapons. They were also given special status and privileges. Designated as independent Texas Rangers attached to the Virginia Cavalry as scouts, they were told they could quit anytime they wanted. By this time their members had dropped to 15, with two of their previous number known to be sailing to-ward a rendezvous with the Union blockade. By July 6, just 5 of the Guerillas had moved to a forward position, to Fairfax Court House, the earlier scene of a small skirmish on June 1. Both sides withdrew from that engagement, but the Confederates sent most of a brigade to reoccupy the area in late June. By July 6, Lubbock, Terry and Goree were among the five Texans that left a more secure camp in Warrenton for the forward post guarding access to Bull Run. Dr. J.T. Matchett had remained in War-renton nursing an illness and wrote from there on July 6 to E.H. Cushing of the *Houston Telegraph* an account of his surroundings. He noted, "Col. Terry says that all Texians coming here have to fight like h—ll to maintain the reputation the State has already won. [sic]. The reputation had been made through Lubbock and Terry's involvement in an incident that occurred the first evening they reached Fairfax Court House. The incident and its retelling might have resembled that of an episode of Don Quixote and Sancho Panza if it had not been so successful and useful for propaganda purposes. According to Goree, on the first evening the small band of Texans reached the forward outpost, Terry and Lubbock decided to take a handful of Virginia Cavalry on a scouting expedition. Passing by the Un-ion sentries within 4 or 5 miles of Alexandria, Lubbock and Terry charged a picket camp of six men, thinking their Virginia comrades were going with them, right behind them. The Texans shot one man and captured two others before they re-alized that the Virginians had stayed out of the fight; they were positioned some distance away just watching the action. It was then that Terry and Lubbock noticed they were alone only 300 yards away from the main Union camp. They swiftly made their retreat, taking with them the two prisoners as well as a horse and a fine Sharp's rifle. The incident was widely covered by the Southern press in the follow-ing weeks as an example of Texan bravery rather than impetuousness.[11]

Nothing much else happened to the Texan volunteers in the buildup to the major battle to come, except the involvement of the Guerillas in a friendly fire incident on July 4 while attached to the 2nd South Carolina Regiment under Colonel Kershaw. Two of Kershaw's men were killed. Thomas Lubbock had left the camp on July 16 and checked into the Spotswood Hotel in Richmond. That very day the Union troops began their offense but did not reach their objective until the following day when they appeared in large numbers at Fairfax Court House. The Confederate command had been warned by spies on the night before of their adversary's advance, so they quickly ordered their forces to retreat, pulling back to a large creek called Bull Run. The Texans took their positions on the night of the 17, and the following day were involved in a skirmish at a crossing known as Blackburn's Ford. This was defended by General Longstreet, whose reconnaissance detected the Union advance and was prepared for the contact on July 18, successfully repelling the enemy with minor losses. U.S. forces suffered 83 casualties. The following day Longstreet sent Thomas Goree on a reconnaissance mission; the former member of Lubbock's Guerillas had been promoted to Captain and was made an aide to General Longstreet. The first battle of the war was just beginning.[12]

On the 20th, Longstreet received orders to take the offensive. Early the following day he took up a position on the other side of Bull Run creek and sent Lubbock and Terry on reconnaissance of the enemy's movements. Returning from that mission the two spies offered to reconnoiter the Federal artillery batteries. The resulting intelligence was forwarded to command. The following day the action in other sections of the battlefield became heated, and casual-ties on both sides were severe. Confederate General Bernard Bee, father of Texas General Hamilton Prioleau Bee became the highest-ranking fatality of the battle. In the late afternoon – early evening of July 21st, the commander of U.S. forces was forced to concede failure and order a general retreat. The final casualties were for the Union, 2,896, including 460 killed, 1,124 wounded and 1,312 captured or missing. Losses for the Confederates were 1,982 inclusive of 387 dead, 1,582 wounded and 13 missing. Also captured by the Confederates were 27 artillery pieces, 500 rifles, 500,000 rounds of ammunition and significant supplies. Overall, Longstreet's 4th Brigade had seen limited fighting, with others, such as Bernard Bee's 3rd Brigade suffering much higher losses as substantial as 16% of those engaged. The citizens of the Confederacy were jubilant while those in the North were panicked.[13]

General Longstreet commended the efforts of Lubbock, Terry and Goree in his official report to Headquarters of the events in the battle and the following day in some mop-up action. Although they had seen limited action, the Texas Guerillas returned home with the momentum to recruit the troops they had sought to bring to the fight. They had accomplished their mission, but it was early in the war. Terry and Lubbock returned to Texas in August and began to build what became the Eighth Texas Cavalry, also commonly known as Terry's Texas Rangers. Terry served as the regimental colonel and Lubbock as the lieutenant colonel. Thomas Goree stayed with Longstreet as his aide until the end of the war and survived. Colonel Terry, who Goree had described in a letter to his mother from Virginia as "a very bold, fearless man, in whose discretion & valor we have the greatest confidence," was killed in battle leading a charge on December 17, 1861, killed by a bullet through the neck. Thomas S. Lubbock became chronically ill and died in his sick bed in Nashville, Tennessee on January 9, 1862. John A. Wharton, another one of the original Lubbock Texas Guerillas, was elected to replace Lubbock as colonel of Terry's Texas Rangers. He too would die violently before the end of the war, but in his instance, it was at the hands of a fellow KGC member, murdered in a fit of uncontrollable rage.[14]

Notes

Chapter One

1. Kennedy, Paul, *The Rise and Fall of the Great World Powers* (New York. Vintage, 1987) pp. 179-181. Davis, William C. *Battle at Bull Run*, (Baton Rouge, Louisiana State, 1977).

2. King, Alvy L. Louis T. Wigfall, *Southern Fire-Eater*, (Baton Rouge, Louisiana State University Press, 1970), pp. 113-114. Kline, Michael J. *The Baltimore plot*, (Yardley, Westholme Publishing, 2008), pp. 91-93.

3. C. A. Bridges, "The Knights of the Golden Circle: A Filibustering Fantasy," *The Southwestern Historical Quarterly*, Vol. XLIV No. 3 (January, 1941), pp. 287-302.

4. Linda Sybert Hudson, *Military Knights of the Golden Circle in Texas, 1854-1861*. Master's Thesis in American History, Stephen F. Austin University, Nacogdoches, Texas, 1990.

Chapter Two

1. Berlin, Ira. *Slavery in New York* (New York, The New Press, 2005) p. 6. "Slavery in Massachusetts," *Slavery in the North*, http://www.slavenorth.com/massachusetts.htm. (accessed January 30, 2013).

2. Doris Y. Kadish, ed. *Slavery in the Caribbean Francophile World* (Athens, University of Georgia Press, 2000) pp. 1-2. Leigh Kimmel, "Slavery as Practiced by the French in Illinois," http://www.geocities.com/Athens/3682/slavery.html?20052. Accessed September 2, 2005. Kathleen Cason, "In Black & White," University of Georgia Research Magazine, Summer 2005. http://www.researchmagazine.uga.edu/summer2005.htm.

3. Berlin, *Slavery in New York*, pp.10-14, 61, 63, 85. Keehn, David C. *Knights of the Golden Circle: Secret Empire, Southern Secession, Civil War* (Baton Rouge, LSU Press, 2013) pp. 58-59.

4. Ambler, Charles Henry. *George Washington and the West* (Chapel Hill, University of North Carolina Press, 1936) p. 132. Shepperson, Archibald Bolling. *John Paradise, and Lucy Ludwell of London and Williamsburg* (Richmond, The Dietz Press, 1942) p. 21. Berlin, *Slavery in New York*, p. 15. Waugh, John C. *The Class of 1846: from West Point to Appomattox* (New York, Warner Books, 1994) p x. "KGC Address to the Citizens of the Southern States." *Dallas Herald*, February 13, 1861.

5. Hunemorder, Marcus. *The Society of the Cincinnati: conspiracy and distrust in early America* (Berghahn Books, 2006), pp. 15-19, 31, 44. Keehn, *Knights of the Golden Circle*, p. 9.

6. Hunemorder, op. cit.., pp. 63-64. Schuyler, John, *Institution of the Society of the Cincinnati...With Extracts, from the Proceedings of its General Meetings and from the Transactions of the New York State Society*

(New York, the Society, 1886) p. 6. Hume, Edgar Erskine, *Sesquicentennial History and Roster of the Society of the Cincinnati in the State of Virginia 1783-1933* (Richmond, the Society, 1934) pp. 24, 25.

7. Edwin Patrick Kilroe, "Saint Tammany and the Origin of the Society of Tammany or Columbian Order in the City of New York," PhD Thesis, Columbia University, New York, 1913. pp. 130-131, 140-143, 157-159. Lause, Mark A. *A Secret Society History of the Civil War.*(Chicago, University of Illinois Press, 2011) p. xi. Keehn, *Knights of the Golden Circle*, p. 10.

8. Kilroe, "Saint Tamanany," pp. 141-146. Powell, H. Jefferson. "The Principles of '98: An Essay in Historical Retrieval" (http://www.jstor.org/stable/1073630), 80 Virginia Law Review 689, pp. 705-719. Anderson, Frank Maloy. "Contemporary Opinion of the Virginia and Kentucky Resolutions," American Historical Review, pp. 45-63, 225-244. Fehrenbacher, Don E. *Slavery, Law, and Politics: The Dred Scott Case in Historical Perspective* (New York, Oxford University Press, 1981) p. 11. Finkelman, Paul. *Slavery and the Founders: Race and Liberty in the Age of Jefferson* (Armonk, M. E. Sharpe, 1996) p. x.

9. Robinson, John. *Proofs of a Conspiracy Against All The Religions and Governments of Europe, Carried on in the Secret Meetings of Free Masons, Illuminati, and Reading Societies, collected from good authorities* (New York, George Forman, 1798). George Washington to George Washington Snyder, 25 September 1798. George Washington Papers at the Library of Congress, http://memory.loc.gov/cgi-bin/query/r?ammem/mgw:@field(DOCID+@lit(gw360346)) accessed on January 3, 2014. Uzzel, Robert L., Ph.D. *Eliphas Levi and the Kabbalah* (Lafayette, Cornerstone Book Publishers, 2006) p. 141, n146.

10. Robinson, *Proofs of a Conspiracy, op. cit.*. Fay, Bernard. *Revolution and Freemasonry, 1680-1800* (Boston, Little, Brown, and Company, 1935) pp. 279-284.

11. Fay, *Revolution and Freemasonry*, pp. 314-315.

12. Robinson, op. cit..

13. Uzzel, *Eliphas Levi and the Kabbalah*, pp. 41-43.

14. 32° Masons, Valley of Detroit, "What is the Scottish Rite?" http://www.32nddegreemasons.org/what-is-the-scottish-rite/ Accessed on January 13, 2014. Mackey, Albert G., M. D. *The History of Freemasonry in South Carolina, From Its Origin in the Year 1736 to the Present Time* (Columbia, South Carolina Steam Power Press, 1861) pp. 494-497.

15. 32° Masons, op. cit.. Robinson, *Proofs of a Conspiracy*, p. 112.

Chapter Three

1. John P. Kaminski, ed. "The Documentary History of the Ratification of the Constitution Digital Edition," *Commentaries on the Constitution,* Vol. XIII, No. 1 (Charlottesville, University of Virginia Press, 2009) http://rotunda.upress.virginia.edu/founders/RNCN-03-13-02-0049 (accessed 10 May 2011) "Treaty of San Lorenzo/Pinckney's Treaty, 1795" U.S. Department of State, Office of the Historian. http://history.state.gov/milestones/1784-1800/pickney-treaty (accessed on January 15, 2014. *The Western Star*, October 11, 1851.

2. Sibley, Marilyn McAdams. *Travelers in Texas, 1761-1860* (Austin, University of Texas Press, 1967.) p. 111.

3. Raine, William MacLeod. *Famous sheriffs & western outlaws* (Garden City, Garden City Publishing Company, 1929.) pp. 59-60.

4. Handbook of Texas Online, s.v. "Philip Nolan," http://www.tsha.utexas.edu/handbook/online/articles/NN/qynrh.html (accessed September 10, 2006).

5. Manning, *Some History*, p. 31.

6. Ibid, s.v. "James Wilkinson," http://www.tsha.utexas.edu/handbook/online/articles/WW/fwi87.html (accessed December 24, 2006).

7. Maurine T. Wilson and Jack Jackson. *Philip Nolan and Texas: Expeditions to the Unknown Land* (Austin, Texian Press, 1987.) p. 5.

8. Wilson, Jackson, *Philip Nolan*, p. 6.

9. Ibid, p. 7.

10. Handbook of Texas Online, s.v. "Philip Nolan," http://www.tsha.utexas.edu/handbook/online/articles/NN/qynrh.html (accessed September 10, 2006).

11. Wilson, Jackson, Philip Nolan, p. 10.

12. Handbook of Texas Online, s.v. "Philip Nolan," http://www.tsha.utexas.edu/handbook/online/articles/NN/qynrh.html.

13. Sibley, *Travelers in Texas*, p. 89.

14. Ibid, footnote 12.

15. Wilson, Jackson, *Philip Nolan*, p. 10.

16. Ibid, p. 88, 111.

17. Ibid, p. 21, 88.

18. Ibid, pp. 70-73.

19. Manning, *Some History*, p. 33.

20. Wilson, Jackson, *Philip Nolan*, p. 110.

21. Handbook of Texas Online, s.v. "Philip Nolan," http://www.tsha.utexas.edu/handbook/online/articles/NN/qynrh.html.

22. Jennie O'Kelly Mitchell and Robert Dabney Calhoun. "The Marquis de Maison Rouge, the Baron de Bastrop, and Colonel Abraham Morhouse: Three Ouachita Valley Soldiers of Fortune. The Maison Rouge and Bastrop Spanish Land 'Grants.'" *The Louisiana Historical Quarterly*. Volume 20, No. 2 (April 1937), p. 291.

23. Handbook of Texas Online, s.v. "Baron De Bastrop" http://www.tsha.utexas.edu/handbook/online/articles/BB/fbaae.html (accessed December 31, 2006).

24. Fehrenbach, T. R. *Lone Star: A History of Texas and the Texans* (Boulder, Da Capo Press, 2000) pp. 118-119.

25. Handbook of Texas Online, s.v. "Aaron Burr," http://www.tsha.utexas.edu/handbook/online/articles/BB/fbu57.html (accessed December 31, 2006). New York State Society of the Cincinnati Institution and By-Laws and General Information. (New York, 1957) p. 35.

26. Chidsey, Donald Barr. *The Great Conspiracy; Aaron Burr and his strange doings in the West* (New York, Crown Publishers, 1967), p. 39.

27. Ibid, p. 52.

28. Ibid, pp. 59.

29. Ibid, p. 41. Normand, Pete. *The Texas Masons: the Fraternity of Ancient Free & Accepted Masons in the history of Texas* (College Station, Brazos Valley Masonic Library and Museum Association, 1986) p. 4.

30. Melton, Buckner F. *Aaron Burr: Conspiracy to Treason* (New York, John Wiley& Sons, 2002.) p. 126.

31. Mitchell, Calhoun, "The Marquis de Maison Rouge" pp. 409-410.

32. Fehrenbach, *Lone Star*, p.120.

33. Handbook of Texas Online, s.v. "James Wilkinson," http://www.tsha. utexas.edu/handbook/online/articles/WWfwi87_print.html. (accessed December 24, 2006).

34. Handbook of Texas Online, s.v. "Gutierrez-Magee Expedition," http://www.tsha. utexas.edu/handbook/online/articles/GG/qyg1_print.html. (accessed September 10, 2006).

35. Fehrenbach, *Lone Star*, pp. 125-127.

36. Handbook, "Gutierrez-Magee" ibid.

37. Fehrenbach, *Lone Star*, p. 126.

38. Handbook of Texas Online, s.v. "Augustin De Iturbide," http://www.tsha. utexas.edu/handbook/online/articles/II/fit1_print.html. (accessed January 1, 2007).

39. *Maryland Gazette and Political Intelligen*cer, February 24, 1819.

40. Handbook of Texas Online, s.v. "Jean Lafitte," http://www.tsha.utexas.edu/ handbook/online/articles/LL/fla12_print.html. (Accessed September 10, 2006).

41. Eugene C. Barker "The African Slave Trade in Texas" *Southwestern Historical Quarterly*. Volume 6, number 2. pp. 1-8.

42. Sibley, *Travelers in Texas*, p. 90f.

43. Owsley, Jr., Frank Lawrence. *Filibusters and expansionists: Jeffersonian manifest destiny* (Tuscaloosa, University of Alabama Press, 1997.) p. 178.

44. Fehrenbach, *Lone Star*, p. 128.

45. Warren, Harris Gaylord. *The Sword Was Their Passport: A history of American filibustering in the Mexican revolution* (Baton Rouge, Louisiana State University Press, 1943.) pp. 235-236. Brands, H.W. *Lone Star Nation: The Epic Story of the Texas Battle for Independence* (New York, Anchor Books, 2004) pp. 17, 124.

46. Fehrenbach, *Lone Star*, p. 129.

47. *Maryland Gazette and Political Intelligencer*, March 2, 1820.

48. Handbook of Texas Online, s.v. "Long Expedition," http://www.tsha.utexas.edu/ handbook/online/articles/LL/qy11_print.html. (Accessed on September 10, 2006).

49. Fehrenbach, *Lone Star*, pp. 130-131.

50. Chaitkin, Anton. *Treason in America: from Aaron Burr to Averell Harriman* (New York, New Benjamin Franklin House, 1984.) The author was kind enough to email his book in file form, hence no pagination. Email received March 31, 2006. Manning, *Some History*, pp. 193-194.

51. Adam Wasserman, "The 1810 West Florida Annexation Scheme," libcom.org, http://libcom.org/history/1810-west-florida-annexation-scheme-0 (accessed on January 15, 2014). Lause, A Secret Society History of the Civil War, pp. 58, 107.

52. Brands, *Lone Star Nation*, pp. 106, 200-203, 412-413. Thomas H. Kreneck, "Houston, Samuel," Handbook of Texas Online, http://www.tshaonline.org/handbook/online/articles/fho73) accessed January 16, 2014. Thomas W. Cutrer, "Quitman, John Anthony," Handbook of Texas Online, (http://www.tshaonline.org/handbook/online/articles/fqu07), accessed January 23, 2013. Dunbar Rowland, editor, *Encyclopedia of Mississippi History*, Vol. I. (Madison, Selwyn A. Brant, 1907) pp. 486-487. Robert E. May, "John Quitman and His Slaves: Reconciling Slave Resistance with the Proslavery Defense," *The Journal of Southern History*, Vol. XLVI, No. 4, November 1980, p. 555. Robert Bruce Blake, "Green, Thomas Jefferson," Handbook of Texas Online (http:www.tshaonline.org/handbook/online/articles/fgr39), accessed January 29, 2014.

53. Miller, Edward L. New Orleans and the Texas Revolution. (College Station, Texas A&M University Press, 2004) pp. 24-26, 62-63, 202. Thomas W. Cutrer, "Christy, William H.," Handbook of Texas Online, (http://www.tshaonline.org/handbook/online/articles/fch39), accessed January 16, 2014.

54. Kreneck, op. cit.. Normand, *The Texas Masons*, p. 5. Keehn, Knights of the Golden Circle, pp. 35-37. Fehrenbach, *Lone Star*, pp. 247, 265. W. W. White, "Green, Duff" Handbook of Texas Online, accessed August 29, 2013. "British Correspondence Concerning Texas, XVIII. Edited by Ephraim Douglass Adams. *Southwestern Historical Quarterly*, Vol. XIX, No. 4, April 1916, pp. 419-414. Introduction to The Duff Green Papers, Southern Historical Collection, University of North Carolina Library, Chapel Hill, North Carolina. Haley, James L. Sam Houston (Norman, University of Oklahoma Press, 2002) p. 310.

55. "Monroe" to William M. Smyth, 15 August 1884. *The Papers of Jefferson Davis* (Baton Rouge, Louisiana State University Press, 1971) Vol. 2, pp. 199-202; 203f14.

56. Greenburg, Amy S. *A wicked war: Polk, Clay, Lincoln, and the 1846 U.S. invasion of Mexico* (New York, Alfred A. Knopf, 2012) pp. 11-17. *The Papers of Jefferson Davis*, pp. 106-107, f104. Carolyn Hyman, "Greer, Elkanah Bracken," Handbook of Texas Online (http://www.tshaonline.org/handbook/online/articles/fgr42), accessed on January 29, 2014. "Good, John Jay," Handbook of Texas Online (http://www.tshaonline.org/handbook/online/articles/fgo08), accessed February 05, 2014. Thomas W. Cutrer, "Wilcox, John Allen," Handbook of Texas Online.

57. Handbook of Texas Online, "Mirabeau Buonaparte Lamar," http://www.tshaonline.org/handbook/online/articles/LL/fla15_print.html. (accessed on March 27, 2009).

58. Gulick and Elliot, *Papers of Mirabeau Buonaparte Lamar*, Volume III, pp. 19-20.

59. Ibid, Volume II, p. 41.

60. Ibid, pp. 292-293.

61. Virginia Louise Glenn, "James Hamilton, Jr., of South Carolina: A Biography". Ph. D. Thesis submitted 1964, University of North Carolina at Chapel Hill. pp. 285-287.

62. Robertson, David. *Denmark Vesey* (New York, Alfred A. Knopf, 1999) p. 112.

63. Starobin, Robert S. *Denmark Vesey; the slave conspiracy of 1822* (Englewood Cliffs, Prentice-Hall, 1970) p.96. Lofton, John. *Insurrection in South Carolina: the turbulent world of Denmark Vesey* (Yellow Springs, Antioch Press, 1964) pp. 212-213, 222-223.

64. Glenn, James Hamilton, p. 290.

65. Gulick, Elliott, *Papers of Mirabeau Buonaparte Lamar*, Volume II, pp. 274 Glen, James Hamilton, p. 273.

66. Glen, James Hamilton, p. 284. Handbook of Texas Online, s. v., "Retrieve Plantation," http://www.tsha.utexas.edu/handbook/online/articles/RR/acrl_print.html. (accessed on March 23, 2007).

67. "Kentucky on George N. Sanders," *New York Times*, August 10, 1860. Melinda Squires, "The Controversial Career of George Nicholas Sanders" (2000) Master's Theses & Specialist Projects. Paper 704. http:// digitalcommons.wku.edu/theses/704. *Letter of Gen. Mirabeau B. Lamar, Ex-President of Texas, on the Subject of Annexation, Addressed to Several Citizens of Macon, Geo.* (Savannah, Printed by Thomas Purse, 1844) pp. 3-15.

68. Glenn, James Hamilton, pp. 386, 388.

69. Brands, H. W. *Lone Star Nation* (New York, Anchor Books, 2004) p. 424.

70. Amelia W. Williams and Eugene C. Barker, *The Writings of Sam Houston, 1813-1863*, Volume II. (Austin, Jenkins Publishing Company, 1970) pp. 206-207.

71. Bill, Alfred Hoyt. *Rehearsal for Conflict: The War with Mexico 1846-1848* (New York, Alfred Knopf, 1947) p. vii.

72. Syndor, *History of The South*, pp. 281-282.

73. John Sayles to Thomas Sayles, 15 August 1847. Sayles Collection, Baylor University Archives, Waco, Texas.

74. Handbook of Texas Online, s.v. "John Sayles," http://www.tsha.utexas.edu/handbook/online/articles/SS/fsa42_print.html. (accessed February 11, 2007).

75. Virtual American Biographies, s.v. "John Sayles," http://www.famousamericans.net/johnsayles/ (accessed July 16, 2005).

76. Cleland, Robert Glass. *A History of California: The American Period* (New York, The Macmillan Company, 1922.) pp. 81, 323-325.

77. Connelly, William Elsey. *Doniphan's Expedition and the Conquest of New Mexico and California.* (Topeka, self-published, 1907.) pp. 126, 184.

78. Glass, *History of California*, op. cit..

79. Dusinberre, William. *Slavemaster President: the double career of James Polk* (New York, Oxford University Press, 2003.) p. 145.

80. Glass, *History of California*, p. 322.

81. Handbook of Texas Online, "Mirabeau Buonaparte Lamar," op. cit..

82. Glenn, James Hamilton, pp. 9, 269-270, 393, 398, 405. Freehling, William W. *The Road to Disunion.* Vol. II (New York, Oxford University Press, 2007) p. 384.

83. Breithaupt, Richard H. *The Aztec Club of 1847: military society of the Mexican War* (Universal City, Walika Publishing Co., 1998) pp. 1-3. *The Constitution of the Aztec Club of 1847* (Washington D.C., Judd & Detweiler, 1896) pp. 7, 20-24. Aztec Club of 1847: History of Its Founding. Aztec Club website (http:www.aztecclub.com/bios.htm). Mackey, Albert G. *The History of Freemasonry in South Carolina* (Columbia, South Carolina Steam Power Press, 1861) pp. 337-341. Mackey, Albert G. *An Encyclopedia of Freemasonry* (New York, The Masonic History Company, 1913) p. 113. Chaitkin, Anton. *Treason in America* (New York, New Benjamin Franklin House, 1984) p. 209. Greenburg, *A Wicked War*, pp. 104, 195, 248-249. Fuller, John Douglas Pitts. *The Movement for the Acquisition of All Mexico, 1846-1848* (Baltimore, John Hopkins Press, 1936) pp. 94, 114. May, Robert E. *John A. Quitman: Old South crusader* (Baton Rouge, Louisiana State University Press, 1985) p. 76.

Chapter Four

1. Lewis Publishing, History of Texas: together with a biographical history of Milam, Williamson, Bastrop, Travis, Lee and Burleson counties. (Chicago, Lewis Publishing, 1893) p. 88.

2. Lause, *A Secret Society History of the Civil War*, pp. 61, 86, 144-145. Keehn, *Knights of the Golden Circle*, pp. 9, 51, 152-153, 189-190. May, Robert E. *The Southern Dream of a Caribbean Empire* (Gainesville, University Press of Florida, 2002) p. 150. Fornell. Earl Wesley. *The Galveston Era: The Texas Crescent on the Eve of Secession* (Austin, University of Texas Press, 1961) p. 201 John J. Good to John A. Quitman, 30 May 1850. John Anthony Quitman Papers, Harvard University, Boston. *Lexington Observer*, June 5, 1850. Dallas City Directory, 1878. Publisher, Dallas, Texas Directories. Richard G. Badger, *American Dictionary of Dates*, 458-1920: 1880-1920. Vol. 2. (Boston, Gorham Press, 1921) p. 266. *Dallas Herald*, August 23, 1856.

3. Hudson, Linda S. *Mistress of Manifest Destiny: a biography of Jane McManus Storm Cazneau, 1807-1878* (Austin, Texas State Historical Association, 2001) p. 135. *Lexington Observer*, June 5, 1850, May 7, 1851, September 10, 1851, September 17, 1850, October 14, 1851, and October 18, 1851. Carr, Albert H. Z. *The World and William Walker* (New York, Harper & Row, 1963) p. 39.

4. May, Robert E. *Manifest destiny's underworld: filibustering in antebellum America* (Chapel Hill, University of North Carolina, 2002) pp. 32-34. *Constitution and By-Laws of the Order of the Lone Star* (New Orleans, Daily Delta, 1851). From a copy at the Center for American History, Austin, Texas. *Lexington Observer*, May 7, 1851. *Galveston Civilian & Gazette*, June 17, 1851 and September 21, 1851. Port-Gibson correspondent, November 30, 1844. *Texas State Gazette*, July 1, 1854. *Texas State Times*, April 7, 1855. *Weekly Telegraph*, September 9, 1857, May 1, 1860. Keehn, *Knights of the Golden Circle*, p. 12. *Dallas Herald*, August 23, 1856, August 29, 1857. "John Jay Good," *Biographical Encyclopedia of Texas* (New York, Southern Publishing Co., 1880) p. 117. Vertical file, "John Jay Good," Dallas Historical Society. Dallas Morning News, September 6, 1908. "Edward Porter," U.S. and Canada, Passenger and Immigration Lists, Index, 1500s-1900s. (Ancestry.com) accessed March 10, 2014. 1850 and 1870 United States Census for Williamsburg, South Carolina, op. cit.. McGill, Samuel D. *Narrative of Reminiscences in Williamsburg County* (Columbia, The Bryan Printing Co., 1897) p. 244. "Mary Jane Plowden Lesesne," Ancestry.com, Accessed on March 13, 2014. Confederate Citizen File for E. J. Porter. (www.fold3.com/image/#50370514) accessed on March 10, 2014. Jordan, Weymouth Tyree. *Rebels in the making: planters' conventions and southern propaganda* (Tuscaloosa, Confederate Publishing

Co., 1958) pp. 28, 42-43. May, Robert E. *John Quitman: Old South crusader* (Baton Rouge, Louisiana State University Press, 1985) pp. 272, 280, 290.

5, May, Manifest Destiny's Underworld, p. 33. "The Order of the Lone Star," *U.S. Democratic Review*, Vol. 32 Issue 1, January 1853, pp. 80-86.

6. May, op. cit.. Keehn, *Knights of the Golden Circle*, pp. 10-13. Lause, *A Secret Society History of the Civil War*, pp. 45, 61.

7. Hudson, *Mistress of Manifest Destiny*, pp. 111,117. May, Robert E. *John A. Quitman: Old South crusader*. (Baton Rouge, Louisiana State University Press, 1985) p. 271. Chaitkin, *Treason in America*, pp. 214-218. Frank Wagner, "Cazneau, William Leslie," Handbook of Texas Online (http://www.tshaonline.org/handbook/online/articles/fcaae) , accessed February 18, 2014. Robert E. May, "Cazneau, Jane Maria Eliza McManus," Handbook of Texas Online (http://www.tshaonline.org/handbook/articles/fcaad), accessed February 18, 2014. Freehling, *The Road to Disunion*, p. 309.

8. May, *Manifest Destiny's Underworld*, pp. 35-38. "Merchants War," Handbook of Texas Online (http://www.tshaonline.org/handbook/online/articles/gym01) accessed February 18, 2014. *Lexington Observer*, October 15, 1851. J. A. Quitman and Felix Huston to P. h. Bell, 21 August 1852. Governor's Papers, P. Hansford Bell, Texas State Archives. Ernest C. Shearer, "The Carvajal Disturbances," *Southwestern Historical Quarterly*, Vol. 55 No. 2 (October 1951) pp. 217, 230. Proceedings of the K.G.C. Texas State Convention, held at San Antonio, February 22, 1861. Devine, David. *Slavery, Scandal, and Steel Rails* (New York, iUniverse, Inc., 2004) pp. 46, 77, 80, 83-84, 90, 92.

9. May, *Manifest Destiny's Underworld*, p. 34. C. R. Wheat to J.A. Quitman, 30 January 1854. John Anthony Quitman Papers, Harvard University.

10. May, *John A. Quitman: Old South crusader*, pp. 279-280. T.S. Anderson to J.A. Quitman, 24 April 1854. John Anthony Quitman Papers, Harvard University.

11. May, op. cit., pp. 282-283. John Marshall to J. A. Quitman, 14 June 1854. Quitman Papers, Harvard University.

12. *New York Herald*, July 2, 1854 and July 10, 1854. Davis, Jefferson. *The Papers of Jefferson Davis*. Vol. 2. (Baton Rouge, Louisiana State University Press, 1971) p. 193 f25.

13. Lause, *A Secret Society History of the Civil War*, pp. 52-56. George Bickley, Address to the Citizens of the southern States by Order of the Convention of Knights of the Golden Circle, held at Raleigh, N. C. May 7-11, 1860. James Pinckney Henderson to J. A. Quitman, 6 October 1854. Quitman papers, Harvard University. May, *John A. Quitman: Old South Crusader*, p. 273.

14. May, *John A. Quitman: Old South crusader*, pp. 293-294. *New York Herald*, July 4, 1854.

15. John Marshall to Gen. J. A. Quitman, 18 September 1854. Quitman Papers, Harvard University. Charles W. Moore, "Triennial Meetings," *The Freemasons' Monthly Magazine*, Vol. XIII, 1854, pp. 7-20. Chaitkin, *Treason in America*, p. 221. Chaitkin concluded that Van Rensselaer, not Bickley, started the KGC.

16. Chaitkin, op. cit., pp. 222-223. *Ohio State Historical Marker*, "The Scottish Rite in Ohio," HMdb.org, the Historical Marker Database. (http://www2.historyarchives.org/marker.asp?marker=1045) accessed January 21, 2014. Jim S. Deyo, "Scottish Rite; The First Two Hundred Years," *Valley of Detriot Valleyvoice*. January 2014. Berlin and Harris, *Slavery in New York*,

pp. 31, 37. Rev. Maunsell Van Rensselaer, *Annuals of the Van Rensselaers in the United States* (Albany, Charles Van Benthuysen & Sons, 1888) p. 8. Goslinga, Cornelis Ch. *The Dutch in the Caribbean and On the Wild Coast, 1580-1680* (Gainesville, University of Florida Press, 1971) p. 361. Moore, *The Freemasons Monthly Magazine*, p. 122. *New York State Society of the Cincinnati Institution and Bylaws and General Information* (New York, the Society, 1957) pp. 35, 43, 44. Hume, Edgar Erskine, *Sesquicentennial History and Roster of the Society of the Cincinnati in the State of Virginia 1783-1933* (Richmond, the Society, 1933) p. 88.

17. *New York Herald*, July 2, 1854. Bickley, op. cit.. Melinda Jane Squires, "The Controversial Career of George Nicholas Sanders," Master's Thesis, Western Kentucky University, 2000, p. 91.

18. Melinda Jane Squires, "The Controversial Career of George Nicholas Sanders," pp. 12, 14, 25, 37, 82-84, 88-91. Lause, *A Secret Society History of the Civil War*, p. 24. J. A. Quitman to G. W. Mimms et. al, 21 October 1854. John Anthony Quitman Papers, Harvard University. Thomas W. Cutrer, "Smith, Persifor Frazer," Handbook of Texas Online (http://www.tshaonline.org/handbook/online/articles/fsm36), accessed July 13, 2013. United States, Letter from The Secretary of War, Transmitting Report of Lieut. Thomas Bradley, examiner of State claims, on the claims of States against the United States, in response to an inquiry from the Committee on Claims, United States Senate. Ex. Doc. No. 74, 46th Congress, 2nd Session, p. 82. This page of the document contains a list of papers from September 30, 1852 to February 5, 1855, "from and to whom."

Chapter Five

1. Christian Watchman, July 6, 1854. Quitman, John A to Lamar, C. A. L. John Anthony Quitman Papers, 1833-1858. Harvard University, Cambridge, Mass. January 5, 1855 *New Orleans Picayune*, quoted in January 10, 1855 *Charleston Courier*.

2. Proceedings of the Southern Commercial Convention, Held in The City of New Orleans, on the 8th, 9th, 10th, 11th, 12th,13th, and 15th of January, 1855. New Orleans, Office of The Crescent, 1855. Davis, "Ante-Bellum Conventions," Vol. V. *Transactions of the Alabama Historical Society, 1904* (Montgomery, Alabama Historical Society, 1904) p. 181. Paul N. Spellman, *Forgotten Texas leader: Hugh McLeod and the Texas Santa Fe Expedition* (College Station, Texas A&M University Press, 1999) p. 178.

3. McLeod, Bremond, De Cordova. *Proceedings*, p. 4. *Sun* (Baltimore) January 17, 1855. Property Tax Records for Galveston County, Texas, 1861, Texas State Archives. *Weekly Advocate*, (Baton Rouge) April 8, 1860.

4. Orval Walker Baylor and Henry Bedinger Baylor, *Baylor's History of the Baylors* (Le Roy, Le Roy Journal, 1914) pp. 29-31.

5. Proceedings, op. cit..

6. Ibid, p. 6. *Times-Picayune*, January 11, 1855.

7. *Proceedings*, pp. 14-17.

8. *Times-Picayune*, January 21, 1855. *Proceedings*, op. cit., p. 17. *Daily National Intelligencer*, February 28, 1855. Petersburg, *Virginia Daily Express*, February 13, 1855. *Report of the Secretary of Finance of the United States of Mexico of the 15th of January 1879, on the actual condition of Mexico, and the increase of commerce with the United States, Rectifying the Report of the Hon. John W. Foster, envoy extraordinary and minister plenipotentiary*

of the United States in Mexico, The 9th of October, 1878 (N. Ponce de Leon, New York, 1880) pp. 164-165. *New York Times*, January 16, 1855.

9. Handbook of Texas Online, Kristl Knudsen Penner, "Whitfield, John Wilkins," accessed July 07, 2017, http://www.tshaonline.org/handbook/online/articles/fwh38. *Dallas Weekly Herald*, April 3, 1861. *Lexington observer and reporter*, July 5, 1854. *Leavenworth Daily Times*, September 14, 1879. Cutler, William G. "Territorial History, Part 2 First Political Movements," History of the State of Kansas. (http://www.kancoll.org/books/cutler/terrhist/terrhist-p2.html) accessed on March 17, 2007.

10. *Daily Illinois State Journal*, September 16, 1856. *Leavenworth Daily Times*, September 14, 1879. Testimony of John Scott, "Secret Societies" Report of The Special Committee Appointed to Investigate the Troubles in Kansas; with The Views of the Minority. House of Representatives Report No. 200, 34th Congress, 1st Session. p. 896.

11. *History of Greene County, Missouri* (Western Historical Company, St. Louis, 1883). p. 241. *New York Times*, July 23, 1860. Dale E. Watts, "How Bloody Was Bleeding Kansas? Political Killings in Kansas Territory, 1854-1861" *Kansas History: A Journal of the Central Plains* 18 (2) (Summer 1995) pp. 124-125. Robinson, Sara T. L. *Kansas; Its Interior and Exterior Life* (Boston, Crosby, Nichols and Company, 1857) p. 168. *Daily Commercial Register* (Sandusky, Ohio), December 17, 1855.

12. Watts, op. cit.. *Daily Atlas* (Boston) February 18, 1856. Monaghan, Jay. *Civil War on the western border, 1854-1865* (Lincoln, University of Nebraska Press, 1985) pp. 23-25.

13. *Cadiz Sentinel*, September 11, 1867. Frank L. Klement, "Ohio and the Knights of the Golden Circle: The Evolution of a Civil War Myth" *The Cincinnati Historical Society Bulletin* Vol. 32, Spring-Summer 1974, p. 7. Ohio Historical Society, Library of Congress, "About The Portsmouth inquirer." www.chroniclingamerica.loc.gov/lccn/sn85026203/ (accessed on July 24, 2017).

14. *Spirit of the Times*, December 11, 1855. *Daily Ohio Statesman*, February 13, 1856. Mayo Fesler, "Secret Political Societies in the North during the Civil War," *Indiana Magazine of History*, Vol. XIV, No. 3 (September, 1918). p. 186.

15. Felter, Harvey Wickes, *History of the Eclectic Medical Institute Cincinnati, Ohio 1845-1902* (Cincinnati, Alumnal Association of the Eclectic Medical Institute, 1902) p. 111. *McArthur Democrat*, August 21, 1856. "About the Portsmouth Enquirer," op. cit..

16. *History of Lower Scioto Valley, Ohio* (Chicago, Inter-State Publishing Co., 1884) p. 225. *Cooper's Clarksburg register,* May 17, 1854. Confederate Service Record for Edwin M. Horrell, NARA. Confederate States of America, "[Resolutions transmitted] to the Hon. Speaker of the House of Representatives: Decatur, Georgia, January 27, 1864," https://catalog.hathitrust.org/Record/010945047, (accessed July 25, 2017); from the original at Duke University.

17. Johnson, John Lipscomb, *The University Memorial Biographical Sketches of Alumni of the University of Virginia Who Fell in the Confederate War* (Baltimore, Turnbull Brothers, 1871) pp. 578-580. *National Era*, June 19, 1856. Library of Congress, "The Weekly Patriot," https://lccn.loc.gov/lccn/sn85042313/ (accessed on July 24, 2017).

18. *Lecompton Union*, October 18, 1856, quoted in the *Charleston Mercury*, November 11, 1856. *Kansas Weekly Herald*, September 13, 1856. Biographical Directory of the United States Congress, "Bowdon, Franklin Welsh, (1817-1857)," accessed December 17, 2018, www.bioguide.congress.gov/scripts/biodisplay.pl?index=B000680. Brewer, W. *Alabama: Her History, Resources, War Record, and Public Men* (Montgomery, Barrett & Brown, 1872) p. 539. *State Gazette*, November 22, 1856.

Handbook of Texas Online, Thomas W. Cutrer, "Shelley, Nathan George," accessed December 17, 2018, http://www.tshaonline.org/handbook/online/articles/fsh20. *State Gazette*, June 18, 1859. *Biographical Encyclopedia of Texas* (New York, Southern Publishing Company, 1880) p. 30. "Brief biography, John Lingard Hunter, circa 1950," University of Alabama Library Special Collections. South Carolina Encyclopedia, Michael S. Reynolds, "St. Bartholomew's Parish," accessed June 15, 2020, www.scencyclopedia.org/sce/entries/st-bartholomews-parish/

19. May, John Quitman, p. 323. "Aztec Club," *The Encyclopedia of the Mexican-American War*, p. 41.

20. *New York Times*, December 5, 1856.

Chapter Six

1. Manning, *Some History of Van Zandt County*, p. 193. *Proceedings of the K.G.C. Texas State Convention*, p. 10.

2. Overdyke, William Darrell. *The Know-Nothing Party in the South* (Baton Rouge, Louisiana State University Press, 1950) pp. 34, 35, 43. Desmond, Humphrey. *The Know-Nothing party; a sketch* (Washington, New Century Press, 1905) pp. 54, 55.

3. Desmond, op. cit., pp. 66-68. Overdyke, op. cit., pp.27-28, 115, 136. Ralph A. Wooster, "An Analysis of The Texas Know Nothings," *Southwestern Historical Quarterly*, Vol. 70 No. 3, January, 1967, pp. 414-423. *La Grange The True Issue*, February 23, 1856. Duff Green to John Anthony Quitman, 11 August 1856. John Anthony Quitman Papers, Harvard University. Linda S. Hudson, "The Knights of the Golden Circle in Texas, 1858-1861: an Analysis of the First (Military) Degree Knights." *The seventh star of the Confederacy: Texas during the Civil War*. Ed. By Kenneth W. Howell. (Denton, University of North Texas, 2009) p. 55. *Official Proceedings of the National Democratic Convention, Held in Cincinnati, June 2-6, 1856* (Cincinnati, Democratic Convention, 1856) pp. 25, 66-67. May, John A. Quitman, pp. 300, 324. Wright, Edmund. *Narrative of Edmund Wright: his adventures with and escape from the Knights of the Golden Circle* (New York, R. W. Hitchcock, 1864) p. 55. Heck, Frank H. *Proud Kentuckian: John C. Breckinridge, 1821-1875* (Lexington, University Press of Kentucky, 1976) pp. 46-48, 104-105.

4. Cecil Harper, Jr., "Runnels, Hardin Richard," Handbook of Texas Online (http://www.tshaonline.org/handbook/online/articles/fru13), accessed March 19, 2014. *Laws of the State of Texas* (Austin, 1858) pp. 220-222. Keehn, *Knights of the Golden Circle*, pp. 89-95, 154. James N. Hammond, "The Aims and Activities of the Knights of the Golden Circle in Texas Leading Up to the Civil War," Master's Thesis, Midwestern State University, 12012. pp. 40-41. Overdyke, *The Know-Nothing Party in the south*, p. 84. *San Antonio Daily Herald*, June 16, 1859. John B. Floyd to T.S. Anderson, 19 April 1858. Governor's Papers for Hardin Richard Runnels, Texas State Library and Archives, Austin. Perrine, C. O. *An Authentic exposition of the "K.G.C.," "Knights of the Golden Circle": or, a history of secession from 1834 to 1861* (Indianapolis, C. O. Perrine, 1861) p. 47.

5. Sam Houston to John Hancock, 7 July 1856. Sam Houston Hearne Collection, Center for American History, University of Texas, Austin. *Houston Weekly Telegraph*, February 24, 1858. Brice, Donaly E. *The Great Comanche Raid: Boldest Indian Attack of the Texas Republic* (Austin, Eakin Press, 1987) pp. 22-26, 35, 48, 69. Farmer, From Blackland Prairie to Blacktop, p.13. Perrine, op. cit., pp. 86, 87.

6. Lause, *A Secret Society History of the Civil War*, pp. 64-65, 93-95. May, John A. Quitman, pp. 335-339, 448f21. William Walker to J.A. Quitman, 19 January 1858. John Anthony Quitman papers, Harvard University. *Register of Officers and Agents, Civil, Military, and Naval, in the Service of the United States, on the Thirtieth September, 1859...* (Washington, William A. Harris, printer, 1859) p. 10. Columbus, Texas *Colorado Citizen*, January 9, 1858 and February 6, 1858. Friend, Llerena B. *Sam Houston: The Great Designer* (Austin, University of Texas Press, 1954) pp. 298-300. *Dallas Herald*, July 10, 1858. *New York Times*, January 13, 1860.

7. *Brownsville Flag* in *Houston Weekly Telegraph*, January 27, 1858. *Waco Southerner* in *Weekly Telegraph*, March 17, 1858. *Philadelphia Ledger* in *Colorado Citizen*, March 20, 1858. Edward J. Berbusse, "The Origins of the McLane-Ocampo Treaty of 1859," *The Americas* Vol. 14 No. 3 (January 1958) p. 226, 229. May, John A. Quitman, p. 315, 443f20. Roy Sylvan Dunn, "The KGC in Texas, 1860-1861," *Southwestern Historical Quarterly*, Vol. LXX No. 4, (April 1967) p. 545.

8. John A. Wilcox to Hardin R. Runnels, op. cit.. A. M. Campbell to H. R. Runnels, 4 January 1858. Governor's Papers, Hardin R. Runnels, Texas State Library and Archives, Austin. Dunn, op. cit., p. 556. Ad for B & J. S. Shropshire, Attorneys and Counselors at Law, *La Grange True Issue*, February 12, 1859. H.R. Runnels to Thomas C. Frost, 31 December 1857. Thomas C. Frost to Hardin R. Runnels, 8 January 1858. *Weekly Telegraph*, May 26, 1858. Harper, "Runnels," op. cit.. T.S. Anderson to Gustave Cook, et. al., 21 April 1858. Governor's Papers, op. cit..

9. *Weekly Telegraph*, March 24, 1858; March 27, 1858; March 31, 1858; April 14, 1858; May 5, 1858. M. B. Highsmith to H. R. Runnels, 8 May 1858. Governor's Papers, op. cit.. "Capt. Malcijah Benjamin Highsmith," Find A Grave (http://www.findagrave.com), Accessed on June 20, 2013.

10. John T. Coit to W.B. Smith, 16 April 1858; A. Patterson to John T. Coit, 17 April, 1858; W.L.T. Prince to John T. Coit, 13 May 1858; John T. Coit to Catherine Coit, 18 June, 1858. Coit Family Papers, Dallas Historical Society, Dallas, Texas. Cheraw, *South Carolina Gazette*, in *New York Times*, September 10, 1856. William H. Bell, "Knights of the Golden Circle, Its Organization and Activities in Texas Prior to the Civil War," Master's Thesis, Texas A & I, August 1965, pp. 72-73. *Upshur Democrat*, quoted in *The Weekly Telegraph*, June 15, 1859. *Belton Independent*, June 6, 1858. Simpson, *Colonel Harold B. Gaines Mill to Appomattox* (Waco, Texian Press, 1963) p. 43. *San Antonio Texan*, October 18, 1855. Colonel M. L. Crimmins, "Colonel Charles Anderson Opposed Secession in San Antonio," *West Texas Historical Association Yearbook*, Vol. 29, October 1953, p. 67. Coit, John Eliot. *Lineage of the descendants of John Calkins Coit of Cheraw, South Carolina, 1799-1863*, prepared and edited by John Eliot Coit. (Coit family, 1945) p. 27.

11. Aragorn Storm Miller, "Weaver, William M.," Handbook of Texas Online, (http://www.tshaonline.org/handbook/online/articles/fwe81), accessed on October 11, 2013. Obituary for William Mack Weaver, *McKinney Courier-Gazette*, January 24, 1908. "Weaver, Colonel William M." *Biographical Souvenir of the State of Texas* (Chicago, F. A. Battey & Company, 1889) p. 874. W. M. Weaver to J. A. Quitman, 7 February 1855. Quitman Papers, Harvard University. Rita Roose and Jeanette Bland, "The Bickley Book: A Family Scrapbook" (Farmersville, privately published, 1988) pp. 9, 12, 29, 43, 44.

12. Property tax roll for Dallas County, Texas, 1859. State Library and Archives, Austin, Texas. John J. Good to Governor E.M. Pease, 20 June 1854. Governor's Papers, Texas State Library and Archives. *Dallas Morning News*, June 23, 1963. Mary Jane Walsh, "Anderson, Thomas Scott," Handbook of Texas Online, op. cit.. *Dallas Herald*, January 9, 1861. Muster roll cards for Texas State

Militias, Texas State Library and Archives, Austin (accessed by Ancestry.com). *Memorial and Biographical History of Dallas County, Texas* (Chicago, The Lewis Publishing Company, 1892) pp. 193, 212. Jackson, George. *Sixty Years in Texas* (Dallas, Wilkinson Printing Co., 1908) pp. 205, 212, 231. Keehn, *Knights of the Golden Circle*, pp. 3, 24, 27, 65, 157-158. Guess, George W. Papers, Texas State Library and Archives, Austin. Wright, Narrative of Edmund Wright, p. 69. Williams, R. H. *With the Border Ruffians, Memories of the Far West, 1852-1868* (Lincoln, University of Nebraska Press, 1982) pp. 198-199.

13. Thomas W. Cutrer, "Quitman, John Anthony," Handbook of Texas Online (http://tshaonline.org/handbook/online/articles/fgu07), accessed January 23, 2013. *Dallas Herald*, July 10, 1858. Letter to the Mayor and Alderman of the City of Austin, 28 July 1858. Letter from N. A. Davis to Wm. Byrd (http://4thtexascob.com/Archives/Quitman_Eulogy.htm), Source: Texas State Library and Archives. Accessed on May 7, 2013. Barry Compton and Crossfire No. 27 (April 1993) pub. By American Civil War Round Table UK, "John Mitchel – Rebel With Two Causes," (http://www.acwrt.org.uk/profile_John-Mitchel---Rebel-With-Two-Causes.asp), accessed on May 20, 2013. McGovern, *Bryan P. John Mitchel: Irish nationalist, Southern secessionist* (Knoxville, University of Tennessee press, 2009) pp. 172-173, 176-180. i, May 15, 1858.

14. *Weekly Telegraph*, April 28, 1858. *The Frontier News*, June 26, 1858, in John Jay Good Papers, University of Texas at Arlington. Harrison Flag, October 1, 1858. Hudson, "Military Knights of the Golden Circle," pp. 184, 210. Proceedings of the K.G.C. Texas State Convention, *State Rights Democrat* Print, pp. 2, 12.

Chapter Seven

1. Smith, F. Todd. *The Caddo Indians* (College Station, Texas A&M University Press, 1995) p. 138. Manning, Some History, p. 57.

2. *Weekly Herald*, July 20, 1859. Manning, *Some History*, pp. 69-71, 193-194. Katheder, Thomas, *The Baylors of Newmarket: The Decline and Fall of a Virginia Planter Family* (New York, iUniverse, Inc., 2009) pp. 1, 56, 62,129, 134. Hume, Edgar Erskine, *Sesquicentennial History and Roster of the Society of the Cincinnati in the State of Virginia 1783-1933* (Richmond, the Society, 1933) pp. 272, 303.

3. Black, Geneal Hamner. *Hamner heritage: beginning without end* (Bear Creek, Cesco Press, 1981.) p. 32.

4. Jack County Genealogical Society, *The History of Jack County, Texas* (Dallas, Curtis Media Corporation, 1985.) p. 19.

5. Middleton, *History of the regulators and moderators*, pp. 34-36.

6. Abel, Anne Heloise. *The American Indian as slaveholder and secessionist* (Cleveland, A.H. Clark Company, 1919.) p.32.

7. John C. Paige, "Wichita Indian Agents, 1857-1869." *Journal of the West*, Vol. XII, No. 3 (July, 1973) p. 404.

8. James Buckner Barry and James K. Greer. Buck Barry, *Texas ranger and frontiersman* (Lincoln, University of Nebraska Press, 1978.) p. 111.

9. Coombes, Zacharia Ellis. *The diary of a frontiersman, 1858-1859* (Newcastle, Texas, 1962.) p. 24.

10. Neighbours, Kenneth F. *Indian exodus: Texas Indian affairs, 1835-1859* (Nortex Offset Publications, 1973.) pp. 110, 116.

11. Rister, Carl Coke. *Robert E. Lee in Texas* (Norman, University of Oklahoma Press, 1946.) p. 138.

12. Neighbours, *Indian exodus*, p. 131.

13. Coombes, *diary*, p. 48.

14. Neighbours, *Indian exodus*, p. 131.

15. Coombes, *diary*, p. 148.

16. Ibid, p. 53.

17. Neighbours, *Indian exodus*, p. 133.

18. McConnell, Joseph Carroll. *The west Texas frontier; or, A descriptive history of early times in western Texas; containing an accurate account of much hitherto unpublished history* (Jacksboro, Gazette Print, 1933.) p. 324.

19. Coombes, *diary*, p. 55. *The Campaign Chronicle*, June 14, 1859. Ironically, Oliver Loving was killed by Indians in 1868 while on a cattle drive.

20. Neighbours, *Indian exodus*, p. 134. *Northern Standard*, June 4, 1859.

21. Barry, Greer, *Buck Barry*, p. 111.

22. Neighbours, *Indian exodus*, p. 135. Middleton, *History of the regulators and moderators*, p. 41.

23. Neighbours, op. cit.. Maddux, Vernon R. *John Hittson: cattle king on the Texas and Colorado frontier* (Niwot, University Press of Colorado, 1994.) p. 37. *The Campaign Chronicle*, June 29, 1859.

24. *Daily Herald*, May 25, 1859 and Jun 16, 1859. *By-Laws of the San Antonio Castle, "K.G.C," Approved [sic] June 15, 1861*. San Antonio, Printed at Ledger & Texan Office, 1861. From a copy at the Evans Library, Texas A&M University. *Dallas Times Herald*, July 13, 1859. Neighbours, *Indian exodus*, pp. 136-139.

25. Handbook of Texas Online, Thomas H. Kreneck, "Samuel Houston," accessed September 28, 2017, http://www.tshaonline.org/handbook/online/articles/fho73. *Daily Herald*, March 19, 1859, July 19, 1859 and August 10, 1859. *Texas Republican*, June 24, 1859. *Proceedings of the M. W. Grand Lodge of Texas at its Twenty-Fourth Annual Communication* (Galveston, The "News" Book and Job Office, 1860) pp. 220-221. *By-Laws of the San Antonio Castle, "K.G.C."* op. cit.. John M. Carolan was responsible for Masonic operations supervision in Comal, Kerr, Gillespie, Blanco, Bexar, Atascosa, Medina, Bandera, Uvalde, Kinney and Maverick counties as District Deputy Grand Master for Masonic Districts Four and Eighteen, which was attached to the Fourth District. He was also a Past Master of the Alamo Lodge in San Antonio, and Captain of one of the KGC Castles in that city.

26. James N. Hammond, "The Aims and Activities of the Knights of the Golden Circle in Texas Leading Up to the Civil War," Master's thesis, Midwestern State University, 2012, pp. 40-41. *Montgomery Daily Confederation*, August 31, 1859.

27. Keehn, *Knights of the Golden Circle*, pp. 24-25. Hudson, "Military Knights of the Golden Circle in Texas," pp. 50-51, 125, 174. *Proceedings of the K.G.C. Texas State Convention*, pp. 1, 9.

28. *Daily Herald*, August 10, 1859.

29. Robert Emmett Bledsoe Baylor to John Robert Baylor, 7 September 1859. Baylor Family Papers, Baylor University, Waco, Texas. Edward J. Gurley to Governor H. R. Runnels, 5 May 1859. Indian

Depredations file, Texas State Library, in C. L. Greenwood Collection, University of Texas, Austin, Texas.

30. *Northern Standard*, June 4, 1859.

31. John J. Good to Governor H. R. Runnels, 7 August 1859. Governors Papers, Texas State Library, Austin, Texas. C. Waller Jr. to R, H. K. Whiteley Esq., 12 September 1859. H. R. Runnels Papers, Governors Papers, Texas State Library.

32. Wesley Norton, The Methodist Episcopal Church and the Civil Disturbances in North Texas in 1859 and 1860. *Southwestern Historical Quarterly*, Vol. 68. Austin, Texas pp. 324-329. E. L. Shettles, "The Disturbance in Texas," *Texas Methodist Historical Quarterly*, Vol. II No. 3 (January, 1911) pp. 191-203. Ridgaway, Henry B. *The Life of Edmund S. Janes, D.D., LL.D.* (New York, Phillips & Hunt, 1882) pp. 224-228.

33. Lause, *A Secret Society History of the Civil War*, pp. 87, 96. Keehn, *Knights of the Golden Circle*, pp. 30-31.

34. *New York Herald*, October 5, 1859. *The Standard*, November 5, 1859.

35. *Dallas Weekly Herald*, November 2, 1859. Rex S. Lewis, "History of Dallas Commandery No. 6," Dallas Commandery No. 6, Grand Commandery of Texas, Knights Templar. www.dallascommandery.org (Accessed on October 20, 2017). *Transactions of the Grand Commandery of Texas of Knights Templar, at the Sixth Annual Conclave.* pp. 34-37. *Proceedings of the K.G.C. Texas State Convention*, pp. 1, 9.

36. *Baltimore Sun*, June 23, 1859. *Weekly Wisconsin Patriot*, October 1, 1859. *Baltimore Sun*, December 6, 1859. *New York Herald*, December 9, 1859. *Southern Intelligencer*, December 28, 1859. Greer, Jack Thornton. *Leaves from a family album*, Holcombe and Greer. (1975.) p. 34.

Chapter Eight

1. *Daily Telegraph*, January 2, 1860. Handbook of Texas Online, Donald E. Reynolds, "Cushing, Edward Hopkins,' accessed November 30, 2017, http://www.tshaonline.org/handbook/online/articles/fcu34. Keehn, *Knights of the Golden Circle*, pp. 73-74.

2. *Louisville Daily Courier*, November 27, 1859. Runnels, Hardin R. *Message of the Hon. Hardin R. Runnels Governor of Texas* (Austin, John Marshall & Co., 1859.) pp. 17, 22, 25, 28, 29.

3. Keehn, *Knights of the Golden Circle*, pp.33-35.

4. Greer, *Leaves From a Family Album*, pp. 34-35. *New Orleans Daily Crescent*, February 3, 1860. *Nashville Patriot*, April 9, 1860. *Nashville union and American*, January 22, 1860. *New York Herald*, October 29, 30, 1859. John Tyler, Jr. to Col. Earl Van Doren, enclosure from E. C. Wharton, April 9, 1861. *The War of the Rebellion*, Vol. 1, Chapter VII, pp. 624-625. Gloria Jahoda, "The Bickleys of Virginia," *Virginia Magazine of History and Biography* 66, no. 4 (October 1958) p. 478. US Census for Harris County, Texas, 1870. US Census for New Orleans, Louisiana, 1880. Confederate Service Record for Charles Bickley, accessed December 4, 2013, www.fold3.com/image/#16609713. Jefferson County Historical Commission, "Officers of the 21st Regiment," accessed October 2, 2017, https://www.co.jefferson.tx.us/Historical_Commission/files/History/Jefferson_County-History-

2015-12-03.pdf. Charles L. Bickley handwritten note, Bickley Papers, NARA. *Dallas Herald*, February 1, 1860. The census data and Confederate service record establish Charles Bickley's age, and the year of his birth is thereby determined to have been 1835. Others have suggested that Charles L. Bickley was a child from an unknown sibling of the KGC Commander, G.W.L. Bickley, which contradicts his established biography. Could Charles have been illegitimate?

5. *Yazoo Democrat*, January 14, 1860, quoting the *New York Tribune*, January 7, 1860. *New York Herald*, January 17, 1860. *Rome Tri-weekly Courier*, February 4, 1860. American Civil War Round Table UK, "Lord Lyons and Civil War Diplomacy 1859-1865," accessed December 6, 2017, www.acwrt.org.uk/profile_Lord-Lyons-and-Civil_War_Diplomacy-1859-1865.asp.

6. *Houston Weekly Telegraph*, January 25, 1860, quoting *State Gazette*. Jack W. Gunn, "Ben McCulloch: A Big Captain," *Southwestern Historical Quarterly*, Vol. 58 No. 1 (July, 1954) pp. 14-15. *San Antonio Daily Herald*, February 4, 1860. McCaslin, *Richard B. Fighting Stock: John S. "Rip" Ford of Texas* (Ft. Worth, TCU Press, 2011) pp. 82, 90-91. Collins, Michael L. *Texas devils: Rangers and regulars on the lower Rio Grande, 1846-1861* (Norman, University of Oklahoma Press, 2008) p. 181.

7. *Navarro Express*, January 28, 1860. *San Antonio Daily Herald*. The officers of the Atascosa County company included Captain D. J. Tobin, 1st Lieutenant V. Welden, 2nd Lieutenant Levi English, 1st Sergeant Thomas Shelton, 2nd Sergeant E. M. Johnson, 3rd Sergeant Sixto Navarro, and Edward Walker, Sutler. Ranger Service Record for H. A. Hamner, Texas State Archives. Special thanks to Donly Brice of the State Library for its location and retrieval. Handbook of Texas Online, David Minor, "White Man," accessed December 11, 2017, http://www.tshaonline.org/handbook/online/articles/eew11. *Dallas Herald*, February 29, 1860.

8. Larry Jay Gage, "The Texas Road to Secession and War: John Marshall and the Texas State Gazette, 1860-1861," *Southwestern Historical Quarterly*, Vol. LXII (October 1958) p. 198. *Houston Weekly Telegraph*, February 21, 1860. *Marshall Texas Republican*, January 14, 1860. Larry Van Horn, "Richard Abbey Van Horn," Find A Grave, accessed December 11, 2017, https://www.findagrave.com/memorial/68628834. Sibley, Marilyn McAdams. *Lone Stars and State Gazettes: Texas Newspapers Before the Civil War* (College Station, Texas A&M University Press, 1983) pp. 317, 344. *Proceedings of the K.G.C. Texas State Convention*, pp. 1, 8, 10, 12. *Navarro Express*, March 17, 1860.

9. Collins, *Texas Devils*, p. 189. Dunn, Roy Sylvan. "The Knights of the Golden Circle in Texas, 1860-1861." *Southwestern Historical Quarterly*, LXX, No. 4 (April 1967) pp. 549-550. Bonham Era, quoted in *Clarksville Standard*, March 10, 1860. Era quoted in *Houston Weekly Telegraph*, April 3, 1860. Era quoted in *State Gazette*, July 7, 1860. The Era listed the officers as L.C. Delisle, Captain; A.M. Gass, 1st Lieutenant; D.M. Waddill, 2nd Lieutenant; T. W. Cobb, 3rd Lieutenant; W.F. Kilbourn, Orderly Sergeant; J.L. Smith, 2nd Sergeant; Rufus Glover, 3rd Sergeant; Isaac Cox, 4th Sergeant; Jesse Cox, 1st Corporal; James Boyet, 2nd Corporal; J.J. Goodin, 2rd [sic] Corporal; William Webber, 4th Corporal. *The Weekly Telegraph* referred the following month to "The Era mentions the leaving of a detachment of K.G.C. for Mexico."[sic] Months later, the *State Gazette* quoted the Era identifying two KGC members as "Messrss [sic] Cobb and Smith, who left Bonham in the spring for the scene of action on the Rio Grande, have returned." T. W. Cobb was identified previously as 3rd Lieutenant and J. L. Smith as 2nd Sergeant of the Bonham company. DeLisle had sold his interest in the Era in the month of the *Gazette* report and was not mentioned. Handbook of Texas Online, "Taylor, Marion

DeKalb," accessed December 12, 2017. http://www.tshaonline.org/handbook/online/articles/fta23.

10. Collins, *Texas Devils*, pp. 183-184. *Weekly Herald*, February 29, 1860.

11. Collins, *Texas Devils*, p. 217. Sam Houston to President Buchanan, 8 March 1860. *The Writings of Sam Houston, 1813-1863*. Volume VII. p. 502. Sam Houston to Citizens of the Frontier, 8 March 1860, op. cit.., pp. 503-504.

12. *San Antonio Daily Herald*, March 8, 1860. Washington, D. C. Constitution, March 9, 1860 quoting the Montgomery Confederation. *Daily Times-Picayune*, March 14, 1860. *New Orleans Daily Crescent*, March 16, 1860. *Daily Times-Picayune*, March 13, 1860. *Daily Crescent*, March 13, 1860. See Handbook of Texas Online for Wyche, Texas, William Henry Stewart, William Washington Moon, Leander Calvin Cunningham, J.G. Coleman, James E. Shepard, Samuel Gabriel Ragsdale, Robert Reese Neyland, Blackstone Hardeman, Sr. et. al., "Lawsonville, Texas," ibid, and John Austin Corley.

13. *Dallas Weekly Herald*, March 21, 1860 and March 28, 1860. 1850 and 1860 Census for Rusk County, Texas. M.D. Graham to J.B. Magruder, 6 December 1862, Confederate Citizen file for Thomas M. Likens, NARA. 1860 U.S. Federal Census Slave Schedules for Rusk County, Texas. Compiled Service File for Volunteers in the Mexican War for Thomas M. Likens. Neyland, James, *Once Around the Square: A Walking Tour of Palestine's Old Town Business District* (Palestine, Anderson County Historical Commission, 1992) p. 28. Anderson County Deed Records, Vol. D., pp. 272, 275. Anderson County District Clerk, Palestine, Texas. Avera, Carl L. *My Journey's End* (Palestine, 2013) pp. 57-59. T.T. Gammage also owned land in Marshall, Texas and in Cass County, both of which he advertised for sale in the Marshall Star State Patriot, July 24, 1852. He purchased his land in Magnolia in February and April 1852. *Knights Templar of Texas, Transactions of the Grand Commandery of Texas, of Knights Templar, at the Seventh Annual Conclave, Held in Huntsville* (Houston, 1860) p.10. Sulphur Springs Monitor, quoted in *Dallas Weekly Herald*, March 28, 1860. Handbook of Texas Online, J. E. Jennings, "Sulphur Springs, TX (Hopkins County)," accessed December 16, 2017, http://www.tshaonline.org/handbook/online/articles/hes08. *Navarro Express*, April 21, 1860. Bell, "Knights of the Golden Circle," p. 78. *Dallas Weekly Herald*, April 11, 1860. The Dallas newspaper carried two stories referencing the company for Bowie, the other being found in *Weekly Herald*, April 18, 1860. *The San Antonio Ledger and Texan*, April 21, 1860 quotes the Paris, *Texas Press* of April 7, 1860 as noting "Twenty K.G.C. passed through our town on Thursday last, on their way somewhere" which seems to indicate that they were not locally recognized. Bowie County is the most easterly county on the Red River, so a path westward would take that KGC company through Paris, Texas in Lamar County, which also borders the Red River. The April 18 story in the Dallas paper notes that one of the Bowie County men had been killed by another KGC in fight near Lancaster, Texas, just south of Dallas. U.S. Census, 1860 Slave Census for Hopkins County, Texas. 1859 Property Tax Records for Upshur County, Texas. Confederate Service Record for Isaiah T. Davis. I.T. Davis enlisted in the Confederate Army in Gilmer, Upshur County, which is adjacent to Hopkins County; by 1870 he was living in Hopkins County.

14. Sam Houston to John B. Floyd, 12 March 1860. *The Writings of Sam Houston*, pp. 519-522.

15. *New Orleans Times Picayune*, March 18, 1860. This same story was carried by *The New York Times*, March 23, 1860 and *The Navarro Express*, April 7, 1860. *Proceedings of the K.G.C. Texas State Convention*, pp. 1, 8, 9, 12. U.S. Census, 1860 Slave Schedule for DeWitt County, Texas.

16. Heintzelman, Samuel Peter; Jerry D. Thompson. *Fifty Miles and a fight: Major Samuel Peter Heintzelman's journal of Texas and the Cortina war* (Austin: Texas State Historical Association, 1998) p. 237f26. *Dallas Herald*, April 11, 1860.

17. "A. Bradshaw" (Amzi Bradshaw) represented Ellis County at the Secession Convention, and appeared in New Orleans during the KGC convention there on March 15, 1860; "R.B. Hubbard" (Richard Bennett Hubbard, Jr.) supported secession in the Eighth Legislature as representative from Smith County; "C. M. Winkler" (Clinton McKamy Winkler) organized the secession movement in Navarro County; "P. Murrah" (Pendleton Murrah) was the last Confederate Governor of the Confederate State of Texas, elected in 1863; "J. Gregg" (John Gregg) of Freestone County was one of the signers and publishers of the call for the State Secession Convention, as was D.M. Pendergast, C.M. Winkler, John R. Baylor, his brother George W. Baylor and John J. Good. All 61 signers of the published "Call For a State Convention" were said to be KGC. Later, John Gregg commanded Hood's Texas Brigade (all biographical information from Handbook of Texas Online; "Call For a State Convention" from the Clarksville Standard, November 22, 1860.) "B. F. Forney" was an officer in the Lamar County Secession Club (Ralph Dice, "Lamar County and Secession," research paper, May 5, 1984, Texas A&M University-Commerce Archives, Commerce, Texas.) "A.J. Hood" of Cherokee County commanded a company of Ben McCulloch's "Buffalo Hunters" that captured the Federal Arsenal at San Antonio (*The Standard*, March 23, 1861).

18. *Cadiz Sentinel*, September 11, 1867. Library of Congress, Ohio Historical Society, "About The Portsmouth inquirer," chroniclingamerica.loc.gov/lccn/sn85026203. (accessed November 15, 2017). Scharf, J. Thomas. *History of Saint Louis City and County* (Philadelphia, Louis H. Everts & Co., 1883) p1718f1. *Southern Churchman*, June 3, 1836. *Philadelphia Recorder*, May 6, 1826. *National Police Gazette*, July 29, 1848. *Flag of Our Union*, August 18, 1849. 1850 US Federal Census for Pulaski County, Missouri. 1850 US Federal Census – Slave Schedules for Cape Girardeau, Missouri. *Daily Missouri Republican*, September 16, 1841, February 23, 1850. 1850 US Federal Census – Slave Schedules for Pulaski County, Missouri. Property Tax Records for Anderson County, Texas, 1858, 1859, 1860. Anderson County Deed Records, Vol. H. County Clerk, Palestine, Texas. pp. 128-129. *Palestine Trinity Advocate*, April 29, May 6, June 10, June 17, July 15, September 16, 1857; June 13, 1860. Ancestry Library Edition, "Elizabeth Florida Mead – Facts," https://www.ancestrylibrary.com/family-tree/person/tree/11467811/person/27331400371/facts. (accessed on May 13, 2017. Will for E. H. Horrell, Anderson County Probate Records, Palestine, Texas.

19. May, Robert E. *The Southern Dream of a Caribbean Empire* (Gainesville, University Press of Florida, 2002) p. 152. Dunn, *The KGC in Texas*, pp. 550-551. Keehn, *Knights of the Golden Circle*, p. 42. *New York Herald*, March 21, 1860.

20. *Daily Times Picayune*, March 22 and March 24, 1860. Handbook of Texas Online, Aragon Storm Miller, "Runnels, Howell Washington," accessed December 27, 2017, http://www.tshaonline.org/handbook/online/articles/fru44. Dan Norfleet Rhome, Sons of the American Revolution Membership Applications, 1889-1970. Ancestry Library Edition, accessed December 22, 2017. Peter G. Rhome (1806-1875), Find A Grave Memorial, https://www.findagrave.com/ memorial/42470754. 1860 US Federal Census – Slave Schedules for Cherokee County, Texas. Journal of the Secession Convention of Texas 1861. Ed. by Ernest William Winkler, State Librarian. Texas Library and Historical Commission, the State Library, Austin, Texas. (Austin Print Co., 1912) p. 20. Handbook of Texas Online, Thomas W. Cutrer, "Walker, John

George," accessed December 21, 2017, http://www.tshaonline.org/handbook/online/articles/ fwa20. op. cit., "Gillaspie, James," accessed December 22, 2017, http://www.tshaonline.org/ handbook/online/articles/fi18. "A Call For A State Convention," *Standard*, November 22, 1860. H. E. McCulloch was one of the signers of the KGC's call to the people, as were John J. Good, A.T. Rainey, D.M. Pendergast, John Gregg, C.M. Winkler, John R. Baylor, George W. Baylor, George W. Guess and 52 others. *Weekly Telegraph*, September 18, 1861. 1860 U.S. Federal Census – Slave Schedules for Guadalupe County, Texas. To further muddy the waters, in 1860 there was a John Caffery Walker who served in the Texas House of Representatives for Harris County. He was also referred to as "Captain" J. C. Walker. He died at the age of 65 the following year - December 18, 1861, never serving as a Confederate soldier. – "John Caffery Walker," Texas State Cemetery. For the writer's money, the individual in New Orleans for the 1860 KGC meeting was 31-year old John G. Walker of Terry's Texas Rangers, the cousin of future General John George Walker of Walker's Texas Division.

21. *Times Picayune*, March 28, 1860. *Daily Crescent*, March 27, 1860. Rochette, Patricia Atkins. *Bourland in North Texas and Indian Territory During the Civil War* (Broken Arrow, self-published, 2005) p. A-9. Handbook of Texas Online, Mark Dallas Loeffler, "Cone, Horace," accessed October 25, 2017, http://www.tshaonline.org/handbook/online/articles/fcorq. *Dallas Herald*, April 4, 1860. Harrison Flag, March 23 and March 30, 1860. *Texas State Gazette*, April 14, 1860. *Dallas Weekly Herald*, April 18, 1860. Journal of the Secession Convention, op. cit.. Handbook of Texas Online, Anne J. Bailey, "Parsons, William Henry," accessed December 1, 2017, http://www.tshaonline.org/handbook/ online/articles/fpa43.

22. *Texas State Gazette*, April 14, 1860. Hudson, "Military Knights of the Golden Circle in Texas," p.199. Billy S. Ledbetter, "Slavery, Fear, and Disunion in the Lone Star State: Texans' Attitudes Toward Secession and the Union, 1846-1861," Dissertation, University of North Texas, Denton, Texas 1972, pp. 187-188. *Daily Herald*, April 18, 1860. Ronnie C. Tyler, "Cotton on the Border, 1861-1865," *Southwestern Historical Quarterly*, Vol. 73 No. 4 (April 1970) p. 458. J. A. Quintero to John Anthony Quitman, 27 January 1855. John Quitman Papers, Mississippi Department of Archives and History, Jackson, Miss. Handbook of Texas Online, James W. Daddysman, "Quintero, Jose Augustin," accessed December 30, 2017, http://www.tshaonline.org/handbook/online/ articles/fqy95.

23. Keehn, *Knights of the Golden Circle*, p. 42. *Old-Line Democrat*, April 5, 1860.

24. *Alexandria Louisiana Democrat*, March 21, 1860 quoting *New Orleans Courier*. *Daily Gazette & Comet*, April 6, 1860 quoting *Baltimore American*. *Yazoo Democrat*, April 7, 1860. *Macon Telegraph*, April 4, 1860. *Daily Commercial*, April 10, 1860, quoting *New Orleans True Delta*, April 5, 1860. *Tyler Reporter*, May 16, 1860. *List of Patents for Inventions and Designs Issued by the United States from 1790 to 1847* (Washington, J. & G.S. Gideon, 1847) pp. 112, 132, 449. *Daily Crescent*, February 3 and 25, 1860. *Belmont Chronicle*, April 17, 1856. *The Daily Exchange*, September 9, 1858. Washington, D. C. *Evening Star*, January 12, 1909. *Tri-Weekly Telegraph*, April 23, 1862. Keehn, *Knights of the Golden Circle*, p. 43. *Daily Crescent*, April 4, 6, 7, 9, 10, 1860. Heintzelman, *Fifty Miles and a Fight*, pp. 230-231, 237f26. *K.G.C., A Full Exposure of the Southern Traitors*, pp. 4-8. *Daily Gazette & Comet*, April 13, 1860. *Houston Telegraph*, March 24, 1860.

25. *Dallas Weekly Herald*, April 11, 1860. *Weekly Telegraph*, March 27, 1860. George Stoneman to Major S. P. Heintzelman, 25 April 1860. Correspondence, Heintzelman Papers, Library of Congress. Pike,

James, The Scout and Ranger: Being the Personal Adventures of Corporal Pike of the Fourth Ohio Cavalry (Cincinnati, Hawley, 1865) pp. 137-139. Dayton Kelley, editor, and Ellen Kuniyuki, research associate, The Handbook of Waco and McLennan County, Texas (Waco, Texian Press, 1972) p. 82. McLennan County Court Record 1. McLennan County Clerk, Waco, Texas. p. 42. Texas, Muster Roll Index Cards for Davis, James F., Captain. Texas State Library and Archives, Austin, Texas. Confederate Service Records, Company E. 4th Texas Infantry. Ancestry Library, accessed July 2, 2013, www.fold3.com/image/#12240811. Handbook of Texas Online, Jeffrey William Hunt, "Fourth Texas Infantry," accessed July 2, 2013, http://www.tshaonline.org/handbook/online/articles/qkf01.

26. Weekly Telegraph, April 3, 1860, quoting Austin Intelligencer. Arkansas True Democrat, May 5, 1860. Ranger Service Record for H. A. Hamner, Texas State Archives, Austin, Texas.

27. Sam Houston, Amelia W. Williams, ed. and Eugene Campbell Barker, joint ed. The Writings of Sam Houston, 1860. (Austin, University of Texas Press, 1938-1941) p. 13.

28. Houston, The Writings of Sam Houston, op. cit.. Dallas Herald, May 2, 1860. Handbook of Texas Online, David Minor, "White Man," accessed December 30, 2017, http://www.tshaonline.org/handbook/online/articles/eew11. Texas Muster Roll Index Cards for H. A. Hamner, Texas State Library and Archives, Austin, Texas.

29. New York Times, April 20, 1860. Freehling, The Road to Disunion, p. 291.

30. Starobin, Paul. Madness Rules the Hour: Charleston, 1860 and the Mania for War. (New York, Public Affairs, 2017) pp. 41, 43, 48. Cutrer, Thomas W. Ben McCulloch and the Frontier Military Tradition (Chapel Hill, University of North Carolina Press, 1993) pp. 172-173.

31. Starobin, Madness Rules the Hour, p. 49. Freehling, The Road to Disunion, pp. 278- 280, 284-285. Keehn, Knights of the Golden Circle, pp. 30, 57.

32. Freehling, The Road to Disunion, pp.297-298, 301-303. Washington, D.C. Constitution, May 5, 1860.

33. Starobin, Madness Rules the Hour, pp. 57, 66-67. Keehn, Knights of the Golden Circle, p. 50.

34. McCaslin, Fighting Stock, pp. 96-98. Heintzelman, Fifty Miles and a Fight, p. 236.

35. Address to the Citizens of the Southern States by Order of the Convention of Knights of the Golden Circle. Copied from the original in the Texas State Library by Rev. E.L. Shettles, Austin, Texas, 1932. pp. 2, 25, 28, 30, 43. Nacogdoches Chronicle, August 29, 1854, quoting the Red Lander. Clarksville Standard, June 19, 1858.

36. Address to the Citizens of the Southern States, p. 43. Hudson, Military Knights of the Golden Circle in Texas, pp. 58-60. Nacogdoches Chronicle, August 29, 1854, quoting Red Lander. Clarksville Standard, June 19, 1858, quoting Harrison Flag. Handbook of Texas Online, George C. Werner, "Railroads," accessed January 4, 2018, http://www.tshaonline.org/handbook/online/articles/eqr01.

37. Address to the Citizens of the Southern States, pp. 44-75.

38. John J. Good to My dear Wife, 22 May 1860. John Jay Good Papers, University of Texas at Arlington, Arlington, Texas. Grand Junction, Tennessee – Official Site, "History of Grand Junction," accessed on January 3, 2018 www.grandjunctiontn.com. Dallas Weekly Herald, May 2, 1860 and May 9, 1860. John J. Good to My dear Wife, 25 May 1860. John Jay Good Papers. John G. Parkhurst, Official Proceedings of the Democratic National Convention, Held in 1860, at Charleston and

Baltimore. Proceedings at Charleston, April 23-May 3 (Cleveland, Nevins Print, 1860) pp. 29, 62. Keehn, *Knights of the Golden Circle*, pp.95, 213f33.

39. John Jay Good to wife, May 27, 1860 and May 29, 1860, op. cit.. H. L. Wilson, "President Buchanan's Proposed Intervention in Mexico," *The American Historical Review*, 5 (1900) p. 696.

40. *Dallas Weekly Herald*, May 30, 1860. Campbell, Randolph B. *An empire for slavery: the peculiar institution in Texas, 1821-1865* (Baton Rouge, Louisiana State University Press, 1989) pp. 192-193. Ray, G. B. *Murder at the Corners* (Austin, Nortex Press, 1957) p. vi. Ziza Moore to Charles B. Moore, 3 June 1860. Charles B. Moore Papers, University of North Texas, Denton, Texas.

41. John Jay Good to wife Sue, 7 June 1860. Notes to correspondence. John Jay Good Papers, op. cit.. Vertical File on John Jay Good, Dallas Historical Society, Dallas, Texas.

42. Halstead, M. *A History of the National Political Conventions of the Current Presidential Campaign* (Columbus, Follett, Foster and Company, 1860) pp. 154-156. *New York Times*, June 13, 1860. Hudson, *Military Knights of the Golden Circle in Texas*, pp. 50-51.

43. Halstead, *A History of the National Political Conventions*, pp. 156-158. *Richmond Whig*, June 15, 1860.

44. *La Grange True Issue*, May 11, 1860 and June 12, 1860. *San Antonio Ledger and Texan*, June 30, 1860, quoting *The Galveston News*. *New Orleans Evening Picayune*, June 5, 1860.

45. Freehling, *The Road to Disunion*, pp. 282-283, 329. Cairnes, John Elliott. *The slave power: its character, career, and probable designs; being an attempt to explain the real issues involved in the American contest* (New York, Harper & Row, 1969; reprint of the 2nd ed.. 1863) p. 95. *Richmond Whig*, May 22, 1860.

46. *Dallas Weekly Herald*, June 13, 1860. Farmer, Randolph W. *From Blackland Prairie to Blacktop: A History of Collin County* (San Antonio, Historical Publishing Network, 2011) pp. 17, 25.

47. Margaret Kean Monteiro, "The Presidential Election of 1860 in Virginia," *Richmond College Historical Papers*, Vol. 1, No. 2, June 1916, pp. 246-248. Vertical File on John Jay Good, Dallas Historical Society. Cutrer, Ben McCulloch, op. cit..

48. Grand Lodge of Texas, *Proceedings of the M.W. Grand Lodge of Texas* (Galveston, "News" Book and Job Office, 1860) pp. 18-251. *Standard*, November 22, 1860. Hudson, *Military Knights*, pp. 199-200. *Proceedings of the K.G.C. Texas State Convention*, pp. 1, 9, 12. Lause, *A Secret Society History*, p. 129. William R. Baker Commission, 1860, Center for American History, Austin, Texas. Diana J. Kleiner, "Baker, William Robinson," Handbook of Texas Online,(http://www.tshaonline.org/handbook/online/articles/fba42), accessed July 23, 2013. Baker held various executive positions with the Houston and Texas Central Railway from 1852 to 1877. He owned 23 slaves in 1860 and was married to Hester Eleanor Runnels in 1845.

49. Grand Commandery of Texas, Knights Templar. *Transactions of the Grand Commandery of Texas* (Houston, Office of the Telegraph, 1860) pp. 1, 12, 51-55. Dallas Commandery No. 6, "The Masonic Knights Templar," Grand Commandery of Texas, Knights Templar, (www.dallascommandery.org), accessed January 2, 2018. Grand Commandery of Texas, Knights Templar, *Transactions of the Grand Commandery of Texas* (Houston, 1858) pp. 9-11.

50. Philip I. Barziza to Charles A. Russell, 11 April 1861. Quoted in "Charles Russell," A.A. Neighbours Papers, pp. 31-32, Center for American History, University of Texas, Austin. Grand Commandery of Texas, *Transactions of the Grand Commandery of Texas of Knights Templar* (Houston, 1859) pp. 7-8. Valentine J. Belfiglio, "The Nature and Impact of Italian Culture Upon Galveston Island,"

East Texas Historical Journal, Vol. 27: Issue 1, Article 8, p. 44. Charles L. Robards and A. M. Jackson, *Reports of Cases Argued and Decided in The Supreme Court of The State of Texas* (St. Louis, Gilbert Book Company, 1881) pp. 136-138. Francis Barziza was also Trustee for 9 slaves in Robertson County in 1860, for the estate of "R. Graves, dec'd" according to the 1860 US Federal Slave Census. Grand Commandery, *History of the Grand Commandery, Knights Templar of Texas* (Houston, Dealy & Baker, 1899) pp. 1-14, Constitution of the Grand Encampment of Texas, Appendix, p. 5. *Standard*, November 22, 1860. *Proceedings of the K.G.C. Texas State Convention*, op. cit.. Robert Morris, "The Regulations of Knight Templary," *The Masonic Review*, Vol. XIX, August, 1858: No. 5, p. 154.

Chapter Nine

1. Handbook of Texas Online, Donald E. Reynolds, "Texas Troubles," accessed November 15, 2017, http://www.tshaonline.org/handbook/online/articles/vetbr.

2. Handbook of Texas Online, Lisa C. Maxwell, "Dallas County," accessed February 20, http://www.tshaonline.org/handbook/online/articles/hcd02.

3. Reynolds, Donald E. *Editors make war: Southern newspapers in the secession crisis* (Carbondale, Southern Illinois University Press, 2007) pp. 98-99. ----*Texas Terror: The Slave Insurrection Panic of 1860 and the Secession of the Lower South* (Baton Rouge, Louisiana State University, 2007) p. 33.

4. *Texas State Gazette*, July 7, 1860. *Memorial and Biographical History of Dallas County, Texas* (Chicago, The Lewis Publishing Company, 1892) pp. 289-290. *Times-Picayune*, March 24, 1860. Shettles and Janes, "The Disturbance in Texas," *The Methodist Historical Quarterly*, p. 202. Reynolds, *Texas Terror*, p. 33.

5. Original Muster Roll, Dallas Light Artillery, March 12, 1859. Muster Roll, Dallas Light Artillery, Feb. 22, 1861 When Commanded Tendered to State [sic] John J. Good Papers, University of Texas at Arlington, Special Collections, Arlington, Texas. Keehn, *Knights of the Golden Circle*, p. 59. Hudson, "Military Knights of the Golden Circle in Texas," pp. 53, 222. Bates, Ed. F. *History and Reminiscences of Denton County* (Denton, McNitzky Printing Company, 1918) pp. 348-349. C.A. Williams, a forty-four year resident of Denton in 1894 gave an interview to E. F. Bates and stated by that time, it was "fully proven" that the abolitionists were falsely accused of setting the fires in Denton and other towns. the fires were caused by the volatile "prairie matches" spontaneously igniting.

6. *Marshall Texas Republican*, July 28, 1860, quoting *Bonham Era* of July 17, 1860. *New Orleans Times-Picayune*, March 20, 1860. *Handbook of Texas Online*, David Minor, "Ferris, Justus Wesley," accessed December 22, 2017, http://www.tshaonline.org/handbook/online/articles/ffe09. 1860 U.S. Federal Census – Slave Schedule for Dallas County, Texas. Muster Roll, Dallas Light Artillery, Feb, 22, 1861. Original Muster Roll, Dallas Light Artillery, March 12, 1859.

7. *Texas Republican*, July 28, 1860. Reynolds, *Texas Terror*, pp. 36-37. Campbell, *An empire for slavery*, pp. 264-266. Crowell, Evelyn Miller, *Texas Childhood* (Dallas, Kaleidograph Press, 1941) p. 68. Keehn, *Knights of the Golden Circle*, p. 67.

8. *Texas State Gazette*, July 7, 1860. *Richmond Whig*, July 20, 1860. *Evening Transcript*, July 19, 1860. *Philadelphia Enquirer*, July 19, 1860. *Alexandria Gazette*, July 20, 1860. Samuel A. Lockridge to Major Heintzelman, 27 April 1860. Correspondence, Heintzelman Papers, Library of Congress.

9. Reynolds, *Texas Terror*, pp. 83-84. Campbell, *An empire for slavery*, p. 266. Terrell, Capt. J. C. *Reminiscences of the Early Days of Fort Worth* (Fort Worth, Texas Printing Co., 1906) p. 39. *Navarro Express*, August 25, 1860.

10. Reynolds, *Texas Terror*, pp. 80-83. *Memorial and Biographical History of Dallas County*, p. 292.

11. *Texas Republican*, August 11, 1860, quoting Rusk Enquirer. *Semi-Weekly Mississippian*, August 7, 1860, quoting *Houston Telegraph* of July 31, 1860. Bell, *Knights of the Golden Circle*, pp. 65-66. Wesley Norton, "The Methodist Episcopal Church and the Civil Disturbances in North Texas in 1859 and 1860," *The Southwestern Historical Quarterly*, Volume 68, July 1964-April 1965, p. 333.

12. *Houston Telegraph*, August 9, 1860, quoting Columbus Citizen, August 4, 1860. Bell, *Knights of the Golden Circle*, p. 65. Campbell, *An empire for slavery*, pp. 264-265. *Houston Weekly Telegraph*, August 18, 1860, quoting Sulphur Springs Monitor, August 4, 1860. *Navarro Express*, August 11, 1860, quoting *Fairfield Pioneer Extra*, August 7, 1860. *Weekly Telegraph*, August 14, 1860, quoting *Fairfield Pioneer*, op. cit.. *Semi-Weekly Mississippian*, August 17, 1860. *Alamo Express*, August 18 and August 25, 1860. Handbook of Texas Online, Diana J. Kleiner, "Matagorda County," accessed March 2, 2018, http://www.tshaonline.org/handbook/online/articles/hcm05. *Texas Republican*, August 18, 1860.

13. Garrett, Julia Kathryn, *Ft Worth: A Frontier Triumph* (Austin, Encino Press, 1972) pp. 177-178. Arlington Heights Junior Historians, *Downtown Historic Trails of Fort Worth and Tarrant County* (Ft. Worth, Dudley Hodgkins Company, 1949), pp. 21-22. Slave Schedules, 1850 U.S. Census for Shelby County, Texas. *Texas State Gazette*, August 11, 1860. Handbook of Texas Online, Aragorn Storm Miller, "Welch, Otis G.," accessed February 26, 2018, http://www.tshaonline.org/handbook/online/articles/fwe82. *Memorial and Biographical History of Dallas County*, pp. 293-294. Reynolds, *Texas Terror*, pp. 34, 156-157.

14. *Clarksville Standard*, September 29, 1860. Captain George Stoneman to Major S. P. Heintzelman, 25 April 1860. Correspondence, Heintzelman Papers, Library of Congress.

15. Rev. Charles Elliott, "The Martyrdom of Bewley," *Methodist Quarterly Review*, Vol. 45, October Number, 1863, pp. 633-634.

16. Elliott, *Methodist Quarterly Review*, pp. 635-639. Reynolds, *Texas Terror*, pp. 151-152. Fannin County Commissioner's Court Minutes, Book B, p. 550, Bonham, Texas.

17. Garrett, *Fort Worth: A frontier triumph*, pp. 179-181. Reynolds, *Texas Terror*, p. 118. *Proceedings of the K.G.C. Texas State Convention*, pp. 10, 12. Newcomb, James Pearson, *Sketch of secession times in Texas and Journal of travel from Texas through Mexico to California* (San Francisco, 1863) p. 6.

18. Davis, Richard Harding, *Real Soldiers of Fortune* (New York, Charles Scribner's Sons, 1912) pp. 184-187. Keehn, *Knights of the Golden Circle*, p. 12.

19. Garrett, *Fort Worth: a frontier triumph*, pp. 181-182. Elliott, *Methodist Quarterly Review*, p. 640. Reynolds, *Texas Terror*, pp. 118, 152-153, 160-161. *Texas Republican*, October 13 and 20, 1860.

20. *Texas Republican*, August 25, 1860 (pp. 1, 2). Bell, *Knights of the Golden Circle*, pp 207-217.

21. Bell, op. cit., pp. 104-107. *Washington, D.C. Constitution*, September 5, 1860. *New York Tribune*, September 8, 1860. *Little Rock Old-Line Democrat*, September 20, 1860, quoting *Norfolk Day Book*. *Galveston News*, undated fragment with Charles Bickley's obituary. Another obituary indicated he died November 11, 1880. *Dallas Daily Herald*, November 18, 1880. Reynolds, *Texas Terror*, p. 127. *Navarro Express*, October 5, 1860. Carland Elaine Crook, San Antonio, Texas, 1846-1861, Master's Thesis,

Rice University, Houston, 1964, p. 64. Handbook of Texas Online, Donald E. Reynolds, "Texas Troubles," accessed November 15, 2017, http://www.tshaonline.org/handbook/online/articles/ vetbr.

22. *Weekly Telegraph*, October 9, 1860. *Baton Rouge Daily Gazette & Comet*, October 12, 1860, quoting *Corpus Christi Ranchero. The Ranchero*, October 27, 1860.

23. *Ranchero*, ibid. Keehn, *Knights of the Golden Circle*, p. 212, f5. Bell, *Knights of the Golden Circle*, pp. 104, 107.

24. *Ranchero*, November 3, 1860. *Alamo Express*, November 5, 1860. Frank W. Smyrl, "Unionism in Texas, 1856-1861," *Southwestern Historical Quarterly*, Vol. LXVIII (October 1964) p. 179. *Texas State Gazette,* October 20, 1860.

25. Williams and Barker, eds., *The Writings of Sam Houston, 1813-1863*, pp. 145-156. Keehn, *Knights of the Golden Circle*, pp. 68-69, 75. *Washington, D.C. Constitution*, August 9, 1860, quoting *St. Louis Republican.* The *St. Louis Republican* quoted "A Texas gentleman". *Texas State Gazette*, August 25, 1860. *The Houston Telegraph*, August 9, 1860. *Texas State Gazette*, September 8, 1860 and October 6, 1860. Smythe, H. *Historical Sketch of Parker County and Weatherford, Texas* (St. Louis, Louis C. Lavat, 1877) pp. 138-140.

26. Campbell, *An empire for slavery*, p. 264. Handbook of Texas Online, Paula Mitchell Marks, "Bastrop County," accessed March 07, 2018, http://www.tshaonline.org/handbook/online/articles/hcb03. *The True Issue*, November 1, 1860, quoting *Bastrop Advertiser. Texas State Gazette*, November 3, 1860, quoting *Bastrop Advertiser. Alamo Express*, October 23, 1860. *Houston Tri-Weekly Telegraph*, November 1, 1860. *Dallas Weekly Herald*, November 14, 1860, quoting *Houston Telegraph*, November 3, 1860. Hudson, *Military Knights of the Golden Circle*, pp. 178, 184, 190-191, 196, 205-206. James M. Hammond, The Aims and Activities of the Knights of the Golden Circle in Texas Leading Up to the Civil War, MA Thesis, Midwestern State University, Wichita Falls, Texas, p. 78. Handbook of Texas Online, Carole E. Christian, "Chappell Hill, TX," accessed March 7, 2018, http://www.tshaonline.org/handbook/online/articles/hlc21.

27. Keehn, *Knights of the Golden Circle*, pp. 69-70, 100-101, 117. *Springfield Republican*, November 5, 1860. William C. Yancey, The Old Alcalde: Oran Milo Roberts, Texas's Forgotten Fire-Eater. PhD dissertation, University of North Texas, Denton, Texas, 2016, pp. 114-115.

28. Jeffrey A. Jenkins and Irwin L. Morris, "Running to Lose? John C. Breckinridge and the Presidential Election of 1860," *Electoral Studies*, Vol. 25 (2006) pp. 306-328. *Harrison Flag*, November 10, 1860. *Houston Tri-Weekly Telegraph*, November 8, 1860. Barry, *A Texas Ranger*, p. 124. Campbell, *An empire for slavery*, p. 264.

29. *Navarro Express*, November 9, 1860. Yancey, *The Old Alcalde*, pp. 116-117. Newcomb, James Pearson, *Sketch of secession times in Texas and Journal of travel from Texas through Mexico to California* (San Francisco, 1863) p. 10.

30. *Dallas Herald*, November 21, 1860. Original Muster Roll, Dallas Light Artillery, March 12, 1859. John Jay Good Papers.

31. *Dallas Herald*, ibid. *Dallas Weekly Herald*, February 29, 1860. *Texas Republican*, November 17, 1860. *Indianola Courier*, November 24, 1860. *Houston Tri-Weekly Telegraph*, December 27, 1860. *Standard*, November 22, 1860. Bancroft, Hubert Howe, *History of the north Mexican states and Texas* (New York, Arno Press, 1967) p. 436. Versions of Bancroft's book were published as early as 1886. The following

is the complete list of sixty-one names published by the *Standard*, on November 22, 1860, with their home counties, where indicated: Wm Byrd; John A. Wharton, Brazoria Co.; B S Whitaker, M S Cooksey, T C Jackson, R J Moore, John Burleson, S Fletcher, Mark Bean, all of Lampasas County; Thomas Moore, Burnet Co.; H E McCulloch, C. Reich, Guadalupe Co.; S G Sneed, John T. Pruit, Geo W. White, Jas. P. Neal, J B Banks, Travis Co.; C E Burns, T D Robertson, P H Smith, Robertson Co.; A T Rainey, Anderson Co.; John J Good, Geo W Guess, Dallas Co.; R M Bomar, Caldwell Co.; Edward Bailey; D M Pendergast, Limestone Co.; John Gregg, Freestone Co.; L K Preston, Galveston Co.; A. A. Kemble, Waxahachie [sic; Ellis Co.]; W S Oldham, Washington Co.; James H Fry, Webberville [sic; Travis Co.]; Jesse Billingsley, John C. Higgins, Bastrop Co.; Roger Q. Mills, C M Winkler, Navarro Co.; Clement R. Johns, J E McCord, Hays Co., T D Mosely; C H Randolph, Houston Co.; George Flournoy; John R. Baylor, George Baylor, Parker Co.; Joseph Lee; S Crosby; Wm. P. Stapp, Calhoun Co.; W.W. Apperson; Louis Hoast; John B. Costa; Thomas Green; R. Brownrigg; A H Parish; J E Rector; Wm Lee Chambers; Morris R Reagan; John A Green; George D Durham; W C Pitts; Ed Clark; T J Chambers, Chambers Co.; W M Hardeman; Junius W Smith, Tarrant Co.

32. Anderson, Charles, *Texas, Before, and on the Eve of the Rebellion* (Cincinnati, Peter G. Thomson, 1884) pp. 9, 14-17. Handbook of Texas Online, Thomas W. Cutrer, "Wilcox, John Allen," accessed March 9, 2018, http://www.tshaonline.org/handbook/online/articles/fwi10. Proceedings of the K.G.C. Texas State Convention, pp. 1, 9. Handbook of Texas Online, T.R. Fehrenbach, "San Antonio," accessed March 9, 2018, http://handbook.org/handbook/articles/hds02. Handbook of Texas Online, "Upson, Christopher Columbus," accessed March 9, 2018, http://www.tshaonline.org/handbook/online/articles/fup01. Newcomb, Sketch of secession times in Texas, p. 5, footnote +.

33. Zenas Randall Bliss Papers, 1854-1898, Dolph Briscoe Center for American History, The University of Texas at Austin, Vol 2, pp. 35-38. Anderson, Texas, Before, and on the eve of rebellion, op. cit.. Confederate Citizens File for W.R. Story, NARA, Accessed via Fold3, June 25, 2013. *Proceedings of the K.G.C. Texas State Convention*, op. cit.. "Call for a State Convention," *Standard*, November 22, 1860.

34. *Navarro Express*, December 21, 1860, quoting letter to the Editor of the *State Gazette*, November 28, 1860. *Tri-Weekly Telegraph*, December 8, 1860, quoting Charles Bickley to *The Telegraph*, November 29, 1860.

35. *Washington, D.C. Constitution*, December 29, 1860, quoting V.D. Groner to J.J. Pettus, November 30, 1860. *Dallas Herald*, December 5, 1860. Starobin, *Madness Rules the Hour*, pp. 126-127. Keehn, *Knights of the Golden Circle*, p. 4. *Indianola Courier*, November 24, 1860. *Texas Republican*, November 17, 1860. *Navarro Express*, December 7, 1860.

36. *Navarro Express*, op. cit.. *Proceedings of the K.G.C. Texas State Convention*, p. 1. *Dallas Herald*, December 5, 1860, quoting *Marshall Texas Republican*.

37. *Colorado Citizen*, December 22, 1860. *Proceedings of the K.G.C. Texas State Convention*, pp. 1, 9. Handbook of Texas Online, Allen Kibler and Dawn Kibler, "Redgate, Samuel Joseph," accessed on March 9, 2018, http://www.tshaonline.org/handbook/online/articles/frehu. Handbook of Texas Online, Charles Christopher Jackson, "Herbert, Claiborne C.," accessed on March 9, 2018, http://www.tshaonline.org/handbook/online/articles/fhe25. *Colorado Citizen*, December 22, 1860. Among "the most aged and respectable citizens" mentioned by the *Colorado Citizen* as being enrolled

in their "military companies" were "Col. Robson, Col. Wallace, Col. Garner, Isam Tooke, Dr. Banks, Gen. Jones, Hon. C.C. Herbert, Dr. C.W. Tait, and others too numerous to mention."

38. Tom L. Holman, James Montgomery, 1813-1871, PhD dissertation, Oklahoma State University, Stillwater, Oklahoma, 1973, pp. 120-131. Leavenworth, *Kansas Daily Times*, October 20, 1860. *Dallas Herald*, December 12, 1860. *Navarro Express*, December 14, 1860. Actually Charles R. Pryor had been promoting the story of "Indians and Abolitionists" working together against Texans since July 1860, when one of his letters was published in the *Colorado Citizen* on July 28, 1860.

39. *Texas State Gazette*, December 15, 1860. *Navarro Express*, December 7 and 14, 1860. *Dallas Herald*, December 16, 1860 and December 19, 1860.

40. *The Citizen*, December 22, 1860. *Proceedings of the K.G.C. Texas State Convention*, p. 9. Wharton County Historical Commission, Frazarville Historical Marker, accessed on February 10, 2018, www.whartoncountyhistcomm.com.

41. Dickey, Christopher, *Our Man in Charleston: Britain's Secret Agent in the Civil War South* (New York, Crown Publishers, 2015) pp. 179, 191-195, 362. Adam Goodheart, "The Happiest Man in the South," *The New York Times*, December 16, 2010. *Dallas Herald*, December 5, 1860. Keehn, *Knights of the Golden Circle*, p. 35.

42. *Dallas Herald*, December 26, 1860. Dickey, *Our Man in Charleston*, pp. 198-199. *Houston Tri-Weekly Telegraph*, December 27, 1860.

Chapter Ten

1. *Navarro Express*, January 2, 1861 and March 20, 1861. *Proceedings of the K.G.C. Texas State Convention*, p. 1. *Biographical Sketches from Limestone, Freestone, and Leon Counties, Texas* (Chicago, Lewis Publishing Company, 1893) pp. 11-13. Property Tax Records for Freestone County, Texas 1858 and 1860. 1860 U.S. Federal Census – Slave Schedules for Freestone County and Henderson County, Texas. In Henderson County, he is listed as John Carner.

2. Keehn, *Knights of the Golden Circle*, pp. 94-95. Anderson, *Texas, Before, and on the eve of rebellion*, p. 25. Freehling, *The Road to Disunion*, p. 483. King, Alvy L. Louis T. Wigfall: *Southern Fire-eater*, (Baton Rouge, Louisiana State University Press, 1970) p. 114. *Navarro Express*, January 9, 1861, quoting *Austin Intelligencer*. Sandbo, "First Session of the Secession Convention of Texas, p. 181. H.A. Hamner to Hon. A. Nelson, 31 January 1861, in *Journal of the Secession Convention*, p. 384.

3. Merrick, Morgan Wolfe, *From desert to bayou: the Civil War journal and sketches of Morgan Wolfe Merrick* (El Paso, Texas Western Press, 1991) pp. ii, 3, 4, 101 f6. *San Antonio Express*, August 22, 1975. Hudson, *Military Knights of the Golden Circle in Texas*, p. 216. *Proceedings of the K.G.C. Texas State Convention*, pp. 2, 9.

4. *Navarro Express*, January 16, 1861 and February 13, 1861. Mayo Fesler, "Secret Political Societies in the North during the Civil War," *Indiana Magazine of History*, Vol. XIV No. 3, September 1918, p. 201. Coit, John Eliot, *Lineage of the descendants of John Calkins Coit of Cheraw, South Carolina, 1799-1863* (n.p. 1945) pp. 7-9. Chapman, F.W. *The Coit family* (Hartford, Lockwood & Brainard Co., 1874) pp. 188-189. S.S. Lyons and Eli Witt to John T. Coit, 9 January 1861. Coit Family Papers, Dallas Historical Society, Dallas, Texas. Farmer, From Blackland Prairie to Blacktop, pp. 22, 26-29.

5. *Philadelphia Inquirer*, February 12, 1861, quoting *Louisville Journal. Daily Telegraph*, January 2, 1860. Campbell, *An empire for slavery*, pp. 264-265. *Standard*, August 20, 1859; September 10, 1859 and March 16, 1861. *San Diego Union*, July 1, 1875 and May 11, 1898. San Diego Sun, November 16, 1881. Obligations of the Knights of the Golden Circle, George W. Guess Papers, Center for American History, Austin, Texas. "Civil War Letters of George W. Guess to Sarah Horton Cockrell," op. cit.. Williams, R. H. *With the Border Ruffians: Memories of the Far West 1852-1868* (London, John Murray, 1907) pp. 155, 160, 199. Handbook of Texas Online, George P. Isbell, "Mitchell, Asa," accessed March 27, 2018, http://www.tshaonline.org/handbook/online/articles/fmi51.

6. *The Standard*, January 26, 1861. Handbook of Texas Online, Michael M. Ludeman, "Lamar County," accessed March 27, 2018, http://www.tshaonline.org/handbook/online/articles/hc101. Neville, A. W. *The History of Lamar County (Texas)* (Paris, North Texas Publishing Company, 1986) pp. 80-83, 89-90.

7. Texas Library and Historical Commission, *Journal of the Secession Convention of Texas*, pp. 1-19. Bancroft, *History of the north Mexican states and Texas*, p. 436. "Call for a State Convention" in *The Standard*, November 22, 1860. *Daily Times-Picayune*, March 24, 1860. *San Antonio Weekly Herald*, February 2, 1861.

8. Handbook of Texas Online, Anne J. Bailey and Bruce Allardice, "Carter, George Washington," accessed March 29, 2018, http://www.tshaonline.org/handbook/online/articles/fac70 . Anderson, *Texas Before, and on the Eve of the Rebellion*, pp. 19-21. Handbook of Texas Online, Walter L. Buenger, "Secession Convention," accessed May 6, 2005, http://www.tsha.utexas.edu/handbook/online/articles/view/SS/mis1.html.

9. *Tri-Weekly Alamo Express*, February 4, 1861 and February 13, 1861. Dictionary of North Carolina Biography, William S. Powell, "Clarke, William John," accessed October 2, 2017, www.ncpedia.org/biography/clarke-william-john. *San Antonio Ledger and Texan*, October 9, 1858; October 8, 1859 and December 22, 1860. *Proceedings of the K.G.C. Texas State Convention*, pp. 9, 12. Bowden, J. J., *The Exodus of federal forces from Texas, 1861* (Austin, Eakin Press, 1986) p. 36. Handbook of Texas Online, Paula Mitchell Marks, "Maverick, Samuel Augustus," accessed June 1, 2018, http://www.tshaonline.org/handbook/online/articles/fma84.

10. Marks, Paula Mitchell, *Turn Your Eyes Toward Texas: Pioneers Sam and Mary Maverick* (College Station, Texas A&M Press, 1989) p. 5. *Journal of the Texas Secession Convention*, pp. 20-22, 28 ,41-50. "A Call for a State Convention," op. cit.. Sprague, Major J. T. *The Treachery in Texas, the Secession of Texas and the Arrest of the United States Officers and Soldiers Serving in Texas* (New York, New York Historical Society, 1862) pp. 112-113. *Proceedings of the K.G.C. Texas State Convention*, p. 10. Hudson, *Military Knights of the Golden Circle*, p. 219. Slavery in the North, "Slavery in Massachusetts," accessed January 30, 2013, http://www.slavenorth.com/massachusetts.htm.

11. Daniel, Lewis E. *Personnel of the Texas State Government, with Sketches of Distinguished Texans* (Austin, City Printing Company, 1887) p. 244. *Proceedings of the K.G.C. Texas State Convention*, p. 9. *Journal of the Secession Convention of Texas 1861*, p. 277. Sprague, *The Treachery in Texas*, p. 110. *War of the Rebellion*, Series 1 Vol. 3, p. 639.

12. *Journal of the Secession Convention*, pp. 60, 71, 80. United States Senate, *Journal of the Congress of Confederate States of America, 1861-1865*. Volume 1, (Washington, Government Printing Office, 1904) pp. 40, 43, 54. 60, 64. *San Antonio Weekly Herald*, February 2, 1861.

13. *Navarro Express*, March 13, 1861, quoting *Dallas Herald*. Post Return of Camp Colorado, Texas, U.S. Returns from Military Posts, 1806-1916, September and October 1856, and February 1860. Handbook of Texas Online, Harold B. Simpson, "Second United States Cavalry," accessed April 11, 2018, http://www.tshaonline.org/handbook/online/articles/qls03. *Proceedings of the K.G.C. Texas State Convention*, pp. 2, 12. Keehn, *Knights of the Golden Circle*, p. 210n42. 1860 U.S. Census for Bexar County, Texas. *Seguin Southern Confederacy*, February 22, 1861. *Tri-Weekly Alamo Express*, April 15, 1861.

14. Handbook of Texas Online, Aragorn Storm Miller, "Denton, Ashley Newton," accessed April 11, 2018, http://www.tshaonline.org/handbook/online/articles/fdeal. *Navarro Express*, op. cit.. Civil War Service Record for Franklin L. Farrar, 18 Cav. Texas (Darnell's Regiment). *Navarro Express*, March 20, 1861. Civil War Service Record for Jerome B. McCown, 5th Texas Mounted Volunteers. Murrah, David J., *C. C. Slaughter: Rancher, Banker, Baptist* (Austin, University of Texas Press, 1981) p. 15. Texas Legislators; Past & Present, Legislative Reference Library, "J. B. McCown," accessed April 12, 2018, http://www.lrl.state.tx.us/mobile/memberDisplay.cfm?memberID=5185. Service records for Franklin L. Farrar and Jerome B. McCown. Index to Compiled Service Records of Volunteer Soldiers Who Served During The Mexican War. 1860 U.S. Federal Census – Slave Schedule for Ellis County, Texas. Gardner, Charles K., *A Dictionary of All Officers, Who Have Been Commissioned, or Have Been Appointed and Served, in the Army of the United States...* (New York, G.P. Putnam and Company, 1853) p. 540.

15. Thos. J. Devine, Sam. A. Maverick, P.N. Luckett, Commissioners of Committee of Public Safety to Ben McCulloch, 8 February 1861. Same to John C. Robertson, Chairman Committee of Public Safety, 10 February 1861. Both quoted in Sprague. *The Treachery in Texas*, pp. 115-116, 126-127. *Southern Confederacy*, February 15, 1861.

16. S.D. Carpenter to Major W.A. Nichols, 14 February 1861, *Records of the War of Rebellion*, Vol. 1 Series 1, p. 523. 1860 U.S. Federal Census – Slave Schedule for Presidio County, Texas contained on the last page of the Slave Schedule for Ellis County (listed as El Paso County). S.D. Carpenter had one male slave at Fort Davis in 1860. *Southern Confederacy*, February 15, 1861 and February 22, 1861. David Paul Smith, Frontier Defense in Texas: 1861-1865. Ph.D. Dissertation, University of North Texas, Denton, 1987, p. 55. *Southern Confederacy*, op. cit.. 1860 U.S. Census for Seguin, Guadalupe County, Texas. The *Seguin Gazette Enterprise*, February 5, 1981. *Seguin Gazette-Enterprise*, November 13, 1963. Return for Guadalupe Lodge No. 109, *Proceedings of the M. W. Grand Lodge of Texas at its Twenty-Fifth Annual Communication*, p. 179. *Proceedings of the K.G.C. Texas State Convention*, p. 9.

17. *Southern Confederacy*, op. cit.. "Reports of the Committee on Public Safety, Journal of the Secession Convention, p. 277, f3. *Proceedings of the K.G.C. Texas State Convention*, p. 9. U.S., Returns from Military Posts, 1806-1916. Post Return for Fort Mason, for December 1860. 1850 U.S. Federal Census for Bexar County, Texas. 1860 U.S. Federal Census for Guadalupe County, Texas; 1860 U.S. Federal Census – Slave Schedules for Guadalupe County, Texas. Johnson, Andrew, *The Papers of Andrew Johnson: September 1865-January 1866* (Knoxville, University of Tennessee Press, 1991), pp. 159-160. *The War of the Rebellion: A Compilation of the Official Records of the Union and Confederate Armies. Additions and Corrections to Series I*, Volume IV (Washington, Government Printing Office, 1902) p. 125. J.F. Minter, "To the People of the Trans-Miss. Department," September 15, 1863, National Archives, War Department Collection of Confederate Records. Cutler, William G. "Territorial History, Part 2 First Political Movements," History of the State of Kansas. (http://www.kancoll.org/

books/cutler/terrhist/terrhist-p2.html) accessed on March 17, 2007. Arnold, James. *Jeff Davis's own: cavalry, comanches, and the battle for the Texas frontier* (Edison, Castle Books, 2000) p. 299. Sam Houston to D. E. Twiggs, January 20, 1861, in *Writings of Sam Houston*, 1861, Vol. VIII, p. 234.

18. *Southern Confederacy*, op. cit.. Newcombe, *Secession Times*, p. 11. *Journal of the Secession Convention*, op. cit.. Handbook of Texas Online, Aragon Storm Miller, "Yager, William Overall," accessed May 10, 2018, http://www.tshaonline.org/handbook/online/articles/fya08. VMI Archives Historical Rosters, "William Overall Yager," accessed May 10, 2018, https://archivesweb.vmi.edu/rosters/record.php?ID=334. Students of the University of Virginia, 1825-1874, "Yager Family of Page County, Virginia," accessed May 10, 2018, https://uvastudents.wordpress.com/2013/03/26/yager-family-of-page-county-virginia/. King, James L. *History of Shawnee County, Kansas and Representative Citizens* (Chicago, Richmond & Arnold, 1903) pp. 37, 56-60. First and Second Sessions, Thirty-Fourth Congress, *Executive Documents*, Printed by Order of the Senate of the United States...1855-'56, (Washington, A. O. P. Nicholson, 1856) pp. 687, 690, 713, 793. "Call for a State Convention," Standard, November 22, 1860. 1860 U.S. Federal Census, Caldwell County, Texas and Comal County, Texas. Handbook of Texas Online, Crystal Sasse Ragsdale, "Lindheimer, Ferdinand Jacob," accessed May 11, 2018, http://www.tshaonline.org/handbook/online/articles/fli04. Handbook of Texas Online, "Bracht, Viktor Friedrich," accessed May 11, 2018, http://www.tshaonline.org/handbook/online/articles/fbr07. Lonn, Ella. *Foreigners in the Confederacy* (Ann Arbor, University of Michigan Press, 1965) pp. 48-49. *Alamo Express*, November 5, 1860, quoting *Southern Intelligencer*.

19. 1860 U.S. Census for Gonzales County, Texas. – Slave Schedule, Gonzales County. Civil War Service Record for William H. Stewart, NARA. Journal of the Secession Convention, op. cit.. *Southern Confederacy*, op. cit.. 1860 U.S. Census for Hays County. 1850 U.S. Census – Slave Schedules for DeWitt County, Texas. *Nashville Christian Advocate*, October 23, 1908. *San Antonio Light*, October 7, 1908. *Minutes of the Annual Conferences of the Methodist Episcopal Church, South for the year 1859* (Nashville, Southern Methodist Publishing House, 1860) p. 175. Lieut. Colonel T.S. Anderson, Major A.H. Phillips and Capt. J. Rupley, Order No. 23, Civil War Service Record for Rev'd Buckner Harris, NARA.

20. *Southern Confederacy*, op. cit.. George T. McGehee, "A Brief History of One Branch of the McGehee Family from 1771 to the Present...1899," *Hays County Historical and Genealogical Society, Inc. Fall Quarterly*, Vol. VII, No. 3, (September 1973) pp. 7-20. 1860 U.S. Census for Hays County, Texas – 1860 Slave Schedules for Hays County, Texas. Frances Stovall, et. al, Clear Springs and Limestone Ledges, *A History of San Marcos and Hays County* (San Marcos, Hays County Historical Commission, 1986) pp. 90-91. Texas, Muster Roll Index Card for Clem R. Johns, Jr. Texas State Library and Archives, Austin, Texas. 1860 U.S. Census for Hays County and Travis County, Texas - Slave Schedules for Hays and Travis County, Texas. Handbook of Texas Online, Lura N. Rouse, "Johns, Clement Reed," accessed May 5, 2018, http://www.tshaonline.org/handbook/online/articles/fjo02. Call for a State Convention, op. cit.. *Dallas Herald*, February 27, 1861, quoting *San Antonio Herald*, February 16, 1861. *San Antonio Ledger and Texan*, June 1, 1861. Handbook of Texas Online, Geraldine F. Talley, "Logan, John Davis," accessed August 24, 2018, http://www.tshaonline.org/handbook/online/articles/flo43.

21. Thomas J. Devine, et. al to J. C. Robertson, 18 February 1861, in *The Treachery in Texas*, pp. 116-117. *Standard*, March 9, 1861, quoting *Galveston News*. Zenas R. Bliss, Bliss Papers, Center for

American History, Austin, Texas, Volume 2, pp. 234-241. S.D. Carpenter to Maj. W.A. Nichols, 16 February 1861, *War of the Rebellion*, Vol. 1 Series 1, pp. 541-542. Dalrymple, William C., Texas, Muster Roll Index Cards, 1838-1900, Texas State Library and Archives, Austin, Texas. Dalrymple's Muster Roll card lists "Companies in his regiment, Capt. C. Mays's, Thos. Harrison's, D.L. Sublett's, E.W. Roger's after E. H. Moore's Co., J.M. Wright's and A. B. Burleson's Co." The regiment's Adjutant, James C. McCord, served from January 7, 1861 until the regiment was disbanded May 10, 1861. *New York Herald*, January 17, 1861: "Governor Houston has accepted the services of the Waco Mounted Guard, commanded by Captain Thomas Harrison.... Capt. Ross will also return at once. Captain Dalrymple, of Williamson; Captain A.B. Burleson, of Travis, and Captain Berry of Bosque will soon be at Fort Belknap. Captain Rogers, of Ellis, is raising a company, and also Capt. Stockton, of Young. The entire force of about 350 men will be concentrated at Fort Belknap as soon as possible." Sam Houston, "Message to the Legislature of Texas in Extra Session," January 21, 1861, in *The Writings of Sam Houston*, op. cit.., pp. 237-239. W.C. Dalrymple to S.D. Carpenter, 18 February 1861; S.D. Carpenter to W.C. Dalrymple, 19 February 1861. *War of the Rebellion*, op. cit.. McCaslin, John S. *"Rip" Ford of Texas*, pp. 107-108. E. B. Nichols to John C. Robertson, *War of the Rebellion*, Series 1 Vol. 53, pp. 657-665. Ivey, Darren L. *The Ranger Ideal, Volume 1: Texas Rangers in the Hall of Fame, 1823-1861* (University of North Texas Press, Denton, 2017) p. 537 f121. General Sherman to J. C. Robertson, 6 March 1861, in *Journal of the Secession Convention*, pp. 394-395.

22. Biography of Ebenezar Bacon Nichols, "Past Grand High Priest," The Grand Royal Arch Chapter of Texas, accessed May 17, 2018, www.yorkritetexas.org. Handbook of Texas Online, Julia Beazley, "Nichols, Ebenezar B.," accessed May 17, 2018, http://www.tshaonline.org/handbook/online/articles/fmi01. *State Gazette*, June 16, 1860. McCaslin, Ford, op. cit.. *History of the Grand Commandery, Knights Templar of Texas*, pp. 2-4. The Friends of Glasgow Necropolis, Ashley Jameson, "Archibald St. Clair (Sinclair) Ruthven," accessed January 2, 2018, www.glasgownecropolis.org. *Proceedings of the M.W. Grand Lodge of Texas* (1860) p. 152. *Proceedings of the Grand Commandery of Texas of Knights Templar* (1856) p. 22. *Proceedings of the Grand Commandery of Texas Knights Templar* (1861) pp. 13-14.

23. Peterson, Dorothy Burns, *Daughters of the Republic of Texas patriot ancestor index* (Paducah, Turner Publishing Company, 1995) p. 242. Biographical Sketch of Charles Arden Russell, Charles Arden Russell Papers, Center for American History, Austin, Texas. L. B. Russell to Mr. Winkler, 20 November 1930, Russell Papers, op. cit.

24. *Proceedings of the K.G.C. Texas State Convention*, pp. 1-12. Charles A. Russell to Emeline C. Russell, 4 March 1861, quoted in "Russell as a Member of the K.G.C.," A.A. Neighbours Papers, Center for American History, op. cit.. Civil War Service Record for John E. Park, NARA. 1860 U.S. Federal Census – Slave Schedule for Guadalupe County, Texas.

25. *Proceedings of the K.G.C. Texas State Convention*, pp. 1-12. Neighbours, "Russell as a Member of the K.G.C." pp. 28-30. Philip I. Barziza to General Chas. A. Russell, 11 April 1861, quoted in Neighbours, "Russell as a Member of the K.G.C.', pp. 31-33. Hudson, *Military Knights of the Golden Circle in Texas*, p. 174. *Navarro Express*, March 20, 1861, quoting *States Rights Democrat*. Sprague, *The treachery in Texas*, p. 110.

26. *Proceedings of the K.G.C. Texas State Convention*, op. cit.. Art in Colorado County, Texas, Bill Stein, "Tatum, H. A.," in biographical sketches of Colorado County artists, Nesbitt Memorial Library, Columbus, Texas. Lillian Grace Schoppe, The History of Bee County, Texas, Master's Thesis,

University of Texas, 1939, pp. 61, 62, 153, 198. Find a Grave, "William Baker Cone," memorial no. 71023808, accessed January 2, 2018, https://www.findagrave.com.

27. Proceedings of the K.G.C. Texas State Convention, ibid. Handbook of Texas Online, Martin Hardwick Hall, "Jordan, Powhatan," accessed May 18, 2018, http://www.tshaonline.org/handbook/online/articles/fjo72. Ledger and Texan, September 10, 1859. 1860 U.S. Census for Victoria County – Slave Schedule. Rice, A. J., Texas Muster Roll Cards, Texas State Library, Austin, Texas. *Fort Worth Daily Gazette*, July 25, 1887. Handbook of Texas Online, Craig H. Roell, "San Antonio and Mexican Gulf Railroad," accessed May 18, 2018, http://www.tshaonline.org/handbook/online/articles/eqs08. *San Antonio Weekly Herald*, February 2, 1861. Crook, San Antonio, pp. 44-45, 64, 121, 128. *Ledger and Texan*, April 4, 1857 and January 2, 1858. Sprague, *The treachery in Texas*, p. 129. Handbook of Texas Online, Bruce Allardice, "Sweet, George Henry," accessed April 26, 2013, http://www.tshaonline.org/handbook/online/articles/fsw10.

28. Proceedings of the K.G.C. Texas State Convention, ibid. Sprague, *The treachery in Texas*, p. 140. Bell, *Knights of the Golden Circle*, p. 182. *Journal of the Secession Convention*, p. 89. Hudson, *Military Knights of the Golden Circle*, p. 91. Rebecca W. Danvers, The Charles B. Moore Collection: Interpretation and Annotation, Ph.D. dissertation, University of Texas at Dallas, 1985, pp. 212-213. Anderson, *Texas, Before, and on the eve of rebellion*, p. 50. Newcomb, *Secession Times in Texas*, p. 8.

29. H. E. McCulloch to John A. Robertson, 1 March 1861, in *Journal of the Secession Convention*, pp. 375-376; 389-390. *Philadelphia Public Ledger*, March 26, 1861.

30. *Proceedings of the K.G.C. Texas State Convention*, ibid. *Dallas Herald*, February 20, 1861.

31. *Proceedings of the K.G.C. Texas State Convention*, ibid. Sprague, *The treachery in Texas*, p. 139. August 30, 1842 arrival of Schooner Lelia, and April 6, 1846 arrival of Brig Empressario, in New Orleans, Passenger List Quarterly Abstracts, 1820-1875. May 31, 1842 arrival of A. Brown from Galveston, New York Passenger and Immigration Lists, 1820-1850. Property Tax Rolls for Gonzales County, Texas from 1855 to 1866, Texas State Library and Archives, Austin, Texas. 1860 U.S. Federal Census - Slave Schedule for Gonzales County, Texas. Tombstone for James T. Mathieu, Gonzales Masonic Cemetery, Find A Grave, accessed May 29, 2018, https://www.findagrave.com/memorial/61918007. 1850 U.S. Census for Gonzales. James T. Mathieu, Texas Muster Roll Cards, Texas State Library and Archives. *Navarro Express*, March 20, 1861. Handbook of Texas Online, Jennifer Bridges, "Davidson, Alexander Hamilton," accessed May 30, 2018, http://www.tshaonline.org/handbook/online/articles/fdabd. "W. L. Davidson," Daniell, L.E., *Texas: The Country and Its Men* (Austin, 1918) pp. 530-536.

32. *Proceedings of the K.G.C. Texas State Convention*, ibid. 1860 U.S. Federal Census – Slave Schedule for Colorado County, Texas. Spurlin, *Texas Veterans in the Mexican War*, p. 38. 1860 U.S. Federal Census – Slave Schedule for DeWitt County, Texas. Obituary for Lawrence E. LeTulle, Colorado Citizen, January 1, 1912. Colorado County Historical Commission, *Colorado County Chronicles*, Volume 1 (Austin, Nortex, 1986) p. 105. Handbook of Texas Online, Thomas W. Cutrer, "Highsmith, Malcijah Benjamin," accessed May 31, 2018, http://www.tshaonline.org/hnadbook/online/articles/fag03. Sam Houston, *Writings*, Vol. 7. p. 206. Proceedings of the M. W. Grand Lodge of Texas, [1861], p. 210. *Weekly Houston Telegraph*, January 25, 1860. 1860 U.S. Census for Bell County, Texas.

33. *Proceedings of the K.G.C. Texas State Convention*, ibid. Handbook of Texas Online, Craig H. Roell, "Concrete, TX (DeWitt County)," accessed June 1, 2018, http://www.tshaonline.org/handbook/

online/articles/hnc89. Marriage for Andrew J. Hodge and Salina Thomas, 1 July 1857, DeWitt County, Texas, Texas Marriage Collection, 1814-1909. Civil War Service Record for A. J. Hodge, Atchison's Cavalry Company, 5 Regiment Texas Volunteers. Proceedings of the M. W. Grand Lodge of Texas, [1861], pp. 188-189. James Kilgore Death Certificate, Texas Death Certificates, 1903-1982 for James T. Kilgore. Mattioli Family Public Member Tree, "James T. Kilgore," Ancestry.com, accessed May 29, 2018, http://search.ancestrylibrary.com. 1860 U.S. Federal Census for DeWitt County, Texas. Civil War Service Record for John R. Pulliam, 2nd Texas Cavalry. Civil War Service Record for E. J. Pitts, 8th Texas Cavalry.

34. *Proceedings of the K.G.C. Texas State Convention*, ibid. . Philip I. Barziza to General Chas. A. Russell, 11 April 1861, quoted in Neighbours, "Russell as a Member of the K.G.C.," pp. 31-33.

35. "General Henry Eustace McCulloch," in Daniell, L. E., *Personnel of the Texas State Government* (Austin, Press of the City Printing Company, 1887), p. 246. Henry E. McCulloch to John C. Robertson, 26 February 1861, in *War of the Rebellion*, Series I – Volume 3, pp. 639-640; ibid, Series I Volume 1, pp. 543-544. "R. B. Halley, Captain," Texas, Muster Roll Index Cards, 1838-1900, Texas State Library. Sprague, *The treachery in Texas*, p. 135.

36. Bliss, *Bliss Papers*, Part III, p. 75. W. T. Mechling to Devine, Luckett and Maverick, March 1, 1861, in Sprague, *Treachery in Texas*, p. 130. Ibid, March 2, 1861, *Treachery in Texas*, pp. 129-130. Texas, Muster Roll Index Cards for Captain Trevanion T. Teel's Company, Texas State Library and Archives. Proceedings of the K.G.C. Texas State Convention, ibid.

37. *Journal of the Secession Convention*, op. cit.., pp. 85-87. *Proceedings of the K.G.C. Texas State Convention*, ibid. Texas, Muster Roll Index Cards for Captain Matt Nolan's Company, Texas State Library and Archives. Charles Russell to Emeline C. Russell, 2 March 1861, in Neighbors Collection, p. 30.

Chapter Eleven

1. Kline, Michael J., *The Baltimore plot: the first conspiracy to assassinate Abraham Lincoln* (Yardley, Westholme, 2008) pp. 24, 25, 60, 91, 92, 259-261, 292. Keehn, *Knights of the Golden Circle*, p. 134. Chestnut, Mary Boykin, *A Diary from Dixie* (New York, D. Appleton and Company, 1905) p. 18. Wright, Mrs. D. Girard, *A Southern Girl in '61* (New York, Doubleday, Page and Company, 1905) p. 59. Mrs. Wright was Louis T. Wigfall's daughter.

2. Ben McCulloch to J. C. Robertson, 18 February 1861, in *War of the Rebellion*, Series II, Vol. 1, pp. 34-35. Ben McCulloch to John H. Reagan, 25 February 1861, in *War of the Rebellion*, Series I Vol. 1, p. 609.

3. Milo Mims, "The Ben McCulloch Colts...1,000 Six-Shooters for Texas," *The Texas Gun Collector*, 1997, accessed June 15, 2018, www.morphyauctions.com. Proctor, Ben H. *Not Without Honor; the life of John H. Reagan* (Austin, University of Texas Press, 1962) p. 127. *Journal of the Provisional Congress*, 1st Session, p. 97. L. P. Walker to Ben McCulloch, *War of the Rebellion*, op. cit., p. 610. H. E. McCulloch to L. P. Walker, 30 March 1861, op. cit., pp. 617-618. *Journal of the Secession Convention*, pp. 125-127.

4. Louis T. Wigfall to Jefferson Davis, 11 March 1861, in *War of the Rebellion*, op. cit., p. 273. *Journal of the Provisional Congress*, 1st Session, pp. 112, 122, 154. *Atlanta Southern Confederacy*, March 8, 1861.

5. *Journal of the Provisional Congress*, 1st Session, pp. 154-156. Handbook of Texas Online, Steve Hooper, "Sorley, James," accessed June 25, 2018, http://www.tshaonline.org/handbook/online/

articles/fsorl. 1860 U.S. Federal Census – Slave Schedules, Galveston County, Texas. Jennifer M. Murray, "The Civil War Begins, Opening Clashes 1861, Center of Military History, (Washington, United States Army, 2012) p. 10. Wright, Edmund, *Narrative of Edmund Wright: his adventures with and escape from the Knights of the Golden Circle* (Cincinnati, J. R. Hawley, 1864) pp. 79, 87. Samuel A. Lockridge to S. P. Heintzelman, 27 April 1860, Heintzelman Papers.

6. *Journal of the Provisional Congress*, op. cit.. Cozzens, Peter, *The Darkest Days of the War, the Battles of Iuka & Corinth* (Chapel Hill, University of North Carolina Press, 1997) p. 10. Hudson, *Military Knights of the Golden Circle in Texas*, 129.

7. *Writings of Sam Houston*, pp. 271-278. *Proceedings of the K.G.C. Texas State Convention*, p. 10. *Journal of the Secession Convention*, pp. 179, 184.

8. *Journal of the Secession Convention*, pp. 8, 184, 401. Sackfield Maclin to President of the Convention, 16 March 1861, John S. Ford to John C. Robertson, March 20, 1861, in *Journal of the Secession Convention*, p. 401. *Tri-weekly Alamo Express*, February 19, 1861 and February 25, 1861. Handbook of Texas Online, Jeanette H. Flachmeier, "Briggs, Elisha Andrews," accessed July 5, 2017, http://www.tshaonline.org/handbook/online/articles/fbr47.

9. *Dallas Weekly Herald*, April 3, 1861, quoting the *Galveston Civilian*, March 18, 1861. *Journal of the Secession Convention*, pp. 200-205. *State Gazette*, March 23, 1861. Mims, *Ben McCulloch Colts*, p. 15. Charles D. Spurlin, "Waller, Edwin, Jr.," Handbook of Texas Online, accessed September 12, 2013, Index Cards, 1838-1900, Texas State Library.

10. *States Rights Democrat*, March 21, 1861. John Rosenheimer to Edward Clark, 22 March 1861. Governor's Papers, Texas State Archive, Austin, Texas. *San Antonio Ledger and Texan*, November 26, 1859 and July 3, 1858. *Journal of the Secession Convention*, p. 8. Mims, "The Ben McCulloch Colts," p. 13. *San Antonio Express*, November 20, 1870. Wright, *A Southern Girl in '61*, p. 34. Keehn, *Knights of the Golden Circle*, p. 129.

11. Wright, op. cit.. Mims, "The Ben McCulloch Colts," p. 15. Otis G. Welch to Edward Clark, March 24, 1861, Governor's Papers. McCaslin, Richard B. *Tainted Breeze: The Great Hanging at Gainesville, Texas, 1862* (Baton Rouge, LSU Press, 1997) p. 112.

12. Thomas Hardeman to Edward Clark, March 1861, Governor's Papers. *Atlanta Southern Confederacy*, March 24, 1861. *Journal of the Secession Convention*, p. 452. Handbook of Texas Online, W. H. Timmons, "Hart, Simeon," accessed July 19, 2018, http://www.tshaonline.org/handbook/online/articles/fhaak. Hudson, *Military Knights of the Golden Circle*, p. 223.

13. Earl Van Dorn to L. P. Walker, 26 March 1861; Hugh W. Hawes to John H. Reagan, 30 March 1861; T. N. Waul to Jefferson Davis, 26 March 1861 and 2 April 1861. *War of the Rebellion*, Series 1 Vol. 1, pp 614-617, 668.

14. Wright, *A Southern Girl in '61*, p. 35. *Atlanta Southern Confederacy*, March 7, 1861. Mims, op. cit.. Edward Clark to Jefferson Davis, 4 April 1861, *War of the Rebellion*, Series 1 Vol. 1, p. 621.

15. *Texas State Gazette*, April 6, 1861. Civil War Service Records, Unit Information for 1st Texas Mounted Rifles.

16. Mims, "The Ben McCulloch Colts," p. 15. Chestnut, *A Diary from Dixie*, p. 33.

17. Mims, op. cit.. J. J. Hooper to Edward Clark, 9 April 1861, *War of the Rebellion*, Series 4 Vol. 1, p. 213. Louis T. Wigfall to Colonel____? 9 April 1861; a copy in the Wigfall Papers, Texas State

Archives; original in Old Records Division, Adjutant General's Office, US Army, Washington, DC. E. C. Wharton to John Tyler, Jr., 9 April 1861; H. W. Hawes to John H. Reagan, 9 April 1861 and S. Cooper to Earl Van Dorn, 11 April 1861; *War of the Rebellion*, Series 1 Vol. 1 pp. 623-624.

18. Philip I. Barziza to Charles A. Russell, 11 April 1861, transcribed in Neighbours, "Russell as a Member of the K.G.C.," Texas State Archives, pp. 31-33. Hudson, *Military Knights of the Golden Circle in Texas*, pp. 224-231, 249. *Proceedings of the K.G.C. Texas State Convention*, pp. 5-6. Marriage Record for George Witting [sic], Galveston, Texas. Texas, Select County Marriage Index, 1837-1965. G.W. Whitting is also listed as an artist in Chambers County in *Dictionary of Texas Artists, 1800-1945* (College Station, Texas A&M University Press, 1999), born in 1815. In Hudson's thesis, she identified Castle locations by county, and indicated other counties that needed to be investigated more comprehensively. Among those counties she listed as needing further investigation were Fort Bend and Liberty counties. Like all other research to-date concerning the KGC in Texas, Hudson did not find the Neighbours profile of Charles A. Russell, or the Proceedings of the K.G.C. Texas State Convention. However, her thesis is essential to understanding much about the KGC in Texas and is the foundation for all that follow as she was an early pioneer in this field. Her work and cooperation is much appreciated by this author.

19. *Tyler Reporter*, April 11, 1861. *La Grange States Rights Democrat*, March 7, 1861. *Tri-Weekly Alamo Express*, April 10, 1861 and April 15, 1861. Declaration of Recruit for Robert B. Ward, signed April 1, 1861, in Union Army Service Record for Robert B. Ward, NARA. Ward's service record indicates that by January 1862 he was stationed at Camp Hamilton, Virginia, near Fortress Monroe, Virginia. His reenlistment record also gives his age as 31, born in Illinois (circa 1830?) and listed his occupation as "soldier".

20. *Atlanta Southern Confederacy*, April 13, 1861. Ford, John Salmon, *Rip Ford's Texas* (Austin, University of Texas Press, 1987) pp. 335-337. Cutler, *History of the State of Kansas*, op. cit.. James Bourland to William Quayle, 14 April 1864, William Quayle Papers, University of Alabama Special Collections Library, Tuscaloosa.

21. *Knights of the Golden Circle*, Coded Message, April 14, 1861, Hobart Huson Collection, Archives, Texas State Library, Austin, Texas. Texas, Muster Roll Index Cards for Captain William T. Townsend's Home Guard Reserve, St. Mary's, Refugio County. Ben McCulloch to Edward Clark, 14 April 1861, Records of Edward Clark, Archives, Texas State Library, Austin, Texas. Hudson, *Military Knights of the Golden Circle in Texas*, pp. 192, 234.

22. *Richmond Daily Dispatch*, April 29, 1861. *New York Times*, April 29, 1861. Van Dorn filed reports dated April 17 and 26, but they have been lost. See *War of the Rebellion*, Series 1 Vol. 1, p. 573. *Civilian and Gazette*, April 30, 1861. The *Civilian and Gazette* of Galveston listed all the names of the Galveston men who had participated in the capture of the Star of the West in its April 30, 1861 edition. The commanders and their respective companies listed were: Captain Van Buren, Galveston Artillery; Captain James McGrath, Wigfall Guards; Captain John Muller, Island City Rifle Company.

23. Jennifer M. Murray, "The Civil War Begins: Opening Clashes, 1861," Center of Military History, United States Army, Washington, D.C. pp. 17-18. Freehling, *The Road to Disunion*, p. 524. Sprague, *The treachery in Texas*, p. 136. Henry E. McCulloch to L.P. Walker, 17 April 1861, *War of the Rebellion*, Series 1 Vol. 1, p. 627. Daniel, L.E., compiler, *Personnel of the Texas State Government* (Austin, City Printing Company, 1887) pp. 252-255. *Arkansas True Democrat*, May 9, 1861, quoting *Louisville Courier*, April 24, 1861.

24. *Journal of the Secession Convention*, p. 115. Texas, Muster Roll Cards for Milton Webb, Captain of Lamar Cavalry and Lamar Mounted Volunteers. Milton Webb to Edward Clark, 17 April 1861. Governors Papers, Texas State Library.

25. Elkins, John M. *Indian Fighting on the Texas Frontier* (Amarillo, Russell & Cockrell, 1929) p. x. Harris A. Hamner to Edward Clark, 18 April 1861, Governor's Papers, Texas State Library. Hudson, *Knights of the Golden Circle in Texas*, p. 130. *Houston Weekly Telegraph*, April 30, 1861. Richardson, *The Frontier of Northwest Texas*, p. 230. Howell, "James Webb Throckmorton," p. 195. William H. Emory to Lt. Colonel Townsend, May 19, 1861, *War of the Rebellion*, pp. 637, 648.

26. T. J. Thomas to Edward Clark, 20 April 1861, Governor's Papers, Texas State Archives, Austin, Texas. Tignal Jones to Edward Clark, 21 April 1861, Texas State Archives. *Journal of the Secession Convention*, p. 37. D. M. Short to Edward Clark, 22 April 1861, Governor's Papers. Handbook of Texas Online, Robert Bruce Blake, "Short, Daniel , http://www.tshaonline.org/handbook/online/articles/fsh32. Hudson, *Seventh Star of the Confederacy*, p. 61. Texas Muster Roll Index Cards, 1838-1900 for Harvey Yarbrough.

27. General Order No. 1, *War of the Rebellion*, Series 1 Vol. 1, p. 628. Daniell, *Personnel of the Texas State Government*, p. 253. Sprague, *The treachery in Texas*, pp. 137-139. C. C. Sibley, "Memorandum relating to the arrest of Col. Waite, U.S. Army, 23 April, 1861," in *War of the Rebellion*, Series 2 Vol. 1, pp. 45-50. *Tri-Weekly Alamo Express*, February 20, 1861.

28. W. T. Mechling, General Orders No. 4, *War of the Rebellion*, Series 1 Vol. 1, pp. 632-633. Stein, Consider the Lily, Part Six. *Journal of the Secession Convention*, p. 202. Handbook of Texas Online, Stephanie P. Niemeyer, "McDowell, Samuel J. P.," accessed August 11, 2018, http://www.tshaonline.org/handbook/online/articles/fmcsa. Civil War Service Record, Samuel J. P. McDowell, NARA. Shearer, "The Callahan Expedition," p. 583. Perrine, An Authentic exposition of the "K.G.C.," pp. 72, 77. Handbook of Texas Online, Matthew Ellenberger, "Horton, Albert Clinton," accessed August 10, 2018, http://www.tshaonline.org/handbook/online/articles/fho62. Texas Muster Roll Cards, 1838-1900 for G. J. Hampton. Handbook of Texas Online, Brett J. Derbes and Bruce Allardice, "Hampton, George James," accessed on August 10, 2018, http://www.tshaonline.org/handbook/online/articles/fhakb. *Proceedings of the K.G.C. Texas State Convention*, pp. 9, 12.

29. *Proceedings of the K.G.C. Texas State Convention*, op. cit.. Hudson, *Military Knights of the Golden Circle in Texas*, p. 224. Texas Muster Roll Index Cards, 1838-1900 for John T. Holt. Wharton, *History of Fort Bend County*, p. 170. Texas Muster Roll Index Cards, 1838-1900 for Isham G. Jones and W. H. A. Harris. Handbook of Texas Online, Jennifer Eckel, "DeWitt, Christopher Columbus," accessed August 10, 2018, http://www.tshaonline.org/handbook/online/articles/fdebc. Texas Muster Roll Index Cards, 1838-1900 for Joseph C. Williams. Civil War Service Record for Joseph C. Williams, NARA.

30. *War of the Rebellion*, Series 1 Vol. 1, p. A004. Handbook of Texas Online, Barbara Donaldson Althaus, "Kyle, Claiborne," accessed August 11, 2018, http://www.tshaonline.org/handbook/online/articles/fky02. Ibid, "Kyle, Fergus," Texas, Muster Roll Index Cards, 1838-1900, Ferg. Kyle, Texas State Library. War of the Rebellion, Series 1 Vol. 1, p. A005. Handbook of Texas Online, J. L. Bryan, "Stapp, Darwin Massey," accessed August 11, 2018, http://www.tshaonline.org/handbook/online/articles/fstqq. Thrall, *A Pictorial History of Texas*, p. 622.

31. *War of the Rebellion*, Series 1 Vol. 1, p. A005. Dermot H. Hardy and Ingham S. Roberts, eds., *Historical Review of South-East Texas*, Vol 2 (Chicago, Lewis Publishing Company, 1910) p. 874. Find a Grave, Frances Donnelly, "Searcy, Albert Wynne," accessed August 11, 2018, http://www.findagrave.com. Texas Muster Roll Index Cards, 1838-1900 for Oliver C. Searcy and A. W. Searcy. Civil War Service Record, Co. D 27 Tex. Cav., NARA. Handbook of Texas Online, Claudia Hazelwood, "Searcy, Isham Green," accessed August 11, 2018, http://www.tshaonline.org/handbook/online/articles/fse03. Texas Muster Roll Index Cards, 1838-1900 for A. H. Phillips and R. E. Sutton. Jennett, Elizabeth LeNoir, *Biographical Directory of the Texan Conventions and Congresses, 1832-1845* (Austin, Book Exchange, Inc., 1941) p. 153. Handbook of Texas Online, Stephanie P. Niemeyer and Daniel Park, "Phillips, Alexander H., Jr.," accessed August 11, 2018, http://www.tshaonline.org/handbook/online/articles/fph18.

32. *War of the Rebellion*, Series 1 Vol. 1, p. A003. Handbook of Texas Online, Thomas W. Cutrer, "Finlay, George Preston," accessed August 12, 2018, http://www.tshaonline.org/handbook/online/articles/ff11. Texas Muster Roll Index Cards, 1838-1900 for George P. Finlay. Hudson, *Knights of the Golden Circle in Texas*, p. 233. *War of the Rebellion*, Series 1 Vol. 1, p. A005. Shirley Ledwig Brown and Carol Sue Gibbs, *Historic Matagorda County*, Vol. 1 (Houston, D. Armstrong Company, 1986) pp. 158-159. Handbook of Texas Online, Diana J. Kleiner, "Matagorda County," accessed August 13, 2018, http://www.tshaonline.org/handbook/online/articles/hcm05. Texas Muster Roll Index Cards, 1838-1900 for James Selkirk. State of Texas, Special Laws of the Eighth Legislature, (Austin, John Marshall & Co., 1860) pp. 127-128. Ruthven, A. S. *Proceedings of the Grand Lodge of Texas*, Vol. 2 (Galveston, Richardson & Co., 1857) p.210.

33. *War of the Rebellion*, Series 1 Vol. 1, p. A005. Handbook of Texas Online, Stephen L. Hardin, "Owen, Clark L.," accessed August 13, 2018, http://www.tshaonline.org/handbook/online/articles/fow01. Grand Lodge I.O.O.F. of Texas, "Clark L. Owen," accessed August 13, 2018, https://ioof-grand-lodge-texas-pgm,weebly.com/clark-l-owen.html. Texas Muster Roll Index Cards, 1838-1900 for Clark L. Owen. War of the Rebellion, Series 1 Vol. 1, p. A002. Dorothy Burns Peterson and Herbert C. Banks, *Daughters of the Republic of Texas* (Paducah, Turner Publishing Company, 1995) p. 24. Texas Muster Roll Index Cards, 1838-1900 for R. A. Barkley [sic] and L.W. More. *The Civilian and Gazette*, May 14, 1861. Texas Muster Roll Index Cards, 1838-1900 for Jesse S. Gordon [sic]. *War of the Rebellion*, Series 1 Vol. 43, pp. 908-909, 1018. Civil War Service Records, Benavides Regiment of Texas Cavalry, NARA. 1860 U.S. Federal Census for Matagorda County, Texas – Slave Schedules. McCaslin, Fighting Stock, pp. 89, 185-188. Hudson, *Knights of the Golden Circle in Texas*, pp. 120, 239. *Proceedings of the K.G.C. Texas State Convention*, op. cit.. Thompson, Jerry, *Tejano Tiger* (Fort Worth, TCU Press, 2017) pp. 68, 75-77, 153-154.

34. Memorandum for L. A. Thompson, from William F. Austin, 7 May 1861. *War of the Rebellion*, Series 1 Vol. 1, p. 634. General Order No. 4, Ibid, p. 632. Unit Information for 1st Texas Mounted Rifles, NARA. *The Civilian and Gazette*, May 14, 1861. William R. Scurry to Edward Clark, 20 April 1861, Edward Clark Papers. Brown, Indian Wars and Pioneers of Texas, p. 601. *Proceedings of the K.G.C. Texas State Convention*, op. cit.. 1860 U.S. Federal Census for Lavaca County, Texas - Slave Schedules. Veteran Biographies, "York, James Allison," San Jacinto Museum of History. 1860 U.S. Federal Census for Lavaca County and DeWitt County, Texas. Handbook of Texas Online, "Rocky Creek (Gonzales Co.), accessed August 16, 2018, http://www.tshaonline.org/

handbook/online/articles/rbr92. Mexican and Indian War Service Record for Jonathan York, NARA. Civil War Service Record for John P. York, NARA.

35. *War of the Rebellion*, Series 1 Vol. 1, p. 634. General Order No. 4, Ibid, p. 632. Unit Information for 1st Texas Mounted Rifles, NARA. *The Civilian and Gazette*, May 14, 1861. *Proceedings of the K.G.C. Texas State Convention*, op. cit.. Hudson, Military Knights of the Golden Circle, p. 190. "Call for a State Convention," Standard, November 22, 1860. 1860 U.S. Federal Census for Travis County, Texas.

36. *The Civilian and Gazette*, May 14, 1861. Handbook of Texas Online, Aragon Storm Miller, "Carter, Benjamin F.," accessed on August 22, 2018, http://www.tshaonline.org/handbook/online/articles/fcafe. Proceedings of the K.G.C. Texas State Convention, op. cit.. "Call for a State Convention," op. cit.. *Journal of the Secession Convention*, pp. 12-13.

37. *The Weekly Telegraph*, April 30, 1861. *The Civilian and Gazette*, April 30, 1861, May 21, 1861 and June 11, 1861. *Dallas Herald*, May 15, 1861. *War of the Rebellion*, Series 1 Vol. 1, p. 637. *LaGrange States Rights Democrat*, May 16, 1861, quoting *Dallas Herald*, May 5, 1861. Handbook of Texas Online, Stephanie Piefer Niemeyer, "Bass, Frederick Samuel," accessed September 8, 2018, http://www.tshaonline.org/handbook/online/articles/fbafa. Kenneth Wayne Howell, "James Webb Throckmorton: The Life and Career of a Southern Frontier Politician, 1825-1894, PhD dissertation, Texas A&M University, 2005, p. 196. *Galveston News*, May 21, 1861. *War of the Rebellion*, Series 1 Vol. 3, pp. 679, 682. Captain John H. Daniels, Texas, Muster Roll Index Cards, 1838-1900, Texas State Library. Other officers in the White Rock Mounted Rifles included 1st Lieutenant Daniel Miller, and 2nd Lieutenants A. D. Rice and George Barton. This unit had been in existence by February 9, 1861 if not earlier. Some men, like W. T. Johnson and A. Woody who were on this roster had been listed in Asher Carter's Company as late as January 8, 1861. Carter's Company had been present in Dallas during the secession election in November 1860 and may have served to intimidate voters by a show of force.

38. *The Weekly Telegraph*, May 7, 1861. Sprague, *The treachery in Texas*, p. 139. *The Daily Ledger and Texan*, May 7, 1861 and May 13, 1861. Handbook of Texas Online, Robert W. Shook, "Duff, James," accessed September 9, 2018, http://www.tshaonline.org/handbook/online/articles/fdu06. James, Duff, Texas, Muster Roll Index Cards, 1838-1900, Texas State Library. Alvin Gerdes, "Descendants and Relatives of Jose Antonio Navarro," Los Bexarenos Genealogical and Historical Society, Vol. 4 Issue 3 (March 2015), accessed September 9, 2018, www.losbexarenos.org/newsletter/LBGHS_Newsletter_201503.pdf. Chabot, *With the Makers of San Antonio*, pp. 204-205, 286, 409. Bliss, Bliss Papers, Part 3, pp. 5, 10. Confederate Service Records for Angel Navarro, NARA. *San Antonio Daily Herald*, March 3, 1859. Handbook of Texas Online, Aragorn Storm Miller, "Kampmann, John Herman," accessed September 10, 2018, http://www.tshaonline.org/handbook/online/articles/fka17. *Alamo Express*, February 20, 1861.

39. Bliss, Bliss Papers, Part 3, pp. 1-19. Daniell, *Sketches of Distinguished Texans*, pp. 253-255. Handbook of Texas Online, Kevin R. Young, "Adams Hill, Battle of," accessed September 10, 2018, http://www.tshaonline.org/handbook/online/articles/qka01. Oates, Stephen B., *Confederate Cavalry West of the River* (Austin, University of Texas Press, 1961) pp. 11-12. *War of the Rebellion*, Series 1 Vo. 1, pp. 572-573, 634-635. Handbook of Texas Online, Thomas W. Cutrer, "Major, James Patrick," accessed September 10, 2018, http://www.tshaonline.org/handbook/online/articles/ fma19. S.

Cooper to Earl Van Dorn, 15 May 1861, Confederate Service Records for Elkanah Greer, NARA. *The Civilian and Gazette*, June 11, 1861.

40. Confederate Service Record for Victor W. Thompson, NARA. LaGrange True Issue, September 5, 1861. *San Antonio Semi-Weekly News*, January 27, 1862. *The Weekly Telegraph*, May 7, 1861. Handbook of Texas Online, Thomas W. Cutrer, "Thompson, Algernon P.," accessed September 14, 2018, http://www.tshaonline.org/handbook/online/articles/fth15. Mark Dallas Loeffler, "Cone, Horace," op. cit., http://www.tshaonline.org/handbook/online/articles/fcorq. Rudolph L. Biesele, "Fisher, Henry Francis," op. cit., http://www.tshaonline.org/handbook/online/articles/ffi17. The *Civilian and Gazette*, May 7, 1861. Dyer, Dr. J. O., *The Old Artillery Company of Galveston* (Galveston, Dr. J. O. Dyer, 1917) pp. 9-12.

41. The *Civilian and Gazette*, May 3, 1861 and May 7, 1861. Handbook of Texas Online, Jennifer Bridges, "Black, Harvey H.," accessed December 12, 2017, http://www.tshaonline.org/handbook/online/articles/fbl74. Confederate Service Record for H. H. Black, NARA. *Dallas Herald*, May 15, 1861. Property Tax roll for Galveston County, 1861, Texas State Archives. Hudson, Military Knights, pp. 147-150.

42. *Memphis Daily Appeal*, May 7, 1861. *The Weekly Telegraph*, May 7, 1861. *The Ranchero*, May 11, 1861. Delaney, Norman C., *The Maltby brothers' Civil War* (College Station, Texas A&M University Press, 2013) pp. 51, 60. *War of the Rebellion*, Series 1 Vol. 1, pp. 629-630. *The Daily Ledger and Texan*, May 13, 1861 and May 14, 1861. *Proceedings of the K.G.C. Texas State Convention*, p. 10. *Tri-Weekly Alamo Express*, February 25, 1861. *Indianola Courier*, May 25, 1861. *Newcomb, Secession Times*, p. 12. Bliss Papers, Part 3, pp. 33-35.

43. *States Rights Democrat*, May 16, 1861. Keehn, *Knights of the Golden Circle*, pp. 28, 65.

44. *Galveston Civilian and Gazette*, May 21, 1861. Handbook of Texas Online, Julia Beazley, "Sherman, Sidney," accessed September 25, 2018, http://www.tshaonline.org/handbook/online/articles/fsh27. Confederate Service Records for Samuel Boyer Davis and E. Von Harten, NARA. Edward Von Harten to Governor Edward Clark, 23 August 1861, Governor's Papers, Texas State Library. Ben McCulloch to L. P. Walker, 20 May 1861, *War of the Rebellion*, Series 1 Vol. 3, pp. 579-580, 583, 590-591. *Civilian and Gazette*, June 11, 1861. D. J. MacGowan, "Indian Secret Societies," *Historical Magazine*, Vol. 10 (1866) p. 140. Cunningham, Frank, *General Stand Watie's Confederate Indians* (Norman, University of Oklahoma Press, 1959, 1998) pp. 5, 28, 36, 38.

45. *Galveston Weekly News*, May 21, 1861. *The Weekly Telegraph*, May 22, 1861. *San Antonio Ledger and Texan*, June 1, 1861. Bliss Papers, Part 2, pp. 39-43, 51-56, 61-66, 102. *War of the Rebellion*, Series 1 Vol 1. pp. 573-574. T. T. Teel, "Sibleys New Mexico Campaign" in *Battles and Leaders of the Civil War*, Vol. II, (New York, The Century Company, 1884) p. 700. Frazier, Donald S., *Blood and treasure: Confederate Empire in the Southwest* (College Station, Texas A&M University Press, 1995) pp. 43-45.

46. Keehn, *Knights of the Golden Circle*, pp. 77, 80. *Civilian and Gazette*, May 28, 1861. John S. Rudd, Texas, Muster Roll Index Cards, 1838-1900, Texas State Archives. Texas Baptist, June 7, 1861. *Houston Telegraph*, May 31, 1861. *Weekly Telegraph*, June 26, 1861. *Richmond The Daily Dispatch*, "Lincoln, Thomas Blodgett," obituary in *Appleton's Annual Cyclopedia and Register of important events of the year 1888*. Vol. 13, (New York, D. Appleton and Company, 1891), p. 643. Samuel Blodgett, Jr. to Thomas Jefferson, 25 June 1792. Jefferson Papers, NARA, **https://founders.archives.gov/documents/Jefferson/01-24-02-0120**. Deed of J. W. Flanagan to Thomas B. Lincoln, Texas General

Land Office records. *Philadelphia Enquirer*, June 29, 1888. *Fort Worth Gazette*, June 30, 1888. Browning, Charles H. *Americans of Royal Descent* (Philadelphia, Porter & Coates, 1891) pp. 359, 363. M. D. Graham to J. B. Magruder, 6 December 1862, Confederate Citizen File for Thomas M. Likens, NARA.

47. *The San Antonio Ledger and Texan*, June 1, 1861. Keehn, *Knights of the Golden Circle*, p. 190. *New York Times*, April 2, 2012.

Appendix A

1. Handbook of Texas Online, Thomas W. Cutrer, "Lubbock, Thomas Saltus," accessed July 12, 2018, http://www.tshaonline.org/handbook/online/articles/flu02. *Weekly Telegraph*, April 8, 1857.

2. *Dallas Herald*, May 8, 1861.

3. 1860 U.S. Federal Census – Slave Schedules for Harris County, Texas. Journal of the Secession Convention, p. 7. *Weekly Telegraph*, May 7, 1861. *State Gazette*, August 11, 1860; November 20, 1860. *Galveston Weekly News*, April 30, 1861.

4. *Weekly Telegraph*, ibid.

5. Ibid. *Dallas Herald*, ibid. Davis, *Battle at Bull Run*, p. 57.

6. *Weekly Telegraph*, May 29, 1861. *Civilian and Gazette*, June 4, 1861. Thomas Jewett Goree to Sarah Williams Kittrell Goree, 15 June 1861. *Thomas Jewett Goree Letters*, Vol. 1, (Bryan, Family History Foundation, 1981) p. 42.

7. Thomas Jewett Goree to Sarah Williams Kittrell Goree, 23 June 1861, *Thomas Jewett Goree Letters*, Vol. 1, (Bryan, Family History Foundation, 1981) p. 44. *Weekly Telegraph*, June 26, 1861. The Crockett Printer, March 13, 1861. Confederate Service Record for A. A. Aldrich, NARA. *Galveston Daily News*, August 27, 1876. Morrison & Fourmy. Morrison & Fourmy's General Directory of the City of Galveston: 1893/1894; (https://texashistory.unt.edu/ark:/67531/metapth894023/m1/64/ accessed February 6, 2020), University of North Texas Libraries, The Portal to Texas History, texashistory.unt.edu.

8. *The Daily Dispatch*, (Richmond, VA.) July 18, 1861. Handbook of Texas Online, "Smith, Morgan L.," accessed February 18, 2020, http://www.tshaonline.org/handbook/online/articles/fsm33. The *Weekly Telegraph*, November 30, 1859. Handbook of Texas Online, Diana J. Kleiner, "Waldeck Plantation." Accessed February 18, 2020, http://www.tshaonline.org/handbook/online/articles/acw01. Nashville union and American, July 19, 1861. Handbook of Texas Online, Diana Kleiner, "Eagle Island Plantation," accessed February 18, 2020, http://tshaonline.org/handbook/online/articles/ace01. *The Weekly Telegraph*, July 17, 1861. Proceedings of the K.G.C. Texas State Convention, p. 9. Confederate Service Record for Lawrence E. LeTulle, Capt. Jackson's Co. Horse Artillery. Confederate Service Records for Co. A, 3rd Regiment Virginia State Line. *The West Virginia Encyclopedia*, Kenneth R. Bailey, "Moccasin Rangers." Accessed February 20, 2020, https://www.wvencyclopedia.org/articles/2005. L. E. LeTulle was born and raised in Virginia and had been the postmaster in Cabell County in 1855. Cabell County today is in West Virginia, a part of the original State of Virginia that was the scene of guerilla warfare between Unionists and Confederate supporters. The Unionists won, West Virginia became a state and the various guerilla units were incorporated into the 3rd Regiment, Virginia State Lines, whose

limited records indicate the Moccasin Rangers formed July 15, 1861, before incorporation as Company A of the 3rd Regiment on February 28, 1862. LeTulle's formal record begins with his enlistment in Jackson's Virginia Horse Artillery on April 1, 1863 which states, "Recruited from the Va. St. Line" [sic] Both the Richmond, Virginia daily dispatch and Houston, *Texas Weekly Telegraph* stated Mr. LeTulle was present with the Texas Guerillas on June 22, 1861 in Richmond.

9. Thomas Jewett Goree to Sarah Williams Kittrell Goree, 23 June 1861, ibid. *Galveston News* –Extra!, July 5, 1861.

10. Handbook of Texas Online, "Smith, Morgan L.," accessed February 18, 2020, http://www.tshaonline.org/handbook/online/articles/fsm33. The KGC was widely suspected to be behind the Draft Riots that shook New York City during the Civil War. Also, before the war commenced, Mayor of New York City Fernando Wood threatened that New York City might secede from the Union in sympathy with the South.

11. Davis, *Battle at Bull Run*, pp. 34, 55. Thomas Jewett Goree to Sarah Williams Kittrell Goree, 6 July 1861, Thomas Jewett Goree Letters, ibid. *Weekly Telegraph*, July 24 and 31, 1861.

12. *The Daily Dispatch*, July 17, 1861. Thomas Jewett Goree to Sarah Williams Kittrell Goree, 20 July 1861, Thomas Jewett Goree Letters, ibid. Davis, *Battle at Bull Run*, pp. 89, 98, 130. Jennifer M. Murray, "The Civil War Begins: Opening Clashes, 1861," Center of Military History, United States Army, Washington, D. C., p. 26.

13. Brig Gen. James Longstreet to Headquarters, *War of the Rebellion*, Series 1, Vol. 2, pp.543-544. Murray, The Civil War Begins, pp. 39-43. Davis, *Battle at Bull Run*, pp. 246, 250-252.

14. *War of the Rebellion*, ibid. Confederate Veteran, Vol. 13 No.1 (January 1905), p. 238. Thomas Jewett Goree to Sarah Williams Kittrell Goree, 6 July 1861, *Thomas Jewett Goree Letters*, ibid. Memphis daily appeal, January 10, 1862. Handbook of Texas Online, Thomas W. Cutrer, "Lubbock, Thomas Saltus," ibid. *The Weekly Telegraph*, December 25, 1861. Handbook of Texas Online, Robert Maberry, Jr., "Wharton, John Austin [1828-1865]," accessed February 18, 2020, http://www.tshaonline.org/handbook/online/articles/ fwh04. *The Daily Ledger and Texan*, August 8, 1861.

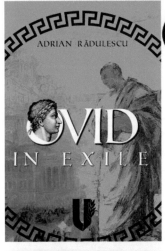

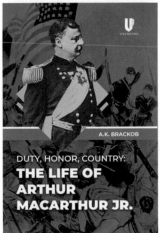
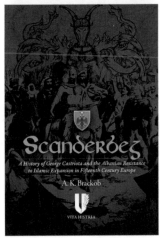